SITUATION CRITICAL

Max Cavitch and Brian Connolly, eds.

SITUATION CRITICAL

CRITIQUE, THEORY, AND EARLY AMERICAN STUDIES

DUKE UNIVERSITY PRESS *Durham and London* 2024

© 2024 DUKE UNIVERSITY PRESS
All rights reserved

Project Editor: Livia Tenzer
Designed by Matthew Tauch
Typeset in Arno Pro and Barlow Condensed by
Westchester Publishing Services

Library of Congress Cataloging-in-Publication Data
Names: Cavitch, Max, editor. | Connolly, Brian, [date] editor.
Title: Situation critical : critique, theory, and early American studies /
Max Cavitch & Brian Connolly, eds.
Description: Durham : Duke University Press, 2024. | Includes bibliographical
references and index.
Identifiers: LCCN 2023027201 (print)
LCCN 2023027202 (ebook)
ISBN 9781478030317 (paperback)
ISBN 9781478026082 (hardcover)
ISBN 9781478059301 (ebook)
Subjects: LCSH: American literature—History and criticism—Theory, etc. |
American literature—17th century—Themes, motives. | American literature—
18th century—Themes, motives. | American literature—19th century—Themes,
motives. | Criticism—United States. | United States—History—17th century. |
United States—History—18th century. | United States—History—19th century. |
BISAC: LITERARY CRITICISM / American / General | HISTORY / United States /
Colonial Period (1600–1775)
Classification: LCC PS88 .S458 2024 (print) | LCC PS88 (ebook) |
DDC 810.9—dc23/eng/20231206
LC record available at https://lccn.loc.gov/2023027201
LC ebook record available at https://lccn.loc.gov/2023027202

Cover art: John Singleton Copley, *Watson and the Shark*, 1778.
National Gallery of Art, Washington, DC, Ferdinand Lammot Belin Fund.

CONTENTS

vii   *Acknowledgments*

1   Introduction: Situation Critical
         MAX CAVITCH AND BRIAN CONNOLLY

I   Theory for Early America

33   ONE · Psychoanalysis and the Indeterminacy of History
         JOAN W. SCOTT

52   TWO · Foucault's Oedipus
         MICHAEL MERANZE

II   Subjects of Early America

73   THREE · Annoyances, Tolerable and Intolerable
         ANA SCHWARTZ

103   FOUR · Michael Wigglesworth's Queer Orthography
         CHRISTOPHER LOOBY

139   FIVE · George Whitefield's Sexual Character
         MARK J. MILLER

III   Fantasies of Realism

177   SIX · Secularism, Hypocrisy, and the Afterlives of Thomas Paine
         JUSTINE S. MURISON

202	SEVEN ·	No Matter: Persisting Rationalisms in Antebellum Black Thought
		BRITT RUSERT
223	EIGHT ·	Queering Abolition
		JORDAN ALEXANDER STEIN

IV Power, Knowledge, Justice

241	NINE ·	Equity in the Time of *Moby-Dick*
		MATTHEW CROW
263	TEN ·	Antebellum or Interbellum?
		JOHN J. GARCIA

287 *List of Contributors*
289 *Index*

ACKNOWLEDGMENTS

The chapters in this volume first took shape at a conference of the same name held at the McNeil Center for Early American Studies in 2016. As the coorganizers of that conference, we are deeply grateful to the center's director Dan Richter, associate director Amy Baxter-Bellamy, and administrator Barbara Natello for their generous support. The McNeil Center has long been one of the most vital institutions for the support of scholarship in the field of early American studies, and we are extremely proud that it was the venue for this timely and wide-ranging conference. Our agreement that it warranted development into a volume of essays was cemented by the generative, often provocative conversations that occurred both during and after the conference. For their essential contributions to those conversations, we join the contributors to this volume in thanking the other conference participants: Herman Bennett, Corey Capers, Lara Langer Cohen, Elizabeth Maddock Dillon, Marcy Dinius, Nicole Eustace, Jonathan Beecher Field, Carrie Hyde, Peter Jaros, Christopher Lukasik, Jen Manion, Meredith McGill, Joe Rezek, Jonathan Senchyne, David Waldstreicher, and Michael Warner. We thank the contributors not only for their excellent chapters but also for their responsiveness and patience throughout the process of making this volume.

We are also delighted that the volume found a home at Duke University Press and are especially grateful for the enthusiasm with which Elizabeth Ault greeted the project, and the editorial acumen that both she and Benjamin Kossak devoted to its development. Their knowledge and insights are woven into the fiber of this book. Warm thanks as well to the press's anonymous reviewers for their close, critical readings of the manuscript. Finally, we would like to thank Susan Albury for copyediting, Matthew Tauch for the terrific cover design, and Livia Tenzer for guiding the book through production. We would also like to thank Sarah Osment for indexing the book.

The first glimmer of this project appeared to Brian Connolly when he was a member of the School of Social Science at the Institute for Advanced Study, where time away from teaching and regular university service provided the perfect opportunity to think through its prospects with Max Cavitch, whose longtime service on the McNeil Center's executive and advisory councils also helped secure the conference venue. Brian would also like to thank the University of South Florida for a Publications Council Grant and his research assistant, Alissa Roy, for help preparing the final manuscript. Max would also like to thank the English Department of the University of Pennsylvania for their unstinting encouragement and support.

INTRODUCTION · *Max Cavitch and Brian Connolly*

Situation Critical

Crisis is a Hair.
—EMILY DICKINSON

LOCATING EARLY AMERICA

"Early America" is neither a specific chronological period nor a discrete geographic region, yet it has been made to stand, in one way or another, for the more or less certain origin point of everything from religious freedom to chattel slavery, settler colonialism, mercantile capitalism, modern democracy, structural racism, economic liberalism, individual sovereignty, national imaginaries, the right to bear arms, disestablishmentarianism, and apple pie. "In the beginning," wrote John Locke, "all the world was *America*."[1] Two centuries later, Max Weber credited New England Puritans with conjuring the "spirit of capitalism" for the global economy.[2] And almost a century after that Anibal Quijano and Immanuel Wallerstein coined the term *Americanity* to designate nothing less than the newness and novelty of the sixteenth-century modern world-system.[3] The academic field of early American studies, too, is replete with origin stories: the origin of secularism, libertarianism, self-reliance, white supremacism, mass media, or what-you-will.[4] Wherever we look, from the far right to the far left, from the classroom to the polling station, from narrative histories to historical novels, some idea of "early America" is being used as the historical justification of someone's fantasy of what America means today.

The contributors to this volume are less interested in proving or disproving those grounds than in better understanding these fantasies and their effects—effects both intended and unintended. That is, instead of dismissing or discrediting such fantasies, we take seriously Joan Wallach Scott's observation that, by lending shape to confusion and incoherence, fantasy is precisely what "enables individuals and groups to give themselves histories."[5] In this light, the critical understanding of any historical narrative—including origin stories—depends, in part, upon reconstructing and interpreting the fantasies that inform and motivate it. This is the work, not of mystical divination, but of critical unsettlement: returning to the archives and texts that bear the legible traces of those fantasies and reflecting in a theoretically informed way on the new experiences of confusion and incoherence they produce in and for us.

Critique, in this sense, is not the opposite (and certainly not the enemy) of empirical research but, rather, its accomplice in a wide range of disciplinary efforts to dislodge the experience of the past from the thick sediment of orthodoxy. These efforts are directed less at "correcting" received opinions than at examining the new fantasies that we as "early Americanists" inevitably generate amid the confusion and incoherence of always having to begin again. Thus, each of the volume's contributors, in their own way, begins again with "early America," in order both to interpret current investments in the field and also to offer their own perspective on contemporary debates over the value of critique to historical and literary scholarship as such.

Many narratives of "early America"—from Puritan epics to Revolutionary hagiographies, liberal teleologies, democratic mythologies, and antifoundational counternarratives—get deployed or redirected in order to facilitate or excuse the operations of the nation-state. In response, some scholars resort to a kind of naïve empiricism, returning to the archives to pursue more or less desperate forms of fact-checking, engaging in the back-and-forth of correction and replacement. In contrast, critique directs attention toward the factitious as well as the factual, and toward the ideological as well as the material. The contributors to this volume are skilled researchers as well as seasoned critical thinkers who have done their best to put aside disabling scholarly anxieties about how to "manage" the past, just as they have rejected the fatuous apologetics of so-called postcritique.

Situation Critical is a volume of interanimating chapters that historicize the present of the early American past. Some are concerned with aspects of human subjectivity, such as interiority, belief, and sexuality. Others focus on ontological and epistemological questions regarding freedom, empiricism, truth-value, and racialization. Others are concerned with matters of ethics and representation relating to imperialism, law, and violence. Crucially, they all refrain from making any further efforts to state "definitively" where early America begins and ends, or to arrogate that authority to any particular historical subject or group.

How, then, might this volume be read and used by scholars, students, and other readers with an interest in early America at a time when the word *America* itself has never sounded more like a misnomer? When the concept of an American national identity has never seemed more riven and compromised? When "truthiness" has given way to "alternative facts"? When devotion to the study of the past seems more and more like sheer escapism or a pathological denial of present catastrophes?

Consider, for example, the bitter contentiousness over "The 1619 Project," with its stated aim "to reframe the country's history by placing the consequences of slavery and the contributions of Black Americans at the very center of the United States' national narrative."[6] "The 1619 Project" initially appeared in the *New York Times* to coincide with the four hundredth anniversary of the twenty or so enslaved and indentured Africans who disembarked at Jamestown in 1619. It was a vital critique of a certain American mythos and its ideological as well as material foundations in white supremacism and chattel slavery. It emphasized the origins of "early America" in the subjection of Black diasporic subjects, while simultaneously offering a vibrant account of the project of radical freedom that emerged from Black liberation struggles. It stands thus far as the most important public intellectual and historical project of the twenty-first century, and reactions to it have ranged from the gracious and enthusiastic reception of a much-needed public reckoning to the visceral rejection of its challenge to white supremacism.

"The 1619 Project" aimed at nothing less than rewriting the origin story of the United States (and the legacies of that origin story), which has structured the nation-state from the eighteenth century to the present day. Its goal was to displace previously enshrined narratives in which the progressive unfolding of democratic freedoms grounded the ostensibly universal ideals of the American Revolution. In their place, it offered a narrative that begins with the "original sin" of chattel slavery and that proceeds with an account of the ongoing reinscription of anti-Black racism into the nation's "DNA"—with consequences for everything from constitutional law to economic policy, social services, infrastructure, and cultural forms. The newspaper venue of "The 1619 Project" and its accessible journalistic survey of recent historical scholarship made it highly visible and widely debated. In 2021 a book version was published, with several new essays and a new subtitle: *The 1619 Project: A New Origin Story*.[7]

The further deluge of responses to this version of *The 1619 Project* has ranged from the sober and well informed to the tendentious and opportunistic.[8] Indeed, the book has become a major cultural event, highlighting at least three of the most urgent matters at stake in our own volume's advocacy for more fully critique-driven accounts of early America. First, *The 1619 Project*, for all of its intellectual force, tends to reify early America as a discrete origin point for the subsequent, continuously unfolding history of the United States. One could argue that the sound and fury of the many reactions against *The 1619 Project* stem from its ostensive "violation" of other cherished origin stories. Second, while *The 1619 Project* itself makes clear that it is an interpretive account, many of its fiercest critics have attacked it on the level of facts, as if history consisted only of matters that can be objectively verified. Third, *The 1619 Project* has called into question, in a way that can't be dismissed as "merely academic," the very standards and methodologies of historical research and writing.

The 1619 Project is but one (influential and effective) effort to reframe the origin story and historical shape of early America, produced at the conjunction of the popular and the academic. Critically and reflexively, the present volume pursues a different agenda, one that doesn't hold itself to the illusory standard of consensus.[9] Indeed, any bid for consensus about the past—particularly against the backdrop of a flailing and failing democracy—must allow for the epistemological uncertainty of all such accounts. In his late lectures at the Collège de France, Michel Foucault explores at length the Greek concept of parrhesia, by which Athenian rhetoricians meant speaking the truth freely and boldly—a concept that resonates with the modern injunction to "speak truth to power." Crucially, though, a parrhēsiastes was someone who speaks the truth and also asks forgiveness for doing so. As Foucault observes, "The subject must be taking some kind of risk [in speaking] this truth which he signs as his opinion, his thought, his belief, a risk which concerns his relationship with the person to whom he is speaking."[10] Parrhesia is thus a complex relation among three elements, described by Foucault as: "forms of knowledge, studied in terms of their specific modes of veridiction; relations of power, not studied as an emanation of a substantial and invasive power, but in the procedures by which people's conduct is governed; and finally the modes of formation of the subject through practices of self."[11] Foucault argues, in other words, that relations between truth, power, and subjectivity can and should be studied without conflating them. Unfortunately, such reductive conflation is the hallmark of our times, taking forms such as trigger warnings, cancel culture discourse, and state censorship, all of which dangerously seek to make a shibboleth of epistemological certainty.[12]

Critique-driven early American studies can help counter such reductivism and the threats it poses both to the journalistic public sphere and to academia, where over the past couple of decades three phenomena have perhaps most strongly elicited the panicky response of naïve empiricism: 1) the prodigious digitization of archival materials, now much more widely accessible and instantaneously searchable; 2) the shift to "vast" extranational scales of analysis, broadly challenging the hegemony of the nation-state; and 3) the emergence of ostensibly posthermeneutic or postsymptomatic reading practices, such as "distant reading," "surface reading," "thin description," and "machine reading."[13] As Brian Connolly has argued elsewhere, these three trends have helped foster a troubling "neoempiricism" in the disciplines—history and English—chiefly responsible for scholarship in the field of early American studies.[14] "Troubling," that is, not because the world isn't full of facts and propositions that need to be discovered and processed, but rather because exponents of this recent empirical turn have so often resorted to the minimization, displacement, vilification, and dismissal of critique—as if it had, in Bruno Latour's notorious phrase, "run out of steam."[15]

Critical history, as practiced variously by each of this volume's contributors, addresses some form of a fundamental question: How can our many theoretical orientations continue to be revisited and revised as part of the never-ending study of the relations of knowledge, power, and subjectivity in our pursuit of the past? As Foucault puts it in an interview from the early 1980s, "The game is to try to detect those things which have not yet been talked about, those things that, at the present time, introduce, show, give some more or less vague indications of the fragility of our system of thought, in our way of reflecting, in our practices."[16] And, he might have added, in the very terms we use to talk about them.

Of course, many scholars of early America have been consistently engaged with critique. For decades, scholarship that fits the bill in one way or another has made a deep impact on the field.[17] Yet the broad force of critique has been waning in the humanities—especially, in recent years, under the guise of "postcritique." Moreover, the critical work of early American studies has often been dispersed across numerous subfields, which tends to make the study of critique a secondary or tertiary concern. This volume's chapters work together to recenter critique in early American studies, not least by demonstrating how archives and texts of early America anticipate and invite critical reflection and theorization in relation to numerous salient categories, including: queerness, sexuality, truth, sovereignty, repression, interiority, war, violence, periodization, facts, empiricism—categories of thought and affect through which the past and present call out, as it were, to one another.

Take the affective and propositional term *crisis*, which sets the tone for all the key terms foregrounded in this introduction ("critical," "criticism," "critique"). Indeed, the legacy of critique has been a persistent consciousness of "crisis" for over two hundred years. "Sapere aude!" Kant demanded, punching up the original Horatian motto: "Have the courage to make use of your own intellect!"[18] Kant strikes a rousing note of progress, of possible historical liberation through the public use of reason. But he also slips a real snake into this imagined garden: the critique of reason, which would become, thanks to Hegel and Marx, Nietzsche and Adorno, the ouroboros of immanent critique.

Yet it's hard to tell the story of the future—a future that would depart from the crippled and crippling present—while swallowing your own tail (tale?). It might well be courageous to treat one's own intellectual substance as a source of nourishment, to devour oneself, as it were, in hope of regeneration and renewal. Yet this hope, this desire, this "very particular need," as Nikolas Kompridis puts it, "to begin anew—a need marking one's time as a time of need," is itself nothing new.[19] Indeed, it might be nothing more than a recursive optimism, akin to Enlightenment utopianism or soft messianism—or a defensive mechanism to be mounted against Kompridis's insight. At the same time, though, a "situation critical" is a situation of desire—a situation not only of defense but also of intimacy—or, as Jacques Derrida might put it, of "hospitality,"[20] the hospitality that we, as this volume's editors, proffer at its threshold.

The contemporary mood of irresolvability (Is there a crisis? Is there not? Are we always in crisis?) recalls an exclamatory moment in one of the key works of contemporary critical theory: the widely assimilated imperative—"Always historicize!"—with which Fredric Jameson opens *The Political Unconscious* (1981). Yet this imperative bears within it its own interrogative ethos precisely in its irreconcilable contradiction: historicization tends to move against the temporal frame of "always." It's the essence of critique to challenge all transhistorical claims, including Jameson's deceptively confident claim on critical theory. Nietzsche, after all, called "critique" a "dark question mark,"[21] and efforts at definition remain highly contested. To some extent, perhaps, this is because the joy as well as the anxiety of destruction, of unmaking, harkens back to the infantile—that is, to the shifting but largely undifferentiated fields of libidinal aggression whose archaic traces inform all of our critical efforts, both destructive and emancipatory. All of which is to say that, precisely in its openness and irresolvability, critique does not and cannot have a single, dominant affect or mood, or a perennial, unquestioned methodology.

For instance, crisis may be apprehended not as an acute, catastrophic scenario, but as the dull immanence of the persistently unbearable. As Emily Dickinson puts it, "Crisis is a Hair"—that is, a hair's breadth, the narrowest of bands, a barely measurable line marking the turning point or zero hour (Walter Benjamin's *Stillstellung*) of quietly impossible decisions, conflicts, or transitions:

> Crisis is a Hair
> Toward which forces creep
> Past which—forces retrograde
> If it come in sleep
>
> To suspend the Breath
> Is the most we can
> Ignorant is it Life or Death
> Nicely balancing—
>
> Let an instant push
> Or an Atom press
> Or a Circle hesitate
> In Circumference
>
> It may jolt the Hand
> That adjusts the Hair
> That secures Eternity
> From presenting—Here—[22]

Some might read this poem as dismissive of worldly conflict and agony (the unspecified "forces" twice referred to in the opening stanza), treating them allegorically as a means of evading responsibility for the here and now. Yet, if the poem's refusal to "historicize" is underscored by the illocal "Here" with which it ends, that doesn't necessarily mean that this deictic punctum seeks maliciously to conceal or obscure the insistent demands of the historical present or culpably to disavow responsibility for making political claims on the present. Indeed, crisis is immanent in every tick of the clock. "Let an instant push," Dickinson recommends. (As if we could do anything but let it!) Yet the poem also suggests that a gesture as simple as the brush of a hand can, at least temporarily, restore the loose strand to its place in the coif that adorns the pate that encloses the mind that, as Benjamin puts it, meets "every second of time [as] the strait gate through which the Messiah might enter."[23]

Another early American, Tom Paine, articulated another mode of political messianism in his Revolutionary-era pamphlet series, published between 1776 and 1783 under the collective title *The American Crisis*. "Even calmness," Paine wrote in the final pamphlet (published shortly after the British ratification of the Treaty of Paris),

> has the power of stunning when it opens too instantly upon us. The long and raging hurricane that should cease in a moment, would leave us in a state rather of wonder than enjoyment; and some moments of recollection must pass before we could be capable of tasting the full felicity of repose. There are but few instances, in which the mind is fitted for sudden transitions: it takes in its pleasures by reflection and comparison, and those must have time to act, before the relish for new scenes is complete.[24]

In our own present case—in the critical situation of past, present, and future prospects that call for our contemplation—we worry about the temptation to taste "the felicity of repose" (offered up to a relatively privileged and mobile class of academicians by deterritorialized global capitalism) and the "relish for new scenes" (e.g., scholarly performances that seek to slough off unfashionable and ostensibly deenergized modes of poststructuralist theory). Indeed, as the chapters in this volume attest, the archives and discourses of early America contain, as do the works of Dickinson and Paine, their own critical lexicons and surprising reformulations. Reflecting upon the intertwining of crisis and calmness might very well be "the most we can."

But, if "crisis" is a hair, then what exactly is critique?

One of the most consequential turns in the history of modern thought can be dated to the late eighteenth century and the fitful emergence, in Kant and others, of immanent critique, which more or less coincided with what A. N. Whitehead considered to be the long-overdue "contact" of speculative and practical reason,[25] or what we would now call theoreticism and empiricism. The intellectual trajectories of critique, from the eighteenth century to the present, are most commonly traced in European intellectual history, although, even before the nineteenth-century emergence of a self-consciously "American" tradition of intellectual history, the shaping of these phenomena in early America has been crucial for current thinking about the history of the present.

The historians, literary historians, and critical theorists contributing chapters to this volume all seek to "advance" (as Whitehead would put it) from this empirico-theoretical impasse toward future methodological instars by speculating, in a disciplined way, on the conjunction of the theoretical and the empirical. America, in the broadest sense, continues to figure in the elaboration of immanent critique, while also serving as a site for thinking through the conditions and limits, the blurry and productive edges, of critical thought. We might think here of Susan Buck-Morss's work on Hegel and Haiti;[26] or Paul Downes's work on Hobbes, sovereignty, and early America;[27] or David Kazanjian's study of the theorizations of freedom in letters of the formerly enslaved from Liberia.[28] These works not only draw on various traditions of critique, from the Frankfurt School to deconstruction, but also challenge our sense of the limits of critique—not least, through their ingenious encounters with the archives of early America. For instance, the critical possibilities of ongoing debates over the psychoanalytic postulate of the death drive are reconfigured in the speculative empiricism of nineteenth-century Black epistemology. Freudian repression finds unexpected antecedents in Puritan settler colonialism. And the contours of heteronormativity are figured in radical abolitionist visions of freedom.

As in academia, so too in the world of mass media, the limits of critique are being debated in relation to new forms of pressure on old historical narratives. For example, in a *Washington Post* op-ed denouncing critical race theory, Marc Thiessen, a conservative pundit, recounts an interview he conducted with the historian Allen Guelzo, himself a critic of *The 1619 Project*. Guelzo told Thiessen that "critical race theory is a subset of critical theory that began with Immanuel Kant in the 1790s. It was a response to—and rejection of—the principles of Enlightenment and the Age of Reason on which the American republic was founded. Kant believed that 'reason was inadequate to give shape to our lives' and so he set about 'developing a theory of being critical of reason.'"[29] It should, perhaps, go without saying that Guelzo's claims are inaccurate and foolish, a combination that counts him among the more dangerous intellectual servants of reactionary conservatism. Guelzo's own wild errors here, along with the wider tumult over critical race theory, belie an anxiety not only over the structural conditions of race and racism, but also over the force and trajectories of critique in the present. Kant was indeed aligned with the reification of racial categories even as he opened up the possibility of immanent critique.[30] But the various trajectories of critique since the eighteenth century cannot be reduced to Kantian epiphenomena. One needn't be concerned with "rescuing" Kant to observe that, even in its periodic alignment with distortions and mythifications, post-Kantian critique continues to have a salutary unsettling force.

This inconvenient truth has led various commentators in academia, as well, to make highly tendentious claims about what critique is and what purposes it serves, claims that often resonate with the doggedly empirical bent of early American studies. Literary critic Rita Felski, for example, has characterized the mindset of critique as one that is "vigilant, wary, mistrustful—that blocks receptivity and inhibits generosity," its operations marked by "an unmistakable blend of suspicion, self-confidence, and indignation."[31] Critics Stephen Best and Sharon Marcus have gone so far as to argue that critique now threatens the perspicacity of political analysis: "Those of us who cut our intellectual teeth on deconstruction, ideology critique, and the hermeneutics of suspicion have often found those demystifying protocols superfluous in an era when images of torture at Abu Ghraib and elsewhere immediately circulated on the internet; the real-time coverage of Hurricane Katrina showed in ways that required little explication the state's abandonment of its African American citizens; and many people instantly recognized as lies political statements such as 'mission accomplished.'"[32] Such claims about the transparency of historical meaning are by no means limited to literary scholarship. Historian Gabrielle Spiegel, for example, has claimed that "the linguistic turn" effected "a profound transformation in the nature and understanding of historical work, but in practice and theory . . . we all sense that this profound change has run its course."[33]

The importance of staging fresh encounters between the field's current neoempiricist tendencies and its frequently arrested or submerged elements of critique has been magnified by often clumsy notions of "postcritique" that have been sweeping through the humanities.[34] Some of these notions are patently false, as Julie Orlemanski, among others, has observed: "I know of no critical reader worth engaging who would agree that one's intellectual task is merely to 'draw out unflattering and counterintuitive meanings,' who would accept 'skepticism as dogma,' or who would recognize her own scholarship as a 'smooth-running machine for registering the limits and insufficiencies of texts' or reading as 'just a diagnostic exercise.'"[35]

But, if many of the most prominent dismissals and caricatures of critique are so distorted and unsound, what has made them so common in the first place? Why have so many humanities scholars turned away from critique at this historical juncture? One explanation focuses on what

Patricia Stuelke calls "the celebrated flight from critique to repair" or "the reparative turn,"[36] an allusion to Eve Kosofsky Sedgwick's influential work on paranoid and reparative reading, another touchstone of postcritique. Stuelke notes that "embracing the reparative meant for Sedgwick, as it has often come to mean for the scholars who write in her wake, ceasing to anticipate trouble to come or hunt for evidence of violence the academy already knows or suspects, instead finding joy where one can, honoring practices of survival, finding comfort in contact across temporal and other scales of difference, and celebrating reforms as a win . . . the reparative seems both perpetually avant-garde and eternally ethical in its generous optimism about texts and feelings."[37] Yet it remains a form of repair—of putting back together (hopefully in better condition) already existing systems and forms. But what if the systems and the forms under which we have lived for centuries are irreparable? Early America is one densely configured site of irreparability, and the contours of modern life continue to resonate with it. And yet, as the contributors to this volume demonstrate, so too do alternative possibilities that aim not merely to repair, but to reimagine and even re-shape the world as it might otherwise be.

What the arguments for postcritique seem determined to forget is that, fundamentally, critique is about attending to the present conditions of the production of knowledge—while also acknowledging that we are never simply writing better or worse accounts of the past, but different accounts of the present, as well. As anthropologist Didier Fassin puts it, "Critique is always, at least in part, a response to a certain state of the world being developed within a certain configuration of power and knowledge in the academic and public sphere."[38] Critique cannot become "exhausted," precisely because the historical present is always interrupting its own trajectories and stumbling upon its own possible futures. As legal scholar Allegra McLeod argues, "Critique . . . holds the potential to be a means of working toward that preliminary transcendence or transformation of the status quo by unmasking, deconstructing, laying bare, describing the world carefully in all its awful and mundane violence, and then refusing together the existing understandings of the world as it is and thereby beginning to make it anew."[39] Critical history attends not only to present, past, and future, but also to the ways in which categories of knowledge accrete and impinge on one another as unanticipated futures continue to become new realities. Critique is concerned less with policing disciplinary boundaries than with political and ethical analyses of the present conditions of knowledge production. It's no accident that several of the contributors to this volume turn their critical energies toward the discourses of fact, documentary, empiricism, and hypocrisy, while others turn to the conditions of the sexual subject and interiority, and still others turn to sovereignty, justice, and violence. For these are conditions of the present, as well as objects of historical inquiry.

This orientation toward critique doesn't map neatly onto discrete disciplinary forms. It requires creative, often unexpected cross-disciplinary attention to the present conditions that shore up these inherited disciplinary forms. For example, Elizabeth Maddock Dillon has pointed to the generativity of cross-disciplinary dissensus and to scholarship produced in the "large area of noncoincidence between the aims and desires of literary studies and historical studies."[40] What might our established disciplinary forms look like from new critical perspectives? Or, as Sedgwick asks: "What if the richest junctures were not the ones where *everything means the same thing*?"[41] *Situation Critical* explores what might be at stake in our methodological questions *before* we start attending to disciplinary and methodological borders. Despite what critique's critics claim, the risk of critique, like that of parrhesia, is that it encourages the kind of free speech that precedes the disciplinary expectations that so frequently yield disguised repetitions of "the same." The volume's contributors pursue patient documentary methods, such as bibliography, book history, and legal studies, that are very much in concert with the more speculative operations of critique, the fundamental aim of which is to unsettle received wisdom.

A GENEALOGY OF CRITICAL EARLY AMERICAN STUDIES

In early American studies the epistemological and analytic force of critique has often been muted by the uneasy alliance of history and literature. Thus, it's worth briefly recalling here the history of this relationship and some of the abiding material and intellectual obstacles to the flourishing of critique in the field. Eric Slauter, concerned with the contemporary material consequences (e.g., funding and institutional support, publication, economies of prestige, and state and private-sector sponsorship) for early American studies, has written of "a trade deficit . . . on the side of literary studies" and acknowledges that "the real division may not be between history and literary studies so much as it is between competing concepts within history and within literary studies about what texts are and do."[42] Questions about the nature of texts and their status as evidence—and as fodder for skirmishes between historians and literary scholars—have been with us for a long time, and they have been exacerbated by the relentless financial degradation of higher education under the aegis of neoliberal austerity. As Rey Chow asks: "What kinds of questions are deemed worthy of funding at a time when resources are dwindling largely because of a historically unprecedented, exponential expansion of the university managerial class, dedicated to entrenching its own indispensability?"[43] How do material circumstances shape the intellectual projects of early American studies? And how do the perceived viability and efficacy of intellectual projects in early American studies further influence the distribution of evaporating material resources?

The intellectual circumstances, and the oft-erected barrier to critique in early American studies, are evident to Slauter, who takes both "literary history and history" to be "historicist enterprises; they are simply committed to historicizing different things."[44] But this historicist premise shouldn't be the uninterrogated ground of the field as such. Are we all historicists simply because we write about the past? Engaging historical narratives—engaging the past in the present—need not be an inherently historicist enterprise. Literary scholars Ed White and Michael Drexler argue that the study of early American literature, broadly speaking, has continued to be "dependent for resources and readers upon a field [History] ostensibly committed to an empirical methodology (however attenuated) and often still relegating theoretical discussions to endnotes," the result of which is that "early American literary critics have often steered clear of nonhistoricist theoretical programs considered too outré by historians and their institutional patrons."[45] While acknowledging Slauter's account of a "trade gap," White and Drexler take issue with his breezy assumption that we're all historicists now, as if all that distinguished the two disciplines were the "different things" they both "historicized." In this regard, one might suggest that the material circumstances of early American studies have created a space for historicist work while marginalizing non- or counterhistoricist work.

Moreover, the early American printed works, manuscripts, and other archival materials studied by members of both disciplines are often the same objects—far more often, indeed, than in fields such as Renaissance studies and Victorian studies, where there has traditionally been a much more clearly demarcated domain of the "literary." Nevertheless, there is nothing about the nature of the early American archive that makes it any less appropriate as a focus of critique. Both within and beyond the field of early American studies, speculative archival work informed by critical theory keeps challenging the prizing of mimetic representation and ontological realism that are so characteristic of contemporary history writing, with its emphasis on the technocratic mastery of the kind of archival work that is performed chiefly in the service of foregone conclusions.[46] Unfortunately, however, speculative historicisms and alternative historical logics continue largely to be unrewarded, discredited, quarantined within "intellectual history," or exceptionalized as maverick or virtuoso.

Writing history—cultural, economic, geographical, intellectual, literary, military, political, social, subaltern, etc.—requires a commitment to the ineluctably dynamic relation between the empirical and the theoretical. It requires acknowledgment of the persistent tension between the vagaries of language and the vagaries of experience—experience both in and of the past. And it requires training in what Jameson once called the "named theories" and the ethos of critique in order to take, in the words of the Wild On Collective, "non-contiguous, non-proximate arrangements, processes, and forces seriously be they social, symbolic, or psychic structures; fields and relations; or 'causes' that may be separated from 'effects' by continents or centuries." "*Critical* history," they continue, "reflects on its own conditions of social and historical possibility. It specifies the theoretical assumptions, orientations, and implications of its claims," and it "elaborates the worldly stakes of its intervention."[47]

Such "worldly stakes" cannot be dissociated from the disciplinary anxieties and defenses that have long marked even the most sophisticated thinking about the future of the past. Even so, there have been important efforts to introduce alternative logics and to disrupt entrenched disciplinary paradigms. As far back as 1993, for example, the *William and Mary Quarterly* published a forum on "The Future of Early American History," in which ten historians speculated on possible future contours of the field. Their hopes and predictions included: a call for synthesis, against the fragmentation of social history; a synthesis of agrarian history that foreshadowed the new histories of capitalism that have helped animate the discipline in recent years; a call for more work on maritime history, which has been answered by an explosion of circum-Atlantic and other oceanic histories; a call for the renewed study of demography and population, which helped reinvigorate the study of biopolitics; a call for the expansion of African American history in early American studies; and a call for materialist intellectual histories of early America.[48]

This list is striking for its prescience: most of the essays marked out paths through subsequent decades of early American scholarship. However, it is telling that almost half of the contributions spent a significant amount of time contemplating theory, critique, and postmodernism in the context of early American history. Daniel Richter's essay, for example, sounded a warning call against what he perceived as a postmodernist threat, not only to his own investment in Native American studies, but to the entire historical enterprise as he understood it. Richter claimed that historians already knew and put into practice the valuable insights of the "postmodernist enterprise," while insisting that very enterprise was inherently antithetical to the discipline of history.

However, the new genealogies, counterhistories, and narratologies made possible by "postmodernism," which Richter's criticism identified as "hopeless" and "meaningless," were for others a source of new critical energy. Saul Cornell, for example, averred that "historians may find it most useful to consider recent theory in terms of its focus on textuality, discourse, and ideology as categories of analysis," and he sympathetically portrayed "post-structuralism's primary goal: to create the potential for political liberation by decentering, dislocating, and disrupting conventional understandings."[49] Cornell championed a "pragmatic hermeneutics" as a means of "adapting our craft to a postmodern age"—though with no mention of challenging the technocratic foundations of the discipline itself.[50] Kathleen Brown's essay celebrated the proliferation of recent work on women's and gender history that emphasized its points of intersection with contemporary feminist theory.[51] And Michael Meranze's essay drew attention to the importance of not simply conceding the irrecuperability of the past to best-effort approximations but, following figures like Benjamin and Foucault, to develop and practice, as historians, an ethics of historical loss grounded in responsibility for the dead as well as the living.[52]

Obscuring this genealogy has, in part, obscured contrary temporalities that connect the early American past to our ever-vanishing present. Indeed, Meranze's invocation of Benjamin opens up a specific way of rethinking the temporality of early America. "The past can be seized," Benjamin writes, "only as an image which flashes up at the instant when it can be recognized and is never seen again."[53] Such a formulation forces a query that connects the present and the past: Why does a particular "image" become visible at a particular "instant"?[54] And what might that mean for conventional historical periodization? Readers may wonder at the characterization of this volume's focus as "early American studies," since a significant number of the contributions focus squarely on the antebellum United States. This in itself raises issues of both periodization and disciplinarity. "Early America" has tended to be confined to the period prior to the early nineteenth century. To take the chronological purview of leading journals in the field, the *William and Mary Quarterly* considers "the early nineteenth century" to be the end of early America, while *Early American Studies* pushes the limit to 1850, and *Early American Literature* settles on a limit (approximately 1830) more or less between WMQ and EAS.[55] However, in the broad, interdisciplinary field of American studies, which skews toward more contemporary scholarship, anything prior to 1900 tends to be classed as "early." Moreover, in recent decades English literature curricula have tended to push the provisional end of early America closer and closer to 1900. In both scholarly and pedagogical domains, early America has a certain elasticity.

Periodization and temporality occupy the chapters in this volume in at least two ways. First, periodization is always a political strategy. As the medievalist Kathleen Davis writes, periodization is "not simply the drawing of an arbitrary line through time, but a complex process of conceptualizing categories, which are posited as homogenous and retroactively validated by the designation of a period divide."[56] The chapters in this volume push against such linear periodization, making political and ethical claims on the present precisely by interrogating contemporary categories in their early American iterations. Second, because critique refuses to ignore the present, connections to early America emerge in unexpected, potentially unsettling manners. As Nancy Bentley writes elsewhere, "While we may forego the most stringent kinds of critical *disenchantment*, it is possible to reimagine critique as *enchantment*" where "we can discover new dimensions of history not by looking strictly at dominant meaning systems (whether hegemonic or counterhegemonic) but at the unexpected connections that stretch across and athwart those systems."[57]

How does returning to an unexpected early America interrogate the present? And how do the problems and possibilities of contemporary life open up new questions for early Americanists? Political theorist Massimiliano Tomba sees critique as wrapped up with "a specific conception of history and time" and borrows the geological term *subduction* to characterize its "image of history as an overlapping of historical-temporal layers [standing] in opposition to the unilinear image of historical time."[58] This is a helpful way to think of the work of this volume's contributors, which tracks various concepts, events, ideas, and idioms from early America as they shift the ground of our own disciplinary present—a present constituted by multiple historical-temporal tectonic layers sliding into, over, and under one another.

The work of critique changes its objects of study, which in turn reconfigures the terms and conditions of critique. One trajectory of early American studies has been to deploy narratives that expand its purview with respect to the recovery of marginalized subjects and expansive geographic framing, in order to challenge dominant narratives both academic and popular. But the values of critique also include humility and forbearance. One need only think of the much-ballyhooed "deaths" of the author, the subject, and God. As Leo Bersani puts it, "We can, and should, will ourselves to be less than what we are; an expansive diminishing of being is the activity of a psychic utopia."[59] This, too, is an underlying aim of this volume in relation to the forces that have sustained modernity and secured conventional wisdom about early America.

The modern, normative subject—autonomous, rights-bearing, rational, property-holding, white, male, with a deep interiority marked by sexuality—has been exhaustively critiqued, both on empirical and theoretical grounds. And over the past half-century early American studies has continued to devote more and more energy to cataloging and describing the social lives of counter- or nonnormative subjects, including women, the enslaved, the propertyless, Indigenous peoples, and queer peoples, among others. Yet while this largely descriptive mode of recovery has very substantially challenged the hegemonic structures of the normative modern subject, much critical and theoretical work remains to be done.

Early America is replete with subtle, unexplored interruptions of this dominant narrative and the critical work undertaken in this volume is exemplary. For instance, the psychic defense we now understand, psychoanalytically, as repression was just as central to the seventeenth-century New England Puritans as it is to the post-Freudian subjects of today. This is not merely an empirical fact, but a fact of human subjectivity for which we now have a range of sophisticated theories—from the beginnings of psychoanalysis to contemporary neuroscience—that continue to challenge and find themselves challenged by ever-shifting accounts of early modern psychology. To better understand the articulation of repression in, say, the traces of the uses of Michael Wigglesworth's diary or the poetic self-making of the Puritan Edward Johnson, then and now, is to better understand the relationship between psychic life, settler colonialism, and the trials of Anglo-Protestant self-scrutiny.

Similarly, the discursive dimensions of sexuality, so frequently studied as part of nineteenth-century Anglo-American subjectivation, have received far less study in histories of early America.[60] For instance, the moral panic over masturbation in the nineteenth-century United States has been much more thoroughly studied than the onanistic discourse of the Great Awakening. And queer subjectivities have yet to be adequately historicized in relation to the textual practices and medical discourses of Puritan self-fashioning. Pre-nineteenth-century Anglo-American subjects developed diverse and sophisticated discourses of sexuality and gender that are impossible to comprehend now if they are quarantined from contemporary critical discourses through which we understand our own psychosexual development.

Of course, the modern subject has been insistently figured as secular, as made possible by the split between the public and the private spheres, a split that often relegated the supposedly nonrational to the precincts of the private—religion, family, emotion, desire. The cultural afterlife of Thomas Paine, as both atheist and as someone deemed a moral hypocrite by others, for instance, works to recalibrate religion and secularism, public and private, insofar as the discourse of moral hypocrisy stems from precisely those dualisms. This kind of critique is not one that empirically proves that a public-private division was not an accurate description of lived experience, but that the public and the private, imbricated in one another, sustained the specific deployment of the secular as a biopolitical regime.

The empirical, the factual, and the documentary are the conditions of the modern regime of truth—a regime that appears increasingly destabilized in our contemporary era of so-called post-truth. However, to attend meaningfully to the empirical, the factual, and the documentary in early America requires attending, as well, to their variability, ideological uses, relations to hierarchies of oppression, and delimitations of freedom—and also, crucially, to their speculative and imaginative possibilities. The imbrication of the descriptive and the interpretive, the empirical and the ideological, has, of course, been accounted for by other scholars. In her history of the modern fact, Mary Poovey has traced the way that "what looks like two distinct functions—describing and interpreting—seem to be different only because one mode of representation (the number) has been graphically separated from another (the narrative commentary)."[61] Or, as Jennifer Morgan has demonstrated, the sciences of numeracy—demography, accounting, political economy—were entirely wrapped up in the justification of slavery and the delimitation of the human: who could be counted and how they were counted were presented as empirical facts, which, precisely in the figuring of the fact as number, as calculable, delimited the borders of humanity.[62]

Again, the origins of another category, that of the representation of reality, are bound up in the epistemic conditions of early America. To claim that factuality, objectivity, disinterested description, and ideologically neutral empiricism are impossible is not a particularly new claim, but this is not being advanced here to bolster the power of constructivism even if that is a side effect. Rather, a critical attention to them in the context of the specific work they do in early America is particularly revealing and not simply to make us all contingent relativists. The point is not, as so many historians have claimed, that the past is always contingent, that our histories can never be fully objective; rather, it is that that contingency is inherent in the past itself—our present has not broken down, it has recirculated and rearticulated already broken-down categories.

Similarly, modern notions of sovereignty, race, justice, and power emerge in early America and the wider Atlantic and have been figured as unfolding in various ways. Sovereignty increasingly attached to the nation-state system that was worked out in a colonial field; race constituted in the interstices of Atlantic slavery and colonialism becoming the dominant categorical organization of the modern world; justice, increasingly attached to law and the nation; power and violence and periodization not so much an aberration as a constitutive feature. The narrative origins of these ideas are often located in the thickets of early America and the Atlantic world, but, again, these origins, under close critical interrogation, are found to be cracked, unstable foundations. Indeed, critical attention to them diminishes the historical narratives, uncovers subjugated knowledges, and in doing so recovers possibilities for thinking the political, justice, the nation-state, violence, and power otherwise.

To attend to critique and early America, then, is to open the major issues of the present—subjectivity, sexuality, truth, empiricism, justice, sovereignty, violence—in their buried, subjugated forms in early America, and it is in that recursive relationship that critique performs its most trenchant work for early America—a past in the present, the present in a past, as it were. Its urgency inheres in the double move in the present, where staid categories calcify and break apart simultaneously. On a precipice, then, critical early American studies could be said to take the risk of the parrhēsiast, a risk that inheres in a persistent recourse to the nonfoundational conditions of knowledge and history.

This brings us full circle—if the conditions of early America are figured as always fragmented, never stable, always able to be diminished, then is there, can there be, a crisis now? Especially one with specific bearing on early America? Do the apparent crises of late modernity around race, capitalism, sexuality, or sovereignty relate to the origin narrative in early America? Surely, what gives early America a place in so many conceptualizations of modernity is that its origins narratives are routed through and refracted in the spatiotemporal formation we call early America. But the critical approach advanced in this volume puts crisis itself into question. Do crisis and critique need to be joined? As the anthropologist Janet Roitman puts it, "The point is to observe crisis as a blind spot, and hence to apprehend the ways in which it regulates narrative constructions, the ways in which it allows certain questions to be asked while others are foreclosed."[63] So rather than the close coupling of crisis and critique, perhaps, as demonstrated here, the operations of critique directed at a specific object—early America—demonstrate that our narratives and conceptualizations of contemporary crisis are misplaced. This is not to offer a rosy picture of the present; far from it. Rather, the sense of contemporary crisis relies, as Roitman suggests, on reifying a stable past and not asking questions, or the right questions, of it.

NEW GENEALOGIES

We invite readers to approach this volume as a series of meditations on desire and truth in the writing of early America, and the first two chapters equip the reader for such an approach. Joan W. Scott begins by exploring the relationship between history and psychoanalysis and highlighting the inevitable indeterminacy of historical knowledge shaped by unconscious as well as conscious motivations. In the next chapter, Michael Meranze directs attention to Foucault's late lectures on parrhesia, sovereignty, and the government of the self as critical aids to historical reflection on the relation between truth-telling and power. By foregrounding the work of two of the volume's intellectual touchstones, Freud and Foucault, these two chapters illuminate some of the most important theoretical and critical stakes for the new critical histories of early America toward which the ensuing chapters embark.

Part II attends to the interrelations of desire, truth, sexuality, and interiority in early America, paying particular attention to seventeenth- and eighteenth-century Puritan and evangelical writings. As Ana Schwartz demonstrates, any discussion of what Perry Miller famously called "the New England Mind" must account for its unconscious as well as conscious dimensions. Indeed, against scholars who argue that these Puritans enjoyed a conscious, emotional freedom, unmarked by repression and the conflicts of the unconscious, Schwartz shows, in a brilliant reading of a poem by Edward Johnson, that repression acted as a defense mechanism against the quotidian struggles and irritations of settler colonialism. Schwartz argues that settler colonialism and its spectacular violence of dispossession are impossible to understand apart from settlers' unconscious struggles with their own internal regimes of psychic displacement and dispossession.

Following Schwartz's exploration of repression, Christopher Looby and Mark J. Miller return to the history of sexuality in the murky period of the seventeenth and eighteenth centuries. Looby focuses on the diary of the Puritan minister Michael Wigglesworth, who recorded what may be homoerotic dreams and his experiences of nocturnal emissions in a "secret cipher" as part of the tachygraphy of the diary. Looby excavates a speculative moment in the history of sexuality that situates queerness at the intersection of the secret discourse of the diary, the material textual practices of shorthand, and the medicalizing impulse in Wigglesworth's writings (he consulted with several doctors about his nocturnal emissions). In this, an emergent moment in the history of queer sexuality is evident precisely in the opacity of the diary. As Looby puts it, "With Wigglesworth we are still far short of the historical emergence of the homosexual as a species of person, but we are at least a step beyond an undifferentiated concept of lust that might attach itself to many different objects but was itself one thing only."

Miller similarly takes up questions of sexuality and textual study in his reading of George Whitefield's autobiography and his public efforts to deal with his own masturbation. Whereas Looby attends to the private diary of Wigglesworth and its later, twentieth-century publication history, Miller focuses on the multiple variants of Whitefield's autobiography, which was written for publication, and questions of the relationship between sex, print, and publicity. Whitefield published what was one of the only first-person narratives of masturbation in the emergent transatlantic print public sphere, offering a particularly germinative site for exploring the emergence of sexuality in the evangelical print public sphere.

Part III focuses on early nineteenth-century critiques of veracity, fact, and empiricism, and on the way such discourses structured secularism, family, freedom, and Black speculative life. Indeed, in the context of emergent secularism and Enlightenment conceptions of reason and freedom, critical histories of this period emphasize the spectacular and speculative, contingent and precarious configurations of fact and belief. As Justine S. Murison shows, emergent secular society was in part configured around hypocrisy as a disconnect between private self and public persona. Attending both to the afterlife of Tom Paine, in which the American Tract Society ventriloquized him as a hypocritical infidel, and to Royal Tyler's 1797 novel *The Algerine Captive*, Murison contends that the cultivation of belief and attempts to verify it follow from disestablishment and the secular organization of privacy. As such, there is a spectacular quality to the efforts to verify real belief that continue to haunt the twenty-first century's obsessions with hypocrisy and moral authenticity. Moreover, as Murison shows, the inherently secular vocations that animate the disciplines of history and English tend to obscure this reading.

Britt Rusert, returning to issues addressed in her book *Fugitive Science*, attends to the "purchase of empiricism . . . for enslaved and nominally free people." Taking her cue from David Walker's use of the term *immaterial*, Rusert traces a deployment of empiricism to speculative ends in Black writing in the nineteenth century, thus critically engaging more conventional uses of the empirical. In doing so, Rusert links the immaterial and the speculative empiricism to a kind of critical nihilism, a questioning of the existence of the world in writings by Walker, Frederick Douglass, Martin Delany, and others, to the death drive. Such an account, linking the speculative and the empirical, limning the boundary between the material and the immaterial, opens a new reading of nineteenth-century epistemologies.

In a similar manner, Jordan Alexander Stein attends to the documentary realism of nineteenth-century abolitionist writing and in doing so uncovers the manner in which the opposite of slavery was not freedom, not contract, not wage labor, but rather the heteronormative family. While the emphasis on the family in antislavery writing is well known, Stein's critique of abolitionist writing here examines the centrality of the "simple referentiality" of antislavery writing, exemplified by Theodore Dwight Weld's *American Slavery as It Is*, and the way it naturalized heteronormativity in an effort to critique slavery. In this figuration, domestic familial life became inevitable and heteronormative gender roles were naturalized.

The final section of this volume attends to the conjunctions of war, violence, and sovereignty to open up entirely new ways, via critique, of conceptualizing possibilities of justice and periodization, of absence and presence. Matthew Crow offers a fresh reading of the tricky and elusive concept of equity. Equity, which raises the question of where the power to do justice sits in an institutional order, offers a space by which to intervene in liberal accounts of justice and the law. Crow, leaning on Adorno's and Benjamin's work on allegory, turns to the writings of Herman Melville, and in particular, *Moby-Dick*, to excavate a natural history of justice situated in the chasm between the history of law and the history of justice. In doing so, Crow attends to the oceanic conditions of justice in an effort to critically interrogate the human and beyond human aspects of justice. The radical strangeness of equity, in particular its off-kilter temporality, opens up possibilities for rethinking justice itself, borne of Melville's allegories.

This question of time, and in particular of periodization, is of particular concern to John J. Garcia in his critical reading of the Mexican War. Situating it in the context of emergent war reporting and spectacle, Garcia argues that the Mexican War is a vanishing public event, marked by its occlusion and disappearance in historical memory, which furthers the effort of erasing atrocity. In a critical revaluation of periodization itself, Garcia suggests that interbellum, which emphasizes an in-betweenness, is perhaps preferable to the much more common antebellum. However, this is no mere corrective; instead, Garcia merges critical theory and critical bibliography to trace out the different temporality of the war in the writings of soldiers, reporters, and Franklin Pierce that set the war at odds with the time of the nation-state. In doing so, this new effort at periodization, which Garcia reads through Georges Bataille's work on sacrifice, centered the disappeared and reappearing violence of the Mexican War as an extraterritorial refiguring of both early and antebellum America.

NOTES

Epigraph: Emily Dickinson, "Crisis is a Hair," *Poems of Emily Dickinson*, 2:934.

1. Locke, *Two Treatises*, 301.
2. Weber, *Protestant Ethic*.
3. Quijano and Wallerstein, "Americanity," 550.
4. See, for example, Smith-Rosenberg, *This Violent Empire*; Berkin, *A Sovereign People*; Calloway, *Indian World*; Breen, *The Will of the People*; Fox-Amato, *Exposing Slavery*.
5. Scott, "Fantasy Echo," 51.
6. "1619 Project."
7. Hannah-Jones et al., *1619 Project*.

8   For serious, critical engagements, see Karp, "History as End"; Jackson, "1619 and Public History."
9   Without constraining the meanings of critique, it is worth provisionally noting here that it is worth distinguishing the project of critique from criticism or from being critical. Eric Fassin makes a useful distinction between critique and criticism. As Fassin puts it, "This is what critical thought is about. It is not merely about the denunciation of our opponents' positions, which would only amount to *criticism. Critique* also entails questioning the imposition of the very terms of debate." Fassin, "From Criticism to Critique," 267.
10 Foucault, *Courage of Truth*, 11.
11 Foucault, *Courage of Truth*, 9.
12 Laws regulating and dictating what can and cannot be taught, laws that have determined that critical accounts of the history of the United States are forms of indoctrination, have emerged in numerous states over the past several years. Nowhere is this more evident than in Florida, exemplified both in the passage of the so-called Stop WOKE Act, as well as new posttenure regulations that include indoctrination and violation of state law, as grounds for dismissal of tenured faculty. For a sampling of how early America is conceptualized, here is former state secretary of education Richard Corcoran and now president of New College: "Instruction on the required topics must be factual and objective and may not suppress or distort significant historical events, such as the Holocaust, and may not define American history as something other than the creation of a new nation based largely on universal principles stated in the Declaration of Independence." For Corcoran's comments, see "Education Proposal Targets Efforts to 'Indoctrinate,' for the Stop WOKE Act," https://www.flsenate.gov/Session/Bill/2022/7; for posttenure review, see https://www.flbog.edu/wp-content/uploads/2022/11/NoticeofProposedNewRegulation_10.003_Nov2022.pdf.
13 In recent years, the social media hashtag #VastEarlyAmerica has galvanized debate about the advantages and disadvantages of the field's sheer breadth, prompting some to wonder whether the expanding geographical, cultural, linguistic, and chronological scope of early American studies leaves sufficient space for coherent, sufficiently reflexive early American historiographies.
14 Connolly, "Against Accumulation," 172.
15 Latour, "Why Has Critique Run Out of Steam?"
16 Foucault, "What Our Present Is," 137.
17 See, e.g., Bennett, *Colonial Blackness*; Best, *Fugitive's Property*; Bhandar, *Colonial Lives of Property*; Burnham, *Folded Selves*; Cahill, *Liberty of the Imagination*; Castronovo, *Propaganda 1776*; Crow, *Thomas Jefferson*; Dillon, *Gender of Freedom*; Drexler and White, *Traumatic Kernel*; Fuentes, *Dispossessed Lives*; Kazanjian, *Colonizing Trick*; Morgan, *Reckoning with Slavery*; Rusert, *Fugitive Science*; Schwartz, *Unmoored*; Shapiro, *Culture and Commerce*; Wertheimer, *Underwriting*; White, *Backcountry and City*; and Wong, *Neither Fugitive nor Free*.

18 Kant, "Answer to the Question," 17.
19 Kompridis, *Critique and Disclosure*, 3.
20 Derrida, *Of Hospitality*.
21 Nietzsche, *Twilight*, 155.
22 Dickinson, "Crisis is a Hair," 2:934.
23 Benjamin, "Theses," 264.
24 Paine, "Last Crisis," 348.
25 Whitehead, *Function of Reason*, 34.
26 Buck-Morss, *Hegel, Haiti, and Universal History*.
27 Downes, *Hobbes, Sovereignty*.
28 Kazanjian, *Brink of Freedom*.
29 Thiessen, "The Danger of Critical Race Theory."
30 Moten, "Knowledge of Freedom."
31 Felski, *Limits of Critique*, 188.
32 Best and Marcus, "Surface Reading," 2.
33 Spiegel, "Task of the Historian," 3.
34 See Felski, *Limits of Critique*; Anker and Felski, *Critique and Postcritique*; and Castronovo and Glimp, "Introduction: After Critique." Recently, a range of scholars has, in various ways, tried to conceive of new reading practices that would move beyond what they take to be the tired, predictable, and outdated practice of "symptomatic reading" closely associated with Louis Althusser and Fredric Jameson. See, for example, Best and Marcus, "Surface Reading:"; and Love, "Close Reading." For skeptical responses, see, for example, Rooney, "Live Free or Describe"; Weed, "Way We Read Now"; and Robbins, "Not So Well Attached."
35 Orlemanski, "A Reader's Love," 9.
36 Stuelke, *Ruse of Repair*, 4.
37 Stuelke, *Ruse of Repair*, 4.
38 Fassin, "How Is Critique," 14.
39 McLeod, "Law, Critique, and the Undercommons," 255.
40 Dillon, "Atlantic Practices," 208.
41 Sedgwick, *Tendencies*, 6; see also Farred, "'Science Does Not Think,'" 58.
42 Slauter, "History, Literature," 154.
43 Chow, *Face Drawn in Sand*, 8.
44 Slauter, "History, Literature," 154.
45 White and Drexler, "Theory Gap," 472.
46 See, for instance, Connolly and Fuentes, "Introduction"; Helton et al., "Question of Recovery."
47 Jameson, *Postmodernism*, 184; Wild On Collective, "Theses on Theory and History."
48 "Forum: The Future of Early American History."
49 Cornell, "Early American History," 329.
50 Cornell, "Early American History," 341.

51 Brown, "Brave New Worlds."
52 Meranze, "Even the Dead Will Not Be Safe." For another influential effort to address the conjunction of theory and early American studies from this period, see St. George, *Possible Pasts*.
53 Benjamin, "Theses," 255.
54 For more on this in the context of early American studies, see Kazanjian, *Colonizing Trick*, 27–34.
55 See the websites for the *William and Mary Quarterly* (https://oieahc.wm.edu/publications/wmq/), *Early American Studies* (https://eas.pennpress.org/home/), and *Early American Literature* (https://uncpress.org/journals/early-american-literature/).
56 Davis, *Periodization and Sovereignty*, 3.
57 Bentley, "Critique as Enchantment," 149. Bentley cites James, *Black Jacobins*, and Buck-Morss, *Hegel, Haiti*, as examples.
58 Tomba, "Critique as Subduction," 114.
59 Bersani, "I Can Dream," 69.
60 See, for instance, LaFleur, *Natural History of Sexuality*.
61 Poovey, *History of the Modern Fact*, xii.
62 Morgan, *Reckoning with Slavery*.
63 Roitman, *Anti-Crisis*, 94.

BIBLIOGRAPHY

Anker, Elizabeth S., and Rita Felski, eds. *Critique and Postcritique*. Durham, NC: Duke University Press, 2017.

Benjamin, Walter. "Theses on the Philosophy of History." In *Illuminations: Essays and Reflections*, edited by Hannah Arendt, translated by Harry Zohn, 253–64. New York: Schocken Books, 1969.

Bennett, Herman L. *Colonial Blackness: A History of Afro-Mexico*. Bloomington: Indiana University Press, 2009.

Bentley, Nancy. "Critique as Enchantment: Introduction." *J19: The Journal of Nineteenth-Century Americanists* 1, no. 1 (Spring 2013): 147–53.

Berkin, Carol. *A Sovereign People: The Crises of the 1790s and the Birth of American Nationalism*. New York: Basic, 2017.

Bersani, Leo. "I Can Dream, Can't I?" In *Thoughts and Things*, 58–76. Chicago: University of Chicago Press, 2015.

Best, Stephen M. *The Fugitive's Properties: Law and the Poetics of Possession*. Chicago: University of Chicago Press, 2004.

Best, Stephen, and Sharon Marcus. "Surface Reading: An Introduction." *Representations* 108, no. 1 (Fall 2009): 1–21.

Bhandar, Brenna. *Colonial Lives of Property: Law, Land, and Racial Regimes of Ownership*. Durham, NC: Duke University Press, 2018.

Breen, T. H. *The Will of the People: The Revolutionary Birth of America*. Cambridge, MA: Harvard University Press, 2019.

Brown, Kathleen M. "Brave New Worlds: Women's and Gender History." *William and Mary Quarterly* 50, no. 2 (April 1993): 311–28.

Buck-Morss, Susan F. *Hegel, Haiti, and Universal History*. Pittsburgh: University of Pittsburgh Press, 2009.

Burnham, Michelle. *Folded Selves: Colonial New England Writing in the World System*. Hanover, NH: Dartmouth University Press, 2007.

Cahill, Edward. *Liberty of the Imagination: Aesthetic Theory, Literary Form, and Politics in the Early United States*. Philadelphia: University of Pennsylvania Press, 2012.

Calloway, Colin G. *The Indian World of George Washington: The First President, the First Americans, and the Birth of the Nation*. New York: Oxford University Press, 2018.

Castronovo, Russ. *Propaganda 1776: Secrets, Leaks, and Revolutionary Communications in Early America*. New York: Oxford University Press, 2014.

Castronovo, Russ, and David Glimp. "Introduction: After Critique?" *English Language Notes* 51, no. 2 (Fall/Winter 2013): 1–5.

Chow, Rey. *A Face Drawn in Sand: Humanistic Inquiry and Foucault in the Present*. New York: Columbia University Press, 2021.

Connolly, Brian. "Against Accumulation." *J19: The Journal of Nineteenth-Century Americanists* 2, no. 1 (2014): 172–79.

Connolly, Brian, and Marisa Fuentes, eds. "Introduction: From Archives of Slavery to Liberated Futures?" *History of the Present: A Journal of Critical History* 6, no. 2 (Fall 2016): 105–16.

Cornell, Saul A. "Early American History in a Postmodern Age." *William and Mary Quarterly* 50, no. 2 (April 1993): 329–41.

Crow, Matthew. *Thomas Jefferson, Legal History, and the Art of Recollection*. Cambridge: Cambridge University Press, 2017.

Davis, Kathleen. *Periodization and Sovereignty: How Ideas of Feudalism and Secularization Govern the Politics of Time*. Philadelphia: University of Pennsylvania Press, 2008.

Derrida, Jacques. *Of Hospitality*. Translated by Rachel Bowlby. Stanford, CA: Stanford University Press, 2000.

Dickinson, Emily. "Crisis is a Hair." In *The Poems of Emily Dickinson: Variorum Edition*, 3 vols., edited by R. W. Franklin, 2:934. Cambridge, MA: Harvard University Press, 1998.

Dillon, Elizabeth Maddock. "Atlantic Practices: Minding the Gap between Literature and History." *Early American Literature* 43, no. 1 (2008): 205–10.

Dillon, Elizabeth Maddock. *The Gender of Freedom: Fictions of Liberalism and the Literary Public Sphere*. Stanford, CA: Stanford University Press, 2004.

Downes, Paul. *Hobbes, Sovereignty, and Early American Literature*. Cambridge: Cambridge University Press, 2015.

Drexler, Michael J., and Ed White. *The Traumatic Colonel: The Founding Fathers, Slavery, and the Phantasmatic Aaron Burr*. New York: New York University Press, 2014.

Farred, Grant. "'Science Does Not Think': The No-Thought of the Discipline." *South Atlantic Quarterly* 110, no. 1 (2011): 57–74.

Fassin, Didier. "How Is Critique?" In *A Time for Critique*, edited by Didier Fassin and Bernard Harcourt, 13–35. New York: Columbia University Press, 2019.

Fassin, Eric. "From Criticism to Critique." *History of the Present: A Journal of Critical History* 1, no. 2 (2011): 265–74.

Felski, Rita. *The Limits of Critique*. Chicago: University of Chicago Press, 2015.

"Forum: The Future of Early American History." *William and Mary Quarterly* 50, no. 2 (1993): 298–424.

Foucault, Michel. *The Courage of Truth: The Government of Self and Others II. Lectures at the Collège de France, 1983–1984*. Translated by Graham Burchell. New York: Picador, 2012.

Foucault, Michel. "What Our Present Is." In *The Politics of Truth*, edited by Sylvère Lotringer, 129–44. New York: Semiotext(e), 2007.

Fox-Amato, Matthew. *Exposing Slavery: Photography, Human Bondage, and the Birth of Modern Visual Politics in America*. New York: Oxford University Press, 2019.

Fuentes, Marisa J. *Dispossessed Lives: Enslaved Women, Violence, and the Archive*. Philadelphia: University of Pennsylvania Press, 2016.

Hannah-Jones, Nikole, Caitlin Roper, Ilena Silverman, and Jake Silverstein, eds. *The 1619 Project: A New Origin Story*. New York: Random House, 2021.

Helton, Laura, Justin Leroy, Max A. Mishler, Samantha Seeley, and Shauna Sweeney, eds. "The Question of Recovery: Slavery, Freedom, and the Archive." *Social Text* 33, no. 4 (December 2015): 1–18.

Jackson, Lauren Michelle. "The 1619 Project and the Demands of Public History." *New Yorker* (December 8, 2021). Accessed November 3, 2022. https://www.newyorker.com/books/under-review/the-1619-project-and-the-demands-of-public-history.

James, C. L. R. *The Black Jacobins: Toussaint L'Ouverture and the San Domingo Revolution*. New York: Vintage, 1963.

Jameson, Fredric. *Postmodernism; or, the Cultural Logic of Late Capitalism*. Durham, NC: Duke University Press, 1990.

Kant, Immanuel. "An Answer to the Question: What Is Enlightenment?" In *Toward Perpetual Peace and Other Writings on Politics, Peace, and History*, edited by Pauline Kleingeld and translated by David L. Colclasure, 17–23. New Haven, CT: Yale University Press, 2006.

Karp, Matthew. "History as End." *Harper's Magazine* (May 2021). Accessed November 3, 2022. https://harpers.org/archive/2021/07/history-as-end-politics-of-the-past-matthew-karp/.

Kazanjian, David. *The Brink of Freedom: Improvising Life in the Nineteenth-Century Atlantic World*. Durham, NC: Duke University Press, 2016.

Kazanjian, David. *The Colonizing Trick: National Culture and Imperial Citizenship in Early America*. Minneapolis: University of Minnesota Press, 2003.

Kompridis, Nikolas. *Critique and Disclosure: Critical Theory between Past and Future.* Cambridge, MA: MIT Press, 2006.

LaFleur, Greta. *The Natural History of Sexuality in Early America.* Baltimore: Johns Hopkins University Press, 2018.

Latour, Bruno. "Why Has Critique Run Out of Steam? From Matters of Fact to Matters of Concern." *Critical Inquiry* 30, no. 2 (2004): 225–48.

Locke, John. *Two Treatises of Government.* Edited by Peter Laslett. Cambridge: Cambridge University Press, 1988.

Love, Heather. "Close Reading and Thin Description." *Public Culture* 25, no. 3 (Fall 2013): 401–34.

McLeod, Allegra M. "Law, Critique, and the Undercommons." In *A Time for Critique*, edited by Didier Fassin and Bernard Harcourt, 252–70. New York: Columbia University Press, 2019.

Meranze, Michael. "Even the Dead Will Not Be Safe: An Ethics of Early American History." *William and Mary Quarterly* 50, no. 2 (April 1993): 367–78.

Morgan, Jennifer L. *Reckoning with Slavery: Gender, Kinship, and Capitalism in the Early Black Atlantic.* Durham, NC: Duke University Press, 2021.

Moten, Fred. "Knowledge of Freedom." In *Stolen Life*, 1–95. Durham, NC: Duke University Press, 2018.

Nietzsche, Friedrich. *Twilight of the Idols, or How to Philosophize with a Hammer.* In *The Anti-Christ, Ecce Homo, Twilight of the Idols, and Other Writings*, edited by Aaron Ridley and Judith Norman, translated by Judith Norman, 153–230. Cambridge: Cambridge University Press, 2005.

Orlemanski, Julie. "A Reader's Love." *American Book Review* 38, no. 5 (2017): 8–9.

Paine, Thomas. "The Last Crisis." In *Collected Writings*, edited by Eric Foner, 348–54. New York: Library of America, 1995.

Poovey, Mary. *A History of the Modern Fact: Problems of Knowledge in the Sciences of Wealth and Society.* Chicago: University of Chicago Press, 1998.

Quijano, Anibal, and Immanuel Maurice Wallerstein. "Americanity as a Concept, or the Americas in the Modern World System." *International Social Science Journal* 44, no. 4 (1992): 549–57.

Robbins, Bruce. "Not So Well Attached." *PMLA* 132, no. 2 (March 2017): 371–76.

Roitman, Janet. *Anti-Crisis.* Durham, NC: Duke University Press, 2013.

Rooney, Ellen. "Live Free or Describe: The Reading Effect and the Persistence of Form." *differences: a journal of feminist cultural studies* 21, no. 3 (2010): 112–39.

Rusert, Britt. *Fugitive Science: Empiricism and Freedom in Early African American Culture.* New York: NYU Press, 2017.

Schwartz, Ana. *Unmoored: The Search for Sincerity in Colonial America.* Chapel Hill: University of North Carolina Press, 2023.

Scott, Joan Wallach. "Fantasy Echo: History and the Construction of Identity." In *The Fantasy of Feminist History*, 45–67. Durham, NC: Duke University Press, 2011.

Sedgwick, Eve Kosofsky. *Tendencies.* Durham, NC: Duke University Press, 1993.

Shapiro, Stephen. *The Culture and Commerce of the Early American Novel: Reading the Atlantic World-System*. State College: Penn State University Press, 2007.

"The 1619 Project," *New York Times*. https://www.nytimes.com/interactive/2019/08/14/magazine/1619-america-slavery.html.

Slauter, Eric. "History, Literature, and the Atlantic World." *Early American Literature* 43, no. 1 (2008): 153–86.

Smith-Rosenberg, Carroll. *This Violent Empire: The Birth of an American National Identity*. Chapel Hill: University of North Carolina Press, 2010.

Spiegel, Gabrielle M. "The Task of the Historian.*" American Historical Review* 114, no. 1 (February 2009): 1–15.

St. George, Robert Blair, ed. *Possible Pasts: Becoming Colonial in Early America*. Ithaca, NY: Cornell University Press, 2000.

Stuelke, Patricia. *The Ruse of Repair: US Neoliberal Empire and the Turn from Critique*. Durham, NC: Duke University Press, 2021.

Thiessen, Marc A. "The Danger of Critical Race Theory." *Washington Post*, November 11, 2021. Accessed November 6, 2022. https://www.washingtonpost.com/opinions/2021/11/11/danger-critical-race-theory/.

Tomba, Massimiliano. "Critique as Subduction." In *A Time for Critique*, edited by Didier Fassin and Bernard E. Harcourt, 114–31. New York: Columbia University Press, 2019.

Weber, Max. *The Protestant Ethic and the Spirit of Capitalism: And Other Writings*. Translated by Talcott Parsons. London: Routledge, 1992.

Weed, Elizabeth. "The Way We Read Now." *History of the Present: A Journal of Critical History* 2, no. 1 (2012): 95–106.

Wertheimer, Eric. *Underwriting: The Poetics of Insurance in America, 1722–1872* Stanford, CA: Stanford University Press, 2006.

White, Ed. *The Backcountry and the City: Colonization and Conflict in Early America*. Minneapolis: University of Minnesota Press, 2005.

White, Ed, and Michael J. Drexler. "The Theory Gap." *American Literary History* 22, no. 2 (Summer 2010): 480–94.

Whitehead, Alfred North. *The Function of Reason*. Princeton, NJ: Princeton University Press, 1929.

Wild On Collective [Ethan Kleinberg, Joan Wallach Scott, and Gary Wilder]. "Theses on Theory and History." May 2018. http://theoryrevolt.com/.

Wong, Edlie L. *Neither Fugitive nor Free: Atlantic Slavery, Freedom Suits, and the Legal Culture of Travel*. New York: NYU Press, 2009.

I THEORY FOR EARLY AMERICA

ONE · *Joan W. Scott*

Psychoanalysis and the Indeterminacy of History

At the meeting of the Vienna Psychoanalytic Society on March 27, 1907, the presentation by a Dr. Sadger was about somnambulism (sleepwalking) and its relationship to dream life. Freud made the concluding remarks, cautioning against accepting the statements of patients at face value; these always represented, he said, "a falsified picture, compounded of fantasy and reality." "Fantasy," he continued, "fills in memory gaps in a plausible, often very clever way . . . we find this in lovers who cannot tolerate the thought that their present state is a new one and who are soon convinced that they have known each other long ago. The hysteric, too, in the etiology of whose illness seduction . . . has played no role . . . does the same thing when he transforms the autoeroticism of his childhood into object love by means of fantasies corresponding to his present thinking. The historian proceeds similarly when he projects the views of his own time onto the past."[1]

Freud's preoccupation with history, the Israeli psychoanalyst Eran Rolnik tells us, came from his interest in the fallibility of human memory "with its unconscious psychic determinants," and his desire to call into question "history's objectifying pretensions"—pretensions that were particularly strong at that moment of the discipline's formation. "The epistemological foundations of psychoanalysis," Rolnik tells us, "were . . . laid in close proximity to the ideas voiced by the leading historians of his day."[2]

For that reason it seems useful to return to some of those ideas as we contemplate questions about critique in our contemporary context. My argument is that Freud's insistence on the ultimate indeterminacy of our knowledge is the best guarantee we have of practicing critique. Freud suggested that the pursuit of knowledge was illusory—the quest for positive knowledge (hard facts we might call them now) was simply a disguise that concealed the primary processes—the drives—which were the true motivation for the quest. Psychoanalysis is "suspicious" of any account that stops with the production of positive knowledge; the cure has nothing to do with the discovery of "the facts." This skepticism about the status of positive knowledge and the insistence that the pursuit of it is ongoing— and itself needs interpretation—enables the kind of critical work that, by constantly interrogating normative concepts, keeps future possibilities open. What does it mean to "know history"? What does the writing of history entail beyond the construction of sequences of events? How far can we take the notion that the pursuit of knowledge itself is symptomatic of something else? Foucault characterized psychoanalysis (along with ethnology) as a "counter-science" which flowed in the opposite direction from the empirical human sciences: "They lead them back to their epistemological basis, and . . . they ceaselessly 'unmake' that very man who is creating and re-creating his possibility in the human sciences."[3]

Freud's comments on history recur throughout his work, whether he is talking about individual cases (the Wolfman, the Ratman), historical figures (Leonardo da Vinci) or "group psychology" ("Totem and Taboo"; "Moses and Monotheism"; *Civilization and Its Discontents*). A word he uses often is "tendentious" (meaning biased, promoting a particular interest or set of beliefs) to characterize the motives of those writing history in the service of a nation; they are producing fantasized memories in much the way an individual adult does about his childhood. The analogy is a strong one: "Closer investigation," he wrote, "would perhaps reveal a complete analogy between the ways in which the traditions of a people and the childhood memories of the individual come to be formed."[4] Men became concerned with their past, Freud suggests, when they "felt themselves to be rich and powerful, and now felt a need to learn where they had come from." So they

> gathered traditions and legends, [and] interpreted the traces of antiquity that survived in customs and usages . . . It was inevitable that this early history should have been an expression of present beliefs and wishes rather than a true picture of the past; for many things had been dropped from the nation's memory, while others were distorted, and some remains of the past were given a wrong interpretation in order to fit in with contemporary ideas. Moreover people's motive for writing history was not objective curiosity but a desire to influence their contemporaries, to encourage and inspire them, or to hold up a mirror before them.[5]

Just as he grappled with distinguishing the truth of a patient's past from his or her unreliable recollections of it, so Freud thought it possible to discern "the historical truth behind the legendary material" in a nation's history.[6] Sometimes he suggested that traditions were analogous to an individual's unconscious: "Tradition is a repository of facts and ideas left out by official historians."[7] "They owe their power to the element of historical truth which they have brought up from the repression of the forgotten and primeval past."[8] Sometimes he thought it was necessary only to get at the "tendentious purposes" of historians: "By recognizing the distortions produced by those purposes we shall bring to light fresh fragments of the true state of things lying behind them."[9] This truth was not about what happened, but why. In either case, the work was archaeological: transforming incomplete and imperfect bits of found objects into a plausible construction (or reconstruction) of the motives and meanings of past experience.

Freud distinguished between interpretation and construction, the one addressing a single element of the material under analysis, the other the creation of a fuller narrative.[10] If memory is a psychic process, informed by such things as repression, displacement, condensation, fantasy, desire, conflict, envy, aggression, and ambivalence, the analyst's job is to make sense of it. Yet that sense is not pursued for itself, but only as a way of weaving together scattered elements to achieve an affective transformation in the patient. This is what Freud, speaking of the interpretation of dreams, referred to as "secondary revision," and what François Duparc defines as "a rearrangement of the seemingly incoherent element of the dream into a form serviceable for narration. This involves logical and temporal reorganization in obedience to the principles of non-contradiction, temporal sequence, and causality which characterize the secondary processes of conscious thought."[11] Here there is a similarity to history, but the end is different—affective transformation, not a closed narrative that stands on its own.

Freud's case histories are themselves narratives, as they describe the uneven process of construction by which the analyst helps a patient rewrite his life story in order to account for troubling behavior in the present that necessarily has its roots in the past. Freud's attempts at more conventional histories—"Totem and Taboo" and "Moses and Monotheism" are examples—are also constructions, efforts, that is, to explain contemporary phenomena (the origins of the social contract; the reputation of Jews) by critically revisiting accounts of the past, but then writing them in familiar chronological form. For the disciplined historian there is a fascinating tension between what appears to be wild speculation (based on a variety of texts) and the familiar chronological form in which it is presented. It is all the more fascinating because Freud is fully aware of the pitfalls of his approach:

> I am very well aware that in dealing so autocratically and arbitrarily with Biblical tradition—bringing it up to confirm my view when it suits me and unhesitatingly rejecting it when it contradicts me—I am exposing myself to serious methodological criticism and weakening the convincing force of my argument. But this is the only way in which one can treat material of which one knows definitely that its trustworthiness has been severely impaired by the distorting influence of tendentious purposes. It has to be hoped that I shall find some degree of justification later on, when I come upon the track of these secret motives. Certainty is in any case unattainable and moreover it may be said that every other writer on the subject has adopted the same procedure.[12]

Here again, we have a direct refusal of the claims of an objective science of history—it is the "tendentious" practice that conceals the "secret motives" that must be explored, but that exploration has no finite end. Instead, it is a recognition that the "construction" achieved in analysis is not objective, but not untrue either. The selection, weaving, and reweaving rewrites the analysand's sense of her history, but it does not foreclose subsequent narrations as fantasies and repressed material continue to come to light in the course of the analysis. Could we think about the process of historical revisionism in similar terms—as a process in which the desire to contest prevailing orthodoxies leads the historian to long forgotten or overlooked material that then becomes the basis for a new understanding of some aspect of the past?

Freud's insistence on the validity of his approach came from his sense that the psychic realities of human existence had been given short shrift in historians' accounts. In 1938 he noted "the modern tendency . . . towards tracing back the events of human history to more concealed, general and impersonal factors, to the compelling influence of economic conditions, to alterations in food habits, to advances in the use of materials and tools, to migrations brought about by increases in population and climatic changes."[13] He had no objection to these, only to the attempt to identify a single cause that eliminated any consideration of an individual's influence on events (Moses was the case in point here), since these events, he argued, were always "overdetermined, . . . the effect of several convergent causes."[14] The point was not to try to account for what Michel de Certeau called "the areas where an economic or a sociological explanation forcibly leaves something aside,"[15] but rather to include the irrational as a fundamental principle of human behavior—psychic reality was a vital aspect of human experience. "In spite of all the distortions and misunderstandings," Freud wrote of legends of early history, "they still represent the reality of the past: they are what a people forms out of the experience of its early days and under the dominance of motives that were once powerful and still operate today; and if it were only possible, by a knowledge of the forces at work [he means the ones uncovered by psychoanalysis], to undo these distortions, there would be no difficulty in disclosing the historical truth lying behind the legendary material."[16]

The distinction between reality and truth is important here—reality is a set of manifest beliefs and the practices that follow from them; truth is the underlying psychic—we might say critical—explanation that refers to repressions, fantasies, delusions. Finding "truth" meant looking beyond the self-justification offered by actors, not in order to impugn their motives or discredit their aims, but to uncover the desires and anxieties they contained, the collective representations they appealed to, in order to better understand how psychic processes—those of the people in the past as well as of their historians—enabled and informed what has come to count as history.[17]

THE POST-FREUDIAN FREUD

I came late to psychoanalysis personally and professionally, having for a long time refused it as a useful way of thinking either about myself or about history. In retrospect I think that's fortunate, because the Freud I discovered was what Adam Phillips calls the "post-Freudian" Freud, the one read through the lenses of poststructuralism (Jacques Lacan, Jean Laplanche, Michel Foucault, and certain feminists—Naomi Shor, Joan Copjec, Renata Salecl), postcolonialism (Frantz Fanon), and theories of race and racism (Hortense Spillers, Sylvia Wynter). This is the Freud who, according to Phillips, questions "the very idea of the self as an object of knowledge." "The inevitability of infancy, the unruliness of instinctual life, the puzzling acquisition of language and its link with sexuality, the unconscious dreamwork; all of these suggested to Freud a radical and formative insufficiency, something that cannot be solved by knowledge."[18] In terms of identity, we cannot know in advance how subjects will identify. Social attribution (cultural construction in the jargon of the 1980s and 1990s) is not psychic determination. Foucault tells us that the modern subject is "always open, never finally delimited, yet constantly traversed."[19] Certeau puts it this way: "The labor by which the subject *authorizes* his own existence is of a kind other than the labor for which he receives *permission* to exist. The Freudian process attempts to articulate this difference."[20] Joan Copjec insists as well that subjects are not reducible "*to* the images social discourses construct *of* [them]."[21] Within this frame, Peter Coviello reads the contributions of W. E. B. Du Bois: "All that is certain is that the black citizen will be compelled to include among his or her other attachments in the world, a relation to the shifting imperatives of race. That relation can be described . . . but never presumed."[22] He conceives of the relation in terms of form—the truncation of possibility by normative restrictions—and content—an affective register, consisting of "variance and surprise."[23] Hortense Spillers, looking to add race to psychoanalytic theorizing, suggests that "the question . . . is not so much why and how 'race' makes the difference—the police will see to it—but how it carries over its message onto an interior, how 'race' as a poisonous idea insinuates itself not only across and between ethnicities, but within."[24]

The post-Freudian Freud refuses the conflation of social construction with subjectivity. Social construction presumes an external causality for the constitution of subjects that is challenged by the operations of the unconscious in the formation of individual subjects. The post-Freudian Freud asks us not to read diagnostically (Oedipus complex, family romance, developmental stages) because these labels tend to close down interpretive possibilities. (I realize that these kinds of readings continue to be offered, but they are not the ones I am referring to.) It asks us instead to read openly, expecting to encounter the unforeseen and the unknown. This reading practice involves acute attention to language. It refuses categorical explanations and reductive causalities, opening itself instead to the vagaries of linguistic expression and to theories of psychic representation that seek to make them intelligible. Rolnik writes that "psychoanalysis is not a reservoir of answers but a language, which touches on, yet allows itself to be surprised by, a wide range of human uncertainties and illogicalities."[25]

Foucault noted that the Freudian approach led to considerations that exceeded the bounds of the empirical knowledge of Man. It exposed "what is there and yet is hidden . . . what exists with the mute solidity of a thing, of a text closed in upon itself, or of a blank space in a visible text."[26] Exceeding the bounds of empirical knowledge means taking into account what Elizabeth Wilson calls the "unruly unconscious,"[27] and recognizing that human histories and history writing itself have something in common with

Freud's description of "a day-dream or a phantasy," in which "past, present and future are strung together, as it were, on the thread of the wish that runs through them."[28] The wish (an unconscious expression) at once links past, present, and future *and* undermines any permanent linkage. This is not to say that anything goes in historical accounts, only that our relationship to the realities of history is more complex than the one that locates the historian's truth solely in the excavation of documents from archives, in quantitative measures of such events as births, deaths, marriages, prices, strikes, and wars, or in the literal acceptance of testimony offered in courts of law, memoirs, or oral history interviews. The evidence of experience is neither transparent nor self-evident; it is only grist for the historians' analytic mill.

I think it is important to add, in this moment of "alternative facts," that neither psychoanalysis nor the history influenced by it denies "reality" in the manner of Donald Trump or other authoritarian types. The point is to introduce another register of interpretation, an attempt to understand the psychic underpinnings of the stories we tell, of the ways we account for events and actions—individual and collective. This is what Freud was after when he pondered the story of Moses and the founding myths of nations. What is at stake, he asked, in the need to locate an origin or to define a set of national character traits? This kind of question does not deny the existence of Moses or of nation-states, rather it asks: How do unconscious processes influence politics? How do they influence the work of historians? The critical role of psychoanalysis here is to attempt to account for the unconscious motives that play into and define what counts as an event or a fact, and that color the debates—on all sides—about their meaning.

INCOMMENSURABLE DIFFERENCES

Having said this, I do not want to suggest that psychoanalysis is the only way for historians to approach their task, though I think it adds a necessary dimension precisely by underlining the aspect of the ultimate uncertainty or indeterminacy of all knowledge. There are significant, even incommensurable, differences between the disciplines of history and psychoanalysis. Freud may have taken history writing as an object for analytic attention and he certainly constructed narratives in a way familiar to historians, but as epistemological projects and as disciplines they differ in important ways.

Like psychoanalysis, the discipline of history acknowledges that facts are in some sense produced through interpretation, but each understands this production to take place differently. For historians events are the starting point of the analysis—the taken for granted occurrences whose effects come afterward.[29] (Here I am referring to disciplinary orthodoxies, not to the Foucauldian notion that discursive conditions produce events that become detached from their conditions of production as objects in themselves.) For psychoanalysts it is the other way around: events are deduced from their effects. Analysts attend to what Freud called nachträglichkeit (translated as "deferred action") to indicate the way in which events acquire significance through revision, "rearrangement in accordance with fresh circumstances . . . a re-transcription."[30] As he wrestled with the timing of the primal scene in the Wolf Man case, Freud insisted on "the part played by phantasies in symptom-formation and also the 'retrospective phantasying' of later impressions into childhood and their sexualization after the event."[31] While he concluded that the obsessional neurosis of his patient must have originated when he witnessed his parents' coitus, there was no way finally to establish the fact that the event had actually occurred. Freud acknowledged the difficulty of attributing the dream of a four-year-old boy, recalled by a grown man undergoing analysis some twenty years later, to a trauma experienced by a one-and-a-half-year-old child. (Indeed, the trauma happens only retrospectively when the boy—witnessing copulating animals—makes the connection to what he thought he saw earlier.) But, finally, Freud dismissed the effort at precision as beside the point: "It is also a matter of indifference in this connection whether we choose to regard it as a primal *scene* or a primal *phantasy*."[32] The actual witnessing of an event, in other words, is not the issue; it is the role it plays in unconscious manifestations (symptoms) that matters. As Certeau puts it, "Analysis establishes history by virtue of a relation among successive manifestations."[33]

If historians assume that the linear narratives they create capture the past's relationship to the present (and, in some cases, the present's to the past), psychoanalysts operate in more than one temporal register. There is the time of the analysis and the times remembered in analysis and these do not add up to a single chronology. Brady Brower puts it this way: "Within the practical time of the analysis, the analysand's speech designated a second temporality, one that made it possible for the analyst's speech to be attributed a role with little or no correspondence to his actual personal characteristics or his formal capacities as an analyst."[34] Unlike historians who make an object (an other) of the denizens of the past (and who rarely consider their own reasons for studying those objects), analysts refuse objectification, seeking instead to bring analysands to recognition of the unconscious agency—the condition and limits—of their own subjectivity. It is not, as some have noted, that for Freud, the past always haunts the present, but that the objective times of past and present are confused, often indistinguishable. The point is that time is a complex creation, a constructed dimension of subjectivity, not, as for historians, a chronological given. Freudian theory is skeptical of the evolutionary chronology that shapes professional historians' presentations, instead attending to the role repression or nostalgia play in the construction of memory and of the historian's version of events, as well as to the interruptions and discontinuities that characterize the necessarily uneven and often chaotic interactions of past and present in the psyche.

And there is no end to the individual's story. Although an analysis itself may eventually terminate, the patient is not cured, only better aware of how to deal with her symptoms. This is different from the arbitrary closure that historians provide at the end of their accounts, whether by drawing boundaries of periodization between one age and another, or tracing the lives and deaths of institutions, groups, and individuals subsumed into set categories of identity. In our accounts, for the most part, it is the operations of finite changes (their causes and effects) that demand our attention.

Although Freud likened human memory to an archive in 1898, he soon preferred the concept of archaeology. And there is good reason for this, as pointed out compellingly by Carolyn Steedman in *Dust*, her response to Derrida's *Archive Fever*. Archives, she notes, are formal repositories, ordered by "principles of unification and classification." The human memory, in contrast, is a "fathomless and timeless place in which nothing goes away," whereas the archive, she writes, "is made from selected and consciously chosen documentation from the past and also from the mad fragmentations that no one intended to preserve and that just ended up there."[35] This means that the space of the archive is not the fetishized container that, for many historians in these days of Big Data, Big History, and the so-called empirical (re)turn, has come to be seen as the indisputable, because transparent, source of complete historical knowledge. It is instead, in Steedman's words, full of "stories caught half way through: the middle of things, discontinuities."[36] The archive is a space, she says, "of dreams, of imaginative play," where historians pursue lost objects that are ultimately impossible to retrieve in their original completeness. Yet it is the quest for completeness (to say nothing of the sheer pleasure of the journey) that drives us from archive to archive, text to text, and it is the manner of writing our stories—the conventions of narrative itself—that ensures a sense of completeness or at least of closure. There is no recognition (as there would be in the analytic setting I am thinking of) that the closure is necessarily imaginary, imposed on the materials, unifying them to defy their multiplicity. This is a different imperative from the one that drives the psychoanalyst.

Unlike the analyst, who confronts his patient and works with him through the transference, there is no transference for historians in the archive.[37] There is, instead, a one-sided relationship to the dead, who are made (in the French historian Jules Michelet's depiction of it) "to walk and talk again."[38] Michelet wrote, "I have given to many of the disregarded dead the assistance that I myself shall need. I have exhumed them for a second life."[39] Certeau reflects on the relationship of history to death this way: "Historiography tends to prove that the site of its production can encompass the past: it is an odd procedure that posits death, a breakage everywhere reiterated in discourse, and that yet denies loss by appropriating to the present the privilege of recapitulating the past as a form of knowledge. A labor of death and a labor against death."[40]

On the question of life and death, time and causality, subject and object, there is thus an incompatibility between the aims of psychoanalysis and of the discipline of history. Certeau captures the disparity: "Now I must ask: what disturbing uncanniness does Freudian writing trace within the historian's territory, where it enters dancing? Reciprocally, in what fashion will my question, born of an archival and scriptural labor that cultivates this territory, and seduced by the fiction of psychoanalytical history, be enlightened/distorted through Freud's analysis?"[41] For Certeau the seductive dance of Freudian analysis necessarily distorts even as it sheds new light on the territory of the historian. He designates writing as "fiction" in the sense both of fabrication and deception. The Freudian "dance" is counterposed to the historians' "labor"; "dance" refers to the multiple and mobile forms taken by imaginative representation and also to a certain artful pleasure, while "labor" stresses the imposition of order on (the disciplining of) the materiality of archives and their transcription. Historical writing, he says, is the unconscious or unacknowledged way of working through the historian's relationship to death, at once erasing it by resurrecting the past and avowing it through its very erasure. For Certeau the crucial term is "uncanniness"—psychoanalysis brings back something once familiar, but now estranged through the operations of distance and repression.

It is the clash, not the compatibility, of the two different concepts of history that proves productive for Certeau. "The interdisciplinarity we look toward would attempt to apprehend epistemological constellations as they reciprocally provide themselves with a new delimitation of their objects and a new status for their procedures."[42] The clash is effectively disruptive in both directions, although Certeau's interest (and mine as well) is in bringing psychoanalytic disruption to the attention of historians.

GENDER

The immediate question that drew me to psychoanalysis had to do with my work on gender. Dissatisfied with arguments about cultural construction, economic interest, and patriarchy (though all of these have relevance and utility), I turned increasingly to what seemed to me *the* source for thinking about sex and sexuality—psychoanalytic theory. It was in the theorizing of sexual difference and, beyond that, in philosophical discussions of the formation of subjects that I found the perspective I was seeking. In that theorizing—Freud's and the Lacanian rereading of Freud—the difference of sex is ultimately inexplicable. It is the riddle that defies fixed meaning, the understanding that always seems to escape control, the dilemma that gives rise to myth and fantasy. It is the place where questions of the relationship of mind and body are confounded. Psychoanalytic theory refuses a separation between the biological and the social or cultural, attending instead to what Alenka Zupančič describes as "the zone where the two realms overlap; i.e., where the biological or somatic is already mental or cultural and where, at the same time, culture springs from the very impasses of the somatic functions which it tries to resolve (yet, in doing so, creates new ones). In other words ... the overlapping in question is not simply an overlapping of two well-established entities ('body' and 'mind'), but an intersection which is generative of both sides that overlap it."[43] Sex and sexual difference are generated by this intersection. The mind/body, culture/nature oppositions don't work here. Anatomy is not a fact apart, but rather a fantasy about the body's meaning that follows from gender assignment (naming, gender designation—the identification as male or female at birth) and from a child's efforts to account for what he or she sees or does not see (imagined as castration).[44] Jean Laplanche (invoking history to think psychoanalysis) refers to "the contingent, perceptual and illusory character of anatomical sexual difference," which cannot ground the gender assignment that precedes it.[45] Zupančič points out that "the central point of Freud's discovery was precisely that there is no 'natural' or pre-established place of human sexuality. . . . The sexual is not a substance to be properly described and circumscribed, it is the very impossibility of its own circumscription or delimitation.... Sexual is not a separate domain of human activity or life, and this is why it can inhabit all the domains of human life."[46] But precisely because it is impossible to describe or limit, great effort has been expended to fix its meaning, locating anatomy as an explanation for gender. (This, I take to be the effort of the so-called new materialism, which invokes "the body" as the ground on which sex is built.) Entire social and cultural edifices are built on the shaky foundations of so-called immutable gender difference. Whether taken as God's word or Nature's dictate, gender—the historically and culturally variable attempt to insist on the duality of sex difference—becomes the basis for imagining social, political, and economic order.

By thinking gender in these terms, I found I could gain insight not only into the articulation, implementation, regulation, and transgression of what used to be called "sex roles," but also into the ways difference (at least in modern times) organizes perceptions of societies, polities, and economies. This, of course, meant assuming the fragility of these perceptions, and it required reading for specific, contextual articulations of what male/female differences were taken to mean.

That gender plays a crucial definitional role in the organization of societies and politics is evident these days in the anguished warnings from opponents of feminist and queer theories, who argue that "gender theory" is an assault against the very foundations of civilized life. To take only two examples: During the debates that led to the creation of the International Criminal Court in 1999, one commentator noted that if gender were allowed to refer to anything beyond biologically defined male and female, the court would be in the position of "drastically restructuring societies throughout the world."[47] This same concern about the radical potential of the concept was expressed by the opponents of a French curriculum that aimed at gender equity in 2011 and of France's law on gay marriage in 2013. The "theory of gender," they argued, "by denying sexual difference, [would] overturn the organization of our society and call into question its very foundations."[48]

It is not only that gender is a primary way of conceiving of differentiation, extending beyond sex to race, class, and nation, it is also that the illusory nature of anatomical sex difference introduces ambivalence, anxiety, indeterminacy, and instability into these organizing conceptual systems. Knowing that this is the case opens the way to thinking about the dynamic operations of these systems, reading for their points of tension and contradiction, for the ways devised to deny or displace norms and regulations, and thus for the sources of their transformation.

I do not think of my work as exclusively psychoanalytic (it is not psychohistory), nor is psychoanalysis only supplementary, accounting for reason's leftovers or deviations, those pathological outbursts that otherwise do not fit within conventional frames. Rather, psychoanalysis has become an integral aspect of my thinking about the past. (And, my friend, the psychoanalyst seeking to historicize gender for his clinical practice, adds: "And your historian's perspective is a fundamental aspect to our rethinking of psychoanalysis.")[49] It is probably most useful at this point to offer some examples of what I mean by this. They come from my current work on secularism, a book that is a synthetic history, based on reading and rereading lots of work—feminist, postcolonial, queer theory, theories about race and racism—on the foundational place of gender in the emergence of modern nation-states.

The first example has to do with the politics of the nuclear family from the eighteenth century on, particularly the idea that the only legitimate aim of sexual activity was reproduction, confined to a married, heterosexual couple. What Lee Edelman, invoking Freud and Lacan, calls "reproductive futurism" helps me account for this far-reaching phenomenon. Edelman's is a manifesto for a queer politics; my interest in his work has to do with understanding historical developments. It is his emphasis on reproduction as a denial of the death drive that inspires my thinking.[50] To put it all too briefly, the advent of the discourse of secularism, what Max Weber called "disenchantment"—the substitution of rational calculation for religious belief—brought with it questions about the meaning of life. In the discourses of secularists, there was no longer a guarantee of immortality, of some kind of spiritual life after death, nor was it possible to imagine death as continuous with life. This led, Weber observed, to a sense not only of the "meaninglessness of death," but also to "the senselessness of life itself." He writes, "The stronger, the more systematic the thinking about the 'meaning' of the universe becomes, the more the external organization of the world is rationalized, and the more the conscious experience of the world's irrational content is sublimated."[51] Sublimation in the classic Freudian sense is the turning of unappeasable anxiety to socially constructive ventures. A. K. Kordela describes it as the "administration and management of the subject's relation to mortality and immortality, as compensation for the loss of eternity."[52] In this discourse, biological reproduction becomes not only the sole legitimate aim of sexual intercourse, but the guarantee of immortality—securing life's meaning by deferring its realization to succeeding generations. This is what Edelman means by "reproductive futurism": "Children secure our existence through the fantasy that we survive in them." Edelman notes that it is not so much real children as an iconic Child that embodies this promise, "the promise of a natural transcendence of the limits of nature itself."[53] From this secular insistence on the importance of reproduction follows what Jacques Donzelot has called "the policing of families"—the intervention of state power in the supposedly private life of individuals.[54] "The old power of death that symbolized sovereign power," Foucault wrote, "was now carefully supplanted by the administration of bodies and the calculated management of life."[55] The "unruly unconscious" refuses to disappear. But the question of what counted as a man or woman could never be entirely settled, it persisted in challenging and undermining those calculated management schemes. Reading for the rearticulations of gender in these terms and, of course, in the context of political, economic, and social developments from the eighteenth century on provides critical insight into that politics and history.

The second example has to do with political institutions and citizenship and takes off from Claude Lefort's observation about the "indeterminacy" of democracy. In the discourse of disenchantment, the loss of preeminent religious authority meant the loss of a transcendent affirmation for political power. Possession of the phallus, the symbol of the ruler's power, was no longer the prerogative of God's representative on earth. And, as the reign of kings (and the occasional queen) gave way to representative systems of government (parliaments, constitutional monarchies, republics, democracies), the physical body of the ruler as the incarnation of sovereignty was replaced by a set of disembodied abstractions: state, nation, citizen, representative, individual. Lefort puts it this way: "The locus of power becomes an empty place. . . . It is such that no individual and no group can be consubstantial with it—and it cannot be represented."[56] The impossibility of representation, he continues, leads to a permanent state of uncertainty: "The important point is that democracy is instituted and sustained by the dissolution of the markers of certainty. It inaugurates a history in which people experience a fundamental indeterminacy as to the basis of power, law and knowledge and as to the relations between *self* and *other* at every level of social life."[57] Indeterminacy is a feature of democracy, not a denial of its history or institutions. It can help account not only for the longstanding exclusion of women and minorities from access to political office, but also for the populist appeal of figures like Trump and Berlusconi.

Freud theorized in "Totem and Taboo" that social contracts emerged when the original band of brothers, fed up with their father's monopoly of women, killed and ate him. The equal distribution of power among them, however, remained a challenge.[58] Although there have been many attempts to equate the phallus with the penis and therefore political power with masculinity, the fit has not been as persuasive as when a single ruler wielded all the power. Indeed, the penis might be seen as a poor substitute for the large, central, and singular authority of the king. In any event, making the literal case for the penis as phallus has required continuous effort, the invention and reinvention of explanations. And it has not solved the matter of competition among the brothers. Can one of them ultimately take the father's place and so be exempt from or above the law? If so, which one? What are the signs of what Lacan called "phallic exceptionalism"?[59] The search for answers to these questions plays out in the writing of constitutions, in the structure of political parties, in competition for office, in debates about the access of women to politics, in politicians' sexual liaisons, and in varieties of political conflict, some of which have shaken the very foundations of nation-states.

To the extent that those foundations rest, at least in the Western imaginary, on notions of naturalized, immutable sex differences, they will remain indeterminate (and that is probably all to the good). It is not (as I once argued) gender that itself constitutes a useful category for historical analysis, but gender understood as the impossible resolution to what psychoanalysis tells us is the enigma of the difference of sex. Far from imprisoning our history in closed diagnostic categories, this approach opens us to new readings of the past, and it also reminds us that those readings are never entirely definitive, never the last word. For Lefort, the indeterminacy of democracy was its hallmark and its guarantee. Perhaps we can say that the indeterminacy of interpretation insisted upon by psychoanalysis offers a similar guarantee for the practice of history.

NOTES

An earlier version of this chapter appeared as "The Incommensurability of Psychoanalysis and History," *History and Theory* 51, no. 1 (2012): 63–83.

1. Nunberg and Federn, *Minutes of the Vienna Psychoanalytic Society*, I:156.
2. Rolnik, "Between Memory and Desire," 130. Rolnik's work led me to the *Minutes* cited in note 1.
3. Foucault, *Order of Things*, 379.

4 Freud, "Psychopathology of Everyday Life," 148. Childhood memories, Freud maintained, "correspond, as far as their origins and reliability are concerned, to the history of a nation's earliest days, which was compiled later and for tendentious reasons" (84).
5 Freud, "Psychopathology of Everyday Life," 83.
6 Freud, "Psychopathology of Everyday Life," 84.
7 Freud, "Moses and Monotheism," 69.
8 Freud, "Moses and Monotheism," 269.
9 Freud, "Moses and Monotheism," 42.
10 Freud, "Moses and Monotheism," 261.
11 Duparc, "Secondary Revision."
12 Freud, "Moses and Monotheism," 27. Elsewhere in this same text he writes: "Once again I am prepared to find myself blamed for having presented my reconstruction of the early history of the people of Israel with too great and unjustified certainty. I shall not feel very severely hit by this criticism, since it finds an echo in my own judgement. I know myself that my structure has its weak spots, but it has its strong points too. On the whole my predominant impression is that it is worthwhile to pursue the work in the direction it has taken" (41).
13 Freud, "Moses and Monotheism," 107.
14 Freud, "Moses and Monotheism," 107.
15 Certeau, *Writing of History*, 289.
16 Freud, "Leonardo da Vinci," 84.
17 There is no collective unconscious for Freud and I don't mean to imply that here. Rather, it is the case that individual unconscious processes can involve identification between members of a group or with a particular leader, producing collective action in certain instances. Historically specific representations provide a common repertoire or vocabulary for this kind of collective action. See Freud, *Group Psychology*, 67–143.
18 Phillips, *Terrors and Experts*, cited in Coviello, "Intimacy and Affliction," 24.
19 Foucault, *Order of Things*, 322.
20 Certeau, *Writing of History*, 303.
21 Copjec, "Cutting Up," 241–42.
22 Coviello, "Intimacy and Affliction," 15.
23 Coviello, "Intimacy and Affliction," 31.
24 Spillers, "All the Things You Could Be by Now," 88.
25 Rolnik, "Between Memory and Desire," 148.
26 Foucault, *Order of Things*, 394.
27 Wilson, "Another Neurological Scene," 156.
28 Freud, "Creative Writers and Day-Dreaming," 147–48.
29 This is how Philip Rieff put it: "If for Marx the past is pregnant with the future, with the proletariat as the midwife of history, for Freud the future is pregnant with the past, with the psychoanalyst as the abortionist of history." Rieff, "Meaning of History and Religion," 28.
30 Cited in Laplanche and Pontalis, *Language of Psychoanalysis*, 112.

31 Freud, *History of an Infantile Neurosis*, 103.
32 Freud, *History of an Infantile Neurosis*, 120.
33 Certeau, *Writing of History*, 303.
34 Brower, "Science, Seduction," 172.
35 Steedman, *Dust*, 68.
36 Steedman, *Dust*, 45.
37 This is a disagreement with the idea of transference offered by LaCapra, "Is Everyone a Mentalité Case?," 72–73.
38 Cited in Steedman, *Dust*, 150.
39 Steedman, *Dust*, 150.
40 Certeau, *Writing of History*, 5.
41 Certeau, *Writing of History*, 309.
42 Certeau, *Writing of History*, 291.
43 Zupancic, *Why Psychoanalysis*, 7.
44 Samuel Weber's 1973 reading of Freud's essay on the uncanny points out that the phallus is not an object, but instead symbolizes the structure of castration itself. "Not only do the eyes present the subject with the shocking 'evidence' of a negative perception—the absence of a maternal phallus—but they also have to bear the brunt of a new state of affairs"—the subject "will never again be able to believe its eyes, since what they have seen is neither simply visible nor wholly invisible . . . What is involved here is a restructuring of experience, including the relation of perception, in which the narcissistic categories of identity and presence are riven by a difference they can no longer subdue or command." Weber, "Sideshow," 1133.
45 Laplanche, "Gender, Sex and the Sexual," 159–202.
46 Zupancic, *Why Psychoanalysis*, 19.
47 Rome Statute of the International Criminal Court, July 17, 1998. https://legal.un.org/icc/statute/99_corr/cstatute.htm.
48 "La Théoricienne du gender honoré par l'université Bordeaux 3," a protest circulated by the Association pour la Fondation de Service politique, a Catholic organization, protesting the award to Butler; accessed November 23, 2011, www.libertepolitique.com.
49 Private email communication with Thamy Ayouch. See Ayouch, "La déportation pour motif d'homosexualité," 89–116.
50 Edelman, *No Future*.
51 Weber, "Religious Rejections," 356–57.
52 Kordela, "(Psychoanalytic) Biopolitics," 19.
53 Edelman, *No Future*, 12.
54 Donzelot, *La police des familles*.
55 Foucault, *History of Sexuality*, 139–40.
56 Lefort, *Democracy and Political Theory*, 17.
57 Lefort, *Democracy and Political Theory*, 19.
58 Freud, "Totem and Taboo," 1–161.
59 Lacan, "Signification of the Phallus," 281–91. See also Fink, *Clinical Introduction*.

BIBLIOGRAPHY

Ayouch, Thamy. "La déportation pour motif d'homosexualité: mémoire et histoire." In *Déportations en héritage, Revue française de Phénoménologie et de Psychanalyse*, 89–116. Paris: L'Harmattan, 2015.

Brower, M. Brady. "Science, Seduction and the Lure of Reality in Third Republic France." *History of the Present* 1, no. 2 (2011): 170–93.

Certeau, Michel de. *The Writing of History*. Translated by Tom Conley. New York: Columbia University Press, 1988.

Copjec, Joan. "Cutting Up." In *Between Feminism and Psychoanalysis*, edited by Teresa Brennan, 227–46. New York: Routledge, 1989.

Coviello, Peter. "Intimacy and Affliction: Du Bois, Race, and Psychoanalysis." MLQ: *Modern Language Quarterly* 64, no. 1 (March 2003): 1–32.

Donzelot, Jacques. *La police des familles*. Paris: Les Editions de Minuit, 1977.

Duparc, Francois. "Secondary Revision." http://www.answers.com/topic/secondary-revision?&print=true.

Edelman, Lee. *No Future: Queer Theory and the Death Drive*. Durham, NC: Duke University Press, 2004.

Fink, Bruce. *A Clinical Introduction to Lacanian Psychoanalysis: Theory and Technique*. Cambridge, MA: Harvard University Press, 1997.

Foucault, Michel. *The Order of Things: An Archaeology of the Human Sciences*. New York: Vintage, 1994.

Freud, Sigmund. "Creative Writers and Day-Dreaming." In *The Standard Edition of the Complete Psychological Works of Sigmund Freud*, Vol. 9, edited and translated by James Strachey, 141–54. London: Hogarth, 1995.

Freud, Sigmund. "From the History of an Infantile Neurosis." In *The Standard Edition of the Complete Psychological Works of Sigmund Freud*, Vol. 17, edited and translated by James Strachey, 3–124. London: Hogarth, 1995.

Freud, Sigmund. "Group Psychology and the Analysis of the Ego." In *The Standard Edition of the Complete Psychological Works of Sigmund Freud*, Vol. 18, edited and translated by James Strachey, 67–143. London: Hogarth, 1995.

Freud, Sigmund. "Leonardo da Vinci and a Memory of His Childhood." In *The Standard Edition of the Complete Psychological Works of Sigmund Freud*, Vol. 11, edited and translated by James Strachey, 59–138. London: Hogarth, 1995.

Freud, Sigmund. "Moses and Monotheism." In *The Standard Edition of the Complete Psychological Works of Sigmund Freud*, Vol. 23, edited and translated by James Strachey, 3–140. London: Hogarth, 1995.

Freud, Sigmund. "The Psychopathology of Everyday Life." Vol. 6 of *The Standard Edition of the Complete Psychological Works of Sigmund Freud*, edited and translated by James Strachey. London: Hogarth, 1995.

Freud, Sigmund. "Totem and Taboo." In *The Standard Edition of the Complete Psychological Works of Sigmund Freud*, Vol. 13, edited and translated by James Strachey, ix–164. London: Hogarth, 1995.

Kordela, A. Kiarina. "(Psychoanalytic) Biopolitics and Bioracism." *Umbr(a): A Journal of the Unconscious* (2011): 11–24.

Lacan, Jacques. "The Signification of the Phallus." In *Écrits: A Selection*, translated by Alan Sheridan, 281–91. New York: Norton, 1977.

LaCapra, Dominick. "Is Everyone a Mentalité Case? Transference and the 'Culture Concept.'" In *History and Criticism*, 71–94. Ithaca, NY: Cornell University Press, 1985.

Laplanche, Jean. "Gender, Sex and the Sexual." In *Freud and the Sexual*, 159–202. London: International Psychoanalytic Books, 2011.

Laplanche, J., and J.-B. Pontalis. *The Language of Psychoanalysis*. Translated by Donald Nicholson-Smith. New York: Norton, 1973.

Lefort, Claude. *Democracy and Political Theory*. Translated by David Macey. London: Polity Press, 1991.

Nunberg, H., and E. Federn, eds. *Minutes of the Vienna Psychoanalytic Society*. 4 vols. New York: International Universities Press, 1962–75.

Phillips, Adam. *Terrors and Experts*. London: Faber and Faber, 1995.

Rieff, Philip. "The Meaning of History and Religion in Freud's Thought." *Journal of Religion* 31, no. 2 (April 1951): 114–31.

Rolnik, Eran. "Between Memory and Desire: From History to Psychoanalysis and Back." *Psychoanalysis and History* 3, no. 2 (2001): 129–51.

Spillers, Hortense J. "All the Things You Could Be by Now, If Sigmund Freud's Wife Was Your Mother: Psychoanalysis and Race." *boundary 2* 23, no. 3 (1996): 75–141.

Steedman, Carolyn. *Dust: The Archive and Cultural History*. New Brunswick, NJ: Rutgers University Press, 2002.

Weber, Max. "Religious Rejections of the World and Their Directions." In *From Max Weber: Essays in Sociology*, edited by H. H. Gerth and C. Wright Mills, 323–85. New York: Routledge, 1998.

Weber, Samuel. "The Sideshow, or: Remarks on a Canny Moment." MLN 88, no. 6 *Comparative Literature* (December 1973): 1102–33.

Wilson, Elizabeth. "Another Neurological Scene." *History of the Present* 1, no. 2 (2011): 149–69.

Zupančič, Alenka. *Why Psychoanalysis: Three Interventions*. Aarhus, Denmark: Aarhus University Press, 2008.

TWO · *Michael Meranze*

Foucault's Oedipus

The figure of Oedipus is a recurrent presence in Foucault's work during the 1970s and 1980s. He made a brief occurrence early in the first year of Foucault's lectures at the Collège de France (*Lectures on the Will to Know*) and then received a fuller consideration in that year's final lecture. Foucault then presented a separate discussion on "Oedipal Knowledge" at a series of occasions in 1971 and 1972. Oedipus figured significantly in lectures on "Truth and Juridical Forms" presented in Brazil in 1973. Then, following a hiatus of several years, Oedipus returned with a vengeance in 1980 and 1981 and crucially was revisited in 1982. I leave aside the brief dismissal of the Oedipus complex in *The Will to Know*.

Oedipus's presence over the last fourteen years of Foucault's life strikes as significant for several reasons. First it gives the lie to the most common depiction of Foucault's intellectual trajectory as a withdrawal from concern with sovereignty and politics. Foucault's reading of Sophocles's *Oedipus Rex*, and it was that version of Oedipus that he was concerned with, consistently foregrounded issues of the relationship of truth to law and sovereignty—indeed if there was any trajectory it was the increasing emphasis on the problem of political power. Second, the readings of Oedipus in 1972–73 and then again in 1980–82 marked crucial moments of transition in Foucault's conceptualization of his problematic, and are examples of criticism of both his own work and the work of others. Third, Foucault's treatment of the play was distinctly historical and genealogical—which set it off against the famous readings of Sigmund Freud and Claude Lévi-Strauss. And finally, it made clear Foucault's ultimate interest in the history of "truth-telling," the point at which Foucault's work on Oedipus opens out onto more contemporary concerns. For his recurrent engagement with *Oedipus Rex* and its themes of truth-telling and sovereignty pointed, in the end, to his rediscovery of the ancient practice of parresia, with its joining together of ethics and politics in risking the truth in the context of political struggle.

Indeed, Foucault's discussions of *Oedipus Rex* functioned as an elementary matrix or privileged object in articulating the concerns of his last decade and a half of work. This is not to say that it provides a key to all mythologies, but rather that in Sophocles's *Oedipus Rex* Foucault found a series of problems, images, and narratives that offered a lens through which to focus his concerns over the history of the truth in its relationship to power, politics, ethics, and the law. In this regard, although there were continuities in his discussion of the play, its contexts and relationships changed in important ways. Both that consistency and the variation are crucial to reapproaching Foucault's work in new and productive ways.

....

Sophocles's play revolved around the efforts of Oedipus to determine the murderer of his predecessor King Laius. Oedipus, assumed by all to be a native of Corinth, had gained the kingship of Thebes after freeing the city from the Sphinx. He did so by answering riddles and therefore demonstrating that he himself was a man of knowledge and skill. As a foreigner who achieved power through his own skill, Oedipus shared the characteristics of the seventh- and sixth-century Greek tyrant whose personal rule often marked the transition of political regimes in Greek city-states. The play opens with Theban priests beseeching Oedipus to save them again—only this time from the plague. As we quickly learn, the Delphic Oracle (Apollo's Oracle) has indicated that the plague is a punishment from the gods for Thebes's failure to locate and punish the murderer of the previous King Laius. But the Oracle refuses to name the killer. That is a task left to the Thebans and *Oedipus Rex* is, in effect, the tale of a murder investigation.

Important for Foucault's analysis, the investigation proceeded through a series of confrontations. First there is the confrontation between Oedipus and Tiresias (the blind prophet of Apollo) whom Oedipus summons to explain the Oracle's message and name the killer. Tiresias, who knows the answer, tries to avoid responding but ultimately—having been forced by Oedipus—names the king. Neither Oedipus nor the Chorus accept Tiresias's claim—indeed Oedipus accuses Tiresias of speaking from envy, an accusation that moves us onto the second challenge—that between Oedipus and his brother-in-law Creon. It was Creon who had gone to Delphi to consult the Oracle, and Oedipus accused Creon of using the Oracle and Tiresias as part of a conspiracy to bring him down. Creon's response was twofold (and this would be important to Foucault's interpretation): first, he pointed out that he had the benefits of rulership without the obligations since—as brother-in-law to the king—people treated him with respect and yet he was not responsible for the city; and second, he offered his oath that he was not conspiring. So if Tiresias spoke as the voice of the gods, Creon spoke from the position of the aristocracy. Next a confrontation between Oedipus and his wife Jocasta. Jocasta, of course, had been the wife of Laius and had been given by the city to Oedipus to mark his conquest of the Sphinx and his sovereignty over Thebes. As both we and the Athenian audience know—although Oedipus and Jocasta do not—she was also his mother. Oedipus and Jocasta do not get to that latter point themselves—but in comparing stories of the death of Laius and Oedipus's accounts of his own travels from Corinth to Thebes, Jocasta begins to understand that Oedipus may have been the murderer of Laius and urges him to stop investigating. But Oedipus, full of a sense of duty and an arrogance built from his own sense of capacity and destiny, ultimately compels testimony of two slaves—one from Corinth, and one from the mountains above Thebes—who describe not only the actual murder of Laius at Oedipus's hands, but reveal that Oedipus was not native of Corinth but of Thebes and in fact the son of Laius and Jocasta. The truth is finally revealed through the witnessing of slaves—clarifying from the lowest position of Greek Society the opaque speech of the god. Confronted with these testimonies Jocasta hangs herself and Oedipus blinds himself. Creon becomes king and takes charge of the city and of Oedipus's children. But that is another story.[1]

Both Freud and Lévi-Strauss made *Oedipus Rex* founding supports for their respective intellectual projects. Lévi-Strauss saw in the play an opportunity—combined with Native American myths—to demonstrate a method that revealed the universal structure of mythologies.[2] Sophocles's importance for Lévi-Strauss lay in how well his play enabled the anthropologist to uncover an ahistorical and repeatable logic of the working out of categories that gave myths their meaning and significance. Freud, of course, also made of Oedipus something of universal significance:

> If *Oedipus the King* is able to move modern man no less deeply than the Greeks who were Sophocles' contemporaries, the solution can only be that the effect of Greek tragedy does not depend on the contrast between fate and human will, but is to be sought in the distinctive nature of the subject matter exemplifying this contrast. His fate moves us only because it could

have been our own as well, because at our birth the oracle pronounced the same curse upon us as it did on him. It was perhaps ordained that we should all of us turn our first sexual impulses toward our mother, our first hatred and violent wishes toward our father. Our dreams convince us of it.[3]

For Freud *Oedipus Rex*, which he called a "misleading secondary revision of the subject matter," made art out of a universal psychological structure.[4] But as with Lévi-Strauss, Freud was most concerned with what happened before the play itself. For Freud, the interest of *Oedipus Rex* was the background prophecy (the boy who would kill his father and sleep with his mother and consequently was condemned to die in order to avoid the curse). The actual dynamic of the play was relatively unimportant. Like Freud if in a very different way, Lévi-Strauss was also less interested in the play than in its prehistory. For both the play merely was an example of a structure of myth or of desire.

....

Foucault makes of *Oedipus Rex* something quite different. In his first sustained interpretation (1971–73) the play is the thing. Foucault argues that the different confrontations between different claimants to the truth are the heart of the play, because it was through them that Sophocles both narrated and philosophized about the different practices of truth and justice that Athenians debated in the sixth and fifth centuries BCE. Foucault argues—through a comparison with Homer and a discussion of Athenian legal procedure—that the confrontations (between Oedipus and Tiresias, between Oedipus and Creon, between Oedipus and Jocasta, and finally between Oedipus and the two slaves) represented three moments of what he called "veridiction" or ways to constitute truth: the prophetic, the oath, and the witness. These, in turn, corresponded to the religious, the aristocratic, and the legal-empirical. In the end, although the slave witnesses merely confirmed what the prophet Tiresias had announced early in the play, it was the triumph of empirical knowledge that *Oedipus Rex* announced and which moved truth from a moment of divine illumination to one of earthly procedure.[5]

Foucault situated this narrative of transition in a complex relationship to the class struggles of seventh- and sixth-century BCE Greece, particularly the three-way conflicts between the popular classes, the aristocracy and the tyrants. Foucault's lectures trace out the different ways that the invention of money, the notion of a law of both society and the order of things, and the development of popular religious rituals focused on the individual served to redefine the understanding of purity and impurity and of the relationship between these, the law, and truth.

This history is a complex one but three points are especially important. First, Foucault contends that there was a crucial change in the meaning of impurity and its ritualistic elimination. In the archaic period, he argues, impurity was concerned primarily with an improper mixing of categories: the washing that warriors did after a battle but before prayers, for example, was not designed to wash away an impurity (say having killed someone) but to prevent the mixture of the spaces of battle from the spaces of the temple. Pollution occurred when boundaries were crossed improperly and occurred within a largely religious landscape that maintained its order through separation and multiple division; there was no act that needed to be purified exactly. Instead, the crossing of boundaries had to be done properly.[6] By *Oedipus Rex*, this system had been overturned. Pollution and impurity occurred at the level of the individual act (murdering Laius, sleeping with Jocasta), and purity demanded expulsion from the undifferentiated space of the law-governed city.

Second, there was a transition in the means to reveal the truth of the action. In the archaic world (and in the play this older form of truth was represented by Creon's oath), truth was declared not by witnesses but by oath-taking, and the proof of the oath was determined not by empirical evidence but by the gods either accepting or punishing an oath. Under the older assumptions, the gods would punish someone (or their families) for swearing a false oath, and the key element of the juridical ritual was ensuring proper procedure to make oaths punishable. The truth of an oath, to put it another way, was established in the flash of a god's punishment. But again, in Sophocles truth was not tied to honor but to witnessing. It was the two slaves—both present and long concealing their knowledge—who struck the blows that ultimately brought Oedipus down. As Foucault put it *Oedipus Rex* brought to light "the political, juridical, and religious requirement to transform the event . . . into established and definitely preserved facts in the *observation* of witnesses. Subjecting the event [what would have been judged by the gods] to the form of observed fact is the first aspect of Oedipal truth."[7]

And third, and arguably most important, *Oedipus Rex* indicated a crucial transformation in the relationship between truth and power. Oedipus famously gained power by defeating the Sphinx. But, as Foucault stresses, he defeated the Sphinx through a knowledge that he contained within himself. Foucault argued that Oedipus's rise—his coming to Thebes having lost everything in an effort to escape his seeming fate in Corinth—was a transposition of the myth of the Hero and the historical figure of the tyrant. It was this skill, the ability as it were to pull the truth out of himself, that linked him to the figure of the tyrant who seized political power through his own knowledge and skill as opposed to birth or election. For the Greeks, the notion of the tyrant was not, as it is for us, necessarily a negative one: it simply indicated a specific way in which an individual could, for good or ill, seize and exercise power. But if Oedipus used this knowledge to free Thebes from the Sphinx, at the moment of the plague he continually sought to privilege his own will to truth in order to defend his own power from attack. But he could not solve the problem with his own knowledge. Instead, the problem had to be subjected to investigation. In the process, Oedipus the king became irrelevant: "Between knowledge conveyed by oracles and knowledge reported by regular inquiry, there is no longer any place for 'royal' knowledge, for a gnōmē that can solve riddles and save cities without calling on anyone—neither on seers and their birds, nor on men of experience who have seen and remember. What is played out in *Oedipus* is a struggle between kinds of knowledge (savoirs) and kinds of power, a struggle between forms of power-knowledge."[8]

As the reference to "power-knowledge" may suggest, Foucault's 1971–73 reading of Sophocles takes place at a moment of important transition in Foucault's own thinking. It is the culmination of a term of lectures designed to test out the relative validity of Aristotelian and Nietzschean perspectives on knowledge (spoiler alert: Nietzsche wins). But following the *Archeology of Knowledge* and the introduction of the concept of the discursive event (a system of relations between knowledges, objects, statements, and speakers) as a critique of the notion of ideology, the reference to power-knowledge not only heightens the sense of knowledge as constructed in, and for, struggle but also announces the series of studies on law, discipline, and sexuality that will have such an impact during the 1970s and 1980s. Both the discursive event and power-knowledge reject the position of textuality (and therefore repudiated Derridian deconstruction) while marking a distance from both structuralism and Marxism. Just as importantly, they replace the problem of the truth of desire with the desire for truth and the subjection of desire to law with the subjection of knowledge to law.

In the early 1970s, then, Oedipus was important as a figure of truth-telling within a historically constituted—if transhistorical—system for determining the relationship between truth, the law, and power. As Foucault put it in his *Lectures on the Will to Know*, Oedipus indicated the "founding [of] the principle of the distribution of power on the knowledge of an order of things to which only wisdom and purity give access . . . The other aspect of this Oedipal system of truth will be to found the nomos on a knowledge-virtue which is quite simply in itself respect for the nomos. Truth will be given only to someone who respects the *nomos* and he will arrive at the truth of the *nomos* only on condition of being pure." The law set up a system of truth to which all were subject—there was no singular insight that placed one above or beside the law of the city. The significance of Oedipus lay in the structure of truth-telling: if discovering the truth freed the city from the plague, it also meant the removal of the source of pollution, Oedipus himself. As Foucault continued,

> Freud thought that Oedipus spoke to him about desire, whereas Oedipus, himself, was talking about the truth. It is quite possible that Oedipus may not define the very structure of desire, but what Oedipus recounts is simply the history of our truth and not the destiny of our instincts. We are subject to an Oedipal determination, not at the level of our desire, but at the level of our true discourse. In hearing the true discourse of desire, Freud thought that he was hearing desire speaking, whereas it was the echo of his own true discourse, whereas it was the form to which his true discourse was subject.[9]

After the Oedipal drama, truth could only be determined in relationship to fact and in accordance with law. But if it determined power, it was not itself—at least in the Western imagination—in the service of power. Ironically, given Foucault's famous dictum concerning the king's head, it would seem that dethroning Oedipus meant that the head of the king had been cut off in western political philosophy far earlier than in Western politics.

....

Foucault returned to Oedipus in the early 1980s. In the interim there had been *Discipline and Punish* and the *History of Sexuality, Volume 1*, as well as the beginnings of his analysis of governmentality (an analysis that has become more important in the decades since his death). He had also rethought the history of sexuality in order to refocus it on the Greco-Roman and early Christian worlds. The shift in time period from *Discipline and Punish* and the *History of Sexuality* to the *Use of Pleasure* and *Care of the Self* combined with the development of governmentality has given rise to two linked claims: one that Foucault left behind a consideration of sovereignty and that he had transitioned from politics to ethics. The return to Oedipus should lead us to rethink both notions. His discussion of Oedipus was centrally concerned with sovereignty; it also established the inextricable connections between ethics and politics in the realm of truth-telling.

Foucault first revisited *Oedipus Rex* in 1980 at the start of *On The Government of the Living*.[10] He continued his discussion in 1981 in the lecture series *Wrong-Doing, Truth-Telling*.[11] Although he renewed some aspects of his reading of the play (the emphasis on conflicting logics of veridiction, the notion that the play proceeded through a game of halves, his interest in the different social positions of the sequence of truth-tellers) the contexts and concepts of his new reading changed in significant ways. Four problems stand out in this revised reading.

First, Foucault's conceptual vocabulary had changed. In place of knowledge-power and discursive events he now spoke of a *regime of truth* and of alethurgy (a term he drew from the work of Marcel Detienne).[12] These new terms marked at least two fundamental changes. First whereas the notion of power-knowledge had functioned both as a disciplined reduction of the glories of sovereignty to the quotidian exercise of localized direction, the regime of truth reinstated the notion of sovereign excess in our pursuit of truth. As Foucault noted, one of the paradoxes of *Oedipus Rex* is that although the prophecy demanded the murderer of Laius be executed or exiled, within the play *Oedipus* suffers neither. As Foucault points out,

> It is not, as the oracle demanded, the exile, suppression, elimination, or murder of the guilty person that was needed to liberate Thebes. The necessary and sufficient condition for the liberation of Thebes was that the truth come out.... The alethurgy in itself—quite apart from the pure and simple effects of knowledge that would have made it possible to determine who was guilty and then, as a result, punish him—goes well beyond the pure and simple effects of useful knowledge.... It suffices that the truth be shown, that it be shown in its ritual, in its appropriate procedures, its regulated alethurgy, for the problem of punishment no longer to be posed and for Thebes to be liberated.[13]

Some claim to the truth, some version of alethurgy is necessary for the government of the city; this excess, this significance of truth beyond the utilitarian is a crucial element in the notion of the regime of truth and its departure from the idea of power-knowledge.

Second, whereas power-knowledge apparently evacuated the subject from the problem of knowledge (or at least the subject as subject), alethurgy made of the subjective incorporation and acceptance of truth a major moment in the process of truth-telling. This incorporation would take at least two forms: the first, and here we can see some continuities with the arguments put forth in *The History of Sexuality: Volume 1*, is in the demand to confess either individual faith or fault.[14] The second form is the effect of truth upon the subject: both in the sense of what hearing and acknowledging the truth would mean to the subject and also what obligations it would place upon the subject who spoke the truth. Unlike knowledge-power, alethurgy contained an inextricable subjective moment. *Oedipus Rex* provided him with access to these problems, or as he put it himself: "These then are the three themes that I wanted to emphasize: [first], the relationship between manifestation of truth and exercise of power; second, the importance and necessity for this exercise of power of a truth that manifests itself, at least in certain of its points, but absolutely indispensably in the form of subjectivity; finally, third, the effect of the manifestation of this truth in the form of subjectivity, the effect of this manifestation beyond, let's say, immediately utilitarian relations of knowledge. Alethurgy, the manifestation of the truth, is much more than making known."[15]

Third, Foucault's reading pressed *Oedipus Rex* into the politics of the city. This relationship to the city turned on two issues that have, if anything, even more contemporary importance than they did when Foucault lectured: the problem of education and the question of the tyrant. As Foucault argues, one central issue for Oedipus (both the figure and the play) was how to move from ignorance to knowledge, "the act by which someone who does not know becomes someone who knows."[16] This issue, in turn, led to a central issue in the preservation of the city, that of education:

> This transformation of the one who did not know into the one who knows is, as you know, the Sophists' problem, Socrates' problem, and will still be Plato's problem. It is the whole problem of education, rhetoric, and the art of persuading. It is ultimately the whole problem of democracy. In order to govern the city, does one need to transform those who do not know into those who know? Is it necessary to transform all those who do not know into people who know? Or in order to govern the city is there a certain knowledge that some need to possess but not others? Does one discover this knowledge and can one form it in someone who does not yet know but will

end up knowing? All of these problems of the technique of transformation of nonknowledge into knowledge are, I think, at the heart of philosophical-political, pedagogical, and rhetorical debate, of the debate on language and the utilization of language in fifth century Athens.[17]

In this telling, *Oedipus Rex* becomes part of a debate about politics and democracy even if it took a mythic form. Foucault's approach to the tragedy does not limit itself to the ethical; instead, it presses irrevocably into the political and into the nature of the relationship between truth and political form. This dimension becomes even clearer if we consider that the problem of knowledge and the city is set against the problem of the knowledge of the tyrant. As in his discussions from the early 1970s, Foucault in 1981 emphasized the ways that the final arrival of the servant and slave witnesses made Oedipus's judgment (the judgment that had overcome the Sphinx) an unnecessary excess. Oedipus's defeat of the Sphinx had established him as protector of Thebes, and in return he demanded and received the gratitude and obedience of the city. But this relationship was one not of transparent truth but of the tyrant's personal bond with his subjects. When Oedipus committed himself to seeking out the murderer through the investigation of clues, Foucault demonstrates, he subjected himself to a procedure that was not in his control. Although he and Jocasta consistently sought to use the clues to convince themselves of their innocence, in the end they could not escape the demands of the law established by the gods: "What is condemned in the drama is that someone should claim to be master of this kind of alethurgy [mastery of the signs of destiny] and wants to use this way of discovery for his own advantage, so as to get away with it."[18] Oedipus is condemned because the truth is connected to the law and it cannot ultimately be used to escape the law. The tyrant who evades the law must be condemned.

Fourth, there is the new emphasis on "avowal" and governance. Although Foucault had consistently emphasized the importance of the character of the witness, in the early 1970s the weight of that discussion had been on its implication for a knowledge based on seeing. Although this theme continued, the growing emphasis on subjectification and in *Wrong-Doing, Truth-Telling* on "avowal" placed the question of the relationship between telling one's own truth and the requirements of the law in sharp focus. There was continuity here with the first volume of the history of sexuality. But there was something more as well. In *Wrong-Doing, Truth-Telling* Foucault points to an important transformation in the position of the chorus in *Oedipus Rex*. The first instance is when Tiresias calls upon the chorus for their support. Despite the fact that Tiresias speaks for the god, the chorus demands proof of his charges because Oedipus had saved the city. At this point, the bond to the tyrant remains; the chorus speaks still in the language of obligation and love: "Never will I convict my King, never in my heart."[19] But later, after Jocasta and Oedipus had attempted to argue away the clues that were emerging and to deny the destiny decreed by the gods, the chorus turns: "Pride breeds the tyrant / violent pride, gorging, crammed to bursting / with all that is overripe and rich with ruin—."[20] For Foucault, the key issue here is the relationship between sovereignty and the truth. When Oedipus first challenged Tiresias and accused him of envy, he argued that Tiresias was envious of Oedipus's possession of "the three elements of wealth, tyranny, and supreme art."[21] Supreme art, in Foucault's reading, is the techne of governance. But techne, Foucault insists, is distinct from the capacity that enabled Oedipus to defeat the Sphinx (that was judgment); it indicates an art or type of practice. In this case, Oedipus unleashes an art of investigation based on clues that will, by virtue of its mobilization of a juridical framework of witnessing, bring about the reversal and recognition central to classical drama.[22] In the end, Oedipus is undone by the avowal of servants and slaves compelled to testify and in testifying uphold the law and cast out the excess of tyrannical power.[23] To be sure, Foucault's lectures of the later 1970s on modern governmentality and neoliberalism had been centrally concerned with the role of knowledge in governing.[24] But these lectures were concerned with the objective knowledge needed to govern. With the return to *Oedipus Rex* Foucault once again puts the subject under examination; but whereas knowledge-power pointed to the subject as object, the revised Oedipus pointed to the investment of the subject into his or her own governance. The importance of tyranny and law in this story should remind us that this move was not simply an ethical one; it was deeply political in that it concerned the necessary conditions of freedom both of the subject and of the city.

....

Foucault's final sustained engagement with *Oedipus Rex*—in 1983—occupied a telling position within the set of lectures on *The Government of Self and Others*. In this last reading, Foucault placed Oedipus against another mythical Greek figure, Ion—as represented in Euripides's play of the same name. But in *Ion*, Foucault argues, the play is structured around the problem of political parresia, that is to say the ability to engage in a particular form of free speech within the context of the politics of the city.

Let me briefly set the stage. *Ion* is set at the Temple of Apollo in Delphi. Ion begins the play as a caretaker of the Temple. As the god Hermes tells the audience to start the play, Ion was the son of Apollo and Creusa. Apollo had raped Creusa and then left her to bear Ion alone. Ashamed and despairing, Creusa had left Ion as a baby to die, but Apollo had arranged for Hermes to bring the child to the Temple at Delphi, where the head priestess took pity on him and kept him alive. In the meantime, Creusa, daughter of the king of Athens, had been given in marriage to Xuthus—a foreigner who had helped Athens in wartime. Following the death of Creusa's father, she and her husband rule Athens. The play's drama is triggered by the desire of both Xuthus and Creusa to come to Delphi to learn if they would have any children. In *Ion*, we see some of the same themes as in *Oedipus Rex*: questions of hidden paternity and maternity (only here Ion's father is Apollo himself, not the murdered king), different forms of veridiction (the oracle and the witness), and the relationship between truth and political power. And we also see some of the same notion of arriving at the truth through what Foucault called—in his discussion of *Oedipus*—the "law of halves," in which different parties hold different pieces of the truth which are only brought together at the end.[25]

But whereas Foucault's discussions of *Oedipus* focused on the conflicts between systems of veridiction and the implications of these forms of truth-telling for Oedipus's sovereignty and his punishment, in *Ion* the stakes are different. Ion's parentage—which is at stake in the play—moves through four moments. The first, Hermes's speech at the start, establishes the truth for the audience immediately. We then have a misdirection in which Xuthus, having come to ask the Oracle if he will have children, is told that the first person he sees after leaving the Temple will be his son. That person, of course, is Ion. Xuthus—in full view of the chorus of Creusa's servants—believes that Apollo has indicated that Ion is his natural son—conceived in a premarital tryst with a dancer at Delphi many years ago. After some understandable reluctance on the part of Ion—who after all is a bit put out by some stranger hugging him and declaring himself his father—Xuthus and Ion agree that Ion will return to Athens and take up a place within the royal household. But they will not tell Creusa his "true" identity so that she will not feel displaced or threatened. Not surprisingly, Creusa's servants tell her of the plan and she is justifiably enraged. She is less enraged by the fact that Xuthus has an illegitimate son, however, than that there is a plan that will ultimately displace her lineage from power. As a result, she plans—prodded on by her old teacher—to have Ion murdered. This effort fails, Creusa is exposed, the people of Delphi attempt to stone her to death, she flees to the Temple of Apollo for sanctuary, Ion pursues her there, they confront each other and—thanks to the timely arrival of the priestess of the temple carrying the basket that had contained the infant Ion—finally piece together the truth of Ion's birth. They now conspire to bring Ion back without telling Xuthus the truth (he will think that Ion is coming back under his plan). Finally, Athena arrives to bless this plan and also to announce that Xuthus and Creusa will have further sons who will be the origins of other Greek communities. These latter lineages of course will be lesser than the Ionians (of Athens).[26]

Despite this complex drama of sexual violence, divine cowardice, parental misplacement, and dynastic instability, Foucault insisted that *Ion* "is entirely devoted to *parresia*, or at any rate . . . is permeated from end to end by this theme of *parresia* (of saying everything, telling the truth, and free-spokenness)."[27] In making this claim Foucault had in mind two key moments in the play. The first concerned Ion's worry that if he went to Athens as Xuthus's son he would be doubly disempowered as both illegitimate and non-Athenian. Of course, as a king, that might not matter (remember the history of tyrants), but Ion didn't just want to be king. As he explained to Xuthus (and at this point he thought Xuthus was his father) he wanted to be a citizen. Especially in Athens, whose citizens prided themselves on being native, he worried that, coming to Athens as both foreigner and illegitimate, if he did not achieve standing on his own he would be "said to be a nothing born of nobodies," if he tried to be "on the first ranks of the city," he would be hated by the lower classes; moreover he would be held in contempt by those who prized society over politics, and if he did achieve political stature the "orators and statesmen" would bring him down as a rival without true standing.[28] For Ion, the key question is whether he will have the status to employ parresia: "Off I go, then. But there's one thing that spoils my happiness, father: If I fail to find my mother, my life won't be worth living. If this is something I should pray for, then I pray that my mother is of Athenian descent, so that from her side I may possess freedom of speech. For if a stranger arrives in a city which is untainted by foreign blood, he may nominally be a citizen, but in fact he has the tongue of a slave, with no freedom of speech."[29] In Foucault's reading this pairing of the structural condition of parresia (birth from an Athenian mother) and Ion's concern over his status in the political realm is crucial. Parresia is only available to a citizen, and its possession enables one to compete for ascendancy within the city.

But there is a second moment of parresia in the play that—combined with Ion's speech—can point us in the crucial direction. Creusa also has her moment of parresia. But where Ion is expressing a forward-looking concern about joining the political life of Athens, Creusa is daring to express her rage toward the god who raped and abandoned her. At the Temple itself Creusa declares Apollo's duplicity, his violence, his abandonment, and his hypocrisy: "Oh yes! I accuse you, son of Leto, whose voice is heard / by the queueing visitors to the golden seat / and the shrine of the earth. I shall proclaim my accusation in the open!"[30] As Foucault notes, "This discourse of injustice, which in the mouth of the weak emphasizes the injustice of the strong has a name. . . . The discourse, through which someone weak, and despite this weakness, takes the risk of reproaching someone powerful for his injustice, is called, precisely, *parresia*."[31]

Ion therefore announces, within the context of a mythic accounting of the ascendancy of Athens, the importance of parresia in the context of the city. On the one hand, Ion himself links the exercise of political parresia to the capacity to intervene in a punctual manner in the politics of the city—to engage in the struggle for leadership through the speaking of truth. On the other hand, in her passion and rage, Creusa demonstrates the link between self and truth-telling and the risk that truth-telling must involve if we are to consider it parresia. This truth-telling is essential to the functioning of the democratic city—citizenship entitles you to parresia, but without parresia the proper order of democracy could not be achieved. And because the parresiastic responds to specific challenges or problems, parresia is punctual—it cannot be a statement of a theory or a general accounting.

Foucault's accounting of parresia, in *Ion* and elsewhere, returns us to the themes introduced in his discussions of *Oedipus Rex*. If you recall, Foucault's first set of readings argued that *Oedipus Rex* marked a transition in the relationships between power and purification, rules of truth-telling, and the transition from gods and oaths to empirical witnessing. But it did so, as it were, on the object side—Oedipus's ultimate purification was an outcome of the truth not its condition. In his second set of readings, Foucault placed greater emphasis on the subjective in its relationship to law, alethurgy, and "regimes of truth." This transition to the question of the subject and avowal in his discussions of *Oedipus Rex* underlined the importance of the political and legal contexts of the subject's side of truth. The final consideration, as *Oedipus Rex* led to the consideration of parresia, opened up the possibility of a new relationship between truth, the subject, and the power of the sovereign. The parresiast, as Foucault puts it, is "the person who has the courage to risk telling the truth, and who risks this truth-telling in a pact with himself, inasmuch as he is, precisely, the enunciator of the truth."[32] There is then, if not exactly a purification, an obligation to the truth for the parresiast, and if, unlike the oath, no god will punish you for speaking falsely, there is for the parresiast the risk of repudiation or worse for telling the truth.[33]

....

These discussions may seem far from the quotidian concerns of scholars of early America. After all, we neither command nor, at least in our roles as teachers and scholars, engage directly in the play of rule and politics. Indeed, Foucault himself provides some reason to doubt that parresia applies to our truth-telling efforts: "The analysis of *parresia* is the analysis of this dramatics of true discourse which brings to light the contract of the speaking structure with himself in the act of truth-telling. In this way I think that one could make an analysis of the dramatics of true discourse and its different forms: the prophet, the seer, the philosopher, the scientist."[34] Here I think it is safe to say that the early Americanist is placed within the category of the scientist and not the parresiast.

But forty years after Foucault made this judgment I think that there are reasons to think differently. As the attacks on *The 1619 Project* and critical race theory make clear, scholars who place slavery at the heart of the American experience face new professional and indeed personal risks. Given the surge in what PEN America has termed "educational gag orders" and what the American Association of University Professors' Committee A has recently characterized as "Legislative Threats to Academic Freedom," the enunciation of truths about early America in some situations and places may now constitute an act of parresia.[35] I do not wish to overstate this issue. For most early Americanists, teaching and writing at this moment remains within the "dramatics" of the scientist. But for increasing numbers of scholars in increasing numbers of states, the separation of scholarly duties and political risks is dissolving. Indeed, in states with "educational gag orders" or for scholars whose work or teaching engages questions about early American slavery, the separation of church and state, the conquest of Native Americans, or the nature of the American Revolution parresiastic risks have grown.

And they have grown for reasons that make Foucault's readings of *Oedipus Rex* and *Ion* even more contemporary today. Remember that in his accounting of both plays, Foucault stressed not only their search for (from the vantage point of the authors and their audiences) the mythic truths of their origins. In this search, this desire to join together truth and rule, decisive blows were struck from below as it were. In *Oedipus Rex* it was the testimony of slaves that revealed not only who Oedipus truly was but what he had done; in *Ion* it is Creusa's biting condemnation of Apollo that makes clear both what was done to her and to Ion. In both plays it is the desire for consoling illusion that must be overcome; not simply to "speak truth to power" as the phrase goes but to establish the proper relationship between governing and being governed. The stories told about early America—especially the Revolution—provide the mythic origins for the United States. Whatever the professional criticisms of the *1619 Project* have been, its larger significance has been as an opening salvo in a larger culture war about the American past.[36] The distinction between scientist and parresiast may be shrinking because the debate over the nature of belonging, the rights of speech and participation, the boundaries of American history and society, and the question of America's origins is once more in play across a range of sites and issues that may fairly be called Oedipal.

NOTES

1. Sophocles, *Oedipus the King*, 159–251.
2. Lévi-Strauss, "Structural Study of Myth," 432–36.
3. Freud, *The Interpretation of Dreams*, 202.
4. Freud, *The Interpretation of Dreams*, 203.
5. Foucault, *Lectures on the Will to Know*, 183–99.
6. Foucault, *Lectures on the Will to Know*, 167–81.
7. Foucault, *Lectures on the Will to Know*, 196.
8. Foucault, "Oedipal Knowledge," in *Lectures on the Will to Know*, 256.
9. Foucault, *Lectures on the Will to Know*, 196–97.
10. Foucault, *On the Government of the Living*.
11. Foucault, *Wrong-Doing, Truth-Telling*.
12. Detienne, *The Masters of Truth in Ancient Greece*.
13. Foucault, *On the Government of the Living*, 74.
14. Foucault, *History of Sexuality, Volume 1*.
15. Foucault, *On the Government of the Living*, 74–75.
16. Foucault, *On the Government of the Living*, 56.

17 Foucault, *On the Government of the Living*, 56.
18 Foucault, *On the Government of the Living*, 66.
19 Sophocles, *Oedipus the King*, 187.
20 Sophocles, *Oedipus the King*, 209.
21 Foucault, *Wrong-Doing, Truth-Telling*, 71.
22 In this emphasis on reversal and recognition Foucault, of course, was following a long tradition back to Aristotle. But his particular reading was deeply influenced by Jean-Pierre Vernant's "Ambiguity and Reversal: On the Enigmatic Structure of *Oedipus Rex*."
23 Foucault, *Wrong-Doing, Truth-Telling*, 76–81.
24 Foucault, *Security, Territory, Population*, and *The Birth of Biopolitics*.
25 Foucault, *On the Government of the Living*, 25.
26 Euripides, *Ion*, 1–47.
27 Foucault, *The Government of Self and Others*, 76.
28 Euripides, *Ion*, 18.
29 Euripides, *Ion*, 20.
30 Euripides, *Ion*, 26.
31 Foucault, *The Government of Self and Others*, 133–34.
32 Foucault, *The Government of Self and Others*, 66.
33 The demands of truth-telling, especially in parresia, will be the central theme of Foucault's final set of Collège de France lectures, as well as lectures given at the University of California, Berkeley. See Foucault, *The Courage of Truth*, and Foucault, *Fearless Speech*.
34 Foucault, *The Government of Self and Others*, 68–69.
35 Sachs, "Steep Rise in Gag Orders"; AAUP, "Legislative Threats to Academic Freedom."
36 For one thoughtful discussion of the meaning of the debate over the 1619 Project see Waldstreicher, "Hidden Stakes of the 1619 Controversy."

BIBLIOGRAPHY

American Association of University Professors, Committee A. "Legislative Threats to Academic Freedom: Redefinitions of Antisemitism and Racism." March 2022. Accessed June 8, 2022. https://www.aaup.org/report/legislative-threats-academic-freedom-redefinitions-antisemitism-and-racism.

Detienne, Marcel. *The Masters of Truth in Ancient Greece*. Translated by Janet Lloyd. Cambridge, MA: Zone, 1999.

Euripides. *Ion*. In *Orestes and Other Plays*. Translated by Robin Waterfield. New York: Oxford University Press, 2001.

Foucault, Michel. *The Birth of Biopolitics: Lectures at the Collège de France, 1978–1979*. Edited by Michel Senellart. Translated by Graham Burchell. New York: Palgrave Macmillan, 2008.

Foucault, Michel. *The Courage of Truth: The Government of Self and Others II; Lectures at the Collège de France, 1983–1984.* Edited by Fréderic Gros. Translated by Graham Burchell. New York: Palgrave Macmillan, 2011.

Foucault, Michel. *Fearless Speech.* Edited by Joseph Pearson. Los Angeles: Semiotext(e), 2001.

Foucault, Michel. *The Government of Self and Others: Lectures at the Collège de France, 1982–1983.* Edited by Frédéric Gros. Translated by Graham Burchell. New York: Palgrave Macmillan, 2011.

Foucault, Michel. *History of Sexuality, Volume 1: An Introduction.* Translated by Robert Hurley. New York: Pantheon, 1978.

Foucault, Michel. *Lectures on the Will to Know: Lectures at the Collège de France, 1970–1971.* Edited by Daniel Defert. Translated by Graham Burchell. New York: Palgrave Macmillan, 2013.

Foucault, Michel. *On the Government of the Living: Lectures at the Collège de France, 1979–1980.* Edited by Michel Senellart. Translated by Graham Burchell. New York: Palgrave Macmillan, 2014.

Foucault, Michel. *Security, Territory, Population: Lectures at the Collège de France, 1977–1978.* Edited by Michel Senellart. Translated by Graham Burchell. New York: Palgrave Macmillan, 2007.

Foucault, Michel. *Wrong-Doing, Truth-Telling: The Function of Avowal in Justice.* Edited by Fabian Brion and Bernard E. Harcourt. Translated by Stephen W. Sawyer. Chicago: University of Chicago Press, 2014.

Freud, Sigmund. *The Interpretation of Dreams.* Translated by Joyce Crick. New York: Oxford University Press, 1999.

Lévi-Strauss, Claude. "The Structural Study of Myth." *Journal of American Folklore* 68, no. 270 (1955): 428–44.

Sachs, Jeffrey. "Steep Rise in Gag Orders, Many Sloppily Drafted." *Pen America*, January 24, 2022. Accessed June 8, 2022. https://pen.org/steep-rise-gag-orders-many-sloppily-drafted/.

Sophocles. *Oedipus the King.* In *The Three Theban Plays: Antigone, Oedipus the King, Oedipus at Colonus.* Translated by Robert Fagles. Introduction and notes by Bernard Knox. New York: Penguin, 1984.

Vernant, Jean-Pierre. "Ambiguity and Reversal: On the Enigmatic Structure of *Oedipus Rex*." In Jean-Pierre Vernant and Pierre Vidal-Naquet, *Myth and Tragedy in Ancient Greece*, 113–40. Translated by Janet Lloyd. New York: Zone, 1988.

Waldstreicher, David. "The Hidden Stakes of the 1619 Controversy." *Boston Review*, January, 24, 2020. Accessed, June 8, 2022. https://bostonreview.net/articles/david-waldstreicher-hidden-stakes-1619-controversy/.

II SUBJECTS OF EARLY AMERICA

THREE · *Ana Schwartz*

Annoyances, Tolerable and Intolerable

If theory, generally speaking, tends to arouse skepticism because the objects it examines have often attained the appearance of normalcy or reached a status quo, we may expect an unusual degree of skepticism, even aversion, toward a theory that claims to account for the costs of the fantasy of happiness. One such theory is the theory of repression, and, in the case of the early modern English Protestants who settled in Algonquian territory, recent critical unease considering their repression is especially curious since these historical figures actively and enthusiastically sought repression out. To repress was costly work, but when they called it "discipline," they learned to imagine it as an investment. It was a practice they hoped would distinguish them in the eyes of history, and they thought it would make them, in the long run, happy. Historians who have argued against their repression have not, of course, been totally in error. They may have been striving to be good Foucauldians, learning from the *History of Sexuality* to avoid claiming that the past was more repressed than the present (perhaps not noticing that one way to avoid this is to entertain the possibility that the present remains repressed, too). Or they may have been trying to avoid anachronism, intuiting that the conditions shoring up the specific repression that Sigmund Freud observed in the early twentieth century (conditions that included the class, racial, and ethnic imperatives at work in domestic family arrangements, or the abstract idea of normative individual freedom) did not so clearly pertain in the seventeenth century, or even in Hawthorne's enduring nineteenth-century caricature of it. What seems much more likely is that cultural historians of seventeenth-century settlement were simply looking in the wrong place. Primed by the more spectacular of Freud's case studies—studies, Freud himself warned, of "repressions that have failed"—many historians remember repression as a pathological, aberrant, and exceptional operation rather than, as the settlers' enthusiasm for "discipline" was, an activity taking place virtually all the time, activity whose success would make identification of its motives all the harder to find.[1] Occasionally, however, a text appears that quietly chastises that faulty memory, proposing that most hours of the waking day were filled with an onslaught of disturbances, and consequently, with the imperative to control, discipline—in other words, to repress—one's consciousness of them. Edward Johnson's poem "New England's Annoyances" is one such text, remarkable not only for its representation of repressible experiences, but the tone in which it represents them. In Johnson's words, the frustrations of settlement are relentlessly, buoyantly annoying.

Repression, like irritation, is ubiquitous and complex. It acts, as one of its first committed witnesses put it, "in a *highly individual* manner."[2] Its spectacular failures can provoke fear. Yet its ambition is to mount a "defense" of the conscious self against the irritations of "unpleasure" through "*turning something away, and keeping it at a distance, from the conscious.*"[3] The goal of that defense was, in Freud's estimation, the preservation of an individual's equanimity, peace, and, perhaps, happiness. Studying repression often appears to risk the opposite outcome, a return to unhappiness. But among the gains of such an inquiry is fresh illumination of the powerful, but often perplexing cultural and political phenomenon we now call settler colonialism.[4] This form of colonialism was at times spectacularly violent, but much more often, it was quietly frustrating, and those frustrations merit attention because their disappearance in the shadow of the spectacle snatches with it an appreciation of the patent audaciousness of the ambition with which these settlers arrived in their new, annoying environment. These Europeans apparently really thought they could achieve substantive peace in the middle of enormous disturbance on a global scale—in the middle of enduring it and also reproducing it. Few early moderns aspired to such disturbance; most felt it to be thrust upon them. Some, however, actively sought it out, and knowingly threw themselves into stressful, life-threatening circumstances. Some wanted gold, others glory. Most of them said they were doing it for their god. Among these adventurers, the ones Johnson lived with and wrote about were unique. What was strangest about them was that despite the struggles they courted, their self-conscious goal in undertaking this project was to live normal, undisturbed, peaceful lives. That quotidian confidence, a dream of living unhassled by conflict or contest, is one way of understanding the hubristic ambition we now identify with the modifier "settle" in "settler" colonialism.[5] And though a robust scholarly literature exists chronicling the violence that this goal of peace required, we lack commensurate understanding of how that antithesis was lived, how the utopian, beatific dream came to seem to them to be remotely plausible, a dream that might stand a chance of enduring, unwoken and unbothered.[6] Few settlers offered anything like a systematic program for reconciling these two features, for closing the gap between material fact and transcendent ideal. Yet the optimistic mood of conventional recent histories of these settlers suggests that they succeeded. One way they did was by undertaking a strange and subtle process of adjustment characterized by strategic but necessarily largely unconscious acts of forgetting the work of adjustment itself. It there was anything "settled" about settler colonialism, if settlement would ever be able to recognize itself as successful, it would only be able to do so because of this prior act of forgetting.

Thus, settler colonialism, to the degree that it succeeds, acutely exemplifies the processes of forgetting that Freudian repression names. It also heightens their stakes. And out of such a context, a poem like "New England's Annoyances" is a vibrant transcript of this work of forgetting, showing how repression consisted not only of rules to live by, but the stories individuals told themselves about why they were following them, and the rewards that would redeem those efforts and cause their catalysts to disappear from memory. This poem, in other words, both describes a set of irritations, and, in its manner of describing them, transforms their meaning to the people enduring those irritating, unpleasant, disturbing conditions. Certainly, the poem antedates the conditions that Freud tried to describe in his elaborate study of repression. But these people did have their own notion of repression—which included the word itself. And this hope of subordinating and forgetting overlapped substantially with Freud's description of repression's structure. More importantly, however, the poem has its finger on the pulse of some nascent stages of those conditions in early modernity. The poem, first, accounts for and affirms the presence of irritations and frustrated desires in the colonial context, distant from the formerly familiar European world individuals knew, irritations like cold, hunger, boredom, unfairness. Unlike many other contemporaneous texts describing and often implicitly promoting colonial settlement, this poem admits frankly: *Things were tough!* But it didn't simply affirm some unpleasant material facts that other literature often disregarded. It also, further, tried to describe a subset of those frustrations that were especially vexing: the strange discomfort of depending on individuals who were supposedly of identical status and substance as oneself. The poem, invoking figurative clichés and commonplaces about these frustrating relationships, insisted that they could be made tolerable through discipline, through force of individual will, fortified by shared pleasures like a jocular folk song. But some of these peculiar, novel frustrations were too elusive for words. These frustrations were strange and new not only in their intensity, but also their origin—individuals who were supposed to be of identical status and substance as oneself yet appeared intensely different. These new conditions and new neighbors were more astonishing and disturbing to early modern settlers than they knew how to put into words. "New England's Annoyances" is one example of their attempt to do so. Johnson's poem works to smooth away that strangeness with humor, and seems, in its innocent simplicity, to have succeeded. Historians who would prefer to remain ignorant of the historical cost of this happiness, who prefer to turn it away and keep it at a distance, may come to understand themselves better in studying this poem. Johnson's annoyances surrender back to history the comfortable peace that forgetful ignorance claims to have won.

THE ANNOYANCES

"New England's Annoyances" is a folk song that delivers what its title promises: a list of features of early colonial life that nagged and frustrated English people who tried to establish a newer, better version of England in Algonquian territories. Meant to be sung, the poem consists of sixteen verses, or stanzas, that in turn consist of two rhyming couplets each. Each line unfolds in anapestic tetrameter, which has the potentially anachronistic effect of sounding childish, if not annoying, to the ear of the modern reader. As a folk song, the circumstances of its composition remain uncertain, though in 1985, Leo Lemay argued that it was written around 1643, mostly likely by Edward Johnson, who returned to these themes in his other works *Good News from New England* (1648, distinct from Edward Winslow's 1624 text of the same name, though eager to spread a similar gospel) and *History of New England* (1654).[7] Topical similarity among the three texts is one of Lemay's significant pieces of evidence. All three share similar thematic preoccupations and similar figurative language. The unhappily cold climate, the startlingly austere resources, and the challenges of social cohesion in a theologically oriented community preoccupy all of Johnson's writings. Closely attending to the chronology of the named frustrations, Lemay argues that "New England's Annoyances" was written before these prose texts. If he is right, that sequence would constitute a subtle challenge to the claims that the poem itself makes. At its conclusion, the poem proposes a method for achieving confidence that settlement was the correct investment. Yet the possibility that he and his fellow settlers had not achieved such confidence appears in his efforts, over the course of the two decades that followed, to insist, in supplementary pieces of writing, that they had succeeded.

Using the conventions of the gently mocking folk song, these verses participated in and torqued a thematic genre that blossomed in England in the early seventeenth century. "New England's Annoyances" is a tidy example of literature promoting colonization, and a dynamic example of that genre's spin-off, literature satirizing the promotional literature. The poem promotes colonization, and it ridicules its own promotion. Along with texts like Christopher Levett's *A Voyage into New England* (1624) and Winslow's *Good News* (1624), "New England's Annoyances" recognized that describing a new land too rosily might lead to unhappy outcomes for those who sought to plant themselves there. These outcomes ranged from vague disappointment to avoidable death.[8] The poem energetically, at times sarcastically, takes the inverse approach to those early promotional tracts. Rather than list felicitous qualities, it operates litotically. It assembles a litany of infelicitous qualities. Better to set low expectations than be unhappily surprised by too-high ones. Yet the poem did not conclude from those examples that it would be better for everyone to stay home in England, as had a similar ballad "A West-Country Man's Voyage to New England."[9] Instead, in its last four stanzas, "New England's Annoyances" proposed discretion in assessing the assembled evidence about the quality of life one might expect on the colonial frontier. Not everyone would flourish. Some might, though even for them, it would be hard work. The poem concluded by addressing those prospective settlers directly, "you whom the Lord intends hither to bring."[10] The poem's conclusion invited them to rise to the challenges the previous stanzas had described. The ultimate quality needed for success, the poem claimed, was a disposition of equanimity to be able to "find" or discern the "blessings" that would recompense settlement's struggles.

Equanimity was desirable because measuring returns was itself hard work. Failure and loss were the most reliable experiences one could expect on the frontier—losses and failures so unpleasant and unrelenting that it might seem prudent *not* to count them anymore. The first such loss was a climate English bodies experienced as relatively hospitable. The territory where they hoped permanently to settle proved to be painfully cold for fully one-quarter of the year, "from the end of November till three months are gone." Unless English settlers modified their ways of living, those three months out of every twelve would be functionally lost to them.[11] The severity of those months threatened further losses. Those who imagined that they were physically or mentally strong enough to "withstand" the cold risked losing important parts of their bodies—"a finger, a foot or a hand"—extremities incrementally more important to the work of making the land livable according to English sensibilities, and extremities that also functioned as mnemonic aids in the work of counting and measuring. But even with relatively able bodies, English settlers found that their efforts in engaging with their environments might still not prove fruitful. In his fourth stanza, Johnson narrated the work of farming, hoeing, planting, and sowing. In that stanza's fourth line he paused, as if in retrospective satisfaction, to observe the crops in their condition of having been planted: "The corn being planted and seed being sown." Would there be any reliable moment of rest and reward for the weary? Not likely. He went on: the "worms destroy much before it is grown." He could not forget that destruction. The fourth stanza's loss of corn and the loss of the work that went into planting it echoed in the conclusion of his fifth stanza too. Some crops survived the worms, growing to be "full corn in the ear." But those crops, settlers found, were "apt to be spoil'd by hog, racoon, and deer." In one variant of the poem, the verb *destroyed* appears instead of *be spoil'd*, thus echoing at the end of two subsequent stanzas—repeated destructions, repeated frustrations to their efforts to survive in the way they thought was best.[12]

If it was possible to count lost months and lost harvests, it would be harder to measure the qualitative experience of bodily discomfort. Early modern bodies were shaped profoundly by their experience of clothing— what Anne Jones and Peter Stallybrass have called a "worn world."[13] Those worlds tended to demand more of the human body that wore them, and to act on it more directly, than many modern critics may experience clothing to do. Early modern European clothing was heavier, stiffer, rougher, more complicated to put on, and, in addition to these qualities, there was quantitatively less of it on the colonial frontier, item-wise, than there had been in the metropole. And on the colonial frontier, settlers watched as those worn worlds wore away before their eyes. The work that survival required took its toll not only on European limbs, but also on the garments that enclosed and protected those limbs, and it would not be easy to replace those clothes as they dissolved. Where would they get the textiles? It would take years before English settlers established reliable, wool-producing flocks of sheep, and in the meantime, they could not rely on ships coming from England to resupply them with sufficiently protective garments. In response to the frustration of this impasse, Johnson jokingly proposed, reaching for the sort of humor that Sigmund Freud would classify as "sophistical," that the rips and tears, fraying and wearing, actually led to *more* clothing rather than less.[14] A patched garment, Johnson argued, could be said (if not actually felt) to be twice as warm than an unpatched one: "Clouts double are warmer than single whole clothing." It would not be easy to measure the pace at which a garment wore through, but one could find consolations in the fantasy of wearing a second garment in the course of forestalling that first garment's decomposition.

Amid all this discomfort, even sources of abundance generated frustration. Although it was difficult to keep corn from spoiling, there were other sources of alimentary sustenance. Yet from the tone of Johnson's eighth, ninth, tenth, and eleventh stanzas, settlers seemed to be sick of most of them. These stanzas ring with repetition. Despite the appearance of variety, to English tongues, eating in the colony was an experience of great monotony. Johnson's eighth stanza surveys America's gastronomic variety. Its second line assembles "carrots and parsnips and turnips and fish" before turning to "clam banks" where, presumably, one could find clams as well as "catch fish" for a "delicate dish." If one was tempted to think that fish complemented those root vegetables happily, one had not been paying attention. "Fish" and "dish" had already been used as a rhyme pair within the same stanza, in the immediately preceding couplet. The next stanza made that monotony clearer. Settlers were tired of pumpkins. Pumpkins, that versatile squash, which he named in the eighth stanza and named again in the tenth one, appeared four times in his ninth stanza. One out of every six syllables in stanza nine pointed to this literal first fruit, which, he observed, settlers could expect to eat for breakfast and for lunch, continuously. They wearied of it, but they depended on it: "If it was not for pumpkins, we should be undone." For all the deliberate austerity imputed to these settlers, caustic passages like these, which are rare in their writings, testify that they noticed, and minded, how few of the former gastronomic pleasures there were to be had in their new home, how profoundly they longed for the fleshpots of England.

Few were the sensory pleasures early modern colonists enjoyed, and small was the likelihood of finding more soon. Perhaps it would not be within the lifetimes of the adults of the first waves of English planters. This was, on one hand, a general likelihood. Settlers knew successful planting would take time.[15] On the other hand, the absence of certain formerly sound material conditions was also a specific, acute challenge for English settlers in the 1640s, when they were, as Perry Miller famously put it, "left alone with America."[16] Despite their lofty spiritual and political ambitions, these self-important colonists found themselves forgotten by the metropole. More immediately troublesome, however, they were forgotten by the English merchants on whom they depended. Colonial administrators noticed this neglect. In his *Journal*, Massachusetts Bay Colony governor John Winthrop recorded news of the start of the English Civil War, which led to "hope of a thorough reformation."[17] This was happy news in theory, but unhappy news in practice: "This caused all men to stay in England in expectation of a new world." The cessation of new ships to the former new world distressed the frontier settlements: "Few coming to us, all foreign commodities grew scarce, and our own of no price."[18] Dearness of currency affected the dearness of services, too. The value of these services, and the value of the social relations they materialized, became harder to measure. Johnson lamented not only that all the money "we brought with us is wasted and gone." He also noticed that its absence made "all our dealings uncertain and strange." Settlers depended even more on borrowing and lending than they had before. They regressed from the credit-emphasizing economies that had characterized early modern English markets back to the debt-emphasizing economies that their parents' generations had known.[19] And it wasn't only the administrators who noticed. Merchants and workers did too, and leveraged that knowledge in ways that threatened to make social relations even stranger. Noting the loss of money, Winthrop expressed irritation toward the "excessive rates of laborers' and workingmen's wages"[20] and the "evil . . . very notorious" in the colony whereby colonists strove "to buy as cheap as they could, and to sell as dear."[21] Settlers were losing material resources, but they were not gaining much for those losses. The material deficit, in turn, was individually annoying, but its effects on mood, Johnson suggests, registered as greater than the sum of its parts. The losses that New England's settlers felt were not just "vexing, troubling, molesting, or injuring."[22] Reviving some of the less-presently obvious qualities of the word *annoying*, they were also "offensive," "odious," and "hateful," too.[23]

THE INTOLERABLE ANNOYANCES

Some settlers found these qualities of life so hateful as to be literally intolerable. They ceased tolerating such an ordeal, and soon left.[24] Johnson noticed this impatience among his contemporaries, and, after twelve stanzas humorously inviting prospective settlers to de-escalate their hopes for happiness, he offered some practical suggestions for succeeding rather than giving up. Though material frustrations would be many, and though it was unlikely that they would decrease in number, it was possible, he suggested, to make them less intense. The poem's last four stanzas describe some of the ways that current settlers dealt with difficulty, and prescribed some ways of its own. These stanzas propose, a little less directly, but a little more evocatively, that attitudes toward collective life were a decisive factor in colonization's success. Proper community-mindedness could make New England's annoying features more tolerable. The poem's thirteenth stanza glossed reform Protestant "covenant" theology, using the language of the initiated. It spoke of saintliness, brotherhood, and spiritual virtues. The next three stanzas offered a wealth of aphorisms and clichés to elaborate the social consequences of that theology. Critics of settlement's frustrations, Johnson chided, were impatient. They "find fault with our apples before they are mellow." Absconders "meet with a lion in shunning a bear." Those who stayed might consider those departures felicitous, since "while liquor is boiling, it must have a scumming." Those who stayed would learn something about themselves, too. According to the proverb that Johnson rehearsed, "birds of a feather" tended to "flock[] together." As his contemporary John Winthrop had put it, "Simile simili gaudet or like will to like."[25] Johnson put more than the usual rhetorical energy in these stanzas of persuasion. The colony might annoy, but prospective colonists, he exhorted, should not "forsake ... the honey for fear of the sting."

That sting—an ache in the belly, frost biting the hand—was useful. It was useful not simply as a principle of selection to scoop away like boiling scum all but the most committed. It could also be productive. According to Winthrop, the colony's most vocal political theorist, pain and suffering could generate a sense of cohesion and togetherness within a population that might otherwise have lacked such conventional reasons to affiliate. Already Plymouth Colony, the Bay Colony's older sibling, had experienced the pull away from communalism.[26] The hypothetical value of shared suffering would reach its most refined articulation in the eighteenth century, when Anglo-American political theorists looked ahead at the challenges of new nationhood.[27] But political leaders in colonization's early years saw value in agony too. Suffering, proposed John Winthrop, was a golden opportunity for settlers to bind themselves together in knots, for settlers to learn to feel in synchrony. But Johnson's poem suggests that the discomfort wasn't simply the object over which settlers would come to recognize themselves as a distinct community. Johnson's poem suggests that discomfort inhered in the mutual recognition. There might, he suggested, be something intolerable, maybe even agonizing, in the fellow feeling itself. Johnson did not describe the social life within the colony, and between the colony and its external critics, directly. His four concluding stanzas turned away from the vividness and humor of his twelve first stanzas, and instead describe social life in a frenetic sequence of clichés—proverbs, analogies, and figurative representations. Discomfort lurked not only in living together, planting crops together, freezing together, and eating pumpkins together. Discomfort also inhered in wondering, together, when—and for whom—the risky endeavor would pay off.

As much as settlers knew they were supposed to like each other, the work of getting to like each other was difficult to bear. That intolerable quality tends to elude most studies of colonial settlement. These literary and intellectual historians have recovered many names for the ideal felicity that colonial settlement required. Phrases like "love of the brethren," "Calvinist fellow-feeling," "a reforming people," a community of "visible saints," all memorably and immersively describe the social ideals that settlers hoped would compensate for frontier life's many annoyances.[28] Many of these are phrases that settlers themselves used to euphemize their ideals. But Johnson's final stanzas suggest the possibility that there was something quietly irritating, maybe even unbearable about those social ideals—that settlers didn't always like each other and, moreover, they didn't like the imperative to like each other much either. Johnson's poem suggests this in his sustained aversion to describing social life within the colony directly. Here is one paraphrase of Johnson's energetically evasive last stanzas: The Bay Colony's "hot protestants" understood their relationship with their deity as a "covenant," a provisional pact with an ultimately unpredictable divine force.[29] That deity's unpredictability expressed itself in an idea that the deity had chosen some individuals for a favorable afterlife and had damned others. This was the "division 'twixt brother and brother" where "some are rejected, and others made Saints." The deity made that division without regard to rank or status. And the consequences of this randomness, Johnson suggested—subtly, across the break between the thirteenth and fourteenth stanzas—was one of the most annoying things about New England theocracy. That feature led many initiates to give up before the community matured and yielded its "mellow" harvest of rewards. And leaving was also a risk, Johnson argued, alluding to the settlers who tried to defect to the Providence Island colony off the coast of what is currently Nicaragua, but who failed and were nearly taken captive by a Spanish fleet.[30] There would always be skeptics, Johnson claimed. And it was fine if they left. All the better a process by which any group of people might get rid of its impurities. Such purging would leave behind a community happier for its uniformity. This paraphrase doesn't reveal anything new about New England that historians have not elaborated at length in the intervening four centuries. Yet what remains unexplained is why it was so difficult for a poem so vivid in its exposition of material struggles to name its social ones explicitly.

Ambient social dissatisfaction is an unglamorous, probably common feature of any community. Modern scholars of colonial New England have tended not to write about it because the texts that chronicle the past tend not to describe it much either. Why should they? Those who felt themselves most responsible for documenting it were also likely to be the most invested in championing its worthiness. Failure, or the possibility of failure, would be embarrassing. But those ambient annoyances might also build to an intolerable pitch. Some people who did not address intolerable unhappiness by leaving expressed that unhappiness in their local communities. Those who stayed were often petty, fractious, and chronically dissatisfied with their neighbors. Again, they probably weren't exceptional in this regard; they have no historical monopoly on mutual dislike. But they were unusual—or at least they wanted to be unusual—in their hopes to overcome those qualities through their ideals. Modern historians have cherished and continue to cherish their ideal, long after its most explicit articulation.[31] Yet provisionally suspending the ideal that was only ever put into words by the agents of colonial governance makes better visible the strong evidence that settlers struggled in acting like they liked each other, and that, given their ideals, they may perhaps have struggled a little more intensely than typical early modern English. As early as 1622, Plymouth's Protestants expressed worry that their neighbors were taking advantage of them within their system of collectively owned labor.[32] Even after they privatized their labor, both the Plymouth and the Massachusetts Colonies—and then their spin-offs at New Haven and Connecticut—were beset with boundary dispute after boundary dispute. Even animals were conscripted into these arguments.[33] Sometimes dissatisfaction expressed itself within households. It was not unheard for a woman to try to drown her children, burn her house, or to beat her children and her servants and her household's enslaved Native and African laborers.[34] The administrators who espoused horizontal fellow feeling were no more exemplary of it than the people they exhorted. Winthrop, perennial governor of the Massachusetts Bay Colony over the first two decades, nurtured many resentments, perhaps most spectacularly toward his longtime rival on the General Court, Richard Bellingham.[35] Winthrop's frequent deputy governor, Thomas Dudley, was just as ready to suspend the injunction to have mercy on those over whom he exercised power. In the winter of 1630, he abandoned his indentured servants before the completion of their contracts, swiftly untying any knots of sympathy he might have felt toward them, and leaving them to die by starvation and exposure to the life-and-limb-threatening cold.[36] His daughter was just as eager to transmit to her own children the values that property-owners could use to rationalize their exploitation and disregard.[37] Day after day, year after year, they encountered provocative evidence of a gap between fact and ideal. These gaps testify to the endurance of horizontal annoyances, and suggest the presence of many more.

Annoyances—hateful, odious relations—didn't simply appear in the failure of achieving early modern Christian ideals. Horizontal aversions, unbearable to name directly, lurked implicitly also in the ideals themselves. The most intense disappointment, Johnson suggested, was the social implications of colonial New England's foundational theological principle—the principle of universal equality that organized Calvinist theology. "The New England Way" frustrated New England's own settlers because it insisted that spiritual equality was best evident in a principle of random selection. It wasn't simply that the Protestant deity selected some for favor and others for literally unending posthumous suffering—rejecting some, making others saints, as the poem put it. It was that there was no evident difference between the individuals subjected to that division, and no material reason for it either. The ultimate, maddening annoyance was the negation of meritorious striving. That negation began from a claim of spiritual equality, what Johnson glossed in the thirteenth stanza as "those that are equal in virtues and wants." What made fellows mad, or angry, was the want, or lack, of what they saw as fairness. Four centuries later, this can seem like a simple, relatively basic claim. Yet Johnson's ambiguous "mad" suggests not simply anger, but a disposition "uncontrolled by reason or judgment."[38] Here the experience of reason reached a limit, and an unhappy one at that. Yet it is a limit that, retrospectively, can be very easy to miss. "Mad fellows" might include those mentally depleted by the social experience of conditions that, according to Stephen Greenblatt, produced the modern, psychoanalytically legible unconscious.[39]

New England's many annoyances were maddening. They frustrated materially, in the embodied experience of an unfamiliar land. They also frustrated socially, in the relations those bodies tried to maintain with each other, yet that, though based on familiar principles, felt "strange." They frustrated, finally, in their psychic implications. The consequences of these strivings were profound. The early modern era, as Greenblatt explained, saw the emergence of a subject who was fundamentally isomorphic, easily interchangeable but for the effects of the material world. This period also saw the emergence of a particularly significant category to name that interchangeable subject, as Sylvia Wynter has observed, the idea of "Man" that would go on to underwrite not only racial distinctions but racial hierarchy.[40] By the nineteenth century, around the time that Karl Marx posed his critique of the formally universal subject, one of the premier effects of those conditions, argues David Kazanjian, was a condition of de facto hostility to other subjects, expressed in what Jacques Lacan has called an "aggressiveness" latent "in all relations with others, even in relations involving aid of the most good-Samaritan variety."[41] As Greenblatt cautions, those conditions were still congealing in the seventeenth century, and these texts do not easily manifest the content that Freud, three centuries later, would develop psychoanalysis in order to trace. Yet if the content of Johnson's poem appears distinct from the elaborate mutations described by Freudian sexuality, that content vividly expresses one of the key mechanisms of those mutations. Most forcefully, "New England's Annoyances" prescribes and itself initiates the work of repressing New England's many frustrations.

THE TOLERABLE ANNOYANCES

New England's annoyances didn't frustrate only English settlers. They also frustrate existing approaches to the self-opacity that characterized settlers' interior life. That disturbance urges revision of one key term that has tended quietly to shape the past century of discussions regarding early modern colonists' interiority, "repression." The poem makes repression evident not despite its buoyancy and humor, but through it. Repression was its goal. Johnson's poem, Lemay observes, addresses itself to English readers, but not to all equally.[42] It offered quick laughs to readers interested in denouncing colonization, but it offered enduring advice to readers interested in how to succeed at it anyway. Success would, in part, require transforming external material conditions. Colonists might eventually build warmer houses, they might eventually overcome monetary dearth, they might eventually be able to import long-lost pleasures from the metropole. Those triumphs, however, would take some time. And to bear discomfort in the meantime, the poem recommended action on internal dispositions: the poem exhorted settlers to cultivate brotherliness, magnanimity, patience, a "contented mind." The word settlers often used to generalize about this activity was *discipline*. But discipline wasn't always penal or punitive. It was also often productive. Cultural work, like poems or folk songs, could help produce that mental contentment. A humorous song could make the meantime laughable. It could do so in its jocular content and form, as in the rhyme and repetition that mimicked the repetitive dullness of frontier life. And it could do so in its performance of levity regarding those circumstances, by representing them as opportunities for laughter, a shared, but fortifying interruption in the taxing reign of repression's demands.[43] The poem doesn't simply describe what's annoying, but attempts to manage that frustration, and to make the annoying things it describes less annoying, more tolerable.

Historicist critics like Greenblatt have proposed that it is unwise to import anachronisms like "psychoanalysis" or "repression" into the study of early texts. But sometimes, in the work of understanding the past more dynamically, Jordan Stein has argued, it can be useful to estrange it by using vocabulary from the present.[44] And anyway, *repression* was a term available already to early modern English to describe how they managed their discomfort. That management often eludes observation often because successful repression would tend to obviate reasons to name it and describe it explicitly—would, "for the most part," Freud observed, "escape our examination."[45] Johnson's poem, to the degree that it tried to enact repression, appears largely to have succeeded. Most settlers who produced documents that now enjoy access to archival longevity rarely seem to be annoyed at the conditions of settlement. There is not a great deal of explicit, personal complaining about the annoyances that Johnson named. But there were many individuals who may have found those features of settlement annoying and whose record of irritation has been lost. There were many more still who simply didn't write them down. Occasionally, however, an early modern English colonist would write about how difficult it could be to keep their eyes on the proverbial prize. Consider one of Johnson's fellow poets, Michael Wigglesworth. Like Johnson, Wigglesworth was skilled in using verse to tell a story that was ideologically powerful but also very compelling.[46] Wigglesworth noticed the many annoyances of frontier life. He loathed the cold, he dreaded exposure, he hated the effects of what he ate on his digestion, and he found it very difficult to have anything but "strange" relations with his metonymic brothers.[47] He tried to address these annoyances with discipline. In addition to ideologically compelling poems, he also invested a great deal of energy in describing these annoyances and pleading with his deity to help him achieve mental contentment about them. In a diary entry from Friday, June 10, 1653, he described these investments as taxing. They "cost" him significant energy and attention.[48] And, provocatively, the word he used to name that work was repression: "to repress costeth me much," he wrote (22). Repression, in the world Wigglesworth and Johnson shared, named the work of making intolerable annoyances tolerable. Literary production was a dynamic tool for achieving it.

Wigglesworth's repression differs from the psychoanalytically derived idea of repression that clings, even in being negated, to analyses of colonial texts. Were reform Protestant colonial settlers, generations of historians have wondered, subject to the complicated afterlives of libidinal instincts they refused to countenance?[49] Wigglesworth's idea of repression preceded psychoanalysis by 250 years, so in a very specific Freudian sense, the answer to that question is probably "no." Yet Wigglesworth's "repression" shares some similarities with its appearance in Freud's thought. For the former, repression was largely conscious and deliberate. And for Wigglesworth, repression included a range of desires that were not reducible to sexual gratification. But Freud was nevertheless compelled by an approach to unconscious life that Wigglesworth would have understood and shared. Freud was fascinated by the possibility that the unconscious, as it attempted to make intolerable libidinal instincts tolerable, followed certain patterns that were more ubiquitous and far-reaching than the drives he most attentively observed. There were many reasons to try to understand the mechanisms of those patterns, Freud proposed. In one of his last theoretical papers, his 1937 essay "Analysis Terminable and Interminable," he observed that these mechanisms could extend the significance and the reach of psychoanalysis, they could integrate the aberrations and pathologies he studied into a range of behaviors that included the less aberrant, more statistically normal.[50] Most individuals, Freud observed, not simply those who behaved strangely or unusually, were burdened with the work of modulating instincts to accord with their society's demands. And there was no stable or bright line to distinguish the abnormal from the normal. Some individuals, like Wigglesworth, were franker and more fastidious in chronicling their experience of annoyances, but they weren't the only ones who ever got annoyed. Johnson's poem attests that being annoyed was a widely shared experience. Likewise ubiquitous was the labor of striving not to be.

But "New England's Annoyances" doesn't simply record the imperative to repress, to redirect energy from burdensome frustrations toward productive striving. The poem also offered representational strategies for effecting that repression. One was the word *annoyance* itself. It wasn't only attractive for the syncopation it brought to the title's most ubiquitous consonant. The word was also attractive because it named, affirmed, and then made diminutive and more bearable all the bodily risks, unhappy labor, and unrelenting social friction of frontier life—a "weaking of what is distasteful" in order to preserve mental and psychic resources for daily life's demands.[51] Another strategic word was *brother*, the figurative name that the poem gave to relations that were made strange in the colony—suffused with aggression as well as with the possibility of desire. Edward Johnson was by no means the first person to use that familial category to designate affectionate horizontal relations. It extended at least as far backward as the early Christian church, such as in the anonymous epistle circulating among early Christians in the first decades of the cult's consolidation that exhorted them to "let brotherly love continue."[52] For Massachusetts's colonists as for the early Christians, brotherhood was a satisfying name for participation in a spiritual community. This, most broadly, is what the poem means when it names "brother and brother" in its thirteenth stanza. But Johnson's language outruns those ambitions, suggesting relations that do not neatly align with theologically redemptive fellow feeling. In the poem's exposition, "brother[hood]" names prior relations that Calvinist theology would sunder rather than affirm, would make "a division 'twixt brother and brother." Johnson's poem invokes the solidarity of Christian community and uses it to denote relations that are not, strictly speaking, relations between Christians themselves, since those relations could in fact be riven by Christian theology's social unfolding. Rather than religion, these "brothers" who experience annoying divisions were yoked by shared English descent. Even as the division was unpleasant, the parties divided knew that they were related to each other through their accidents of birth.

But English settlers were not the only participants of frontier life, not the only candidates for brotherly relations. By 1643, frontier relations included the intimate encounters of people from at least three continents. Here, an idea of national "brother[hood]," like the idea of an "annoyance," could make bearable the strangeness of those intimacies. It could make tolerable a possibly intolerable experience of depending on, even starting to feel affection for, neighbors who were not brothers in either a spiritual or a national sense. In this context, the ambiguity between spiritual and national affiliation that the phrase suggests might not be a simple collapse between brother as metaphor (spirit) and brother as metonym (nation). In the frontier context, the poems' ambiguity may express what Neil Whitehead has called "texture," places of verbal friction that preserve elusive traces of Indigenous epistemology in texts written by colonial agents.[53] In a poem like "New England's Annoyances," that presence is *very* elusive. The poem does not once name or describe Native people directly. That silence exemplifies the notion of "vacuum domicilium" that legal theorists like Winthrop projected onto the environment that they hoped to claim for themselves.[54] English people were eager to imagine the landscape as depopulated of other humans, waiting for the application of English innovation and industry that would eventually coax out of that "wilderness wood" its fruits. From the dissatisfactions of the first stanza, the "much that is wanting" to the repetition of seemingly sui generis pumpkins across the course of the ninth, tenth, and eleventh stanzas, the poem insists on representing a world where there are no people with whom to be brothers except other English. Many colonial texts do this. But this text doesn't simply rehearse that representational strategy, doesn't simply perform neglect. It also positively describes the relations that settlers hoped would take the place of those people whom their scope of attention excluded. Brotherhood, even the strange kind, seems to have required a homogenous population; the alternative seems to have been imaginatively intolerable.

Intimacy with non-Europeans made English settlers uncomfortable—this is not an especially new or insightful premise. But it is easy to take for granted. And its conditions of possibility remain unclear. For many decades of early colonial historiography, intimacy's discomforts were easy to neglect because chroniclers themselves often neglected to note them. In the late twentieth century, literary and cultural historians began to reckon with that question more tenaciously. From the evidence they gathered, historians and literary historians told a story of antagonism and hostility, both latent and manifest. Settlers, they observed, often saw their new neighbors as threats. They responded to those threats with violence, and the sometimes irrational severity of that violence registered an existential experience of perceived threat.[55] In response to that scholarship and its bleak picture of settlers' interiority, a subsequent wave of historians offered more moderated accounts of the relations that settlers tended not to spend much ink preserving. Settlers, these historians have claimed, recognized a shared humanity with their neighbors.[56] They did not exclude non-Christian neighbors from the abstract order of existence in which they recognized themselves. But intellectual confidence regarding likeness and difference does not always translate into a feeling of security. Rather, confidence of an abstract ideal of humanity, as Johnson's poem itself suggested, led to less confidence, more frustration. If the committed historicism of a Greenblatt is to be trusted, the foundational isomorphism of humanity—the idea that there existed an order of formally interchangeable personhood—wasn't even easy for English people themselves to absorb within their own communities. English people would not have found it easy, in turn, to confront the discomforting strangeness of these neighbors who behaved in such a distinct fashion yet who were, at least according to their own theories, of the same humanity as themselves.

It was not simply the idea of equality that troubled English colonists. Those relations were uncomfortable because despite the differences across hypothetical humanity, settlers depended on these relationships for survival, especially during the first decades of settlement. Karen Kupperman, for example, observes that English settlers entered these relationships from a disadvantageous position as "supplicants."[57] Anticipating Jeffrey Ostler's criticism of accounts of settlers eager to depict them as "confident, efficient, supercilious settler bull[ies]," Kupperman describes the earliest English settlers as "doubtful and insecure."[58] Early English settlers, beset with annoyances, were not always or even often in dominant bargaining positions. Kupperman insists that they were weaker and more vulnerable and, to some degree, they knew it. Although promotional literature often claimed superior intellectual sophistication for Europeans, those who lived on the frontier quickly discovered otherwise. And they learned a great deal from the expertise and acuity of Native people.[59] They observed other ways of making the cold less sharp and aggressive than simply cutting trees and inefficiently burning them with what was, at least initially, unsustainable ardor.[60] They saw techniques for caring and maintaining the environment to preserve sources of food, from shellfish to pumpkins.[61] They learned to negotiate with Native ambassadors to acquire the furs that would enable them, they hoped, to acquire the commodities that they thought they needed from Europe.[62]

Yet after eagerly consuming reports that the land of America would be easy to inhabit, the role of "supplicant" would not have been easy to tolerate. It was annoying enough materially—Johnson's poem describes this amply. But the position of "supplicant" was hateful and odious in immaterial ways, too. It rankled early modern English peoples' ideas of national blessedness, their dearly cherished idea that, as one intellectual historian has recently put it, the Christian "God [was] English."[63] Settlers strained to represent their Native neighbors as supplicants, and themselves as sources of wisdom and power. As early as 1588, Thomas Hariot imagined that English possession of machines like "spring clocks that seeme to goe of themselues" would persuade the Carolina Algonquians to "honour, obey, feare and loue vs."[64] And then that venture failed so colossally as to leave barely one material trace. Thirty years later, John Smith liked to recall his relationship with Powhatan as one characterized by the latter's desire for English commodities and English favor.[65] Fifteen years after that, Edward Winslow likewise cherished his memory of healing the sachem Osamequin, and in doing so imagined himself to be provoking the jealous supplication of Osamequin's rivals, too.[66] Such evidence doesn't negate Kupperman's claim of English vulnerability and weakness. Far from it. Passages like these advance her insight by inviting an inquiry into why historians have seen it necessary to make settlers' material vulnerability explicit. The eagerness with which settlers recalled scenes of perceived power, and the enthusiasm with which they satirized their experience lacking power, suggests that they found the prospect of their own supplication, the prospect of admitting their doubtfulness and insecurity, and the possibility of being subjected chronically not only to material discomforts but also ideological ones, beyond what they could bear.

To eventually succeed in making tolerable what was odious required engaging more deeply in relations that would have been humiliating. Some settlers pursued this route, sought to learn from their Native counterparts how to make life materially less annoying. Modern historians have recovered the content of these exchanges, but the labor required to recover it attests to the uneasiness that these exchanges provoked, the distance settlers hoped to put between that reality and their consciousness.[67] Between the direct material annoyances, and the indirect frustrations of engaging with them, settlers, especially the early ones, would have engaged strenuously in the sort of inward activity that Wigglesworth called "repression," and that we might consider calling that, too—at very least to witness the costs of discipline as settlers pursued it. Repression, like discipline, was a skill. It had to be cultivated. There is no reason to expect any given individual to have been particularly efficient at absorbing their unhappy material and psychic conditions smoothly or inexpensively, without costly consequences. For some settlers, those consequences expressed themselves in violent behavior that might appear to be pathological in its intensity and irrationality.[68] Sometimes settlers themselves seemed to intuit, and nearly to confess, that they recognized that behavior to be extreme, to require justification. Why, John Underhill prosopopoeically asked himself after leading a catastrophic assault on a Pequot village at Mystic in 1637, had he been so furious?[69] He knew that a line existed between acceptable and unacceptable behavior, between what was self-evidently rational and what demanded explicit rationalization. And he found himself drawn across that line, not only in what he did, but what he wrote. But that line, the boundary between acceptable and unacceptable, normal and abnormal, isn't always clear to the individuals who move across it. Moreover, it tends not to stay in the same place as time goes by. Fifty years later, during King Philip's War, for example, English settlers tend to show far less self-consciousness regarding their expressions of vehemence. Over time, violence became a less unusual response to the unbearable impotence that settlers experienced on the colonial frontier, the intolerable frustrations of failing to be as masterful as they would have liked.

....

Johnson's poem catalogued experiences of unhappiness, discomfort, and frustrated desire, and it also tried to ease them. One way it attempted this was by rehearsing rational explanations for those infelicities. In an era characterized by increasing enthusiasm for epistemological endeavors, such gratifications were not insignificant.[70] As part of that rationalization, the poem eased discomfort by representing infelicities as humorous, merely "annoyances." In naming them that, Johnson's poem shaped not only the knowledge of what annoyed, but the relationship with that object of knowledge. The poem insisted this relationship need not be disturbing or relentlessly frustrating. English people who enjoyed the song and who sang it could laugh at its content. In that laughing they could worry less about the costs of these frustrations on themselves, on their neighbors, and on the environment that they shared. Eventually, they might not perceive colonization to have been so costly. Eventually these material and psychic costs would fall off the accounting sheet. Eventually, it would be possible to write of them, as Richard Godbeer did at the turn of this century, and as Abram van Engen has echoed fifteen years since then, that they did not repress; that they were not subject to the vagaries of unconscious life; that they deliberately and consciously chose their ideals and their pleasures and just as deliberately and consciously chose how to pursue them; that they were masters, so to speak, of the houses that they recognized as their own.[71] Yet the plausibility of these claims to emotional freedom might, in the same instance, be evidence of the success of their diligent work of repressing obstacles to it. Conceding that a poem like Johnson's might have succeeded in its task would then undermine modern security in the certainty of settlers' own self-knowledge.

The question of Johnson's poem's success—and the success of the other practices that settlers developed and that Johnson's poem metonymically represents here—has profound implications for the study of literature and history, and especially for the study of early America. A recent forum in the *William and Mary Quarterly* poses this challenge incisively. In reflecting on the value of settler colonial theory to illuminate the unique qualities of colonization in North America, historians of early America have foundered on the challenge of understanding interiority. "Settler colonialism," at least as it's been theorized by modern critics, only imperfectly names what came to pass in America, early Americanist historians observe. Settlers in North America did not succeed in what Patrick Wolfe has called "the elimination of the native." And importing the theory casually, historians warn, risks reproducing in our scholarship an erasure similar to what Johnson's poem less accidentally performs. Yet settler colonial theory, some of these leading historians propose, can be a useful heuristic to begin to recognize the consequences of these settlers' desires, both the desires they recognized and those they struggled to forget. Many early colonists, observes Susana Shaw Romney, "lacked the strength to undertake expropriation and extermination."[72] She is describing Dutch settlers, fellow Protestants several hundred miles to the southwest of the early English colonies. That impotence, as Johnson's poem attests, applies to the English settlements, too. If their flesh was weak, their spirits, Romney observes, were willing in their contemplation of violence. Even if they "lacked the strength" for undertaking violence, "many wished they could," making them, in Romney's account "aspirational settler colonists."[73] Settler colonialism, for these historians, takes place in the realm of "wishes," "aspirations," and "desires." Sometimes the pursuit of those desires, as with John Underhill, manifested itself spectacularly. But other times—probably most of the time—settlers pursued those goals far more subtly, more subtly perhaps than they themselves recognized.

But subtlety does not mean total invisibility. "True conquest," observed Ralph Waldo Emerson two centuries later, was not only a matter of matter, it was a matter of memory—what one remembers, and how.[74] Emerson was not thinking of explicitly political conquest, but conquest over resentment, irritation, and inchoate turmoil's claim on the conscious, masterful subject. True conquest, in other words, would require successful repression. Settlers like Wigglesworth were eager to enlist divine aid in pursuit of this goal, and, along the way, poems like Johnson's could make that yoke easy and that burden light. For this reason, finally, Johnson's poem suggests the value of approaching colonial actors with sensitivity toward the limits of their own self-knowledge. There is value, certainly, in considering the past according to the terms historical agents themselves had to perceive it, rather than importing critical anachronisms, and this is especially the case when narrating historical actors who have long been condescended to for their perceived lack of self-knowledge by the agents of colonial reason. But we err, I think, when we imply in our methods that historical agents are fully knowable to themselves, and, second, when we approach human motivations as immune to transformation over deep time.[75] In this context, where great violence was enacted for the sake of "a peacable and quiet resting place," it is worth at least trying to understand the words they used to buy peace, quiet, and rest, the words with which, within a history they hoped would be large and advancing, would cause whatever disturbed that rest to fade and disappear.[76]

NOTES

1. Sigmund Freud, "Repression," 153.
2. Sigmund Freud, "Repression," 150, italics in original.
3. Sigmund Freud, "Repression," 147, italics in original.
4. For ambivalence and interest in the critical value's term to early American studies, see Ostler and Shoemaker, "Forum." For recent field-transcending surveys of settler colonialism, see Byrd, *Transit of Empire*; Kauanui, "A Structure, Not an Event"; Schueller and Watts, *Messy Beginnings*; Veracini, *Settler Colonialism*; Veracini, *Settler Colonial Present*; Wolfe, "Settler Colonialism"; and Wolfe, *Settler Colonialism and the Transformation of Anthropology*.
5. Rudy, "Settled," 199–200.
6. In the colonial New England context, one enduring account of the place of spectacle in settler violence is Kibbey, *Interpretation of Material Shapes*.
7. Lemay, *New England's Annoyances*, 70–87.

8. Christopher Levett, *Voyage into New England*, 159–90; Winslow, *Good News*.
9. Cited in Lemay, *New England's Annoyances*, 27, 128n19.
10. Johnson, "New England's Annoyances."
11. See Wickman, *Snowshoe Country*, and Cronon, *Changes in the Land*.
12. See the version reproduced in Kenney, *Laughter in the Wilderness*, 34–36.
13. Jones and Stallybrass, *Renaissance Clothing*, 3.
14. Freud, *Jokes*, 60–66. See also his discussion of jokes that represent a concept through describing its opposite, 70–74.
15. Downing, "Letter," 64–66; see also Schwartz, "Were There Any Immigrants [...]?"
16. Miller, "Errand," 15.
17. Winthrop, *Journal*, 341.
18. Winthrop, *Journal*, 353.
19. Muldrew, *Economy of Obligation*.
20. Winthrop, *Journal*, 345.
21. Winthrop, *Journal*, 342.
22. "annoyance, n.," *OED Online*, Oxford University Press, June 2020, accessed August 12, 2020, www.oed.com/view/Entry/7939.
23. "annoy, v.," *OED Online*, Oxford University Press, June 2020, accessed August 12, 2020, www.oed.com/view/Entry/7938.
24. Moore, *Pilgrims*; Delbanco, *Puritan Ordeal*.
25. Winthrop, "Modell," 290; see also Schweitzer, "John Winthrop's 'Modell.'"
26. Bradford, *Of Plimoth Plantation*, 162–63.
27. On suffering's instrumentality, see Coviello, "Agonizing Affection"; and Donegan, "As Dying."
28. The most recent such exegesis is van Engen, *Sympathetic Puritans*.
29. See, most recently, Winship, *Hot Protestants*, 54–57.
30. Winthrop, *Journal*, 355–57; see also Kupperman, *Providence Island*.
31. See, for an example of one such highly cherished object, the cliché phrase that condenses this ideal as it appears in several recent monographs: van Engen, *City on a Hill*; Rodgers, *As a City on a Hill*; and Krieger, *City on a Hill*.
32. Bradford, *Of Plimoth Plantation*, 162–63.
33. Anderson, *Creatures of Empire*; Cronon, *Changes in the Land*; Bailyn, "Apologia"; Valeri, *Heavenly Merchandize*, 37–73.
34. On infanticide, see Winthrop, *Journal*, 229–30, 391–92. On arson, see Koehler, *Search for Power*, 144–45, and Schwartz, "Anne Bradstreet, Arsonist"; on domestic violence, see Smyth, "Mrs. Eaton's Trial"; Handlin, "Dissent"; and Schwartz, *Unmoored*, 1–4, 243–59.
35. For flash points revealing Winthrop's long-simmering irritation with Richard Bellingham, colleague on the General Court as deputy governor, treasurer, and eventually governor, see Winthrop, *Journal*, 144, 312, 358, 367, 373–48, 390, and 452. For a survey of the potentially classed dimensions of this animosity, see Staloff, *Making of an American*, 80–85.

36 Dudley, "Governor Dudley's Letter," 8, 13.
37 Bradstreet, "Meditations," 195–209, 202. See also Schwartz, "Anne Bradstreet, Arsonist?"
38 "mad, adj.," OED Online, Oxford University Press, June 2020, accessed August 12, 2020, www.oed.com/view/Engtry/112000.
39 Greenblatt, "Psychoanalysis."
40 Wynter, "Unsettling."
41 Marx, "On the Jewish Question"; Kazanjian, "Notarizing Knowledge"; Lacan, "Mirror Stage," 79.
42 Lemay, *New England's Annoyances*, 21–35.
43 Freud, "Repression," 151.
44 Stein, "How to Undo," 776–77.
45 Freud, "Repression," 153.
46 Wigglesworth, "Day of Doom." On Wigglesworth's successes, see Bosco, "Introduction," ix–xviii.
47 Wigglesworth, *Diary*, 90, 91, 92 (cold), 94 (exposure), 58 (digestion), 94 (strange relations with metonymic brothers).
48 Wigglesworth, *Diary*, 22.
49 For key moments in this ongoing haunting, see Hawthorne, *Scarlet Letter*; Morgan, *Puritan Family*; Morgan, "Introduction"; Verduin, "Our Cursed Natures"; Godbeer, *Sexual Revolution*; van Engen, *Sympathetic Puritans*.
50 Freud, "Analysis Terminable and Interminable."
51 Freud, "Repression," 152.
52 Hebrews 13:1.
53 Whitehead, "Discoverie," 38. For examples of texture's uptake in early American history and literary history, see Kupperman, *Indians and English*, 32; Wisecup, *Medical Encounters*, 11–15, 197–200; Smith, *Black Africans*, 4–5.
54 Winthrop, "Lawfulness," 82–86, 87–89. On "vacuum domicilium," see Tomlins, *Freedom Bound*, 148–56.
55 See, for example, Jennings, *Invasion of America*; Kibbey, *Interpretation of Material Shapes*; Cave, *Pequot War*; Lepore, *Name of War*; Drake, *King Philip's War*; Horne, *Apocalypse of Settler Colonialism*.
56 Chaplin, *Subject Matter*; Kupperman, *Settling with the Indians*.
57 Kupperman, *Indians and English*, 14.
58 Kupperman, *Indians and English*, 14; Ostler and Shoemaker, "Forum," 363.
59 Chaplin, *Subject Matter*; Kelly Wisecup, *Medical Encounters*.
60 Cronon, *Changes in the Land*; Wickman, *Snowshoe Country*; Little, "Shoot That Rogue."
61 LaCombe, *Political Gastronomy*.
62 Thomas, "Fur Trade"; Brooks, *Common Pot*.
63 Winship, *Godly Republicanism*, 14.
64 Hariot, *A Briefe and True Report*, 39, 44.
65 Smith, "A True Relation," 5–36.

66 Winslow, *Good News*, 84, 86; see also Schwartz, "Mercy as Well as Extremity."
67 Chaplin, *Subject Matter*; Rivett, *Unscripted America*.
68 For an example of the challenge of understanding that vehemence without a rubric for understanding unconscious life, see Edmund Morgan's vivid, apostrophic account of Jamestown in *American Slavery, American Freedom*, 90. Morgan's account seems to align very neatly with the one proposed here, but substitutes re-creation of the experience of profound frustration without naming it, and reflection on what Gayatri Spivak has called "the illogic that produces the subject's logic, and also the logic of the subject's illogic" in "Echo," 20.
69 Underhill, *Newes from America*, 40.
70 For exemplary recent scholarship on this epistemological renaissance, see Chaplin, *Subject Matter*; Parrish, *American Curiosity*; Silva, *Miraculous Plagues*; Rivett, *Science of the Soul*; Rivett, *Unscripted America*; Wisecup, *Medical Encounters*; Altschuler, *Medical Imagination*; Farrell, *Counting Bodies*; Gomez, *Experiential Caribbean*; Chico, *Experimental Imagination*; LaFleur, *Natural History of Sexuality*. See also recent dissertations like Trocchio, "American Puritanism"; Takahata, "Skeletal Testimony"; and Orr, "American Intelligences."
71 Godbeer, *Sexual Revolution*, 55; van Engen, *Sympathetic Puritans*, 1.
72 Romney, "Settler Colonial Prehistories," 380.
73 Romney, "Settler Colonial Prehistories," 380; see also Witgen, "A Nation of Settlers"; Spear, "Beyond the Native/Settler Divide."
74 Emerson, "Circles," 183.
75 See, for example, Kupperman, *Indians and English*, 14; Bross, *Dry Bones*, 25; and Bross, *Future History*, 17.
76 Cotton, *God's Promise*, 2.

BIBLIOGRAPHY

Altschuler, Sari. *The Medical Imagination: Literature and Health in the Early United States*. Philadelphia: University of Pennsylvania Press, 2018.

Anderson, Virginia DeJohn. *Creatures of Empire: How Domestic Animals Transformed Early America*. New York: Oxford University Press, 2004.

Bailyn, Bernard. "The Apologia of Robert Keayne." *William and Mary Quarterly* 7, no. 4 (1950): 568–87.

Bosco, Ronald. "Introduction." *The Poems of Michael Wigglesworth*, edited by Ronald A. Bosco, ix–xvii. Lanham, MD: University Press of America, 1989.

Bradford, William. *Of Plimoth Plantation*. Boston: Wright and Potter, 1899.

Bradstreet, Anne. "Meditations." In *The Complete Works of Anne Bradstreet*, edited by Joseph R. McElrath Jr. and Allan P. Robb, 195–209. Boston: Twayne, 1981.

Brooks, Lisa. *The Common Pot: The Recovery of Native Space in the Northeast*. Minneapolis: University of Minnesota Press, 2008.

Bross, Kristina. *Dry Bones and Indian Sermons: Praying Indians in Colonial America.* Ithaca, NY: Cornell University Press, 2004.

Bross, Kristina. *Future History: Global Fantasies in Seventeenth-Century American and British Writings.* New York: Oxford University Press, 2017.

Byrd, Jodi A. *Transit of Empire: Indigenous Critiques of Colonialism.* Minneapolis: University of Minnesota Press, 2011.

Cave, Alfred A. *The Pequot War.* Amherst: University of Massachusetts Press, 1996.

Chaplin, Joyce E. *Subject Matter: Technology, the Body, and Science on the Anglo-American Frontier, 1500–1676.* Cambridge, MA: Harvard University Press, 2001.

Chico, Tita. *The Experimental Imagination: Literary Knowledge and Science in the British Enlightenment.* Stanford, CA: Stanford University Press, 2018.

Cotton, John. *God's Promise to His Plantation.* Edited by Reiner Smolinksi. *Electronic Texts in American Studies* Paper 22. http://digitalcommons.unl.edu/etas/22.

Coviello, Peter. "Agonizing Affection: Affect and Nation in Early America." *Early American Literature* 37, no. 3 (2002): 439–68.

Cronon, William. *Changes in the Land: Indians, Colonists and the Ecology of New England.* New York: Hill and Wang, 1983.

Delbanco, Andrew. *The Puritan Ordeal.* Cambridge, MA: Harvard University Press, 1989.

Donegan, Kathleen. "'As Dying, Yet Behold, We Live': Catastrophe and Interiority in Bradford's *Of Plymouth Plantation.*" *Early American Literature* 37, no. 1 (2002): 9–37.

Downing, Emanuel. "Letter of Emanuel Downing." *Collections of the Massachusetts Historical Society,* ser. 4 (1863) 6:64–66.

Drake, James D. *King Philip's War: Civil War in New England, 1675–1676.* Amherst: University of Massachusetts Press, 1999.

Dudley, Thomas. "Governor Thomas Dudley's Letter to the Countess of Lincoln, March 1631." In *Tracts and Other Papers Relating Principally to the Origin, Settlement, and Progress of the Colonies in North America,* 1–20 (document 4). Washington, DC: Peter Force, 1836.

Emerson, Ralph Waldo. "Circles." In *Essays: First and Second Series,* introduction by Douglas Crase, 173–84. New York: Library of America, 1991.

Farrell, Molly. *Counting Bodies: Population in Colonial American Writing.* New York: Oxford University Press, 2016.

Freud, Sigmund. "Analysis Terminable and Interminable." In *The Standard Edition of the Complete Psychological Works of Sigmund Freud,* translated by James Strachey, 23:211–53. London: Hogarth, 1937.

Freud, Sigmund. *Jokes and Their Relation to the Unconscious.* In *The Standard Edition of the Complete Psychological Works of Sigmund Freud.* Translated by James Strachey, 8:1–247. London: Hogarth, 1905.

Freud, Sigmund. "Repression." In *The Standard Edition of the Complete Psychological Works Works of Sigmund Freud.* Translated by James Strachey, 14:141–58. London: Hogarth, 1915.

Godbeer, Richard. *Sexual Revolution in Early America.* Baltimore: Johns Hopkins University Press, 2002.

Gomez, Pablo F. *The Experiential Caribbean: Creating Knowledge and Healing in the Early Modern Atlantic*. Chapel Hill: University of North Carolina Press, 2017.

Greenblatt, Stephen. "Psychoanalysis and Renaissance Culture." In *Literary Theory/Renaissance Texts*, edited by Patricia Parker and David Quint, 201–24. Baltimore: Johns Hopkins University Press, 1986.

Handlin, Lilian. "Dissent in a Small Community." *New England Quarterly* 58, no. 2 (1985): 193–220.

Hariot, Thomas. *A Briefe and True Report of the New Found Land of Virginia*. London, 1588.

Hawthorne, Nathaniel. *The Scarlet Letter*. New York: Norton, 1988.

Horne, Gerald. *The Apocalypse of Settler Colonialism: The Roots of Slavery, White Supremacy, and Capitalism in Seventeenth-Century North America and the Caribbean*. New York: Monthly Review, 2018.

Jennings, Francis. *The Invasion of America: Indians, Colonialism, and the Cant of Conquest*. Chapel Hill: University of North Carolina Press, 1975.

Johnson, Edward. "New England's Annoyances." In *American Poetry: The Seventeenth and Eighteenth Centuries*, edited by David S. Shields, 17–19. New York: Library of America, 2007.

Jones, Ann Rosalind, and Peter Stallybrass. *Renaissance Clothing and the Materials of Memory*. New York: Cambridge University Press, 2000.

Kauanui, J. Kēhaulani. "'A Structure, Not an Event': Settler Colonialism and Enduring Indigeneity." *Lateral: Journal of the Cultural Studies Association* 5, no. 1 (2016). https://csalateral.org/issue/5-1/forum-alt-humanities-settler-colonialism-enduring-indigeneity-kauanui/.

Kazanjian, David. "Notarizing Knowledge: Paranoia and Civility in Freud and Lacan." *Qui Parle* 7, no. 1 (1993): 102–39.

Kenney, W. Howland, ed. *Laughter in the Wilderness: Early American Humor to 1783*. Kent, OH: Kent State University Press, 1976.

Kibbey, Ann. *The Interpretation of Material Shapes in Puritanism: A Study of Rhetoric, Prejudice, and Violence*. Cambridge: Cambridge University Press, 1986.

Koehler, Lyle. *A Search for Power: The "Weaker Sex" in Seventeenth-Century New England*. Urbana: University of Illinois Press, 1980.

Krieger, Alex. *City on a Hill: Urban Idealism in America from the Puritans to the Present*. Cambridge, MA: Harvard University Press, 2019.

Kupperman, Karen. *Indians and English: Facing Off in Early America*. Ithaca, NY: Cornell University Press, 2000.

Kupperman, Karen. *Providence Island, 1630–1641: The Other Puritan Colony*. New York: Cambridge University Press, 1993.

Kupperman, Karen Ordahl. *Settling with the Indians: The Meeting of English and Indian Cultures in America, 1580–1640*. Totowa, NJ: Rowman and Littlefield, 1980.

Lacan, Jacques. "The Mirror Stage as Formative of the *I* Function as Revealed in Psychoanalytic Experience." In *Écrits: The First Complete Edition in English*, translated by Bruce Fink, 75–81. New York: Norton, 1966.

LaCombe, Michael A. *Political Gastronomy: Food and Authority in the English Atlantic World*. Philadelphia: University of Pennsylvania Press, 2012.

LaFleur, Greta. *The Natural History of Sexuality in Early America*. Baltimore: Johns Hopkins University Press, 2018.

Lemay, J. A. Leo. *"New England's Annoyances": America's First Folk Song*. Newark: University of Delaware Press, 1985.

Lepore, Jill. *The Name of War: King Philip's War and the Origins of American Identity*. New York: Knopf, 1998.

Levett, Christopher. *A Voyage into New England. Collections of the Massachusetts Historical Society*, series 3, vol. 8 (1843): 159–90.

Little, Ann M. "'Shoot That Rogue, for He Hath an Englishman's Coat On!': Cultural Cross-Dressing on the New England Frontier, 1620–1760." *New England Quarterly*, 74, no. 2 (2001): 238–73.

Marx, Karl. "On the Jewish Question." In *Marx: Early Political Writings*, edited by Joseph J. O'Malley, 28–56. New York: Cambridge University Press, 1994.

Miller, Perry. *Errand into the Wilderness*. Cambridge, MA: Harvard University Press, 1956.

Moore, Susan Hardman. *Pilgrims: New World Settlers and the Call of Home*. New Haven, CT: Yale University Press, 2008.

Morgan, Edmund S. *American Slavery, American Freedom: The Ordeal of Colonial Virginia*. New York: Norton, 1975.

Morgan, Edmund S. Introduction to *The Diary of Michael Wigglesworth, 1653–1657: The Conscience of a Puritan*, edited by Edmund S. Morgan, v–xv. New York: Harper and Row, 1965.

Morgan, Edmund S. *The Puritan Family: Religion and Domestic Relations in Seventeenth-Century New England*. New York: Harper and Row, 1966.

Muldrew, Craig. *The Economy of Obligation: The Culture of Credit and Social Relations in Early Modern England*. New York: Palgrave Macmillan, 1998.

Orr, Itai. "American Intelligences: Varieties of Mind Before IQ." PhD diss., Yale University, 2020.

Ostler, Jeffrey, and Nancy Shoemaker, eds. "Forum: Settler Colonialism in Early American History." *William and Mary Quarterly* 76, no. 3 (2019): 361–450.

Parrish, Susan Scott. *American Curiosity: Cultures of Natural History in the Colonial British Atlantic World*. Chapel Hill: University of North Carolina Press, 2006.

Rivett, Sarah. *The Science of the Soul in Colonial New England*. Chapel Hill: University of North Carolina Press, 2011.

Rivett, Sarah. *Unscripted America: Indigenous Languages and the Origins of a Literary Nation*. New York: Oxford University Press, 2017.

Rodgers, Daniel T. *As a City on a Hill: The Story of America's Most Famous Lay Sermon*. Princeton, NJ: Princeton University Press, 2018.

Rudy, Jason R. "Settled: *Dorritt* Down Under." *Nineteenth-Century Literature* 75, no. 2 (2020): 184–206.

Schueller, Malini Johar, and Edward Watts, eds. *Messy Beginnings: Postcoloniality and Early American Studies.* New Brunswick, NJ: Rutgers University Press, 2003.

Schwartz, Ana. "Anne Bradstreet, Arsonist?" *New Literary History* 52, no. 1 (2021): 119–43.

Schwartz, Ana. "'Mercy as Well as Extremity': Forts, Fences, and Fellow Feeling in New England Settlement." *Early American Literature* 54, no. 2 (2019): 343–80.

Schwartz, Ana. *Unmoored: The Search for Sincerity in Colonial America.* Chapel Hill: University of North Carolina Press, 2023.

Schwartz, Ana. "Were There Any Immigrants in New England?" *New England Quarterly* 93, no. 3 (2020): 400–413.

Schweitzer, Ivy. "John Winthrop's 'Model' of American Affiliation." *Early American Literature* 40, no. 3 (2005): 441–69.

Silva, Cristobal. *Miraculous Plagues: An Epidemiology of Early New England Narrative.* New York: Oxford University Press, 2011.

Smith, Cassander L. *Black Africans in the British Imagination: English Narratives of the Early Atlantic World.* Baton Rouge: Louisiana State University Press, 2016.

Smith, John. "A True Relation of Such Occurrences and Accidents of Note [...]." In *Captain John Smith: Writings,* 5–36. New York: Library of America, 2007.

Smyth, Newman. "Mrs. Eaton's Trial in 1644." *Papers of the New Haven Colony Historical Society* 5 (1984): 133–48.

Spear, Jennifer M. "Beyond the Native/Settler Divide in Early California." *William and Mary Quarterly* 76, no. 3 (2019): 427–34.

Spivak, Gayatri Chakravorty. "Echo." *New Literary History* 24, no. 3 (1993): 17–43.

Staloff, Darren. *The Making of an American Thinking Class: Intellectuals and Intelligentsia in Puritan Massachusetts.* New York: Oxford University Press, 1998.

Stein, Jordan Alexander. "How to Undo the History of Sexuality: Editing Edward Taylor's *Meditations.*" *American Literature,* 90, no. 4 (2018): 753–84.

Takahata, Kimberly. "Skeletal Testimony: Bony Biopolitics in the Early Atlantic, 1705–1836." PhD diss., Columbia University, 2020.

Thomas, Peter A. "The Fur Trade, Indian Land, and the Need to Define Adequate 'Environmental' Parameters." *Ethnohistory* 28, no. 4 (1981): 359–79.

Tomlins, Christopher. *Freedom Bound: Law, Labor, and Civic Identity in Colonizing English America, 1580–1865.* New York: Cambridge University Press, 2010.

Trocchio, Rachel. "American Puritanism and the Cognitive Style of Grace." PhD diss., University of California, Berkeley, 2017.

Underhill, John. *Newes from America; or, A New and Experimentall Discoverie of New England.* London: Peter Cole, 1638.

Valeri, Mark. *Heavenly Merchandize: How Religion Shaped Commerce in Puritan America.* Princeton, NJ: Princeton University Press, 2010.

Van Engen, Abram C. *City on a Hill: A History of American Exceptionalism.* New Haven, CT: Yale University Press, 2020.

Van Engen, Abram C. *Sympathetic Puritans: Calvinist Fellow Feeling in Early New England.* Oxford: Oxford University Press, 2015.

Veracini, Lorenzo. *Settler Colonialism: A Theoretical Overview*. London: Palgrave Macmillan, 2010.
Veracini, Lorenzo. *The Settler Colonial Present*. London: Palgrave Macmillan, 2015.
Verduin, Kathleen. "'Our Cursed Natures': Sexuality and the Puritan Conscience." *New England Quarterly* 56, no. 2 (1983): 220–37.
Whitehead, Neil, ed. "The *Discoverie* as Enchanted Text." In *The Discoverie of the Large, Rich, and Bewtiful Empyre of Guiana*, by Sir Walter Raleigh, 8–59. Norman: University of Oklahoma Press, 1997.
Wickman, Thomas M. *Snowshoe Country: An Environmental and Cultural History of Winter in the Early American Northeast*. Cambridge: Cambridge University Press, 2018.
Wigglesworth, Michael. "The Day of Doom." In *The Poems of Michael Wigglesworth*, edited by Ronald A. Bosco, 11–66. Lanham, MD: University Press of America, 1989.
Wigglesworth, Michael. *The Diary of Michael Wigglesworth, 1653–1657: The Conscience of a Puritan*, edited by Edmund S. Morgan. New York: Harper and Row, 1965.
Winship, Michael P. *Godly Republicanism: Puritans, Pilgrims, and a City on a Hill*. Cambridge, MA: Harvard University Press, 2012.
Winship, Michael P. *Hot Protestants: A History of Puritanism in England and America*. New Haven, CT: Yale University Press, 2018.
Winslow, Edward. *Good News from New England: A Scholarly Edition*. Edited by Kelly Wisecup. Amherst: University of Massachusetts Press, 2014.
Winthrop, John. "The Lawfulness of Removing out of England." In *John Winthrop's Decision for America: 1629*, edited by Harold M. Hyman, 82–86. Philadelphia: Lippincott, 1975.
Winthrop, John. "Modell of Christian Charity." In *Winthrop Papers*, 2:282–95. Boston: Massachusetts Historical Society, 1931.
Wisecup, Kelly. *Medical Encounters: Knowledge and Identity in Early American Literatures*. Amherst: University of Massachusetts Press, 2013.
Witgen, Michael. "A Nation of Settlers: The Early American Republic and the Colonization of the Northwest Territory." *William and Mary Quarterly* 76, no. 3 (2019): 391–98.
Wolfe, Patrick. "Settler Colonialism and the Elimination of the Native." *Journal of Genocide Research* 8, no. 4 (2006): 387–409.
Wolfe, Patrick. *Settler Colonialism and the Transformation of Anthropology: The Politics and Poetics of an Ethnographic Event*. London: Cassell, 1999.
Wynter, Sylvia. "Unsettling the Coloniality of Being/Power/Truth/Freedom: Towards the Human, after Man, It's Overrepresentation—an Argument." *CR: The New Centennial Review* 3, no. 3 (2003): 257–337.

FOUR · *Christopher Looby*

Michael Wigglesworth's Queer Orthography

I found myself much overborn with carnal concupiscence nature being suppressed for I had not had my afflux in 12 nights Friday night it came again without any dream that I know of. Yet after it I am still inclined to lust The Lord help me against it and against discouragement by it and against temptations of another nature and disquietments.
—MICHAEL WIGGLESWORTH, "THE DIARY OF MICHAEL WIGGLESWORTH"

"Michael Wigglesworth's diary," according to Alan Bray, "is a document which is far from easy to unravel."[1] This assessment is certainly valid but may even understate the interpretive difficulty, especially if one is trying, as Bray and a few other scholars have sought to do, to turn the diary to advantage for understanding the history of sexuality and, in particular, the early history of queer sexuality.[2] Wigglesworth's diary (1653–57) suggests itself for these purposes because two of his most troubling preoccupations—which seem, in fact, to motivate his initial inscription of the diary, so densely concentrated are they in the text's very first pages—are, first, what he calls in the opening sentence of the text his "*unnatural filthy lust*" (322), which often produces a "*filthy dream*" (324) accompanied by nocturnal seminal emission ("*pollution escaped me in my sleep*" [324]), and, second, what he believes to be his excessive "doting affection *to some of my pupils*" (328) at Harvard, all of whom, of course, were male. His record of both of these preoccupations was entered in the diary mostly using a shorthand cipher, the so-called tachygraphy devised by Thomas Shelton. Multiple scholars, including Bray, have quite reasonably inferred that these two preoccupations—his unsettlingly intense love for the young men he tutored and his troubling wet dreams—had everything to do with one another, that is, that he must have been having homoerotic dreams, and the fact that he used the shorthand cipher to encrypt both matters would seem to support the connection. This is certainly a reasonable inference—but it is an inference, and not a provable conclusion. Because Wigglesworth never confided the *contents* of his erotic dreams to his diary, as his biographer Richard Crowder noted,[3] as Bray also acknowledged (163n1), and because, as I want to suggest, Wigglesworth may not even have remembered (or may only selectively have remembered) the contents of his erotic dreams, the connection is to some degree a speculative one.

It will probably not be possible to determine definitively whether Wigglesworth experienced dreams and fantasies of a homoerotic nature, nor to determine with certainty exactly what he knew about them, never mind what he thought about them (apart from his intense self-loathing on their account). But it ought to be possible to make some progress in understanding this interpretive crux if we employ some critical methods drawn from several fields of inquiry—namely, queer studies and the history of sexuality, which will help to historicize the very concept of "sexuality" and place Wigglesworth's experiences of embodiment and pleasure in sharper perspective; also material textual studies, which will help in understanding aspects of the text itself (e.g., its combination of English, Latin, and shorthand cipher, as well as certain features of its graphic appearance); and the field of medical or health humanities, which will offer an opportunity to look closely at Wigglesworth's hitherto under-studied consultations with three physicians from whom he sought advice and care with respect to his nocturnal emissions, which he regarded as an illness, a *"distemper"* (323) in need of medical treatment, as well as a moral *"iniquity"* (323) inviting God's punishment.

Eventually these three lines of critical inquiry will converge and be brought to bear upon one particular page of the diary, an anomalous page—recorded at a crucial and especially tortured moment in his life in September 1655, soon after his marriage and a short time before his assumption of a ministerial post at Malden, Massachusetts, and just as his recently widowed mother and unmarried sister were about to come to live with him—a page that features what Crowder aptly calls a "strangely phallic" (90) drawing of the so-called Ebenezer Stone or Ebenezer Pillar, accompanied by a poem in Latin and followed by another passage in the shorthand cipher, in which he reports, yet again, "some *night pollution escaped me*" (412). Along the way it will be possible to correct some persistent errors that have lodged themselves in the (still rather limited) secondary literature on Wigglesworth's diary—errors concerning his purported masturbation and his seeming worry about gonorrhea. It should also be said at the start that this essay is avowedly a "symptomatic" one in that it assumes we may be able to discern things about Wigglesworth, on the basis of his diary, that might not have been consciously discernible to him.[4] As intensely introspective and confessional as his diary undoubtedly is, it also seems paradoxically to be a place where he secreted certain aspects of himself—where he externalized and quarantined certain thoughts and feelings that were unwelcome to his waking self.

QUEER ORTHOGRAPHY

Edmund S. Morgan transcribed Michael Wigglesworth's diary in the mid-1940s and published it soon thereafter in the *Publications of the Colonial Society of Massachusetts* (1951). A few years later it was republished in paperback by Harper and Row (1965) for classroom use.[5] This was a diary that Wigglesworth kept as a young man, from 1653 to 1657, while he was a tutor at Harvard and then during the very first years of his ministerial career. The manuscript diary, which survives as a small leather-bound volume, measuring approximately 14.5 by 9 cm, is held by the library of the Massachusetts Historical Society.[6] It had a curious status for Morgan: he was then pursuing a revisionary account of the New England Puritans, arguing that they were not the uniformly dour, joyless figures of popular caricature,[7] but he found that Wigglesworth corresponded to that caricature more than most—"a living embodiment of the caricature" (316). That was the gist of Morgan's introduction to the Colonial Society publication, which was reprinted in the later paperback and then collected much later in a gathering of Morgan's essays.[8] Later generations of scholars have sought to turn the diary to advantage for the history of sexuality, since among other things Wigglesworth recorded in it his nocturnal seminal emissions, alluded to *"filthy dream*[s]*"* (324), and expressed what some have taken to have been his homoerotic interest in his Harvard students. There are some brief minutes printed just before Morgan's introduction in the Colonial Society edition, in which it is reported that he had read his essay at a meeting of the society on December 19, 1946, where it "evoked a lively discussion among the members present" (311). At that time the society's membership was exclusively male;[9] one wonders what was so "lively" about the unreported discussion between the gathered men, given Morgan's complete lack of comment within the introduction upon Wigglesworth's encoded erotic confessions. It would be interesting to know how, in that homosocial setting, Morgan's discussion was received, and whether, in that setting, he was more forthcoming about the diary's encrypted erotic content than he was willing to be in print.

Morgan observed in his editorial note on "The Manuscript" that it contained "numerous passages, varying in length from a single word to several pages, of shorthand code" (321), which was identified as Thomas Shelton's tachygraphy (described in his *Tachygraphy* [1635, with many later editions]). It seems to have been the historian of shorthand William P. Upham, not Morgan, who first identified the particular cipher Wigglesworth employed (more on this below). Shelton's is a shorthand system of some complexity, partly phonetic and partly not. It uses simplified marks to represent the letters of the English alphabet (see figure 4.1), which are understood to correspond to the sounds of spoken English; it mostly elides medial vowels (that is, vowels not at the beginning or the end of a word) but renders them implicitly by placing the succeeding consonant in one or another of five particular spatial positions relative to the preceding consonant, the choice of position indicating which of the five vowels has been elided (see figure 4.2); and it has a glossary of several hundred special non-phonetic marks representing the most frequently used words and stock phrases, including, tellingly, the names of the different books of the Bible, as well as compounds like "the kingdom of God," "the joys of heaven," "the torments of hell," and so forth, and common words like "and," "behold," "come," "dwell," etc. Shelton says explicitly, in his preface "To the Reader," that his shorthand has several religious purposes (see figure 4.3): "the benefit that many thousands enjoy by the works of many worthy Divines, which had perished with the breath that utters them, had not God . . . instructed some to handle the pen of the writer," as well as "the priviledge that diverse enjoy in foraine parts, by using Bibles and other books in this writing, without danger of bloody Inquisitours."[10] Given its design for pious purposes, there is thus some irony in the fact that Wigglesworth used it extensively to record instances of his "*carnal lusts*" (324) and "*pollution* [which] *escaped me in my sleep*" (324), although he also used it for its intended purposes, for example, to record his congregants' confessions of faith, which occupy a good part of the diary.[11] One important feature of Shelton's system for my purposes is that it is, as just mentioned, partly phonetic and partly not. That is, some of its marks correspond to the phonetic symbols of the English alphabet (and thus transitively to the phonemes

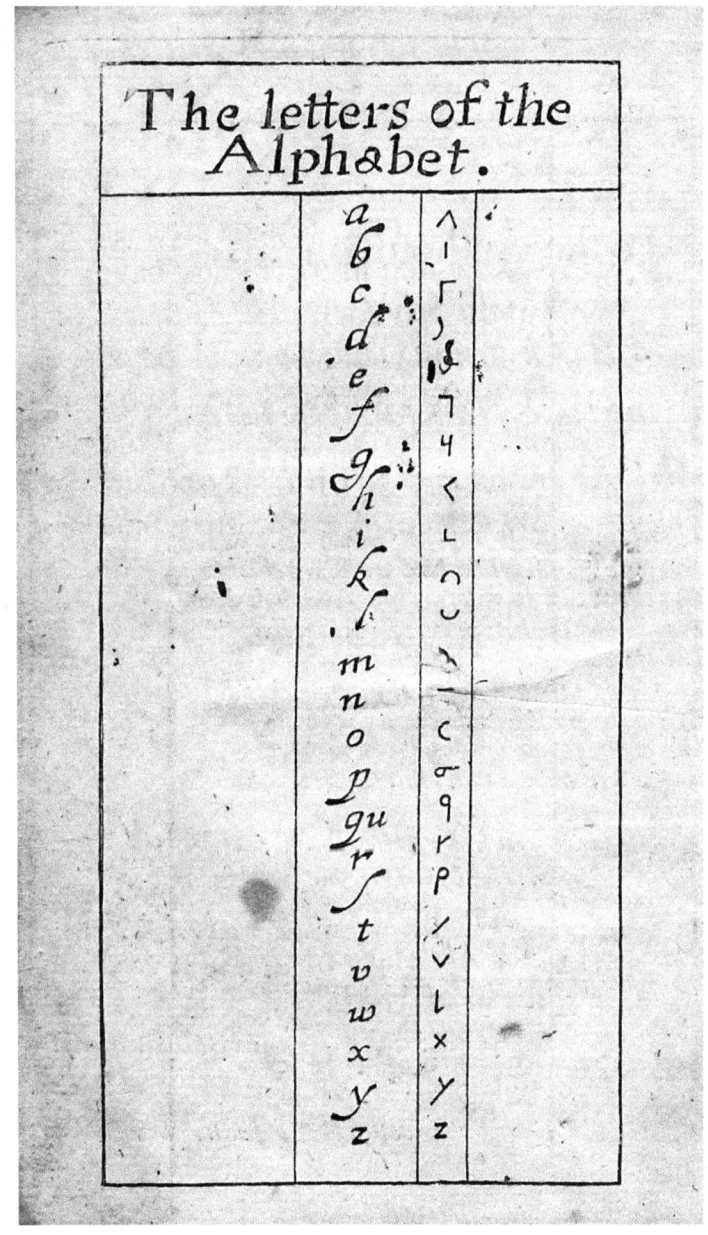

FIGURE 4.1 Thomas Shelton, "The Letters of the Alphabet," *Tachygraphy: The Most Exact and Compendious Methode of Short and Swift Writing That Hath Ever Yet Beene Published by Any* (Cambridge: Roger Daniel, Printer to the Universitie of Cambridge, 1647), facing [1]. The William Andrews Clark Memorial Library, University of California, Los Angeles.

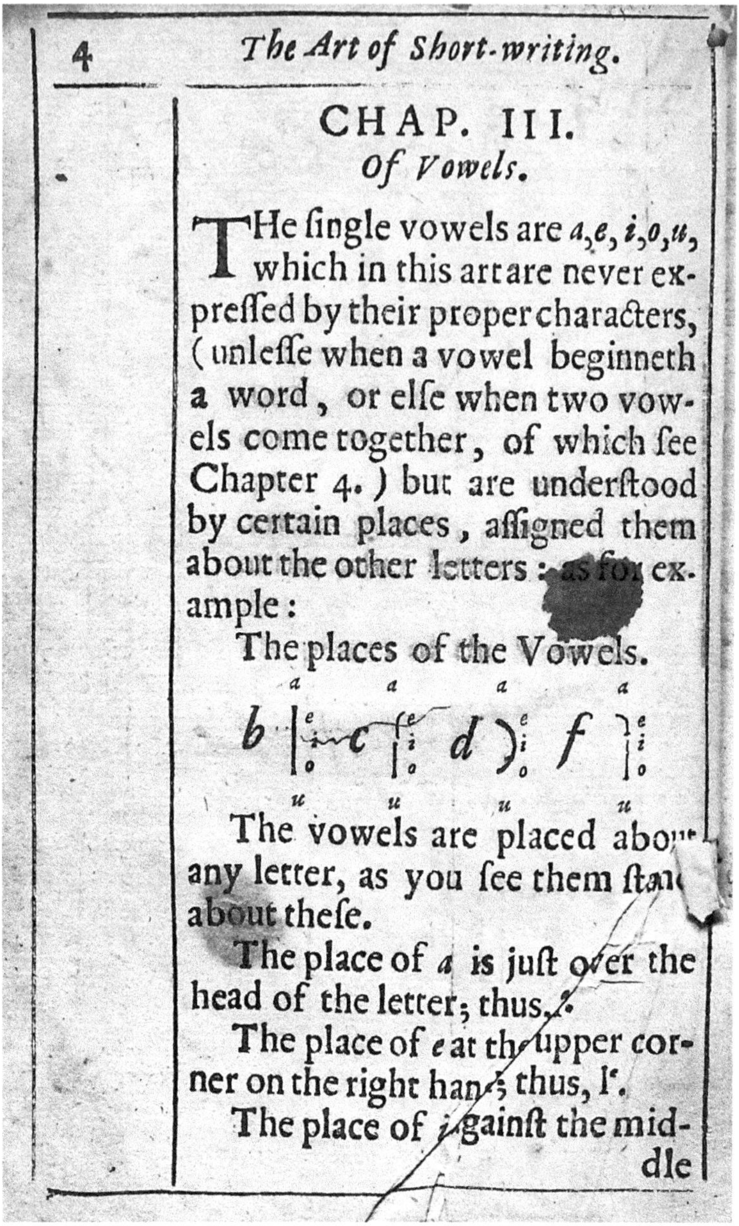

CHAP. III.
Of Vowels.

THe single vowels are *a, e, i, o, u,* which in this art are never expressed by their proper characters, (unlesse when a vowel beginneth a word, or else when two vowels come together, of which see Chapter 4.) but are understood by certain places, assigned them about the other letters: as for example:

The places of the Vowels.

$$b \begin{vmatrix} a \\ e \\ i \\ o \end{vmatrix} \quad c \begin{vmatrix} a \\ e \\ i \\ o \end{vmatrix} \quad d \begin{vmatrix} a \\ e \\ i \\ o \end{vmatrix} \quad f \begin{vmatrix} a \\ e \\ i \\ o \end{vmatrix}$$

The vowels are placed about any letter, as you see them stand about these.

The place of *a* is just over the head of the letter; thus, ⸱
The place of *e* at the upper corner on the right hand; thus, ˙.
The place of *i* against the middle

FIGURE 4.2 Thomas Shelton, "Chap. III: Of Vowels," *Tachygraphy: The Most Exact and Compendious Methode of Short and Swift Writing That Hath Ever Yet Beene Published by Any* (Cambridge: Roger Daniel, Printer to the Universitie of Cambridge, 1647), 4. The William Andrews Clark Memorial Library, University of California, Los Angeles.

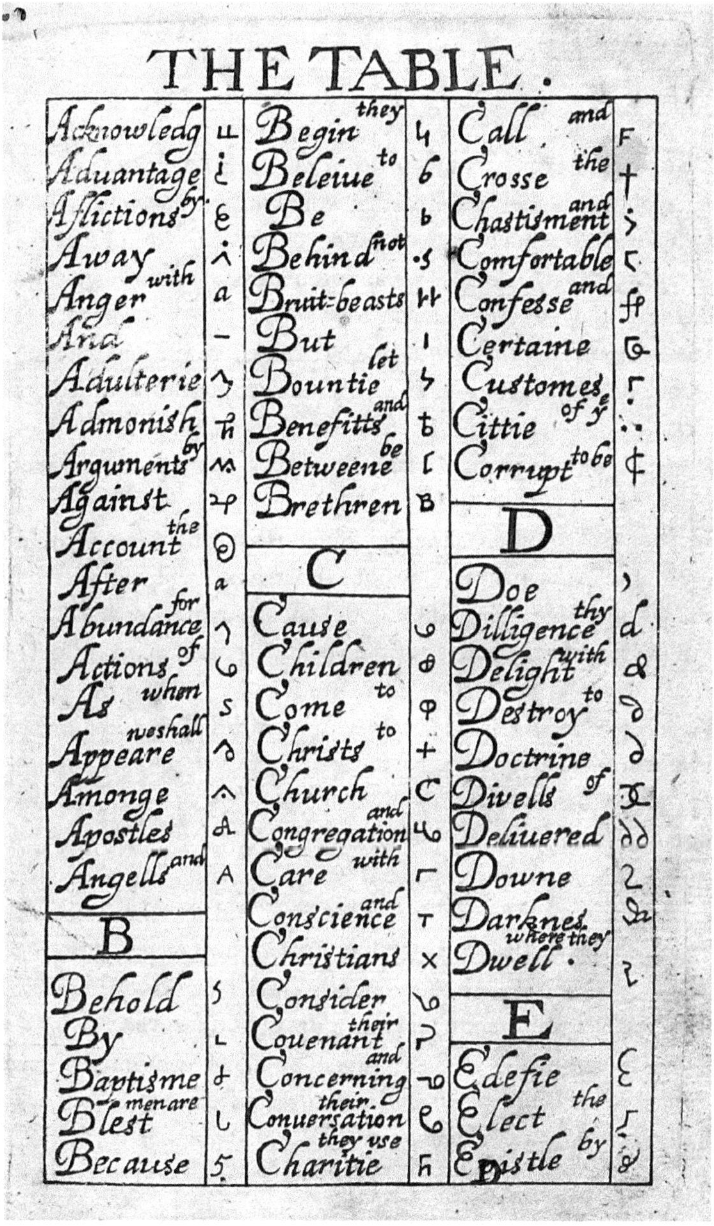

FIGURE 4.3 Thomas Shelton, "The Table," *Tachygraphy: The Most Exact and Compendious Methode of Short and Swift Writing That Hath Ever Yet Beene Published by Any* (Cambridge: Roger Daniel, Printer to the Universitie of Cambridge, 1647), [37]. The William Andrews Clark Memorial Library, University of California, Los Angeles.

thereby represented), and some are more like ideograms or hieroglyphics (i.e., they don't represent speech). More on this later.

Shelton's system was expressly meant to be of use in taking down sermons or lectures in real time, and to keep its contents at least somewhat secret under certain circumstances of religious oppression. But since *Tachygraphy* was widely published, it would not have securely concealed the semantic contents of a given encrypted passage from other readers who were adept at the code. (We can speculate that within Wigglesworth's world there would, therefore, likely have been at least some peers—fellow divines, students—who would have been able to write and read it.) The Shelton code's most famous user was Samuel Pepys, who recorded the vast majority of his celebrated 1660–69 diary in its characters.[12] Thomas Jefferson was also at least an occasional user. As a young man he wrote to his close friend and college classmate John Page, in 1764, "We must fall on some scheme of communicating our thoughts to each other, which shall be totally unintelligible to every one but to ourselves. I will send you some of these days Shelton's Tachygraphical Alphabet, and directions."[13] Considerably later, around 1792, Jefferson used Shelton's system to make brief notes of an agenda for an anti-Hamiltonian meeting of some kind. The editors of the *Papers of Thomas Jefferson* in their annotations of this document aver that Jefferson's tachygraphical skills were by this time rusty and that he made some errors; at a later date, he translated most of this document into English interlinearly.[14]

In his edition, Morgan "expanded" Wigglesworth's shorthand passages, presented them in "modern English spelling," and also "indicated [them] by italics" (321). He discreetly left it to readers, however, to discover that these encoded passages were frequently entries that recorded Wigglesworth's unruly love for, possible queer dreams about, and maybe sexual fantasies concerning his Harvard students, and his torturous experiences of *"ejection of seed"* (323) or *"dreams and self pollution by night"* (398), as well as his *"iniquity"* (323), *"carnal lusts"* (324), *"abomination"* (324), "carnal heart" (331), *"secret vice"* (349), "whoarish affections" (363), "fleshly lusts" (380), "whoarish heart" (381), *"carnal concupiscence"* (399), and "sensuality" more generally (322 and passim)—what he summed up neatly, late in the diary, as the "Sodom within" (423). Morgan also reported that, at six specific "places" in the diary, Wigglesworth employed "many original characters of his own," which had unfortunately "proved undecipherable" (321); these passages were then simply omitted from Morgan's published transcription. He did indicate in brackets eight different times that there were, in one of these locations for example, "[three words in shorthand undecipherable]" (414), or in another, "[Half line undecipherable]" (416).[15]

In the very first sentence of the diary, Wigglesworth wrote of his "*unnatural filthy lust[s] that are so oft and even this day in some measure stirring in me*" (322). I infer from this primacy that the diary was prompted by his distress concerning these "*lust[s]*" and was meant in some manner to be therapeutic, to assist Wigglesworth in monitoring and containing his "*unnatural*" and "*filthy*" lusts. This first passage was probably written in February 1653, when Wigglesworth was twenty-two years old.[16] His shorthand passages also often record his struggles with "pride" (his besetting sin), his chronic lack of love and respect for his parents, and his failure to grieve when they died. As Walter Hughes observes, there is an archaic relationship between "pride" and lust: one of the old meanings of "pride" is "a state of sexual arousal or heat."[17]

Why would Wigglesworth have quarantined his record of sexual fantasy and erotic experience in this queer orthographic fashion? He thereby hid these passages from some eyes, but presumably not from all. And what did Wigglesworth use his additional private code—his "original characters," which Morgan ultimately found "undecipherable"—to memorialize? In the years since Morgan's diplomatic avoidance of the topic of Wigglesworth's possible queer fantasies, several other scholars (Jonathan Katz, Eva Cherniavsky, Walter Hughes, Alan Bray, Nicholas F. Radel, Richard Godbeer, and Taylor Kraayenbrink) have addressed the topic of Wigglesworth's "sexuality" more forthrightly than Morgan did, but none of them has focused very closely on the relationship between sex and orthography in the diary, and they have taken different positions on the character of Wigglesworth's desires and the degree to which we can confidently describe them. Godbeer has been in some ways the most cautious: although it "would be wrong to ignore the possibility that Wigglesworth was drawn sexually to some of his pupils," the diary "contains no unequivocal evidence that such was the case."[18] He thus differentiates himself from those, like Morgan and Crowder, who either didn't recognize the possibility, deliberately avoided it, or actively denied it. But several other scholars, including Bray, believe that despite the inexplicitness of the diary, and despite the importance of historicizing Wigglesworth's desires accurately, there are some passages in which Wigglesworth, in fact, "tells us that the troubling sexual thoughts were directed to the male pupils he lived with so closely" (156). Radel is perhaps the most willing to entertain the notion that we can detect in Wigglesworth's diary "the emergence of discourses of sexuality that seem more modern than we might expect," that "Wigglesworth's diary reveals an early example, indeed perhaps the earliest example, of . . . the self-articulating sodomite in Anglo-American culture," and that "the diary speaks the sodomite as he . . . had never been spoken before in early modern culture, in a discourse of self-defining specificity and secrecy."[19] Radel's reference to "secrecy" does indeed refer to Wigglesworth's use of the shorthand cipher.

My project here is to investigate the relationship between sex and practices of secret writing in Wigglesworth's diary, and if it should prove still impossible to decode these "undecipherable" passages, it nevertheless might be possible to identify their location and present some hypotheses about the function and meaning of Wigglesworth's—and Morgan's—orthographic hygiene. This investigation has several aims. For one, it will try to be more exacting in its analysis of Wigglesworth's "sexuality," stipulating that the very category of "sexuality" is anachronistic when speaking of a mid-seventeenth-century figure. The word *queer* enables us, of course, to avoid ahistorical labels like *gay* or *homosexual*, but it remains especially important to describe Wigglesworth's erotic desires and bodily practices in a way that does full justice to the evident facts that, on the one hand, he was apparently untroubled by what seems to be the same-sex character of his desires, while, on the other, he was deeply ashamed of their very existence and their relentless intensity.

Second, this investigation will attempt to understand the role that *writing* played in Wigglesworth's exemplary self-examination, self-incrimination, and self-constitution. Lee Edelman argued in *Homographesis* for "the rhetoricity inherent in 'sexuality' itself," contending that "a distinctive literariness or textuality, an allegorical relation to the possibility—and, indeed, to the mechanics—of representation, operates within the very concept of 'homosexuality.'"[20] Taking care not to frame Wigglesworth anachronistically as a "homosexual," it should nevertheless be rewarding to investigate Wigglesworth's diary as a textual object, one in which his relationship to his desiring and dreaming and ejaculating body was not accidentally cast (sometimes) in the textual form of a shorthand code, but was itself *constituted* in its specificity by the particular formal qualities of that encoding. Third, Morgan's published transcription will come under scrutiny here, too: he decoded (most of) the shorthand, then rendered the encoded passages in "modern English" and printed them in italics, forming a different kind of published textual object that arguably embodies a kind of 1940s "don't ask, don't tell" ethos. Morgan was famous for being among the revisionary scholars who tried to dislodge caricatured depictions of Puritans as always and everywhere humorless, pleasure-loathing killjoys. Yet even he admits that Wigglesworth, of all Puritans, seems to live up to this reputation. Wigglesworth's "suspicion of pleasure," even "hostility to pleasure" (316), including very notably erotic pleasure, seems to Morgan to support this view. Wigglesworth's biographer, Richard Crowder, using language that is imbued with the normalizing Freudianism of 1960s psychological ideologies of "repression," the "normal," and proper "development," even averred of these passages in Wigglesworth's diary that "everywhere did he try by degrading himself to repress what one must conclude were only the normalities of sexual development" (62).[21] But, of course, Wigglesworth did not simply—never mind effectively—"repress" these sexual experiences, "normalities" or not: he relived them, recorded them for posterity, held on to them with his writing hand. In its own way, Morgan's text *reveals, emphasizes,* and claims to make *transparent* Wigglesworth's sex-related diary entries, even allowing a reader who is so minded to skim the text just for the juicy bits. At the same time, as I stated earlier, Morgan makes no mention in his introduction of the actual substance of these entries, contenting himself with referring in mostly general terms to Wigglesworth's adversarial relationship to pleasure.

None of the historians and critics who have written about sex and Wigglesworth's diary has taken a particularly detailed interest in the *texture* of the diary—especially its multilingual quality (there is a good deal of Latin in addition to English) and its use of shorthand code(s).[22] All scholars have worked from Morgan's invaluable transcription, but without showing any particular curiosity about the "undecipherable" passages nor much curiosity about the meaning of the text's codedness per se. I said earlier that Morgan discreetly left it to the reader to discover that the encrypted passages were sometimes records of Wigglesworth's wet dreams, lusts, and so forth. This might seem peculiar or even blameworthy in the retrospective view of those scholars such as Katz, Cherniavsky, Hughes, Bray, Radel, Godbeer, and Kraayenbrink, who have made, in some fashion, what might seem like the obvious inference: that Wigglesworth's self-castigation during his years as a Harvard tutor—for excessive "sensuality" and "doting upon the creature" (322) or *"love to the creature"* (329), that is, love for the mortal persons of his students rather than for their immortal souls, and "doting affection" (328) or *"fond affection"* (350) for his pupils—was linked to his sexual dreams and his *"pollution by night"* (398).[23] But I think it is quite possible that it simply didn't occur to Morgan and other earlier readers that

Wigglesworth's sexual fantasies and dreams may have involved his male students. After all, Wigglesworth married three times and fathered eight children, and his diary also records his terrible worries about wedlock and even his *"intemperance in the use of marriage"* (407), that is, what he believed to be his too frequent or otherwise unchaste indulgence in sex with his new wife. Morgan and other earlier scholars may simply have thought Wigglesworth's "doting affection" for his students was one (blameless) thing and his sexual dreams another ("normal" or not, to adapt Crowder's term). In fact, Bray was the one scholar who conceded that Wigglesworth's biographer, Crowder, "was strictly right in his claim that Wigglesworth nowhere details the subject matter of his sexual dreams," although Bray then averred that "it is not unreasonable to link the two" (163n1; citing Crowder 62). I agree that it is "not unreasonable." But I also contend that Wigglesworth himself may not have "link[ed] the two." The fact that he never recorded the contents of his wet dreams, the possibility that he may not have remembered them, or may have briefly remembered them before burying them, may mean that he himself did not see a connection between his waking awareness of a worrisomely excessive love for his students and his dreams that, perhaps, he could label "filthy" retroactively because they had resulted in a nocturnal emission.

I agree: not only not unreasonable, but truly quite reasonable. And yet—not *certain*, so I want to stipulate that I am not casting aspersions on Morgan or Crowder or any earlier scholars who saw nothing queer about Wigglesworth. It is even just possible—and this is the more intriguing alternative—that Wigglesworth himself did not link the two (or did not link them thoroughly or consistently). That is, he may have been adept at compartmentalizing and may not have ordinarily recognized any definite relationship between his "doting upon the creature" (322) with respect to his male students and his nocturnal ejaculations. Wigglesworth no doubt had "filthy" erotic dreams, but it is possible that their content was psychologically encrypted—possible that he did not usually or even ever *remember* his erotic dreams—and that therefore he was *unable* to record their contents in his diary. At one point in the diary he mentions having had a nocturnal emission *"without,"* as far as he can remember, *"any dream that I know of"* (399). That's an odd way of putting it: *"any dream that I know of."* Does it imply that he did (usually, or sometimes) remember the content of his sexual dreams and was puzzled by this unusual exception? It is also possible that he sometimes remembered them briefly, as one sometimes does remember a dream upon waking from an interrupted sleep, but that he successfully buried those memories afterward. I have raised the possibility that his own dreams were encrypted in one fashion or another in order to speculate that one hygienic function of his use of shorthand code in his diary was to reencrypt symbolically, so to speak, the fantasies that he did not wish to remain (or to become) conscious.

Were I to pursue this line of speculation I would build upon the impressive work of Eva Cherniavsky, who in an excellent essay from 1989 offered a reading of Wigglesworth's diary and his gendered and erotic life that centered upon a famous passage where he worried himself silly about a neighbor's barn door that was swinging in the wind. For Cherniavsky, the swinging barn door is a metaphor for Wigglesworth's deep "ambivalence"[24] toward his sexual sins: she writes of his "pleasurable indulgence in self-abasement" (18), "his virtual cultivation of the abject" (20), his ability "to turn helplessness into the unrestrained enjoyment of helplessness" (26). "Wigglesworth," Cherniavsky concludes, "learns to delight in that which he repudiates, to constitute himself in sin while purifying himself of it" (32). His use of the Shelton shorthand, I would add, has a fundamental role in this self-cultivation or self-constitution: the code hides his sexual sins to some degree, but of course it also preserves them; it externalizes them and marks them as shameful but also keeps them close at hand for rereading and reexperiencing. Using Shelton's shorthand to record his nocturnal emissions does in some fashion encrypt them, quarantine them, or "sequester" them, to use Walter Hughes's word (121). The shorthand, on the one hand, separates them from the rest of the diary; but on the other hand, it distinguishes them (in a different sense) and makes them more visible, arguably also perversely sacralizing them by employing a shorthand orthography that had as one of its recommended proper uses the stenographic recording of sermons and lectures.

Tachygraphy means "fast writing," so in using it to record his nocturnal emissions Wigglesworth and his writing hand would have dwelled upon them for a shorter length of time; but for most anyone *decoding* these passages (perhaps even for Wigglesworth himself when rereading them), they would have been dwelled upon for a *longer* length of time. I should note here that at one place early in his diary Wigglesworth lamented the fact that he could not even do research about his spermatical illness, as he thought of it, because he found that reading medical texts that addressed it had an erotically inciting effect on him: "*I find such unresistable torments of carnal lusts or provocation unto the ejection of seed that I find myself unable to read any thing to inform me about my distemper because of the prevailing or rising of my lusts. This I have procured to my self*" (323). As is often the case with Wigglesworth's diary, this passage rewards close reading. Does the "this" with which the last sentence begins refer to a *book* that Wigglesworth has procured in an effort to understand his "*distemper,*" a book that nevertheless only serves to incite his lust, as was the case with the later cohort of young men in Jonathan Edwards's congregation who found that a forbidden medical textbook could arouse their desires?[25] Or does "this" refer to his lusts, which he feels he must own as his own, as in another encoded passage later on, where he records "*such filthy lust also flowing from my fond affection to my pupils,*" adding that "*my sin is of my own and pray God make it so more to me*" (350)? Either way, it raises the possibility that rereading these passages in his diary itself could possibly have had a stimulating effect, inducing him or enabling him to relive his erotic dreams and experiences. Does he want to quarantine and neutralize his desires, or does he want to preserve them, even record them in an orthographic fashion that would make it easier to page through the diary and retrieve them on the basis of their standing out visually on the page?

There is one place in the diary—just quoted—where Wigglesworth arguably seems able, at least briefly, to connect his "*unnatural filthy lust*" consciously with his love for his male students. In his entry for July 4–5, 1653, he castigates himself for "*such filthy lust also flowing from my fond affection to my pupils <u>whiles in their presence</u>*" (350; emphasis added). From one perspective, this sounds unequivocal, to be sure: his filthy lust "*flow[s] from*" his "*fond affection to*" his pupils and is aroused "*whiles in their presence.*" But the first point I would make about this passage is its rarity.[26] Part of the fascinating drama of the diary is how successful Wigglesworth usually is at disowning this connection. And that is where the particular qualities of Shelton's shorthand, especially its combination of the phonetic and the nonphonetic, as I mentioned earlier, come in. There is a long history now, thanks to Jacques Derrida, of our skepticism toward the humanist ideology that writing is necessarily tied to voice and presence. Phonetic writing, of course, does tie itself in an arbitrary fashion to this illusion of vocal presence, an illusion that conjures the speaker's body in imaginary proximity. Conjure for yourself, then, if you will, this scene of writing: Wigglesworth watches his hand move his pen as he exerts all of the disciplinary power of writing over his "*filthy lust,*" which for once he briefly recognizes "*flow[s] from* [his] *fond affection to* [his] *pupils whiles in their presence,*" as the ink flows now from his pen; but the phonetic English alphabet with its imagined connection to the body isn't stricture enough to stanch this double flow. In this phrase, rendered in modern English and italicized by Morgan, the words "from" and "to" are expansions of single graphemes, those very common prepositions having their own dedicated nonphonetic marks in Shelton's system. Raymond Williams once wrote truly that there are "relationships embodied in writing."[27] The relationships embodied here—the "to" and "from" between Wigglesworth and his pupils—are dephoneticized, which is to say, imaginarily disembodied as he writes them down, by virtue of the formal qualities of his shorthand characters. By sequestering or quarantining his sexual feelings within a shorthand code that compresses and distorts the alphabet, that has some phonetic characters but also some nonphonetic, Wigglesworth manages both to embody himself and to summon the bodies of his pupils, but also at the same time to disown his embodiment and to distance himself from those other young men: he thereby exercises a queer orthographic hygiene.

THE MEDICALIZATION OF MICHAEL WIGGLESWORTH

Readers of Michel Foucault's *History of Sexuality* will recall that one of his great themes was the central role of rituals and practices of confession—rigorous self-scrutiny leading to the articulation of the truth of the subject—in the nineteenth-century production of categories of sexual subjectivity as such. A related claim was that confession, which began as a practice of Christian penance, later underwent "a considerable transformation," gradually losing "its ritualistic and exclusive localization" in religious circumstances and spreading into a host of other social sites: "It has been employed in a whole series of relationships: children and parents, students and educators, patients and psychiatrists, delinquents and experts."[28] Despite this widespread dissemination of "procedures of confession," one thing always remained constant: "From the Christian penance to the present day, sex was a privileged theme of confession" (61). This held true, for example, when what Foucault called the "medicalization" of confession transpired—the transformation of sex from a matter understood in the moral register as "error or sin, excess or transgression," into a matter of "the normal and the pathological," with sexual morbidity or pathology therefore calling for medical diagnosis and intervention (67). Despite the fact that Foucault located these transformations chiefly in the nineteenth century, it is worth asking whether Wigglesworth's diary—which is manifestly confessional, articulating his truth to himself and to God—figures as a faint early anticipation of this transformed—medicalized—state of affairs. Sex, as we have seen, is certainly one of the diary's privileged themes, and sexual self-inspection one of its chief motives—his sexual distress notably appears in the very first sentence of the text. And although Wigglesworth doesn't, of course, at all abandon the Christian framework of "error or sin, excess or transgression" (he is certainly confessing to all of these), he frequently and simultaneously frames his sexual aberration (alongside his other illnesses or disabilities) as a "distemper" (323, 324, 325, 328, 332, 339, 347, 365, 366, 403, 406, 407, 418), a pathology that calls for medical treatment. He viewed his *"filthy lust"* (322) as at once sin *and* disease, and he confessed not only to himself and to God but, as it happens, to three different physicians of his acquaintance.

Wigglesworth recorded in his diary that, as he contemplated the prospect of marriage, for which he feared his malady unfitted him, he wrote letters in mid-February 1755 to three reputable physicians—John Winthrop Jr., John Alcock, and John Rogers[29]—presumably describing his symptoms and asking them whether he should undergo medical treatment first and postpone marriage till afterward, or could safely go ahead with his betrothal (398–99).[30] (We should remember here, too, that Wigglesworth himself was a practicing physician as well as a minister, so it would be natural for him to contemplate his "distemper" as at once sin and disease, and articulate it in the penitential as well as in the medical register.) At around the same time, he also wrote to his betrothed, his cousin Mary Reyner, describing his distemper, as well as his fear that he might either communicate the disease to her or that it would render him unfit for marriage and fatherhood, and asking her if, in spite of this condition, she would still marry him (399).

On March 13 he recorded that he had received a reply from Alcock (401), which he later discloses advised him to go ahead and marry; he didn't receive a written reply from Winthrop, apparently, but on March 19 he learned that Winthrop had come to New Haven, and so he left for Winthrop's consideration the letter he had previously written (or a copy, perhaps), and then managed, after some difficulty in arranging a face-to-face meeting with the busy man, to confer with him in person on March 24. Winthrop, like Alcock, advised him to proceed to marriage, and Wigglesworth was relieved to find that these two physicians, thankfully, "agree[d] in their counsel" (402). Later that month, he heard from Mary Reyner the happy news that her "heart . . . is toward me as before" (403), and that she was willing to proceed to marriage. In mid-April Wigglesworth conferred with Alcock in person in Roxbury, at which time the physician repeated his advice to marry (404). But soon after—April 25—he "dined and discoursed" (404) with the third physician, John Rogers (who was also a preacher), whose advice, at first, was directly to the contrary. Rogers thought a course of medical treatment was necessary before Wigglesworth could safely marry: "He could by noe means concur with the other physicians in advising first to marriage and afterward to taking physick, for many reasons by him alledged; but thought it meet 1. To rectify the habit of my body and afterward to proceed" (404). Wigglesworth was "distressed at the hearing of his opinion, because it stil made the case more difficult" (404), but after more discussion, "and fuller declaration of my ilness &c" (404), Rogers reversed himself, and joined the consensus of the other two physicians in favor of marriage. One would dearly like to know what that "fuller declaration of my ilness" was all about—what information, perhaps, Wigglesworth had withheld at first, and may belatedly have shared only with Rogers—but in any case it did finally enlist Rogers in the consensus that he could safely go ahead and marry. This seemed to settle the matter, but Wigglesworth nevertheless was haunted by Rogers's initial "scruples" and went yet again to see Alcock for further consultation (405).

One senses from reading this part of the diary that Alcock, having given Wigglesworth advice once in writing and then again in person, was now losing his patience. (One suspects, too, that Wigglesworth may have been actively looking for someone to discourage him from proceeding to marriage.) Alcock seems to have lectured Wigglesworth rather sternly on this occasion, and the diarist carefully numbered four arguments Alcock had made. First, he told Wigglesworth that his disease "might be cured by physick," but that the course of treatment "would be a long and teadious and far more difficult cure, then he hoped it would be by marriage, and astringent cordials afterward" (405). (In the margin Wigglesworth added a manicule here—a graphic symbol representing a pointing hand—presumably to mark what he considered an important point.) Alcock also assured Wigglesworth, second, that he had successfully treated other men with the same malady, mentioning an example of "one just affected like my self before his marriage, who was grievously perplexed with it, yet went on with it and did very wel after, and hath divers children living at this day" (405). He further assured Wigglesworth—this is related in a passage that has been misconstrued by several scholars, which is not surprising given its somewhat opaque exposition—that his disease was not vera Gon: as he could prove nor the excretio (*which happened by the presence of such a friend*) seminis but quasi sudor partium genitatium: as a little alumn wil caus the mouth to fil with water, so a little acrimony gathering there, causeth humours to flow thither amain, which might come away in great quantity, and yet there be plenty of veri seminis behind. (405)

Edmund Morgan first observed, in his introduction, that "Wigglesworth evidently believed that he was suffering from gonorrhea" (314) and then, in a footnote at this place in the diary, observed of the reference to "vera Gon" that "the word intended here is obviously gonorrhea," and he reasoned that it "seems indisputable from the symptoms described and from this direct statement that Wigglesworth thought that he had gonorrhea" (405n42).[31] Biographer Richard Crowder sympathetically exclaimed, "The poor man thought he might have gonorrhea. What a fearful burden to sustain!" (83). But this is a straightforward mistake. In the seventeenth century the word *gonorrhea* had multiple meanings, and did not narrowly signify, as it apparently did for Morgan and Crowder in the mid-twentieth century, the sexually transmitted bacterial infection we customarily know as gonorrhea today. According to the *Oxford English Dictionary*, *gonorrhea* originally signified "involuntary discharge of semen," although in the seventeenth century it was coming to signify a "pox" or "venereal" sore as well.[32] But Alcock and Wigglesworth were clearly using the word in its original sense, to mean involuntary seminal discharge. As one of Wigglesworth's own medical textbooks, Philip Barrough's *The Method of Physicke* (1624), explained:

Gonorrhaea in Greeke, *seminis profluuium* in Latine, it is excretion and shedding of seede or sperme against the patients will, and without sicknesse of the yard. It is caused through imbecilitie and weaknesse of the retentive virtue in the vessels containing the sperme, or through some other disease that moveth the parts of the vessels of sperme, after that sort as the expulsive virtue doth according to nature.... The seede that sheddeth out is watery, thinne, without appetite of carnall copulation: and for the most part without feeling of it, but sometime it cometh out with certaine pleasure.[33]

So Alcock evidently was assuring Wigglesworth (whatever we may think today of his medical wisdom or common sense) that he was not having true gonorrhea (vera Gon), that is, not experiencing true *seminal* emissions ("excretio . . . seminis")—which he seems to imply, somewhat obscurely, would only occur "*by the presence of such a friend*," which I take to mean by the presence of his future wife, whom Wigglesworth refers to as "friend" elsewhere in the diary (see, for example, shortly later, "*dearest friend*" [407])—but rather, he told Wigglesworth, he was merely experiencing something like a sweating of the genital parts ("quasi sudor partium genitatium"), which sweat might even flow in very great quantity but would not deplete his stock of true semen: "Yet there be plenty of veri seminis behind" (405). This helps to explain why, when relating the other case of "the one just affected like my self," Alcock had added that the man went on to father "divers children living at this day," that is, he was fertile and prolific and his children were healthy and thriving precisely because it was not sperm he had been emitting. Wigglesworth wrote here, "And so I found it to be" (405), perhaps adding this brief line sometime later, when rereading the diary, after he had in fact fathered a child of his own. Alcock concluded his case, according to Wigglesworth, with a fourth argument (which might meet with greater approval from modern readers): "That which made me so fearful, made him fearless, and gave him the more hopes, that marriage would take away the caus of that distemper, which was naturalis impulsus seu instinctus irresistibilis" (405), that is, a natural impulse or irresistible instinct. The implication seems to be that what Wigglesworth characteristically regarded as unnatural and sinful excesses of desire were, to Alcock, simply natural urges that, once legitimately satisfied in marriage, might cease to be so troublesome; hence Alcock's insistence on marriage first, and only then, if still necessary, a course of medical treatment—"astringent cordials" afterward.

One of the more touching ironies of the case is that Wigglesworth did therefore go ahead with his marriage (after also worrying that, because Mary Reyner was his first cousin, he might be committing incest [406]); but the morning after his first night with his wife he confided to his diary, using his shorthand cipher, "*I feel the stirrings and strongly of my former distemper even after the use of marriage the next day which makes me exceeding afraid. I know not how to keep company with my dearest friend but it is with me as formerly in some days already*" (406–7). And while he had reasoned to himself that one of the blessings of marriage would be "chastity especially thereby" (406), he soon again was castigating himself for "much frothyness pride, *carnal lusts also exceeding* prevailing *Lord forgive my intemperance in the use of marriage for thy sons sake*" (407). It would be reasonable to infer from this that, despite now enjoying what he even worried was an intemperate indulgence in legitimate marital sex, desires of some other kind—his "*former distemper*"—had, to his surprise, and contrary to the predictions of his physicians, not been obliterated.

Mid-seventeenth-century Massachusetts may seem an unlikely place, at an unlikely time, to find evidence of Foucault's "medicalization" of confession and its "privileged theme" of sex, its relocation from the realm of "error or sin, excess or transgression," to the domain of "the normal and the pathological," but there is one striking fact that makes this at least plausible. And that is the widespread existence of what Patricia A. Watson, adopting a phrase of Cotton Mather's from *Magnalia Christi Americana* (1702), has called the "angelical conjunction," the remarkable prevalence in early colonial New England of "preacher-physicians," that is, divines who also practiced medicine.[34] As Walter W. Woodward has characterized this phenomenon, the medical culture of New England at this time was under the virtually uncontested sway of "medical providentialism—the unwavering conviction among the godly that God played an active role in both inflicting and healing diseases."[35] There were material reasons for this—a vanishingly small number of upper-echelon, formally trained English medical practitioners immigrated to New England during this period, and in their absence the ill relied necessarily upon available healers who had various degrees of education and experience. But in keeping with their religious beliefs, New Englanders also held that "illness was a direct, immediate, and sometimes life-threatening reminder that God monitored personal and collective behavior and intervened medically to call saints' attention to their spiritual estates. Disease was never a mere physical malady; sickness always implied, first and foremost, divine censure or admonition" (164).

In England at the time, the ideology of "medical providentialism" was increasingly contested, at least in urban centers and among elites, by a more secularized understanding of illness and disease. But in New England, "acceptance of a close and direct integration between the spiritual and physical aspects of healing flourished" (166). Thus, presumably, when Wigglesworth consulted the preacher-physician Rogers (and perhaps Alcock and Winthrop as well), he was seeking some combination of medical care and spiritual advice. Frustratingly, he says very little about what exact advice he received from Winthrop, who was certainly the most traditionally learned of them all, except to say that Winthrop's brief response agreed with Alcock's in urging him to go ahead and marry (402). But what is perhaps most striking is that when he consulted Alcock for the third time, and was once again directly assured that he could (and should) proceed to marry, there is little evidence that Alcock addressed his malady at all in terms of "error or sin, excess or transgression," but instead apparently limited himself to what we might call a discourse of the "normal and pathological." In this diary passage we can see, so to speak, Foucault's "medicalization" happening before our eyes: Alcock's advice (and Wigglesworth's record of it) frames Wigglesworth's condition as a matter merely of a "natural impulse" or "irresistible instinct" that is best to be cured mechanically by its licit gratification. It "might be cured by physick" (405), that is, by medicines; but the better, more effective, more efficient cure is by the satisfaction of that natural instinct. Neither solution—physick or marriage—takes any moral attitude toward Wigglesworth's "distemper" (405). The intimacy of the spiritual and the physical in seventeenth-century New England—the dominance of "medical providentialism" under the aegis of the "angelical conjunction"—created an environment in which, perhaps uniquely at the time, a medical model of disease might begin to supplant a moral model.

THE PROBLEMATIC OF THE WILL

We saw a moment ago that one of Wigglesworth's medical texts, Barrough's *The Method of Physicke*, stipulated that gonorrhea (then signifying involuntary seminal emission) was just that, importantly, "a shedding of seede . . . *against the patients will*" (emphasis added). The OED quotes several other sources to the same point—for example, the *Grete Herball* of 1526, which said, "Gomorrea or pollucion is a dyseas where through the sede of man yssueth from hym against his wyll and without hauynge any pleasure"—that make this same stipulation.[36] As Cherniavsky rightly recognized, Wigglesworth "never portrays himself as the agent of his own insistent drive, but always as its object, as that which is acted on by a force it cannot subdue" (23). Cherniavsky observed, "Wigglesworth describes their occurrence in a turn of phrase which literally makes his ejaculate the active element," the turn of phrase in question having several versions: "*a filthy dream and so pollution escaped me in my sleep*," "*some filthiness in a vile dream escaped me*," "*night pollution escaped me*" (Cherniavsky 23; "Diary," 324, 369, 412). Wigglesworth's passive grammatical role does crucial work here, providing Wigglesworth with some small consolation that, while the occurrence of these emissions was surely a sign of his sinful nature, he was at least not actively inducing these ejaculations. This makes it the more curious that one scholar has nevertheless claimed that Wigglesworth "masturbated frequently,"[37] and another scholar has insisted with remarkable pertinacity (and strangely archaic terminology) on Wigglesworth's "masturbation," "onanistic behavior," "auto-erotic activities," and "auto-erotic ejaculations."[38] The diary actually provides no real evidence for such claims; on the contrary, Wigglesworth clearly took some meager satisfaction in the fact that, while he definitely felt worthy of blame for his sinful lusts, he was at least not directly responsible for gratifying them. In several places in the diary Wigglesworth refers somewhat vaguely to *"the sin of my youth"* (324), *"my old iniquity"* (351), *"my former distemper"* (406), and *"my old sins now too much forgotten"* (412), a sin/iniquity/distemper that he apparently fears may return, and it is tempting to read these veiled references as indications of a prior practice of masturbation. It is certainly suggestive that when he refers to *"the sin of my youth,"* he then beseeches the Lord *"not to ... give me into the hands of my abomination"* (324), the word *hand* here perhaps hinting obliquely at manual self-stimulation. But it does not seem certain. At one early place he refers to *"unresistable carnal lusts or provocation unto the ejection of seed"* (323), which might imply his failure to resist the temptation to provoke an ejaculation actively; but again the grammar and diction leave some doubt. Was he the agent of the *"provocation unto the ejection of seed,"* or was he merely unable to stifle the lusts that automatically, so to speak, provoked the ejection? In one other place he refers to *"dreams and self pollution by night"* (398), and again the phrase *"self pollution"* might be construed as implying a voluntary act; but it might also be understood as connoting the inadvertent *"pollution"* of himself by the agency of his *"dreams,"* dreams that he was unable to interrupt or eradicate.

The question of the will's relationship to erotic dreams and nocturnal emissions had its classic exploration in Saint Augustine's *Confessions*, of which we know that Wigglesworth possessed a copy.[39] For Augustine, this attention to dreams and emissions is part of a broader inquiry into sexual desire in general: Why does it arise in us unbidden, unsummoned, and even unwanted? Why is the will sometimes (when we are awake) able to resist such desires, but at other times (when we are asleep) cannot do so—why, as Wigglesworth put it at one place early in the diary, does he experience *"such unresistable torments of carnal lusts or provocation unto the ejection of seed"* (323)? Wigglesworth characteristically described his "filthy lusts" in these involuntary terms, too—they were, for example, *"stirring in me"* (322), he writes, but not stirred by his own actions. One of the central themes of Augustine's *Confessions* is his struggle to subdue his sexual lusts and overcome his youthful sexual indulgences. Addressing God, he writes,

You command me without question to abstain 'from the lust of the flesh and the lust of the eyes[.'] ... And because you granted me strength this was done.... But in my memory of which I have spoken at length, there still live images of acts which were fixed there by my sexual habit. These images attack me. While I am awake they have no force, but in sleep they not only arouse pleasure but even elicit consent, and are very like the actual act. The illusory image within the soul has such force upon my flesh that false dreams have an effect on me when asleep, which the reality could not have when I am awake.[40]

He prays that God will give him strength to "give no assent to such seductions," "so that even in dreams [his soul] not only does not commit those disgraceful and corrupt acts in which sensual images provoke carnal emissions, but also does not even consent to them" (203–4). Wigglesworth must have found this quite recognizable: part of what made even involuntary nocturnal emissions sinful and blameworthy was that, as they were happening and as their pleasure began to be felt, one essentially consented to them in real time. Augustine here, and more extensively in his later *City of God*, assumed that in Paradise a man's erections did not occur unbidden ("not yet did lust move those members without the will's consent");[41] the penis was under the control of the will just as other appendages like hands and feet were. It would be much better if the male member were still "actuated by his volition" (465), but it is a reminder of Adam's sinful disobedience that now his penis "disobediently moved in opposition to the will" (466). Much better it would be if men and women could procreate without lust, at will, and without pleasure. Wigglesworth most likely found such a vision agreeable.[42]

I mentioned near the beginning of this essay that there is one particular location in the diary that is anomalous for several reasons, but chiefly because Wigglesworth made a drawing there of the so-called Ebenezer Stone or Ebenezer Pillar (see figure 4.4), a drawing that Crowder described as "strangely phallic" (90). It is in this place—which, among other things, makes a kind of narrative climax to the diary—that Wigglesworth seems to rally his will to prevent future experiences of involuntary seminal emission. Curiously, Morgan's edition of the diary does not reproduce Wigglesworth's own drawing, but instead features a redrawing of the image, one that resembles the original in most respects but also alters it in certain ways, arguably rendering it somewhat less phallic. It is worth reconstructing Wigglesworth's situation at the time in his life when he drew the

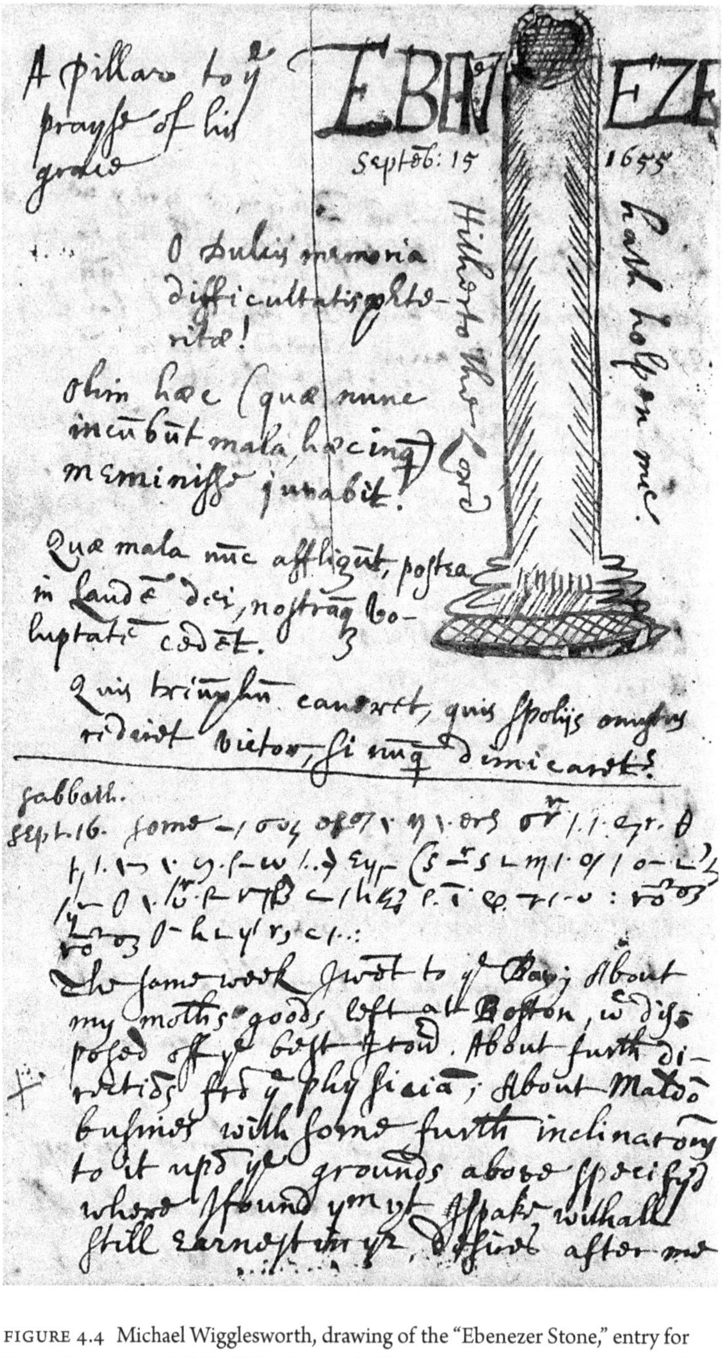

FIGURE 4.4 Michael Wigglesworth, drawing of the "Ebenezer Stone," entry for September 15, 1655, Michael Wigglesworth diary, 1653–1657. Ms.SBd-20. Massachusetts Historical Society, Boston.

pillar, for it was an extremely fraught period (he called it "a time of more than ordinary trouble" [410]), and it may be that this sense of crisis is what precipitated his unusual image. He drew it on September 15, 1655. He had been married in May, on the advice of physicians who had encouraged him to think this would effect a cure of his *"distemper"* (406), but he had immediately discovered that he was not cured. He was now in the final stages of deciding whether to accept an invitation to minister to the congregation at Malden, Massachusetts, but he was hesitating to agree because several different kinds of physical disability rendered him feeble, and he feared he would not be able successfully to discharge his duties to the flock (he had again consulted Alcock about whether his health would allow him to undertake this role [409], and Alcock again urged him to go ahead). Wigglesworth's wife was pregnant (she would give birth to their child, Mercy, in February of the next year), and he needed to get settled into a career.

He and his wife had been living since the wedding in her family's home in Rowley, Massachusetts, and now his widowed mother, Esther, and his unmarried sister Abigail, having settled his father's estate, had come from New Haven to live with them, and they were uncomfortably housed ("I haue no hous to put my own head in much less room for them" [411]). In addition to feeling crowded (and living with his in-laws), there were simply too few beds, which forced Wigglesworth now, of necessity but also to save appearances, to share a bed with his wife, something he ordinarily did not do. *"We can't lay severally without obloquy and reproach neither can we lay together without exposing me to the return of grievous disease"* (411). *"We must lay together constantly which I can't bare"* (413). Think of this: when he shares a bed with his wife he continues to have erotic dreams and nocturnal emissions; now his mother and sister are presumably sharing the other bed, ordinarily Wigglesworth's separate bed, perhaps in close proximity; all of this in the house of his in-laws the Reyners. The situation must have been excruciatingly mortifying.

This confluence of circumstances, and his inability to make decisions, prompts him to "erect" his Ebenezer Pillar, as he phrased it, "In Memoriall of [God's] former mercys received in answer to prayer and off all his goodness" (412). Now, the Ebenezer Stone is known to us from the first book of Samuel, where it is said to have been raised in commemoration of a surprising military victory over the Philistines, after Samuel had encouraged the Israelites to "put away strange gods" and worship the true Lord only, and to fast, to make sacrifices, and to admit their sins. The Philistines attack them, but with the Lord's help the repentant Israelites are victorious.[43] "Then

Samuel took a stone, and set *it* between Mizpeh and Shen, and called the name of it Eben-ezer, saying, Hitherto hath the LORD helped us."⁴⁴

The Bible calls it simply a "stone," but Wigglesworth drew it as a tall pillar. To the left of the drawing of the pillar Wigglesworth inscribed a poem, mostly in Latin, to serve as a sort of caption:

> A pillar to the prayse of
> his grace
> O Dulcis memoria
> Difficultatis praeteritae!
> Olim haec (quae nunc incumbent
> Mala, haec inquam)
> Meminisse juvabit.
> Quae mala nunc affligunt, postea in
> Laudem dei, nostramque voluptatem cedent
> Quis triumphum caneret, quis spoliis onustus
> rederet victor, si nunquam dimicaret?⁴⁵

Although the Ebenezer Stone commemorated a past victory, Wigglesworth seems to have erected it here hopefully, prophylactically, in his "time of more than ordinary trouble," desiring that it might anticipate his future triumph over present anxious circumstances as well as inevitable future difficulties. But that very night it proved a failure. Directly below the drawing he wrote:

> Some *night pollution escaped me notwithstanding my earnest prayer to the contrary which brought to mind my old sins now too much forgotten (as near as I remember the thoughts that then I had) together with my later sins unto seeming one that had received so many mercies from the Lord O unthankfulness unthankfulness when shall I get rid of thee.* (412)

He drew a horizontal line between the "strangely phallic" pillar and his shorthand-encrypted record of its failure—his wet dream in bed with his wife and perhaps in the presence of his female relations—as if to segregate them from one another, as if to deny their relation to one another. And immediately he went to Boston on various items of business but including "further directions from the physician" (412). Then, on October 4, he finally committed himself to go to Malden, feeling, among other reasons, that in Rowley "the room is too strait (here is not a private room for me)" (413). In this place, more than at any other location in the diary, all of the themes of the present essay converge. Wigglesworth had followed his physicians' advice and married, but his combination disease/sin had not abated. He records this return of *"night pollution"* (412) using the shorthand code that encrypts, but also paradoxically makes graphically visible, his record of wet dreams. The unusual drawing, and disposition of the page, appear to bring his wet dreams into proximity to a phallic image, perhaps connecting his nocturnal emissions spatially to an image resembling male genitalia; but the horizontal line attempts to deny the connection. Wigglesworth's complexity and "ambivalence," to borrow Cherniavsky's apt term, are all on display here.

CODA

There is some scattered evidence that others had access to Wigglesworth's diary, at least after his death. It probably remained in the possession of his family for some time, but eventually came into the hands of the Reverend Chandler Robbins, who donated it to the Massachusetts Historical Society on April 30, 1857, according to the bookplate that is pasted inside the front cover.[46] Inside the back cover of the diary is inserted a single folded sheet from a later reader, William P. Upham, a historian of stenography who seems to have been asked at one time to identify the shorthand cipher that Wigglesworth had used. The note reads as follows:

> The Note Book of Rev. Michael Wigglesworth contains some short-hand passages. They are written with the characters of the System of Thomas Shelton, 1641 (See Upham's Brief History of Stenography—Salem, 1877).
> No historical matter of importance is found in them. They appear to consist wholly of the pastor's own penitential reflections, and "relations" (statements of religious experience) made by other persons.
>
> *Wm P. Upham*
DEC. 18, 1894.[47]

Upham's note seems mildly disingenuous in several ways. As an expert on the history of stenography,[48] his statement that the shorthand passages "*appear* to consist" (emphasis added) only of two uninteresting things seems evasive; Upham no doubt discovered exactly what these shorthand passages recorded, which do include "penitential reflections" and relations of his congregants' religious professions, but also, as we have seen, many records of his deep affection for his students, his nocturnal seminal emissions, and his references to "*filthy dream*[s]." Perhaps Upham truly deemed these not to be "historical matter[s] of importance," but his note seems in any case calculated to discourage inspection and decoding of these "short-hand passages." In attempting to divert future scholars' attention in this way he echoed Cotton Mather, who, in composing a funeral sermon for Wigglesworth—and assembling an "Appendix" to its published version containing selected extracts from Wigglesworth's "*Reserved Papers*," comprising "a few MEMORIALS of PIETY"—had this to say by way of explanation:

> The Survivers have often received incomparable Benefits, from the *Reserved Papers* of Good Men, which they have Written only for the Help of their own *Memories* and *Affections*, & without the least Imagination, that they would ever get from under that Character of *Reserved Papers*.
>
> Tis now found that such had our WIGGLESWORTH. Indeed they generally contain his humble, but severe, *Animadversions* upon himself, and such as argue a great Flight of *Holiness* in him from his Youth; and they contain many other *Personal Matters*, in which the Publick is no way concerned.[49]

This certainly sounds like Mather had encountered some of the "*Personal Matters*" that he deemed unsuitable for "the Publick" and therefore scrupulously omitted from the extracts he published in his "Appendix." Whether he had actually decoded any of Wigglesworth's shorthand passages is difficult to determine, although those, as we have seen, certainly contain among the most "severe" of Wigglesworth's "*Animadversions* upon himself."

Later scholars, as we have seen, have sometimes not recognized, or have ignored, or suppressed, or denied the queerness of these "*Personal Matters*"; others have been willing to entertain the possibility, or probability, or near certainty of their queerness, but have taken a range of positions on what evidence counts and how strong a case can be made for Wigglesworth's sexual attraction to his students, his self-awareness about that attraction, or the self-conception that may have been in formation if he was aware of such attractions. In the present essay I have revisited these questions not in hopes of settling them definitively, but with the aim of clarifying the issues where possible, correcting some persistent misconceptions, and introducing some fresh critical approaches drawn from queer studies, material textual studies, the medical humanities, and elsewhere, as well as doing some fine-grained close reading. Although in the end I am of the opinion that Wigglesworth's diary remains somewhat opaque with respect to these questions, I believe that his shorthand encryption of his sexual distress—his orthographic differentiation of those passages—itself suggests some degree of recognition of the specificity of the feelings, sensations, and desires there recorded. In addition, his medicalization of his "distemper" appears to be a critical step in the historical emergence of homosexual desire as a qualitatively different species of desire, one that Wigglesworth could recognize—*"temptations of another nature"* (400); *"I feel the stirrings and strongly of my former distemper even after the use of marriage the next day"* (406)—a kind of desire that was in some degree defined by the gender of its object. With Wigglesworth we are still far short of the historical emergence of the homosexual as a species of person, but we are at least a step beyond an undifferentiated concept of lust that might attach itself to many different objects but was itself one thing only.[50]

NOTES

Epigraph: Michael Wigglesworth, "The Diary of Michael Wigglesworth," 399–400. Further page references will be given parenthetically in the text, referring to the 1951 edition by Edmund S. Morgan. The diary is also available online, courtesy of the Colonial Society of Massachusetts: https://www.colonialsociety.org/node/911. As I discuss below, some parts of the diary—as in the epigraph—were written in a shorthand cipher, which Morgan decoded, rendered into English, and printed in italics. I will preserve those italics.

1. Bray, "To Be a Man," 156. Further page references will be given parenthetically in the text.
2. I agree with Jordan Alexander Stein that "on theoretical as well as historical grounds, *queer* offers an apposite way to describe Puritan forms of affiliation, attachment, desire, and bodily sensation, as well as the representation of any of these, which do not mirror modern, more squarely heterosexual or homosexual versions of similar social forms." This is because of the wide consensus among historians, following on the work of Michel Foucault, that sexual identities "in their person-saturating, modern senses date only as far back as the nineteenth century." Stein, "How to Undo," 753–54, 754. But I am also interested, as will be seen, in the more particular question of whether we can discern in Wigglesworth's diary some faintly emergent early trace of the homo/hetero distinction—not, of course, anything like fully formed sexual identities (or identities at all), but perhaps the beginning of a distinction between different species of sexual desire.
3. Crowder, *No Featherbed*, 62. Further page references will be given parenthetically in the text.

4   The ongoing conversation about "symptomatic" versus "surface" reading was begun by Stephen Best and Sharon Marcus in "Surface Reading."
5   Wigglesworth, "Diary" (1951); and Wigglesworth, *Diary* (1965).
6   Wigglesworth, Michael Wigglesworth diary, 1653–1657.
7   Morgan, "Puritans and Sex." For an insightful discussion of this essay of Morgan's, see Verduin, "'Our Cursed Natures.'"
8   As Morgan, "Puritans' Puritan."
9   There was a "quiet decision during the mid-1970s to admit women." Allis and Tyler, "Historical Sketch," 13.
10 Shelton, "To the Reader," *Tachygraphy*.
11 As Morgan noted in his "Introduction," Wigglesworth's day-by-day and week-by-week chronicle occupies the front of the small volume, but Wigglesworth inverted the book and, starting from the other end, mainly recorded declarations of religious experience, presumably from applicants for church admission, all of which were recorded in the Shelton shorthand (Wigglesworth, "Diary," 320–21). It should be noted that, although Morgan doesn't seem to have known of them, there survive several other diaries in Wigglesworth's hand, now in the collection of the New England Historic Genealogical Society, dating from before as well as after the diary Morgan edited and published. They include "Notebook, 1649," "Notebook, 1650–53," "Notebook, 1652–53," and "Notebook, 1658–1763," the last of which includes later additions by Wigglesworth's son Edward (Mss 71). They also apparently employ Shelton's shorthand for what seem to be various purposes. These diaries have been digitized by the New England's Hidden Histories project but have not been studied, nor have the shorthand passages yet been decoded. http://nehh-viewer.s3-website-us-east-1.amazonaws.com/#/content/WigglesworthFamily/viewer/Notebook2C201649/1.
12 Pepys, *Diary*. For a brisk account of the derivation of Shelton's system and its particular qualities, see xlviii–liv.
13 Jefferson, "To John Page," 14–15.
14 Jefferson, "Note of Agenda," 215–17. See also facsimile following page 404.
15 Because two pairs of the undecipherable passages are in close proximity to one another, Morgan counted six "places" where these eight passages occurred. The undecipherable passages are at 414, 416, 417 (x2), 428 (x2), 431, and 440. It is tempting to imagine that these more deeply encrypted passages record matters that Wigglesworth wanted to render fully inaccessible to all readers, even those who might have known Shelton's shorthand. But it is true, as Morgan states, that they are mostly quite short, and in most contexts they don't, in my judgment, appear likely to contain explosive secrets. It is suggestive that the first four of them come in quick succession in the immediate textual aftermath of the crucial passage including the Ebenezer Pillar drawing that coincided with a severe crisis in Wigglesworth's life, which I indicated above I would be exploring in detail toward the end of this chapter. Although Morgan refers to "original characters," at least one of these "undecipherable" passages looks to

my eyes like merely illegible English script, and another appears likely to be the symbol denoting the name of a book of the Bible (428), since it is followed immediately by numerals ("9:ij" [428]) that appear to indicate chapter and verse. Of the last four undecipherable passages, two of them come from "The relation of Mr Collins" (428), one from notes on a sermon preached by Mr. Dunster (431), and one from "John Green's Relation" (440), i.e., all from the inverted portion of the diary recording mostly professions of conversion.

16 I will follow Morgan in converting all years to the modern calendar, but in Wigglesworth's time this date in February would have been counted as late 1652; his diary announces "Annus Novus 1653" at the beginning of March (327).

17 Hughes, "'Meat out of the Eater,'" 110. Further page references will be given parenthetically in the text.

18 Godbeer, "Wigglesworth, Michael," 278.

19 Radel, "Sodom Within," 42, 45.

20 Edelman, *Homographesis*, xiv.

21 Crowder's disciplinary imperative—"must conclude"—takes up the longstanding project, extending from Cotton Mather to William P. Upham and beyond, to divert curiosity from the queer content of the shorthand passages.

22 Radel is a partial exception, and his essay (as well as that of Hughes) preserves the italics that Morgan employed to distinguish between the coded and uncoded passages. Other scholars have by and large not preserved these italics when quoting from the diary.

23 Bray comments acutely that Wigglesworth's frequent phrase, "fond affection," carries with it in seventeenth-century English usage an implication of "a mad, an unreasoning passion" (156). I would add that the adjective "doting" likewise carries a similar implication of loss of sanity or balance.

24 Cherniavsky, "Night Pollution," 30. Further page references will be inserted parenthetically in the text.

25 Johnson, "Jonathan Edwards"; Chamberlain, "Bad Books."

26 Bray claims that Wigglesworth makes the connection not only here but at two other places—where he cites his *"unnatural filthy lust"* (322), presumably because of the conjunction of the adjective "unnatural" and the noun *lust*, and again when he writes of *"dreams and self pollution by night which my soul abhors and mourns for"* (398), since *"self pollution"* might imply an active role (but also might not—is something polluting his self, or is he polluting himself?). It should be noted, too, that soon after his wedding Wigglesworth confides to his diary, *"I feel the stirrings and strongly of my former distemper even after the use of marriage the next day which makes me exceeding afraid"* (406–7). This is difficult to interpret. He may be thinking that married sex is not helping him to dampen or exhaust his insistent lusts. Or he may be verging upon making a conscious distinction of *kind*, between the opposite-sex pleasures of the marriage bed and another kind of erotic pleasure, same-sex eroticism, that he also continues to want despite the satisfaction of his marital desires. Earlier he

had described himself as at one time *"overborn with carnal concupiscence,"* having then had his first wet dream in twelve nights, yet *"still inclined to lust"* (399) afterward and imploring God to help him against it *"and against temptations of another nature"* (400). Citing these unspecified *"temptations of another nature"* may be an additional example of his distinguishing between *kinds* of lust.

27 Williams, *Writing*, 3.

28 Foucault, *History*, 63. Further page citations will be given parenthetically in the text.

29 John Winthrop Jr. (1606–76) was born in England and educated at Trinity College, Dublin. He was a man of many and varied accomplishments, and later served many terms as governor of Connecticut. Admitted to the bar in London in 1625, he spent the next five years traveling throughout Europe, establishing professional relationships with many scientists and scholars. He sailed for Boston in 1631, following his father, who had established the settlement. See Winthrop et al., "Scientific Notes," 326. See also Steiner, "Governor John Winthrop," and Woodward, *Prospero's America*. John Rogers (1630–84) was born in England and came with his family to Massachusetts as a child. He graduated from Harvard in 1649, two years before Wigglesworth. "As was not uncommon in his time, he studied both medicine and divinity" (Sibley, "John Rogers," 167). He preached at Ipswich for a time, but later gave up the pulpit for the exclusive practice of medicine. He was the first graduate of Harvard to become its president, in 1683. John Alcock (1627–67) was born in England and came to Roxbury, Massachusetts, at a young age. He graduated from Harvard in 1646, five years ahead of Wigglesworth. He established his practice as a physician in Roxbury but later moved to Boston (Sibley, "John Alcock," 124–26). See also Farmer, "John Alcock," *Memorials*, 43.

30 Unfortunately these letters do not appear to have survived.

31 This is puzzling, since Wigglesworth actually described no "symptoms" consistent with what we now understand as gonorrhea, i.e., the sexually transmitted bacterial infection that may cause, for instance, painful urination, a pus-like discharge, or testicular swelling.

32 "gonorrhoea/gonorrhea, n.," OED *Online*, Oxford University Press, 2020, accessed August 13, 2022, https://www.oed.com/view/Entry/79918?redirectedFrom=gonorrhea&.

33 Barrough, *Method of Physick*, 178–79. I have modernized the orthography in this passage slightly, substituting the modern *s* for the long *s*, etc. Barrough's text was listed in the inventory of Wigglesworth's library taken at the time of his death. See Dean, *Memoir*, 152.

34 Watson, *Angelical Conjunction*.

35 Woodward, *Prospero's America*, 164. Further page citations will be given parenthetically.

36 OED *Online*, Oxford University Press, 2020, accessed August 13, 2022, https://www.oed.com/view/Entry/79918?redirectedFrom=gonorrhea&.

37 Godbeer, *Sexual Revolution*, 188. See also Godbeer, "Wigglesworth, Michael," where he writes of Wigglesworth's "masturbatory tendencies" (278).
38 Kraayenbrink, "'Monster of Iniquity,'" 208, 209, 212, 216.
39 Dean, *Memoir*, 152.
40 Augustine, *Confessions*, 203. Further page citations will be given parenthetically in the text.
41 Augustine, *City of God*, 465. Further page citations will be given parenthetically in the text.
42 Augustine's *City of God* does not appear in the inventory of his library made at Wigglesworth's death, but it seems very likely that he would have known it well. These matters are discussed in detail in Foucault, *Confessions of the Flesh*, 256–85. See also the acute aside by Debora Shuger, where she invokes Wigglesworth's diary to support her broad argument for "the synecdochal relation between wet dreams and Augustinian subjectivity: between the filthiness that escapes in a dream, the thoughts that crowd unbidden into consciousness, and the feelings that surge and ebb of their own accord." Shuger, "'Gums of Glutinous Heat,'" 13.
43 1 Samuel 7:3–11.
44 1 Samuel 7:12.
45 "O sweet memory of troubles gone by! / Those troubles (I say this because new sins will press upon me) it will benefit me to have remembered. / Those sins that now dash me to the earth, afterwards may turn into praise of God, and give place to our own pleasure. / Who might sing the triumph, who comes back a victor burdened with the spoils, if he never struggled?" Spires et al., *Broadview Anthology*, 277n6.
46 The plate reads: "Given to the Massachusetts Historical Society by Rev. Chandler Robbins, D.D., Apr. 30. 1857."
47 Wigglesworth, Michael Wigglesworth diary.
48 The citation he gives is to his own *Brief History*.
49 Mather, *Faithful Man*, 28.
50 My thanks to those who listened to or read parts or versions of this work at the McNeil Center for Early American Studies, Philadelphia, Pennsylvania, September 9, 2022, and at the conference of the Society of Early Americanists, Eugene, Oregon, March 1, 2019.

BIBLIOGRAPHY

Allis, Frederick S., Jr., and John W. Tyler. "Historical Sketch of the Colonial Society of Massachusetts, 1952–1992." In *Handbook of the Colonial Society of Massachusetts*, 1–33. Boston: The Society, 1992.

Augustine, Saint. *The City of God*. Translated by Marcus Dods. Introduction by Thomas Merton. New York: Random House, 1993.

Augustine, Saint. *Confessions*. Translated by Henry Chadwick. Oxford: Oxford University Press, 1991.

Barrough, Philip. *The Method of Physick, Containing the Causes, Signes, and Cures of Inward Diseases in Mans Body, from the Head to the Foote*. London: Richard Field, 1624.

Best, Stephen, and Sharon Marcus. "Surface Reading: An Introduction." *Representations* 108, no. 1 (2009): 1–21.

Bray, Alan. "To Be a Man in Early Modern Society: The Curious Case of Michael Wigglesworth." *History Workshop Journal* 41, no. 1 (1996): 155–65.

Chamberlain, Ava. "Bad Books and Bad Boys: The Transformation of Gender in Eighteenth-Century Northampton, Massachusetts." *New England Quarterly* 75, no. 2 (June 2002): 179–203.

Cherniavsky, Eva. "Night Pollution and the Floods of Confession in Michael Wigglesworth's Diary." *Arizona Quarterly: A Journal of American Literature, Culture, and Theory* 45, no. 2 (Summer 1989): 15–33.

Crowder, Richard. *No Featherbed to Heaven: A Biography of Michael Wigglesworth, 1631–1705*. East Lansing: Michigan State University Press, 1962.

Dean, John Ward. *Memoir of Rev. Michael Wigglesworth, Author of The Day of Doom*. 2nd ed. Albany, NY: Joel Munsell, 1871.

Edelman, Lee. *Homographesis: Essays in Gay Literary and Cultural History*. New York: Routledge, 1994.

Farmer, John. "John Alcock." In *Memorials of the Graduates of Harvard University*, 43. Concord, NH: March, Capen and Lyon, 1833.

Foucault, Michel. *Confessions of the Flesh: The History of Sexuality, Volume 4*. Edited by Frédéric Gros. Translated by Robert Hurley. New York: Pantheon, 2021.

Foucault, Michel. *The History of Sexuality, Volume 1: An Introduction*. Translated by Robert Hurley. New York: Vintage, 1990.

Godbeer, Richard. *Sexual Revolution in Early America*. Baltimore: Johns Hopkins University Press, 2002.

Godbeer, Richard. "Wigglesworth, Michael (b. 1631; d. 1705), minister." In *Encyclopedia of Lesbian, Gay, Bisexual, and Transgender History in America*, vol. 3, edited by Marc Stein, 277–79. New York: Scribner/Thomson/Gale, 2004.

Hughes, Walter. "'Meat out of the Eater': Panic and Desire in American Puritan Poetry." In *Engendering Men: The Question of Male Feminist Criticism*, edited by Joseph A. Boone and Michael Cadden, 102–21. New York: Routledge, 1990.

Jefferson, Thomas. "Note of Agenda to Reduce the Government to True Principles, [ca. 11 July 1792]." In *The Papers of Thomas Jefferson*, vol. 24, edited by John Catanzariti et al., 215–17. Princeton, NJ: Princeton University Press, 1990.

Jefferson, Thomas. "To John Page, 23 Jan. 1764." In *The Papers of Thomas Jefferson*, vol. 1, edited by Julian P. Boyd et al., 14–15. Princeton, NJ: Princeton University Press, 1950.

Johnson, Thomas H. "Jonathan Edwards and the 'Young Folks' Bible.'" *New England Quarterly* 5, no. 1 (January 1932): 37–54.

Kraayenbrink, Taylor. "'A Monster of Iniquity in My Self': Queer Sacramental Temporality in Thomas Shepard and Michael Wigglesworth." *New England Quarterly* 94, no. 2 (June 2021): 196–222.

Mather, Cotton. *A Faithful Man, Described and Rewarded: Some Observable and Serviceable Passages in the Life and Death of Mr. Michael Wigglesworth, Late Pastor of Maldon [. . .] and Memorials of Piety, Left behind Him among His Written Experiences*. Boston: B. Green, for Nicholas Buttolph, 1705.

Morgan, Edmund S. "The Puritans and Sex." *New England Quarterly* 15, no. 4 (December 1942): 591–607.

Morgan, Edmund S. "The Puritans' Puritan: Michael Wigglesworth." In *American Heroes: Profiles of Men and Women Who Shaped Early America*, 102–11. New York: Norton, 2009.

Pepys, Samuel. *The Diary of Samuel Pepys: A New and Complete Transcription, Vol. I, 1660*. Edited by Robert Latham and William Matthews. Berkeley: University of California Press, 1970.

Radel, Nicholas F. "A Sodom Within: Gender, Sex, and Sodomy in the Diary of Michael Wigglesworth." In *Other Americans, Other Americas: The Politics and Poetics of Multiculturalism*, edited by Magdalena J. Zaborowska, 38–49. Aarhus, Denmark: Aarhus University Press, 1998.

Shelton, Thomas. *Tachygraphy: The Most Exact and Compendious Methode of Short and Swift Writing That Hath Ever Yet Beene Published by Any*. London: Samuel Cartwright, 1641.

Shuger, Debora. "'Gums of Glutinous Heat' and the Stream of Consciousness: The Theology of Milton's *Maske*." *Representations* 60 (Autumn 1997): 1–21.

Sibley, John Langdon. "John Alcock." In *Biographical Sketches of Graduates of Harvard University, in Cambridge, Massachusetts, Vol. I, 1642–1658*, 124–26. Cambridge, MA: Charles William Sever, 1873.

Sibley, John Langdon. "John Rogers." In *Biographical Sketches of Graduates of Harvard University, in Cambridge, Massachusetts, Vol. I, 1642–1658*, 166–71. Cambridge, MA: Charles William Sever, 1873.

Spires, Derrick R., Christina Roberts, Joseph Rezek, Justine S. Murison, Laura L. Mielke, Christopher Looby, et al. *The Broadview Anthology of American Literature, Volume A, Beginnings to 1820*. Guelph, Ontario: Broadview Press, 2022.

Stein, Jordan Alexander. "How to Undo the History of Sexuality: Editing Edward Taylor's *Meditations*." *American Literature* 90, no. 4 (2018): 753–84.

Steiner, Walter Ralph. "Governor John Winthrop, Jr., of Connecticut, as a Physician." *Connecticut Magazine* 11 (1903): 25–37.

Upham, William P. *A Brief History of the Art of Stenography, with a Proposed New System of Phonetic Short-Hand*. Salem, MA: Essex Institute, 1877.

Verduin, Kathleen. "'Our Cursed Natures': Sexuality and the Puritan Conscience." *New England Quarterly* 56, no. 2 (June 1983): 220–37.

Watson, Patricia A. *The Angelical Conjunction: The Preacher-Physicians of Colonial New England*. Knoxville: University of Tennessee Press, 1991.

Wigglesworth, Michael. "The Diary of Michael Wigglesworth." Edited and with an introduction by Edmund S. Morgan. *Publications of the Colonial Society of Massachusetts*, vol. 85, *Transactions, 1942–46* (1951): 311–444.

Wigglesworth, Michael. *The Diary of Michael Wigglesworth, 1653–1657: The Conscience of a Puritan*. Edited by Edmund S. Morgan. New York: Harper and Row, 1965.

Wigglesworth, Michael. Michael Wigglesworth diary, 1653–1657. Ms.SBd-20. Massachusetts Historical Society, Boston, Massachusetts.

Williams, Raymond. *Writing in Society*. London: Verso, 1983.

Winthrop, John, Geo Starkey, and C. A. Brown. "Scientific Notes from the Books and Letters of John Winthrop, Jr. (1606–1676)." *Isis* 11, no. 2 (December 1928): 325–42.

Woodward, Walter W. *Prospero's America: John Winthrop, Jr., Alchemy, and the Creation of New England Culture, 1606–1676*. Chapel Hill: University of North Carolina Press/Omohundro Institute of Early America History and Culture, 2010.

FIVE · *Mark J. Miller*

George Whitefield's Sexual Character

By the spring of 1739 George Whitefield was used to making news. Though only twenty-four, his field preaching's popularity among London's young and poor made him a lightning rod for concerns about evangelical disruptions of labor, settled pastorates, and other bulwarks of social order. That August, Whitefield sailed from England to Philadelphia to begin a preaching tour of England's North American colonies, raising funds for his Bethesda orphanage in the fledgling colony of Georgia, where he had been designated minister in 1738. Aboard ship, he found himself plagued by unnamed "Temptations" of "the flesh" ("I am never so much tempted," he wrote in his journal, "as when confined on Ship-board") but reasoned such temptations could be a "mercy" if they serve to "keep me in Action."[1] He stayed active, in part, by writing his life story, an extended conversion narrative he entitled "A General Account of the First Part of My Life," perhaps in anticipation of his American second act. After completing his draft manuscript on September 8, Whitefield appended a note commemorating the "great freedom & peace of soul" that overcame him "when [he] resolved to print it."[2] Whitefield regularly (critics would say self-righteously) described his feelings as an index of God's approval, but why would a publishing juggernaut like Whitefield need to "resolve" to enter print, or feel such relief when he did?[3]

One answer lies in Whitefield's sense of print's ability to develop evangelic community, facilitate confession, and structure a particular kind of sex. Whitefield planned to fund his colonial preaching tour by selling books and soliciting donations at outdoor meetings or, when local ministers allowed, from the pulpit. The *Elizabeth*'s hold contained crates of his best-selling *Journals* and *Sermons* for the same purpose. His *General*

Account, however, published in 1740, offered far more intimate autobiographical narrative prose. Given the scrutiny to which he knew his narrative would be subjected, Whitefield's decision to publicize his youthful sexual encounters was particularly significant. During a period of spiritual "backsliding," Whitefield wrote, "Much of my time I now spent in reading plays, & in sauntering from place to place.... Evil communications with my Old Schoolfellows soon corrupted my good manners—By seeing their Evil practices, a sense of the divine presence insensibly wore off my mind & I at length fell secretly into a Sin, for which Onan dyed, & the dismal effects of which I have felt & groaned under ever since."[4] For Whitefield, Onanism was a spiritually significant act that flowed into and out of the nexus of "reading," "plays," "sauntering," and "seeing ... practices"—that is, of mediation in print, stage performance, unstructured public circulation, and unsupervised personal imitation—that transmitted Onanism or allowed for its transmission by degrading "a sense of the divine presence."

This description, along with others in the manuscript, drew from and would soon enter into a series of transatlantic conversations about the meaning and value of Onanism. In the early eighteenth century, Onanism shifted away from its original sense of something like coitus interruptus and toward a range of physical acts that had, since at least the early seventeenth century, been called masturbation, frigging, self-pollution, manufriction, or, as one plainspoken 1616 Protestant catechism elaborates, modes of "fleshly pleasure with ones selfe" that, though *not* Onan's sin, were something "*like* Onans sinne."[5] Titillating references to masturbation were staples of seventeenth-century court satire; in private diaries, Samuel Pepys, Robert Hooke, several Protestant divines, and others used encoded language, idiosyncratic slang, or symbols to record or retrospectively rue their practice. The eighteenth-century shift in nomenclature was accompanied by a change in value. "Onanism" usually signaled the writer's opposition to masturbation, while older terms like frigging developed a more positive gloss as a sociable practice among equals.

Whether denominated Onanism or frigging, the practices seem to have been increasingly demarcated and ritualized in a masculinist erotic social context. The Onanist's supposed isolation or solitude, reflected in Whitefield's description of himself as falling "secretly" into sin, has been crucial to understandings of Onanism as the individuated Enlightenment subject's "dark underbelly," and yet Whitefield's account of his Onanism's nexus of mediation reflects widespread eighteenth-century representations of the practice as intensely, even proverbially, social: "that cursed School-wickedness"; the "first lewd Trick that Boys learn"; a practice familiar to "*Female* readers ... blessed with a Boarding-School Education."⁶ As with the play-reading of informal cliques such as Whitefield's "Old Schoolfellows," this Onanistic socialization continued into adulthood, where it may have been marked by an increasing use of print to help structure, organize, and ritualize a judicious, sociable use of masturbation and phallic display. Commercial pornographic books such as the *Merryland* series (1740–45) were often integrated into the practice of elite societies such as the various "Hell-Fire" Clubs, Scotland's Beggar's Benison (modeled on Masonic and Freemasonic practice), and London's Brotherhood of St. Francis of Wycombe, in which group members participated in the public-sphere discussion and practice of masturbation to attract members, circulate, engage, and produce erotic texts via minute-keeping and dramatic readings, and gather in a public or semipublic manner.⁷ Opponents of Onanism also used print to demarcate the practice and ritualized behaviors to prevent masturbation. Church officials and members of religious societies such as Wesley's "Holy Club," including Whitefield, censured Onanism in oral, print, or manuscript sermons, casuistry manuals, admonitory letters, and rational-critical excerpts.

In eighteenth-century British Christian religious communities, accounts of controlling Onanism and other sexual sins had spiritual and social value. Descriptions of "Abominations" in schools, orphanages, and churches indicated inadequate or corrupt supervision, while their absence or reformation suggested divine favor and justified financial and political support.⁸ Individual control over sexual sin was also a long-standing conversion narrative trope, and the spiritual importance Whitefield granted to Onanism was typical for the genre. For Whitefield, as for St. Augustine, narrating sexual self-control helped demonstrate growing attention to God and away from "worldly" desires.⁹ These narratives emphasized a convert's shifting attention, not toward reproductive sex, but to God: a reorientation of the soul toward the divine that could be achieved, in part, through controlling bodily practice.

Doctrinally, Whitefield's *General Account* was heir to a robust evangelical Puritan-Pietist conversion narrative tradition emphasizing the convert's repeated spiritual "backsliding" or relapse into sin. These conversion narratives demonstrated the inadequacy of personal efforts to escape sin and consequent need to rely entirely on God's grace for redemption and salvation. In virtually all cases, descriptions of masturbation or other sexual sins were impersonal, brief, formulaic, allusive, or even encoded to limit circulation.[10] As with Whitefield's account of the nexus of Onanistic mediation, eighteenth-century catechizing guides and earlier Puritan devotionals often paired sexual sin with "worldly-mindedness," an undue attention to material goods and bodily pleasures that lead to "Uncleanness" or lust.[11] Ministers or, more rarely, laymen writing in this tradition described their ability to escape worldly mindedness and sexual sin as a prerequisite for, or a sign of, conversion, an achievement with spiritual, social, and sometimes political consequences.

Whitefield developed his narrative account of Onanism by illuminating these traditional Christian ideas about sexual practice, conversion, and apostasy under the new glare of the anonymous religio-medical blockbuster *Onania*, more modest sellers such as *The Pure Nazarite* and *Eronania*, and a raft of similar print publications circulating widely in the Anglo-Atlantic.[12] *Onania*, though condemning Onanism as sinful and unhealthy, also reflected the intense cultural ambivalence about masturbation in the period; successive editions added voyeuristic narrative supplements that may have been composed, marketed, or read as pornography.[13] These supplements increased commercial demand for *Onania* and also incorporated, and capitalized upon, women's sexual knowledge, in distinction to medical or religious sexual discourse.[14]

Remarkably, in this welter of writing about masturbation, Whitefield's *General Account* distinguished itself by offering something unusual, and possibly unique at that time. Not only did the *General Account* provide a publicly identifiable first-person description of repeated Onanistic practice, it did so in a narrative intended for, and receiving, the widest possible print circulation. Whitefield's record-breaking print circulation in the 1740s, including an estimated ten thousand North American copies of his conversion narrative alone, suggests he made a substantial contribution to popular understandings of Onanism.[15] So too does the immediate prominence of Whitefield's sexual "sin" in English anti-Methodist erotic satire, from Ralph Jephson's obscene 1740 description of "Satan" lending Whitefield "an *helping Hand* ... so vigorously" that Whitefield was "*bleeding* with the Excess" to Henry Fielding's more restrained alignment of Whitefield's conversion narrative with erotic memoir and the Earl of Rochester's infamous poetry.[16] Taken together, Whitefield's print circulation and appearance in erotic satire indicate that he may have done more to propagate the discourse of Onanism, and personally embody Onanism, than any other public figure at the time. They also suggest that Whitefield's use of the discourse of Onanism contributed to what book historians describe as his material expansion of the print public sphere, especially in England's North American colonies.

SEXUAL CHARACTER AND THE HISTORY OF SEXUALITY

Whitefield employed print as a medium for both rational-critical self-instantiation as well as enthusiastic, affecting performance. As I suggest above, Whitefield's incorporation of Onanism into a Protestant print confessional tradition did something new by narrating Onanistic practice to create affective intimacy with readers, sell books, and attract donations. The *General Account* thereby participated in what Michael Warner describes as Awakening-era evangelical attempts to broaden the social bases or "footings" for public religious address via what Irving Goffman identifies as "dramaturgical" actions or performances.[17] The *General Account* also exemplifies religious societies' attempts to fuse "populist enlightenment notions of spiritual and bodily health," including the discourse of Onanism, with donations, print book sales, and other "liberal capitalist methods of fund-raising."[18] This fusion helped religious societies constitute themselves and, in the process, expand the print public sphere.

Whitefield's *General Account* thereby opens up a space to consider public-sphere evangelism's active contributions to the development of the Onanist as a new type, or prototype, of sexual personhood well before the consolidation of the sexual subject in medicine and the sciences.[19] As I will elaborate below, the *General Account* created Whitefield as an evangelic "sexual character" defined by penitential publicity, or the public performance of sin and redemption in the fraught conjunction of confession and theatricality. This sexual character was prior or adjacent to medico-scientific discourse but not subordinated to a scientific or secularizing logic; it was centrally invested in retaining spiritual agency and promoting the public sphere's spiritual significance. My notion of Whitefield's sexual character grounds the concept of "footing" or dramaturgical action in the rich nexus of print, theater, public display, and other forms of mediation Whitefield associates with the commencement and cessation of Onanistic practice. In the eighteenth century, the notion of "character" helped manage or streamline increasingly complex social roles and material bonds under modern imperial capitalism.[20] For Lisa Freeman, character arises in the absence of a "self-evident or transparent signature" for the self and instead "enter[s] into the gray area of fiction, fabrication, forgery, and fraud. Understanding 'character' now required skills in observation, penetration, and interpretation.... Immediate visual recognition gave way to mediated misprision, and the gap between perception and meaning widened into the space of fiction and theatricality."[21]

Character was performed, acted, or written into being by spiritual, environmental, social, or material forces, including texts and embodied performances. It was pliable, continually maintained or transformed through a range of social influences and, as Susan Manning writes, "reveal[ing] itself in patterns of textual relationship."[22] In contrast to modern subjectivity's wedding of liberal possessive individualism and biological determinism, eighteenth-century character has more in common with early modern notions of the self as "a locus of inscription," in which words instantiate relationships between writer and reader, or between characters on the stage (or page) and characters in the world.[23]

Sexual character was also constructed in and through an interrelated shift in bodily habit in the service of empire and commerce, the eighteenth-century development of racial character or "complexion," which also developed, in part, through the spiritual activity of "compulsive confession."[24] Like racial character, sexual character, though malleable, could condense into particular dispositions; in the case of famous or notorious figures such as the Earl of Rochester, sexual character might become individually recognizable to a wide audience or used eponymously to denote a belief system or trait. Whitefield's critics, for example, tried to make "Whitefieldian" denote "bigotted [sp] Character[s]" or "lewd Characters" and, over the course of the eighteenth century, "the Onanist" became a notorious character type.[25]

Whitefield's sexual character contributes to our understanding of what religion did with and for sex in the mid-eighteenth century by elaborating connections between four interrelated areas of scholarly interest: first, evangelicals' participation in Anglo-Atlantic sex reform movements that shifted sexual practice away from "previously common" sorts of nonreproductive sex; second, sex reform's development alongside other attempts to control bodily habit in the service of British imperial and commercial development; third, early eighteenth-century religious societies' intense spiritual erotics (emotional, psychological, and sometimes physical bonds that grew into and out of spiritual practice within churches, religious societies, or other smaller fellowship communities) and transgressions of gender norms; and, finally, the sexual and gender implications of Whitefield's distinctive performance style.[26]

Before exploring Whitefield's elaboration of a sexual character, I want to briefly recenter eighteenth-century evangelic discourse in histories of sexuality. This recentering is indebted to recent scholarship on early sexualities in unexpected places. Taking Onanism's spiritual and theatrical valences seriously, and crediting the eighteenth century's most popular evangelist with a significant role in the early formation of the Onanist as a social type, offers a new way to facilitate what Greta LaFleur calls the productive tension at the heart of eighteenth-century histories of sexuality: historicizing the alterity of eighteenth-century sex while still finding in it a "usable past."[27] Like LaFleur's work, my study helps explore the "ideological and political territory of sexuality" by considering religious societies' use of commercial print and other public-sphere organizing to act with and against states' established churches "before [sexuality] came into the purview of science and, subsequently, the state." By elaborating Whitefield's work in the nexus of print, performance, public circulation, and imitation, I extend what Chris Looby describes as sexuality's intrinsic literariness, studies of which aim "not to reduce or explain but to observe and appreciate the intractable difficulty of a proper chronological account of the history of sexuality."[28] In some ways, the discourse of Onanism is a traditional starting point for literary and other histories of sexuality that identify Onanism as providing the administrative, intellectual, and affective "technologies" around which modern sexualities crystallized and endured, even after concerns about Onanism waned. However, these histories place Onanism in a liminal cultural space, isolated from both earlier "Christian" masturbation (one of many manifestations of embodied lust) and later medico-scientific sexualities specified by gender and sexual object-choice. Eve Sedgwick, for example, contrasts "Christian" masturbation, a more or less minor sin subject to penance, with Onanism, a terrifying disease and "proto-form" of later sexual identities forming around "disorders *of* attention" that escaped grounding in the body.[29] Laqueur similarly proposes that Swiss physician Samuel-Auguste Tissot's 1760 *L'Onanisme*, the first comprehensive medical treatment of the subject, regarded Onanism as unnatural not in "the traditional Christian sense of going against the natural purpose of a sexual act," but "because the desire that motivates it is ... artificial, made up, chimerical."[30] For Laqueur, Onanism's secular Enlightenment pedigree better positions it as the antetype of modern sexuality, a scientific form matured in the womb of Christianity but born to oppose the old Christian order. And yet Laqueur's attention to Onanism's commercial public-sphere development, as well as his evocative description of Onanism as "artificial, made up, chimerical," gestures at the enduring legacy of an earlier sense of the Onanist as a sexual character, as Laqueur's phrase evokes the triumvirate of theatricality, sexual act, and a traditional conception of lust as "Worldly-minded" desire (a disorder of attention) with which Whitefield's *General Account* grappled. My study corroborates Onanism's singularity but also affirms deep connections between evangelical Onanism, earlier "Christian" masturbation, and later scientific-medical gender and sexuality, helping us see the discourse of Onanism as one more way in which evangelism contributed to modern science and medicine.[31] Neither fish nor fowl but both, Whitefield's sexual character becomes a peculiar facet of what Peter Coviello calls "the erotic as a mode of being not yet encoded in the official vocabularies of the intimate."[32]

One important way Whitefield's *General Account* bridges the gap between seventeenth-century Christian sin and nineteenth-century medico-scientific sexuality is its incorporation of Onanism into a confessional narrative intended to evangelize in a broad commercial print public.[33] As historians have long argued, Protestant publications of "cases of conscience," diaries, and autobiographies had, since at least the seventeenth century, served a similar function to Catholic confession and associated practices.[34] These Protestant print confessional traditions adapted and transformed what Sara Butler, Mayke de Jong, Michel Foucault, and others identify as Catholic confession's simultaneous subjugation and elicitation of desire, inherited from older penitential rites of public penance, ordo paenitentum, and publicatio sui.[35] Foucault does not develop this point in the *History of Sexuality, Volume 1*, but, as with Laqueur's "artificial, made up, chimerical," Foucault's evocative turns of phrase in that volume point to several connections between eighteenth-century public-sphere religion and later sexuality. Whitefield's sexual character, defined by his print confession and performance of a converted sexual self, especially resonates with a much-debated passage from *History of Sexuality, Volume 1*. In that book's English translation, Foucault famously proposed that "the sodomite had been a temporary aberration; the homosexual was now a species." There is both transformation and loss in this translation. The phrase "had been a temporary aberration" is "était un relaps," "was a relapse," or "was a backslider."[36] Derived from the Latin *relapsus*, Foucault uses the original noun form, "a relapse," to indicate a social type, one who *is* a relapse. Contemporary English has lost this meaning, though it retains the notion of a relapse as something one can have, as well as the anthimeria "to relapse," both now most often used in a medical register to characterize behaviors such as addiction or diseased objects such as cancers. The noun form *is* a relapse, had a primarily religious meaning, akin to an apostate heretic who returned to previously renounced heretical beliefs. This noun form also, at least as early as the seventeenth century, applied to adulterers and others whose sexual acts contravened divine law. A person's conviction as "a relapse" by church or civic authorities could entail permanent religious and civil penalties.[37] In other words, Foucault's noun form, "était un relaps," captures the way that religious frameworks since at least the seventeenth century imagined repeated acts, including sexual acts, as signaling heretical "backsliding" in need of penitential rituals of correction and management developed in religion, law, medicine, and education. So, while being "a relapse" is in some sense "a temporary aberration," it is also an enduring identity in which acts are connected to, or constituted by, sinful beliefs or desires.

The long arc of English usage from noun to verb, apostate to illness, encapsulates Foucault's chronicle of the centuries-long development of "productive" medical and scientific discursive power.[38] This journey from noun to verb also encourages us to pause along the way to consider more local or minor intricacies in the relationship between faith, sex, and character that helped constitute, complicate, or resist this shift. Here, again, Foucault may be of some use. *The History of Sexuality, Volume 1*, as later historians of sexuality remind us, attends only to narrow "formal discursive systems" of church and state.[39] Foucault offers a more robust treatment in his Collège de France lectures which, beginning in 1975, outlined his research for a (subsequently abandoned) book on Onanism.[40] In the 1975 lectures Foucault describes Onanism's most important historical feature as the relationship posed between sex and disease: Onanism somatized and pathologized masturbation as the potential ultimate cause of every illness.[41] It thereby became a vessel into which the "Christian flesh" of prior centuries could be distilled before being "transposed into the family element" of Freudian psychoanalysis and the medicalized sexuality of the bourgeois family.[42]

Confessional difference played a vital role in this distillation. Onanism emerged in "Protestant lands," Foucault argues, because Protestants lacked the direct supervision provided, in Catholic countries, by ritualized personal confession and large religious schools. In their absence, the discourse of Onanism developed as a public-sphere alternative to direct supervision.[43] Onanism was "completely different" from both earlier "Christian flesh" and later medical/psychoanalytic "sexuality," then, because it developed within eighteenth-century Protestant cultures' unique print public sphere confessional practices. To whatever extent Onanism was new, evangelical publicity was crucial to its development and circulation. If, as Foucault and other historians propose, the discourse of Onanism left structuring traces in later medical and psychological accounts of sexuality, evangelical publicity played an important role in this process.

CONFESSION IN THE PRINT PUBLIC

Comparing Whitefield's discourse of Onanism to accounts of masturbation and other sexual sins in eighteenth-century Catholic Church trials helps us see why public-sphere Onanist discourse was so valuable, and treacherous, for Methodist and other religious societies. Both Catholic and Protestant attention to masturbation derived from a concept of heresy, a matter of belief and attestation. In societies with established Catholic churches, heresy was the original legal justification for exercising church control over sexual crimes and also the proximate rationale for adjudicating any given case. Zeb Tortorici's discussion of Catholic Church trials in eighteenth-century colonial Mexico, for example, reminds us that sexual sin was still widely understood as heresy and that Catholic confessional practices reinforced church authority against other elements of the state.[44] Whitefield, in contrast, used the evangelical print public as a spiritually efficacious site of confession in order to legitimate religious societies' "outsider" evangelical practice.

One of Whitefield's earliest published sermons, originally delivered to a quarterly meeting of religious societies in 1737, demonstrates the way sexual management facilitated religious societies' self-organization and public legitimation, even in the absence of explicit Onanist discourse. In a section of the sermon denouncing sins of "Worldly-mindedness," Whitefield laments the "many unhappy Instances of young Men, who . . . had escap'd the *Pollutions which are in the World thro' Lust*" when under the "Tuition and Inspection of others," only to relapse "when they have come to be their own Masters." To better extend "Inspection" over sensual "lusts" beyond the school years, Whitefield recommends that his "Brethren . . . would therefore do well . . . frequently to remind each other of this dangerous Snare, and to exhort one another to begin, pursue and end your christian Warfare, in a thorough Renunciation of the World."[45] Circulating in print, the sermon would further encourage mutual "Inspection" by reproducing the call for "frequent" exhortation. Print would also create readerly bonds among the religious societies' "Brethren," evangelize to a broader audience of unaffiliated readers, and legitimate religious societies in the eyes of a broader public interested in controlling sexual sin.

Juxtaposing Whitefield's oblique reference to Onanism in his 1737 sermon with his clear naming and narration of Onanistic practice in the *General Account* reveals a slight but significant shift in emphasis that demonstrates Onanism's emergence within public-sphere evangelical discourse. Whitefield's 1737 rhetoric of pollution, lust, and "Renunciation" primarily designates a spectrum of "Worldly-minded" concupiscence; it connotes "young Men['s]" Onanistic "*Pollutions*" only secondarily and implicitly. When, two years later, Whitefield's *General Account* explicitly specified the "sin of Onan," Whitefield reversed the order of precedence, bringing Onanism into the foreground as an especially dangerous "Worldly-minded" practice. Equally notable is the *General Account's* assertion that Onanism caused him lasting harm ("dismal effects" that he "felt & groaned under ever since"). Onanism's ability to cause physical harm derives from sixteenth-, seventeenth-, and eighteenth-century religio-medical accounts of sexual excess, but the permanence or endurance of this harm long after the cessation of sinful practice was something relatively new, and something that may have literally embodied one Christian solution to relapse: permanent metanoia.[46] While Whitefield's narrative used Onanism in much the same way as earlier conversion narratives used sex or lust, then, later Onanistic discourse severed Onanism's enduring physical effects from Whitefield's public-sphere confession. Once removed from public confessional performances, these physical "effects" appear as manifestations of a penitential ritual that remain stranded in the body or psyche, unable to be incorporated into a reformed sexual character and thereby redeemed by faith.

As I suggest above, Whitefield's engagements with the discourse of Onanism developed an innovative public-sphere evangelical rhetoric of sexual control that helped legitimate religious societies as valuable additions (or, later, alternatives) to established churches. This constituted a reticulated response to English public and established religious attacks on early Methodism's combination of heightened emotional expressivity and austere "methodical" devotion, which critics skewered as a heady mix of "Romish" Catholic theatrical imposture and bigoted Puritan/antinomian disdain for established authority. In the 1730s, as Wesley's Holy Club flourished and Whitefield's celebrity increased, a host of novelists and Enlightenment luminaries intensified these lines of attack, culminating, in the twentieth century, in E. P. Thompson's aspersive description of Methodism as "sanctified emotional Onanism."[47] In this and other ways, critics imagined Methodism as what Misty Anderson calls a "queer technology of desire" because its intensely affective, embodied worship practices seemed to "multipl[y] desires" instead of performing the church's supposed "disciplining" role—or, squaring Thompson and Anderson, because Methodism's emotional and organizational innovations more clearly revealed the way faith could multiply desires by sanctifying that discipline. Opponents of Methodism, as Anderson writes, engaged "the Methodist conversion narrative and its focus on the responsive individual to explain a series of same-sex relationships for which [they had] no clear identity category."[48] The Onanist was one nascent or emergent identity category Whitefield engaged to promote early Methodist organizing and practice and defend against anti-Methodist attack.

The tension between attack and parry, and between discipline and incitement, sits at the crux of Whitefield's groundbreaking evangelism in both oration and print. Even when Whitefield was on safe doctrinal ground in using sexual control to structure his conversion narrative, his prose was so direct, candid, lively, and confidential that it threatened to undermine the conventions of the conversion narrative genre. For example, in a section demonstrating one of his relapses into Onanism, Whitefield sets the scene by invoking virtually the same nexus of print, performance, public circulation, and personal imitation as that which he used to frame his initial account, but with an inverted relationship between cause and effect. He begins by confessing that, despite his growing piety, he had "all this while . . . continued in Secret sin." While, in his first vignette, sustained textual and interpersonal communications "at length" led him into Onanism, in this second vignette it was sustained Onanistic practice that "at length" led to his "acquaintance with a set of such Debauched, Abandoned, Atheistical Youths" whose example encouraged him to "walk about," take "pleasure in . . . lewd conversation," engage in libertine speculations about lust, and generally "make a great proficiency in the school of the Devil," a phrase here recalling both Onanism's proverbial status as "School-wickedness" and Whitefield's former club of "Old Schoolfellows." At a spiritual and doctrinal level, Whitefield's reversal of cause and effect emphasizes the reciprocal reinforcement of all sin and the consequent need to rely on God's grace. In this passage, however, instead of leading to a sense of grace, Whitefield offers a pair of slightly breathless sentences with a knotty timeline and grammar that show him wrestling not only with sin, but with a morphology of conversion itself.[49] "God so deeply convicted me of Hypocrisy," he writes, "that, though I had formed frequent ^but ineffectual^ resolutions before, yet I had then power given me over my secret and darling Sin—Notwithstanding some time afterwards being overtaken in liquor . . . Satan gain'd his usual advantage over me again."[50]

Whitefield's description of Onanism as "my secret and darling Sin" (a lively theological commonplace for a range of sexual sins) is, doctrinally, unexceptional, slotting Onanism into place as a sexual sin whose cessation could signal conversion. Slightly more unusual is Whitefield's beginning with a "convict[ion]" of sin only to note that he had, in fact, experienced the typical series of "ineffectual resolutions," made without God's assistance, before confirming God's gift of "power" over sin. Receipt of God's "power" would usually signal a shift to a new stage of conversion, but Whitefield continues the narrative with yet another turn of the screw, another relapse into Onanism, this time while drunk, and ends the episode in a deeply uncertain spiritual state. Whitefield's series of qualifiers ("though," "yet," "notwithstanding") and insertion, at some later point, of a morphological clarification ("but ineffectual"), moves us back and forth in time and in the salvific process. His confusing temporality and syntax, and his wealth of intimate personal detail, draws readers into a detailed narrative recapitulation of a halting, stuttering, tormentingly unresolved conversion process. His comparatively graphic description of his Onanistic practice also moved Whitefield away from ministerial print precedent and closer to the anonymous, voyeuristic epistolary narratives that padded *Onania*'s "expanded" editions. The *General Account* thereby propels Whitefield's evangelic address by creating an innovative sexual character that fuses the intimacy and narrative irregularity of oral or manuscript conversion accounts with the graphic narrative detail, print form, and wide circulation of *Onania*.

Whitefield subsequently played on this sexual character by using theatricality and relapse as tropes or metaphors elsewhere in his *General Account* as well as in his letters and his sermons, helping audiences unite his written and embodied persona.[51] This troping was scriptural and superficially anodyne but still potentially problematic; if the *General Account's* depictions of sin might be excused as a form of repentance, repeated troping threatened to make light of the practice.[52]

PRINT AS PERFORMANCE

The nexus Whitefield identifies between Onanism, print, performance, public circulation, and personal imitation traces out paths of sin and the way back to redemption. Recent scholarship on Whitefield's print activity, and on speech and print's mutual imbrication in the period, helps us see how classic analyses of Whitefield's oration can inform our understanding of his use of print as a spiritually efficacious type of performance.[53] Like his preaching, Whitefield's commercial success in print was facilitated by his fusion of an apparently "uncontainable" theatrical fluidity of character with the antitheatrical, anti-Onanistic, and moderate oratorical discourses of bodily management he employed.[54] His colonial print engagements epitomized what book historians call an "interchangeability of speech and writing" in the period, perhaps to a fault: Benjamin Franklin, Whitefield's Philadelphia printer and friend, invoked the proverbial contrast between speech's evanescence and writing's endurance ("litera scripta manet") to describe the way Whitefield's "unguarded expressions" in print tarnished his reputation in a manner unguarded oration could not.[55] The manuscript and colonial editions of Whitefield's *General Account* troubled attempts to stabilize and isolate print from oration by "captur[ing] the power of the oratory" through repetitions, corrections, surprising reversals of pat phrases, irregular or "oratorical" punctuation, rhythmic cadences, and other written counterparts of what Franklin portrayed as the seductive, "musick[al]" pleasure of Whitefield's well-rehearsed, affecting, and commercially astute performances. In print and oration, Whitefield's ability to perform in a seemingly "uncontainable" style made him intensely appealing to his supporters, appalling to his detractors, and discomfiting to his fellow early Methodist leaders.[56]

The print history of Whitefield's *General Account* accentuates the degree to which Whitefield's use of print was, like his preaching, intensely commercial, performative, and a product of transatlantic exchange. In a broad sense, all print is performative as a material product of labor, as an intervention in some sort of public, and in its "perpetual re-making" by readers, performers, and auditors.[57] Even Franklin's "*manet*," specifying print's endurance, was most familiar to readers as a bit of print stage direction typically preceding soliloquy ("*Manet* Hamlet"; "*Manet* Bawd"), with its redolence of interiority.[58] Whitefield's use of print in 1740 was conspicuously performative because his narrative broke new print-historical ground in its scale, geographic scope, and coordination with his preaching tour. Furthermore, the high degree of textual variation between the London edition and Whitefield's colonial print editions (including, as I will elaborate below, variations in the depiction of Onanism) not only complemented Whitefield's "uncontainable" preaching style, it was the direct result of Whitefield's decision to publish independently in the colonies to better coordinate with his itinerant preaching tour.[59] In an unexpected way, then, Whitefield's performative use of print can address Anne Myles's call for tracing "performative acts of experimental self-perception and filiation" that might serve as "lens[es] for examining the development of sexual subjectivity and sexual agency." Taking Myles a step farther, Whitefield's development of a sexual character indicates that sexuality may have emerged not only in "parallel to the way people took on identifications in the religious . . . spheres," but in a mutually constitutive dialogue with religious identifications.[60]

The *General Account's* development of a sexual character initially drew on, and then moved away from, Whitefield's earlier, somewhat different print performance of penitential publicity: his serial publication of antitheatrical print "extracts." This link is obscure in the *General Account* itself but comes into focus when we read the *General Account* alongside his personal diary's first mention of Onanism some three years earlier. On April 2, 1736, Whitefield wrote that two of his Oxford friends were "talking of self pollution and the ill effects and put me on abridging Onania." He took up the project a fortnight later and, by April 24, had been "greatly assisted in extracting Onania."[61] Whitefield's description of his writing as "extracting," rather than "abridging," evokes three related meanings—copying out, removing, and distilling—with special resonance in theatrical and Onanistic discourse.[62] Textual extracting, of primary importance to Whitefield here, was a widespread, respectable, and, when printed, reliably profitable method of engaging with texts. Extracting constitutes a selection and "removal" of text as a prelude to continued engagement at some remove. In commonplace books, miscellanies, abridgements, "epitomes," and newspaper and magazine reprinting, extracting helped circulate texts in a new way, often within smaller publics organized by affiliation, interest, or shared experiences of social exclusion. Because these practices of textual manipulation showcased written texts' plastic and dialogic tendencies, they were not uncontroversial; in 1733, for example, John Locke groused that chapter and verse divisions "chopp'd and minc'd" scriptural argument into mere aphorism.[63] Such textual play was a necessary evil, though, as an extractor's judicious character could manifest itself only through careful and rational textual cultivation.

Whitefield's diary account of "extracting Onania" thereby anticipates the nexus between print, performance, circulation, and imitation in his *General Account*'s Onanistic vignettes. In his diary, Whitefield's pious, anti-Onanist conversation with his new Oxford friends leads to his adoption of the highly structured imitative textual practice of "extracting"; in the *General Account*, Onanism leads to (or from) louche "sauntering" (or "walk[ing] about"), unstructured play-reading, imitative "Evil communications" (or "lewd conversation[s]"), and the company of "Old schoolfriends" (or "Youths ... in the school of the Devil"). This parallel structure represents Onanism and anti-Onanism as analogous textual-interpersonal performances mediating between sin and redemption, with God's grace at the fulcrum.

Whitefield's plan to extract *Onania*, as sketched in his diary, would have followed in the footsteps of what his *General Account* describes as his previous serial publication of antitheatrical textual extracts. In his youth, Whitefield explains, he had often acted in stage "Entertainment[s]," which he later came to regard as sinful. When an itinerant theater troupe came to town, he took the opportunity to "extract Mr. Law's excellent little Treatise ... *the absolute Unlawfulness of the Stage Entertainment*" and request a printer "put a little of it in the *News* for six Weeks successively," in order to "give a publick Testimony of my Repentance for seeing and acting Plays."[64] Whitefield's description of his antitheatrical extracts as a "Testimony of my Repentance" echoes his 1736 diary's description of anti-Onanist extracts as "a mark of my repentance" and "a proof of repentance."[65] Had Whitefield gone on to publish those extracts of *Onania*, they, like his published antitheatrical extracts, would have constituted a rational-critical print performance that could have served as a "mark" or "proof" or "testimony" of repentance. Extracts would have externalized (and feminized) his sins in print, fixing them on the page and keeping them at arms' length while allowing him to masculinize himself as an author in the print public, improve his public character as a rational-critical print extractor, and improve his moral standing in the public sphere.

Ultimately, in the case of Onanism, Whitefield does not appear to have published his extracts. His "mark" of repentance instead took shape in the *General Account*'s more complex narrative construction of a sexual character. This sexual character effectively reincorporated his "extracted" Onanism into an intimate personal narrative of sin and its extraction, but it compromised, or complicated, the social prestige Whitefield might expect to derive from print extracts. The complication began with Whitefield's own description of entering print as a form of image management. In a metadramaturgical moment, Whitefield's description of his use of print as "a publick Testimony of my Repentance" incorporates his public-sphere print performance of rational-critical self-instantiation (antitheatrical print extracting) into a theatrical, affecting narrative of transformation in the service of broadening his evangelic and commercial appeal. The evangelic and commercial appeal of Whitefield's decision to move Onanism into a dramatic conversion narrative is thrown into sharp relief when we juxtapose his *General Account* with John Wesley's 1767 extracts of Tissot's 1760 *L'Onanisme*.[66] Whitefield and Wesley both used print treatments of Onanism to develop their public character and legitimate their leadership, but while Wesley's extracts place him above his readers in a position of medico-ministerial expertise by incorporating medical knowledge into an existing Methodist vestibulary public, Whitefield's narrative introduced readers to his own sexual character and employed innovative commercial publication and distribution techniques to extend his evangelic reach and fundraising ability. In commercial evangelical terms, Whitefield's sexual character was far more popular than any extracts could hope to be, but also left him exceptionally open to attack.

GENDER AND THE TEXTUAL MANAGEMENT OF RECURSION

Whitefield's ostentatiously performative description of his fairly unexceptional use of print extracts evinces a specific concern for the gender implications of different types of public performance. Although Whitefield did not publish his extracts on Onanism, the *General Account* reinforces the "extractative" link between Onanism and one subset of his theatrical experience, dressing "in Girl's Cloath's," by suggesting that both practices damaged him permanently. Like Onanism, but unlike any other sin in the *General Account*, acting "in Girl's Cloath's" caused Whitefield persistent and enduring harm, being "a thing which has, and I trust will still cause me much Sorrow even to the End of my Life."[67] This textual parallel between Onanism and acting in girls' clothes marks two ways Whitefield participated in a much longer historical process that Greta LaFleur, Masha Raskolnikov, and Anna Kłosowska describe as a "consolidation of gender expansiveness" limiting "gendered experience[s] that exist outside of the tight bifurcation of male and female." In the eighteenth century, this process was constituted by a shift away from a gender continuum or hierarchy (Laqueur's "one-sex" model) toward a model emphasizing distinct, oppositional genders—that is, the shift that produced "sexual character" in the ontological sense Wollstonecraft famously indicted in 1792.[68] Like the antitheatrical condemnation of dressing in girls' clothes, anti-Onanist discourse participated in this gender shift by strengthening long-standing warnings against masturbation as producing or exploiting "mollicies," or weaknesses, in men. Developed alongside an increasingly ontologized notion of gender difference, these "mollicies" became associated with the rise of a new "third gender" of effeminate adult men.[69]

Although Whitefield treated Onanism and dressing in girls' clothes in similar ways, his consistently optimistic soteriological reasoning complicated his participation in a binarization or consolidation of gender. For example, even as Whitefield condemned his performances in girls' clothes, he insisted that "God brought good afterwards even out of this evil" by making that performance "a means" of developing his "memory," "gesture," and other contemporary theatrical and oratorical performance techniques.[70] We might likewise infer that Onanistic desire could be turned into blessing inasmuch as temptations of the flesh were goads, as his shipboard diary had it, to "keep [himself] in Action." Whitefield's endorsement of theatrical performance's influence on his oratorical performance dovetails with many accounts of Whitefield's distinctive personal style as conspicuously marked by normatively masculine and feminine traits, or what one of Whitefield's ministerial supporters characterized as a "manly" countenance "softened with an uncommon degree of sweetness."[71] This description also evokes Wesley's gendering of oratorical norms in his *Directions Concerning Pronunciation and Gesture* (1749). Much as Wesley would go on to do with his 1767 *Thoughts on the Sin of Onan*, his *Directions* capitalized on the existing English print popularity of an earlier French guide to public bodily management (in this case Le Faucheur's widely translated *Traitté de l'action de l'orateur*) by extracting it in an inexpensive edition aimed at a smaller Methodist public. As with his *Thoughts*, Wesley's *Directions* recommended the careful control of hands ("Your Hands are not to be in perpetual Motion: This the Ancients call'd, The Babbling of the Hands") as well as voice, advising orators to eschew a "whining," "whimsical," or "Theatrical Tone" associated, as Paula McDowell suggests, "with Dissenters and ... women."[72] Wesley's promotion of Le Faucheur's advice on gesture and voice may have been, in part, an attempt to "correct" Methodists influenced by Whitefieldean print and oratorical practice.

By describing and linking his childhood performances in girls' clothes to his commercial public evangelization, Whitefield left himself unusually open to critical satires of his performance and, by association, his Onanism. When printed, the *General Account's* record-breaking circulation helped galvanize these satires by effectively multiplying, in print, a long-standing dilemma in Catholic confession: the way a priest's questions might inadvertently "perpetuat[e] sodomy" (here in its original connotation of a range of sex and gender practices) "by proscribing it."[73] This confessional predicament, familiar from the work of Foucault, Mark Jordan, and others, has been usefully explored as a distinctly material, textual dynamic in a pair of recent trans studies considering gender's historical fluidity and role in sexuality: one by Igor de Souza, who identifies this confessional dilemma as an intertextual "recursive problem" of origins and regress within material texts, and another by Zrinka Stahuljak, who analyzes recursion in medieval and early modern translations of classical manuscripts.[74] In both England and North America, anti-Onanist writers attempted to manage the recursive problem by offering metacritical comments on the materiality of their text. For example, one seventeenth-century ministerial writer, excerpted in *Eronania*, hoped that "this paper" could "become ... more effectual upon you, than other Mens more learned Prescriptions."[75] These attempts to control the recursive problem in Onanist discourse exemplify the wider cultural disquiet about the way print's growing availability and diversity enabled readers' shift away from "hand piety" and other religious reading performances and toward "seductive, dangerous, and enervating" hand and reading practices.[76] Earlier generations of Christian writers had also attempted to manage this recursive problem through a combination of paratextual metacommentary and textual transformation. As Stahuljak writes, Christian translators edited away what they considered "unnatural" Greek and Roman sex in the body of the text while also detailing those editorial changes in introductory or other paratextual materials. The resulting "gap between text and paratext" introduces a "veiling and unveiling dynamic" marked by a "tension ... between an ongoing constitution of [normative] gender systems" in the text and the acknowledgment of gender's "fluidity" in the paratext. That fluidity was obscured in yet another "veiling," when, at a later date, those paratextual pages were literally cut out of the manuscript, and then unveiled in Stahuljak's scholarship itself.[77]

Stahuljak's account of intertextual recursion in a series of material "veilings and unveilings" offers a useful framework for understanding transformations of sexual character in different print editions of Whitefield's narrative, as well as Whitefield's subsequent reception in erotic satire, and possibly in contemporary scholarship as well. The *General Account* seems to have first entered print in June 1740 when Whitefield's traveling companion William Seward, a well-heeled stockjobber and former treasurer of the South Sea Company, returned to London and published a heavily revised, partially redacted edition in a fairly elegant volume under the new title *A Short Account of God's Dealings With the Reverend Mr. George Whitefield*.[78] Acting independently of Seward, Whitefield or someone in his orbit sent a lightly edited manuscript directly to printers in Philadelphia and Boston. In December 1740 and January 1741, this lightly edited manuscript was printed under the title *A Brief and General Account of the First Part of the Life of the Reverend Mr. George Whitefield* in multiple editions at various sizes, prices, and qualities.[79] Collectively, this assemblage of publication, commerce, and oration reproduced the *General Account* in an iterative series of manuscript and print texts, with slightly different sexual characters in each edition. The London edition, which excised or thoroughly revised long passages and added others out of whole cloth, has had an outsized effect on critical interpretation, including an apparent critical consensus that Whitefield "did not say what [his] sin was" or that he only "refer[red] obliquely to" it.[80] The London edition also took Whitefield's consolidation of gender much farther by eliminating his praise of acting as improving his stage performance. Whitefield's rough manuscript, though, is straightforward in its mention of Onan and dressing in girls' clothes; he wrote those passages in a clear hand and made no subsequent editorial marks. All colonial print editions I have seen, including Franklin's well-composed 1740 first edition and a fifth edition from Boston's reputable Kneeland & Green, follow the manuscript's wording more or less exactly. Whitefield's apparent circumlocution, then, is actually a print-historical artifact revealing religious societies' active and conflicted role in shaping a new literary geography of sexual character. Extending Stahuljak's manuscript framework into the increasingly print-saturated eighteenth century, we might say that Whitefield's manuscript production and direct engagement with printers in the colonies allowed for a typically "paratextual" sexual specificity and gender fluidity to slip from manuscript into print before being cut, or moved into innuendo, by London editors, only to be immediately and mercilessly forced back into print in erotic satires.

The London editors' elimination of Whitefield's explicit mention of Onanism and removal of his link between his performance style and acting in girls' clothes attempted to limit the recursion problem by diminishing those passages' implications for Whitefield's sex and gender, but they also minimized God's redemptive power. Whitefield's own attempt to manage the "recursion problem" was more subtle, nuanced, and arguably more pious, as it redeemed his past behavior by showing how it endured in a new way: uplifted and transformed into a blessing by Whitefield and his readers via the action of the public sphere. For example, as part of Whitefield's narration of his past publication of antitheatrical print extracts as a kind of theatrical "publick Testimony," he heightens the contrast between his rational-critical extracting and print engagement and the work of the actors by deriding them as "the Strollers." This common epithet affiliated unlicensed itinerant actors with vagrancy, prostitution, cruising, and related concepts of ostensibly unproductive labor "inseparable from sexual transgression." Anti-revivalists also regularly denounced Whitefield and his supporters as "strollers," an equation his narrative forestalls by repudiating both the current "Offenders" ("the Strollers") and his own past performances in girls' clothes.[81] Whitefield's dramatic account of publishing antitheatrical extracts thereby attempts to simultaneously bolster his rational-critical antitheatrical moral character and theatrically out-stroll the strollers by promoting his own dramatic publishing and preaching in place of both. Whitefield thereby highlights the spiritual activity of the public sphere, entwining acting in girls' clothes and Onanism as uniquely harmful sins best addressed through a series of redemptive print performances, beginning with extracting and capped off by publication, whether of extracts or his *General Account*'s more complex sexual character.

Each of the three main versions of Whitefield's narrative concludes with slightly different passages that, in metacritical fashion, attempted to limit the recursive problem by tying readers' reception to their spiritual condition.[82] Taken individually, these passages each reminded readers of the public sphere's spiritual activity and encouraged them, in different ways, to contemplate the spiritual ramifications of their textual interpretation. Collectively, their various configurations suggest the difficulty with which Whitefield and his London editors attempted to finesse the relationship between self-reflective critique, in the form of confession, and the question of self-confidence, or assurance of grace. These topics, foundational to histories of critique and the hermeneutics of suspicion, were the subject of a running public theological dispute between Whitefield and John Wesley in 1738–41, and raw elements of this dispute are visible in the *General Account*'s different drafts.[83] The rough manuscript's first draft concluded by proposing that readers' interpretations of his sin would indicate their spiritual condition. "Many" readers, Whitefield wrote, "thro' Ignorance, Prejudice, & Unbelief, when they read this will I fear contradict & blaspheme," while pious readers would find salvation. Hailing pious readers directly, Whitefield explains that "thy heart [may] be as ^deeply^[?] alternately affected with grief & joy at the reading, as mine has been at the writing of this short account. . . . Then shall I have good hope of meeting thee with comfort at the Great day of accounts."[84]

With his characteristic wit, Whitefield puns on "account" to suggest that a sympathetic or "affected" reading of his written "account" bodes well for both his own and his readers' salvation on Judgment Day, the "day of accounts." In other words, the print circulation of narratives of triumph over sexual sin creates a gracious circuit from writer to reader that could signal the redemption of both parties. Perhaps because Whitefield had just received sustained criticism for asserting a similar tie, in his recently published *Journals*, between readers' reception of his publication and their prospects for salvation, he crossed out this first conclusion and composed a second draft, which all colonial editions retain. This second draft featured a more modest, scriptural, sexual, and subtly commercial endorsement of print's ability to mediate sin when routed through charitable giving. Whitefield begins this second draft by addressing readers who are "as yet Unspotted from the world," echoing James 1:27 and recalling his 1737 sermon's implicit evocation of Onanism as a type of "Worldly-mindedness." Understood as a dénouement to Whitefield's struggle with Onanism, "Unspotted" also connotes physical markers of the pox, other diseases correlated to sexual sin, and perhaps even ejaculate. Just as importantly, the phrase would remind well-versed readers of James 1:27's prior injunction to "visit the fatherless and widows in their affliction," associating readerly sympathy for his sexual sin with his promise to direct profits from his print editions to his Georgia orphanage.[85] The London editors made yet another revision, replacing the biblical "unspotted" with "uninfected with the Contagion of the World." The terms *uninfected* and *Contagion* back away from the colonial editions' more biblical *Unspotted* to move "Worldly-mindedness" into a medical register that may discreetly allude to a more medicalized concept of Onanism while also reinscribing diseases as, ultimately, caused by sin. The London edition thereby jettisons the dense connections, in Whitefield's manuscript and colonial editions, between sympathetic reading, charitable commerce, and salvation in favor of a straightforward reversal of attacks on Onanism and Methodism as forms of enthusiastic contagion.

As these three revisions suggest, variations in Whitefield's depiction of his sexual character were shaped by geography and cultural norms that likely shaped the work's reception. Considering the *General Account*'s reception in New England and London offers an initial sense of its range of meanings. New Englanders were familiar with Onanism. In Boston, John Phillips first printed *Onania* in 1724; the city's appetite had been whetted in 1723 by Phillips and Thomas Fleet's printing of Cotton Mather's *The Pure Nazarite*.[86] Doctrinally, New England's Congregationalist communities were an ideal proving ground for Whitefield's incorporation of sexual sin into a Puritan-Pietist conversion narrative. Whitefield's Calvinism likely eased his entry into New England's pulpits and presses and shaped readers' reception of his narrative, keeping them focused on traditional understandings of relapse as an expected part of the path to grace. Nevertheless, the print *Brief and General Account*, along with other aspects of his public-sphere evangelism, disrupted the social relationships that had governed conversion in New England.[87] Conversion usually included an initial movement toward faith, a period of relapse and "testing," and finally consolation or certainty in faith that lead to the joining of a congregation and often civil status.[88] Relapse was thus a crucial feature of the normative communal self, incorporated into a routinized practice in which a flexible period of backsliding concluded with entry into the church body, where subsequent relapses could be addressed by direct ministerial discipline.[89] Despite sharing New England's Calvinist beliefs, Whitefield's use of relapse in a broadly circulating evangelical narrative challenged traditional uses of relapse to form congregational communities. Whitefield's itinerant evangelism moved sexual sin and relapse away from cementing ties between a confessional dyad (the stable, socially codified positions of minister and congregant) and toward a less predictable exchange between the unstable positions of speaker, listener, writer, and reader in a transatlantic evangelic public.

Comparing the London and colonial editions reveals a colonial-metropolitan divide in the literary geography of sex, one governed less by morality or theology than commerce and sectarian competition. For example, Whitefield's 1739 manuscript and all colonial printings frankly relate that Whitefield "fell secretly into a Sin for which *Onan* dyed," establishing Whitefield's marketable novelty and cementing his affiliation with imported English books and other goods.[90] The London edition's more circumspect "fell into an abominable secret Sin" antiques Whitefield by harkening back to "abominations" caused by idolatry in Leviticus, Kings, and Deuteronomy, including magic, cross-dressing, and a range of sexual acts.[91] While the London edition's revisions to Whitefield's descriptions of Onanism and theatricality were more extensive and consistent than revisions to any other topic, they were not different in kind. The London edition consistently eliminated more controversial claims about theology, sex, and gender, and moderated Whitefield's style by rearranging words to achieve more conventional turns of phrase, regularized punctuation to slow the pace of reading, and otherwise shifted Whitefield's "oratorical" prose into a more measured, polite, conventionally readerly register. Collectively, these changes indicate that the London edition's representation of Onanism was determined by concerns about public criticism, commerce, and theology.[92] In the colonies, by contrast, printers were unlikely to have evangelical affiliation and more inclined to generate profit through controversy; his colonial critics were primarily ministers focused on his manifest disruption of religious order. In London, greater sectarian competition and pulpit circulation meant that, by moderating Whitefield's style and allowing for a polite façade of readerly uncertainty, Seward could promote the Methodist cause within a narrower elite.

The rapid production of anti-Methodist erotic satires incorporating Seward's more oblique phrasing suggests that his effort to contain Whitefield's sexual character was counterproductive. Satirists moved the London edition's "veiling and unveiling" dynamic forward in order to depict Whitefield as a moralizing charlatan, hypocritically marshaling antitheatrical and anti-Onanist rhetoric to shield himself from accusations of "lewd" character while simultaneously tantalizing an audience entranced by his fluid, theatrical style, and titillated by the possibility of seeing embodied evidence of sexual sin. These and other anti-Methodist erotic satires of Whitefield's narrative, as Anderson notes, regularly structured their critique around Whitefield's self-description in print, and they also may have parodied his use of print, particularly his citational and extractive practices, as a sort of obscene dicta probantia.[93] Jephson, for example, who depicted Whitefield's Onanism as assisted by Satan's hand, begins his satire by quoting the London edition's less overt description of Whitefield's "secret sin" and then obscenely speculating about the nature of that sin in a series of exuberant sexual scenarios structured around confessional phrases from Whitefield's work, phrases that Jephson carefully extracts, ostentatiously cites—"(Page 38)," "(Page 18)," "(Page 21)," etc.—and then reframes in pornographic terms. Hogarth's 1762 engraving "Credulity, Superstition and Fanaticism: A Medley," which has attracted sustained critical attention for its association of Methodism with a range of disordered sexual and gender norms, makes a similar use of quotation and citation: four lines of verse and a direct citation ("Hymn *By* G. Whitefield Page 130") appear on a sheet of paper dangling from a lectern just below a cross-eyed, theatrically winged clerk and his two putti, and just above a book labeled "Whitefields Journal."[94] Hogarth thereby follows Jephson in extracting and citing Whitefield's language of sexual confession and intense spiritual feeling to maximize the punitive potential of Franklin's "litera scripta manet," putting Whitefield's print publication at the visual and metaphorical center of disordered sexual and gender norms. Both Jephson and Hogarth here impugn Methodist confession, of which Whitefield's was the prime example, as an unduly "Romish" or excessively confessional form. Their satires thereby exemplify print's striking amplification of Catholic confession's recursive problem: print circulation and citation allowed satirists to affiliate Methodism with theatrical disruptions of sex and gender by transforming Whitefield's confessional language into pornographic caricature.

Whitefield's obscene reception illustrates the treacherous shoals religious societies navigated in their use of the discourse of Onanism to organize in the evangelic public, particularly in print. Erotic satires therefore help constitute Whitefield's legacy in the history of sexuality, but they do not negate the significance of Whitefield's sincere attempt to use sexual character to evangelize; Whitefield's unexpurgated colonial editions more fully embraced the sinner and the sin as a means to a conversionistic end. We might say that, in the colonies, Whitefield encouraged a sort of confessional voyeurism: by theatrically performing the enduring effects his stage acting had on his emotional state (his sorrow), his sexual excess had on his physiognomy (his famous crossed eye or "squint"), and both had on his gender performance (his "manly" yet "sweet" affect), Whitefield used his voice, his body, and his print publications together as performative modes that could make sin visible and spiritually valuable.[95] The London revisions intensified the abjecting logic of confession that Whitefield's narrative itself set in motion. In altering Whitefield's descriptions of stage performance and Onanism to a greater extent than any other topics, the London revisions deepen the link between Onanism and stage performance by extending it into the realm of editorial practice. This makes the various editions' "veiling and unveiling" of Whitefield's Onanism also appear as a harnessing, channeling, or directing of Whitefield's "uncontainable" expressive power, first by Whitefield himself, in his manuscript and colonial print editions, and then by Seward and a small group of Methodist promoters applying metropolitan elite rhetorical norms, sectarian practices, and print standards. The hypocrisy in Whitefield's simultaneous invocation and denunciation of his Onanism and theatricality was, at least for Whitefield and his supporters, transcended by the spiritual value they saw in disclosing links between religion, theatricality, desire, and print. These links were usually subsumed by other religious writers in the period, but Whitefield insists on exploiting them to extend his salvific reach. Put another way, Whitefield was more scandalous and available for erotic satire because his *General Account* delineated subsumed connections between religion, theatricality, desire, and print more clearly than other religious writers at the time. As William Blake wrote of Samuel Foote's anti-Methodist plays, "Foote, in calling Whitefield hypocrite, was himself one; for Whitefield pretended not to be holier than others, but confessed his sins before all the world."[96]

As Blake and much other scholarship suggests, Whitefield denounced the theater but incorporated theatricality into his preaching (and, as I argue, his writing and publishing). Given that Whitefield yoked Onanism and theatricality together within the narrative itself and in his prior textual extracting practice, and that the London editors' inadvertently yoked them even closer in their editorial excisions and revisions, might we say that Whitefield disavowed Onanism but incorporated Onanism into his preaching, writing, and publishing? If so, Whitefield's anti-Onanist "Action" begins with his shipboard writing and editing (acts that directly substitute for or allay "Temptations" of the "flesh"), continues with his publication and distribution of the book (circulating his intimate narrative), and finishes with his book sales' financial support for his Georgia orphanage (where administrators and students engage and are engaged by Onanistic discourse). The writing, publishing, and circulation of the *General Account* are a practical way to avoid masturbation, spiritual vehicles to transform Onanism into blessing, and a commercial public sphere means to promote religious organizing. Whitefield's Onanist discourse was not sublimating libido in a psychoanalytic sense; rather, he advocated restricting some behaviors (Onanism, reading, acting, strolling, theatergoing) to promote other related behaviors (ecstatic feeling, writing, methodical worship, itinerancy, theatrical preaching). We might, then, conceptualize Whitefield's theatrical Onanistic performance and his anti-Onanistic, antitheatrical extracting as counterbalancing one another. Whereas theatricality relied on invention and persuasive fabrication, extracting could participate in authoritative rational public discourse by virtue of citation, reproduction, accretion of truth, and rejection of artifice.[97] Like an evangelical Diogenes, Whitefield's movement of Onanism from implicit connotation to explicit citation, and from textual extracts into intimate conversion narrative, progressively folded in and resacralized disavowed theatrical and sexual forms. His sexual character thereby grants theatricality and Onanism a protective religious enclosure as a sign of God's grace.

NOTES

1. Whitefield, in Berry, "Whitefield and the Atlantic," 215.
2. Whitefield, *General Account*, 127; Hindmarsh, *Evangelical*, 100–105.
3. On the "feelings" of "certain Modern enthusiasts" such as Whitefield, see Trapp, *Nature, Folly, Sin, and Danger*, 42–45.
4. Whitefield, *General Account*, 22–23.
5. My emphasis; Granger, *Tree of Good and Euill*, 45.
6. Laqueur, *Solitary Sex*, 249; Floyer and Baynard, *Psychrolousia*, 254; Mandeville, *Modest Defence*, 22; Jephson, *Methodism*, 40.
7. Harvey, *Reading Sex in the Eighteenth Century*, 66; Vermeer, "Tiny Symbols," 101–34; Stevenson, "Recording the Unspeakable," 223–39; Bennett and Rosario, *Solitary Pleasures*.
8. Carroll, "'I Indulged My Desire Too Freely,'" 157.
9. Godbeer, *Sexual Revolution*, 64–70; Laqueur, *Solitary Sex*, 143–44.
10. Wesley, *Extract*, 5.
11. Ambrose, *Looking unto Jesus*, 390; *Art of Catechising*, 66; Hindmarsh, *Evangelical*, 105.
12. Laqueur, *Solitary Sex*, 13–16, 25–37; Foucault, *History of Sexuality, Vol. 1*, 117; Stolberg, *Homo Patiens*, 266–67, 286; Stolberg, "Self-Pollution," 37–61.
13. Hitchcock, *English Sexualities*, 14; Foucault, *Power/Knowledge*, 100–101.
14. Crawford, "Sexual Knowledge," 82–106; Crawford, *European Sexualities*, 215–1; Juster, *Disorderly Women*; Winckles, *Eighteenth-Century Women's Writing*.
15. Lambert, *"Pedlar in Divinity,"* 14; Amory, "New England Book Trade," 329; Green, "The English Book Trade," 260–61.
16. Jephson, *Methodism*, 40–41; Anderson, *Imagining Methodism*, 70–99; McInelly, *Textual Warfare*, 40.
17. Warner, "Preacher's," 368–83.
18. Hempton, *Methodism*, 46.
19. Anderson, *Imagining Methodism*, 89.
20. Manning, *Poetics of Character*, 26; Lynch, *Economy of Character*, 23–122.
21. Freeman, *Character's Theater*, 22.
22. Manning, *Poetics of Character*, 5.
23. Goldberg, "Hamlet's Hand," 316; also see de Grazia and Stallybrass, "Materiality," 255–83.
24. LaFleur, *Natural History*; Wheeler, *Complexion of Race*; Kopelson, *Faithful Bodies*; Wood, *Slavery, Empathy, and Pornography*, 23–86.
25. A Gentleman, *Letter to the Reverend*, 47, iv, 3.

26 On evangelical reform and bodily habit see Hitchcock, "Reformulation"; Stone, *Family, Sex, and Marriage*; Foucault, *Power/Knowledge*, 101. On Methodism, eroticism, sex, and gender, see Abelove, *Evangelist of Desire*; Andrews, *Methodists and Revolutionary America*; Gibson and Begiato, *Sex and the Church*; Mack, *Heart Religion*; Larson, "Enthusiastic Sensations"; McInelly, *Textual Warfare*, 146–79; O'Brien, "'A Divine Attraction.'"

27 LaFleur, *Natural History*, 15–16; Miller, *Cast Down*, 6–8.

28 Looby, "Sexuality, History, Difficulty, Pleasure," 253–58.

29 Sedgwick, "Jane Austen and the Masturbating Girl," 818–37.

30 Laqueur, *Solitary Sex*, 213.

31 On evangelicalism and enlightenment, see Hindmarsh, *Spirit*. On religion and medicine, see Griffith, *Born Again Bodies*; Thomson, *Bodies of Thought*.

32 Coviello, *Tomorrow's Parties*, 4.

33 On religious publishing, see Zaret, *Origins of Democratic Culture*. In the colonies, see Amory, "New England Book Trade"; Hall and Martin, "A Note." In England, see Raven, "Publishing and Bookselling"; Rivers, "Religious Publishing."

34 Thomas, *Religion and the Decline of Magic*, 158.

35 Butler, *Pain*, 26–79; de Jong, "Transformations of Penance," 185–224; Foucault, *About the Beginning*, 60–62; Clements, "Foucault's Christianities," 1–40.

36 Foucault, *Histoire*, 164.

37 "relapse," n.1 and adj., OED *Online*, Oxford University Press, 2020, accessed 25 August 2023, www.oed.com.

38 Foucault, *History of Sexuality, Vol. 1*, 104, 117, 121, 154.

39 Halperin, "Forgetting Foucault," 24–47; Trumbach, *Sex and the Gender Revolution*, 19.

40 Many thanks to Michael Meranze for noting Foucault's distinct interests in the Collège de France lectures.

41 Foucault, *Abnormal*, xviii.

42 Foucault, *Abnormal*, 181–82, 233–34, 237, 256.

43 Foucault, *Abnormal*, 233.

44 Tortorici, *Sins against Nature*.

45 Whitefield, *Benefits*, 17.

46 Foucault, *Government of the Living*, 178–87.

47 Thompson, *Making of the English Working Class*, 40. Freeman, *Antitheatricality*; Straub, *Sexual Suspects*; Howard, *Stage and Social Struggle*, 22–46, 94–130.

48 Anderson, *Imagining Methodism*, 72–73.

49 On morphology, see Whitehouse, "Structures and Processes," 103–18.

50 Whitefield, *General Account*, 26–28. Carets mark insertions by Whitefield.

51 See, e.g., Whitefield, "Letter 433," 411–12; Whitefield, "Sermon 14," 204–23.

52 On Methodism and troping, see Dale, *Printed Reader*, 91–120.

53 Cunha, "Whitefield and Literary Affect," 190–206.

54 Ruttenburg, *Democratic Personality*, 91, 97. Also see Stout, *Divine Dramatist*; McDowell, *Invention of the Oral*, 170–74.

55 Reilly and Hall, "Customers and the Market," 406.
56 Green, "The English Book Trade," 261; Franklin, *Complete Works of Benjamin Franklin*, 211.
57 McKenzie, *Bibliography and the Sociology of Texts*, 55. Also see Chartier, "Texts, Printings, Readings," 154–75; Warner, *Letters*, 1–33. On print's reciprocal development with performance see Peters, *Theatre of the Book*.
58 Stern, "Stage Directions," 184.
59 On textual instability and materiality, see Barchas, *Graphic Design*; Runge and Rogers, *Producing the Eighteenth-Century Book*.
60 Myles, "Queering the Study," 202.
61 Hindmarsh, *Spirit*, 283n41; Kidd, *George Whitefield*, 18.
62 Laqueur, *Solitary Sex*, 25–27.
63 On Locke, see Stallybrass, "Books and Scrolls," 42–79. On extracting, see Blair, *Too Much to Know*; Rivers, "John Wesley as Editor and Publisher"; Suarez, "In Good Company."
64 Whitefield, *Brief and General*, 41.
65 Hindmarsh, *Spirit*, 283n41; Kidd, *George Whitefield*, 18.
66 Tissot, *Sin of Onan* (edited anonymously by Wesley). See also Wesley, *Thoughts on a Single Life*, 8.
67 Whitefield, *General Account*, 14.
68 Juster, *Disorderly Women*, 213. Guest, "Eighteenth-Century Femininity."
69 Trumbach, *Sex and the Gender Revolution*, 9, 63.
70 Whitefield, *General Account*, 15.
71 Gillies, *Memoirs of the Life of the Reverend George Whitefield*, 279; Anderson, *Imagining Methodism*, 84–85.
72 McDowell, *Invention of the Oral*, 173.
73 de Souza, "Elenx de Céspedes," 46.
74 Jordan, *Invention of Sodomy*, 92–93.
75 *Eronania*, 3.
76 Brown, *Pilgrim and the Bee*, 71; Williams, *Social Life of Books*, 204.
77 Stahuljak, "Transgender Translation," 213.
78 Whitefield, *Short Account*; Amory, "New England Book Trade," 329; Lambert, "Pedlar in Divinity," 13–14.
79 Whitefield, *Brief and General Account*.
80 Kidd, *George Whitefield*, 17; Hindmarsh, *Spirit*, 283n41; Anderson, *Imagining Methodism*, 89, 91.
81 Nicolazzo, "Henry Fielding's 'The Female Husband,'" 338. On Whitefield as stroller see, e.g., A Gentleman, *State of Religion*, xv.
82 de Souza, "Elenx de Céspedes," 46.
83 Schubert, "The Christian Roots of Critique," 1–11.
84 Whitefield, *General Account*, 126.
85 Whitefield, *General Account*, 128.
86 *Onania*; Mather, *Pure Nazarite*.

87 Holyoke, *Testimony of the President*, 12.
88 Caldwell, *Puritan Conversion Narrative*, 166, 78.
89 Marsden, *Jonathan Edwards*, 31–32, 297, 354.
90 On English goods, see Lambert, *"Pedlar in Divinity,"* 14, 60, 112; Amory, "New England Book Trade," 329.
91 Whitefield, *Short Account*, 17; Whitefield, *General Account*, 26, 28.
92 Lewis, *Anti-Methodism and Theological Controversy*.
93 Anderson, *Imagining Methodism*, 83–84, 89.
94 Castle, *The Female Thermometer*, 33–35.
95 West, "Wilkes's Squint," 65–84; Butler, *Awash*, 188.
96 On Blake, see Anderson, "'Our Purpose,'" 130.
97 Freeman, *Antitheatricality*, 1.

BIBLIOGRAPHY

Abelove, Henry. *The Evangelist of Desire: John Wesley and the Methodists*. Stanford, CA: Stanford University Press, 1990.

Ambrose, Isaac. *Looking unto Jesus: A View of the Everlasting Gospel*. London: Richard Chiswel, Benjamin Tooke, Tomas Sawbridge, 1680.

Amory, Hugh. "The New England Book Trade, 1713–1790." In *A History of the Book in America*, 5 vols., edited by Hugh Amory and David D. Hall, 1:314–46. New York: Cambridge University Press, 2000.

Anderson, Misty. *Imagining Methodism in Eighteenth-Century Britain: Enthusiasm, Belief, and the Borders of the Self*. Baltimore: Johns Hopkins University Press, 2012.

Anderson, Misty. "'Our Purpose Is the Same': Whitefield, Foote, and the Theatricality of Methodism." *Studies in Eighteenth-Century Culture* 34 (2005): 130.

Andrews, Dee E. *The Methodists and Revolutionary America, 1760–1800: The Shaping of an Evangelical Culture*. Princeton, NJ: Princeton University Press, 2000.

The Art of Catechising: or, The Compleat Catechist. 4th ed. London: W. B. for Henry Bonwicke, 1706.

Barchas, Janine. *Graphic Design, Print Culture, and the Eighteenth-Century Novel*. Cambridge: Cambridge University Press, 2003.

Bennett, Paula, and Vernon Rosario, eds. *Solitary Pleasures: The Historical, Literary, and Artistic Discourses of Autoerotism*. New York: Routledge, 1995.

Berry, Stephen R. "Whitefield and the Atlantic." In *George Whitefield: Life, Context, and Legacy*, edited by Geordan Hammond and David Ceri Jones, 207–23. New York: Oxford University Press, 2016.

Blair, Ann M. *Too Much to Know: Managing Scholarly Information before the Modern Age*. New Haven, CT: Yale University Press, 2010.

Brown, Matthew P. *The Pilgrim and the Bee: Reading Rituals and Book Culture in Early New England*. Philadelphia: University of Pennsylvania Press, 2007.

Butler, Jon. *Awash in a Sea of Faith: Christianizing the American People.* Cambridge, MA: Harvard University Press, 1990.

Butler, Sara M. *Pain, Penance, and Protest: Peine Forte Et Dure in Medieval England.* Cambridge: Cambridge University Press, 2021.

Caldwell, Patricia. *The Puritan Conversion Narrative: The Beginnings of American Expression.* New York: Cambridge University Press, 1983.

Carroll, Brian D. "'I Indulged My Desire Too Freely': Sexuality, Spirituality, and the Sin of Self-Pollution in the Diary of Joseph Moody, 1720–1724." *William and Mary Quarterly* 60, no. 1 (2003): 155–70.

Castle, Terry. *The Female Thermometer: Eighteenth-Century Culture and the Invention of the Uncanny.* New York: Oxford University Press, 1995.

Chartier, Roger. "Texts, Printings, Readings." In *The New Cultural History*, edited by Lynn Hunt, 154–75. Berkeley: University of California Press, 1989.

Clements, Niki Kasumi. "Foucault's Christianities." *Journal of the American Academy of Religion* 89, no. 1 (2021): 1–40.

Coviello, Peter M. *Tomorrow's Parties: Sex and the Untimely in Nineteenth-Century America.* New York: NYU Press, 2013.

Crawford, Patricia. *European Sexualities, 1400–1800.* Cambridge: Cambridge University Press, 2007.

Crawford, Patricia. "Sexual Knowledge in England, 1500–1750." In *Sexual Knowledge, Sexual Science: The History of Attitudes to Sexuality*, edited by Roy Porter and Mikuláš Teich, 82–106. Cambridge: Cambridge University Press, 1994.

Cunha, Emma Salgård. "Whitefield and Literary Affect." In *George Whitefield: Life, Context, and Legacy*, edited by Geordan Hammond and David Ceri Jones, 190–206. New York: Oxford University Press, 2016.

Dale, Amelia. *The Printed Reader: Gender, Quixotism, and Textual Bodies in Eighteenth-Century Britain.* Lewisburg, PA: Bucknell University Press, 2019.

de Grazia, Margreta, and Peter Stallybrass. "The Materiality of the Shakespearean Text." *Shakespeare Quarterly* 44, no. 3 (1993): 255–83.

de Jong, Mayke. "Transformations of Penance." In *Rituals of Power: From Late Antiquity to the Early Middle Ages*, edited by Frans Theuws and Janet L. Nelson, 185–224. Leiden: Brill, 2000.

de Souza, Igor. "Elenx de Céspedes: Indeterminate Genders in the Spanish Inquisition." In *Trans Historical: Gender Plurality before the Modern*, edited by Greta LaFleur, Masha Raskolnikov, and Anna Klosowska, 42–67. Ithaca, NY: Cornell University Press, 2021.

Eronania. London: H. Parker, 1724.

Floyer, John, and Edward Baynard. *Psychrolousia, or, The History of Cold-bathing.* 5th ed. London: William and John Innys, 1722.

Foucault, Michel. *Abnormal: Lectures at the Collège de France, 1974–1975.* Translated by Graham Burchell. New York: Picador, 2003.

Foucault, Michel. *About the Beginning of the Hermeneutics of the Self: Two Lectures at Dartmouth College, 1980*. Translated by Graham Burchell. Chicago: University of Chicago Press, 2015.

Foucault, Michel. *Histoire de la sexualité I: La volonté de savoir*. Paris: Gallimard, 1976.

Foucault, Michel. *The History of Sexuality, Volume 1: An Introduction*. Translated by Robert Hurley. New York: Vintage, 1990.

Foucault, Michel. *On the Government of the Living: Lectures at the Collège de France, 1979–1980*. Translated by Graham Burchell. New York: Palgrave Macmillan, 2014.

Foucault, Michel. *Power/Knowledge: Selected Interviews and Other Writings, 1972–1977*. New York: Knopf, 1980.

Franklin, Benjamin. *The Complete Works of Benjamin Franklin, Vol. 1*. Edited by John Bigelow. New York: Putnam's Sons, 1887.

Freeman, Lisa A. *Antitheatricality and the Body Public*. Philadelphia: University of Pennsylvania Press, 2017.

Freeman, Lisa A. *Character's Theater: Genre and Identity on the Eighteenth-Century English Stage*. Philadelphia: University of Pennsylvania Press, 2002.

A Gentleman in New England. *The State of Religion in New-England, Since the Reverend Mr. George Whitefield's Arrival There*. Glasgow: R. Foulis, 1742.

A Gentleman of Pembroke College, Oxon. *A Letter to the Reverend Mr. Whitefield*. London: M. Cooper, n.d.

Gibson, William, and Joanne Begiato. *Sex and the Church in the Long Eighteenth Century: Religion, Enlightenment and the Sexual Revolution*. London: I. B. Tauris, 2017.

Gillies, John. *Memoirs of the Life of the Reverend George Whitefield*. London: Edward and Charles Dilly, 1772.

Godbeer, Richard. *Sexual Revolution in Early America*. Baltimore: Johns Hopkins University Press, 2002.

Goldberg, Jonathan. "Hamlet's Hand." *Shakespeare Quarterly* 39, no. 3 (1988): 307–27.

Granger, Thomas. *The Tree of Good and Euill: or, a Profitable and Familiar Exposition of the Commandments*. London: N.O. for Samuel Man, 1616.

Green, James N. "Part One: English Books and Printing in the Age of Franklin." In *A History of the Book in America*, 5 vols., edited by Hugh Amory and David D. Hall, 1:260–61. New York: Cambridge University Press, 2000.

Griffith, R. Marie. *Born Again Bodies: Flesh and Spirit in American Christianity*. Berkeley: University of California Press, 2004.

Guest, Harriet. "Eighteenth-Century Femininity: 'A Supposed Sexual Character.'" In *Women and Literature in Britain, 1700–1800*, edited by Vivien Jones, 44–68. Cambridge: Cambridge University Press, 2000.

Hall, David D., and Russell L. Martin. "A Note on Popular and Durable Authors and Titles." In *A History of the Book in America*, 5 vols., edited by Hugh Amory and David D. Hall, 1:519–21. New York: Cambridge University Press, 2000.

Halperin, David M. "Forgetting Foucault." In *How to Do the History of Homosexuality*, 24–47. Chicago: University of Chicago Press, 2002.

Harvey, Karen. *Reading Sex in the Eighteenth Century: Bodies and Gender in English Erotic Culture*. New York: Cambridge University Press, 2004.
Hempton, David. *Methodism: Empire of the Spirit*. New Haven, CT: Yale University Press, 2005.
Hindmarsh, D. Bruce. *The Evangelical Conversion Narrative: Spiritual Autobiography in Early Modern England*. New York: Oxford University Press, 2005.
Hindmarsh, D. Bruce. *The Spirit of Early Evangelicalism: True Religion in a Modern World*. New York: Oxford University Press, 2018.
Hitchcock, Tim. *English Sexualities, 1700–1800*. New York: St. Martin's, 1997.
Hitchcock, Tim. "The Reformulation of Sexual Knowledge in Eighteenth-Century England." *Signs: The Journal of Women in Culture and Society* 37, no. 4 (2012): 823–31.
Holyoke, Edward. *The Testimony of the President, Professors, Tutors and Hebrew Instructor of Harvard College*. Boston: T. Fleet, 1744.
Howard, Jean E. *The Stage and Social Struggle in Early Modern England*. New York: Routledge, 2003.
Jephson, Ralph. *Methodism and Enthusiasm Fully Display'd*. London: M. Cooper, 1743.
Jordan, Mark. *The Invention of Sodomy in Christian Theology*. Chicago: University of Chicago Press, 1998.
Juster, Susan. *Disorderly Women: Sexual Politics and Evangelicalism in Revolutionary New England*. Ithaca, NY: Cornell University Press, 1994.
Kidd, Thomas S. *George Whitefield: America's Spiritual Founding Father*. New Haven, CT: Yale University Press, 2014.
Kopelson, Heather. *Faithful Bodies: Performing Religion and Race in the Puritan Atlantic*. New York: NYU Press, 2014.
LaFleur, Greta. *The Natural History of Sexuality in Early America*. Baltimore: Johns Hopkins University Press, 2018.
Lambert, Frank. *"Pedlar in Divinity": George Whitefield and the Transatlantic Revivals, 1737–1770*. Princeton, NJ: Princeton University Press, 1994.
Laqueur, Thomas W. *Solitary Sex: A Cultural History of Masturbation*. New York: Zone, 2003.
Larson, Scott. "Enthusiastic Sensations: Religious Revivals, Secular Bodies, and the Making of Modern Sexualities in Early American Culture." PhD diss., George Washington University, 2017.
Lewis, Simon. *Anti-Methodism and Theological Controversy in Eighteenth-Century England: The Struggle for True Religion*. New York: Oxford University Press, 2022.
Looby, Christopher. "Sexuality, History, Difficulty, Pleasure." *J19: The Journal of Nineteenth-Century Americanists* 1, no. 2 (2013): 253–58.
Lynch, Deidre Shauna. *The Economy of Character: Novels, Market Culture, and the Business of Inner Meaning*. Chicago: University of Chicago Press, 1998.
Mack, Phyllis. *Heart Religion in the British Enlightenment: Gender and Emotion in Early Methodism*. Cambridge: Cambridge University Press, 2008.
Mandeville, Bernard. *A Modest Defence of Publick Stews*. London: T. Read, 1740.

Manning, Susan. *Poetics of Character: Transatlantic Encounters, 1700–1900*. Cambridge: Cambridge University Press, 2013.

Marsden, George. *Jonathan Edwards: A Life*. New Haven, CT: Yale University Press, 2003.

Mather, Cotton. *The Pure Nazarite: Advice to a Young Man*. Boston: T. Fleet for John Phillips, 1723.

McDowell, Paula. *The Invention of the Oral: Print Commerce and Fugitive Voices in Eighteenth-Century Britain*. Chicago: University of Chicago Press, 2017.

McInelly, Brett C. *Textual Warfare and the Making of Methodism*. Oxford: Oxford University Press, 2014.

McKenzie, D. F. *Bibliography and the Sociology of Texts*. London: British Library, 1986.

Miller, Mark J. *Cast Down: Abjection in America, 1700–1850*. Philadelphia: University of Pennsylvania Press, 2016.

Myles, Anne G. "Queering the Study of Early American Sexuality." *William and Mary Quarterly* 60, no. 1 (2003): 199–202.

Nicolazzo, Sarah. "Henry Fielding's 'The Female Husband' and the Sexuality of Vagrancy." *Eighteenth Century* 55, no. 4 (2014): 335–53.

O'Brien, Glen. "'A Divine Attraction between Your Soul and Mine': George Whitefield and Same-Sex Affection in Eighteenth-Century Methodism." *Pacifica* 30, no. 2 (2017): 177–92.

Onania; Or, The Heinous Sin of Self-pollution. Boston: John Phillips, 1724.

Peters, Julie Stone. *Theatre of the Book, 1480–1880: Print, Text, and Performance in Europe*. New York: Oxford University Press, 2000.

Raven, James. "Publishing and Bookselling, 1660–1780." In *The Cambridge History of English Literature, 1660–1780*, edited by John Richetti, 11–36. Cambridge: Cambridge University Press, 2005.

Reilly, Elizabeth Carroll, and David D. Hall. "Customers and the Market for Books." In *A History of the Book in America*, 5 vols., edited by Hugh Amory and David D. Hall, 1:387–98. New York: Cambridge University Press, 2000.

Rivers, Isabel. "John Wesley as Editor and Publisher." In *The Cambridge Companion to John Wesley*, edited by Randy Maddox and Jason Vickers, 144–59. New York: Cambridge University Press, 2010.

Rivers, Isabel. "Religious Publishing." In *The Cambridge History of the Book in Britain: Volume V, 1695–1830*, edited by Michael F. Suarez and Michael L. Turner, 579–600. Cambridge: Cambridge University Press, 2009.

Runge, Laura L., and Pat Rogers, eds. *Producing the Eighteenth-Century Book: Writers and Publishers in England, 1650–1800*. Newark: University of Delaware Press, 2009.

Ruttenburg, Nancy. *Democratic Personality: Popular Voice and the Trial of American Authorship*. Stanford, CA: Stanford University Press, 1998.

Schubert, Karsten. "The Christian Roots of Critique." *Le foucaldien* 7, no. 1 (2021): 1–11.

Sedgwick, Eve Kosofsky. "Jane Austen and the Masturbating Girl." *Critical Inquiry* 17, no. 4 (1991): 826–27.

Stahuljak, Zrinka. "Transgender Translation, Humanism, and Periodization: Vasco da Lucena's Deeds of Alexander the Great." In *Trans Historical: Gender Plurality before the Modern*, edited by Greta LaFleur, Masha Raskolnikov, and Anna Klosowska, 207–31. Ithaca, NY: Cornell University Press, 2021.

Stallybrass, Peter. "Books and Scrolls: Navigating the Bible." In *Books and Readers in Early Modern England: Material Studies*, edited by Jennifer Andersen and Elizabeth Sauer, 42–79. Philadelphia: University of Pennsylvania Press, 2002.

Stern, Tiffany. "Stage Directions." In *Book Parts*, edited by Dennis Duncan and Adam Smyth, 177–90. New York: Oxford University Press, 2019.

Stevenson, David. "Recording the Unspeakable: Masturbation in the Diary of William Drummond, 1657–1659." *Journal of the History of Sexuality* 9, no. 3 (2000): 223–39.

Stolberg, Michael. *Homo Patiens: Krankheits- und Körpererfahrung in der Frühen Neuzeit*. Weimar: Böhlau, 2003.

Stolberg, Michael. "Self-Pollution, Moral Reform, and the Venereal Trade: Notes on the Sources and Historical Context of *Onania* (1716)." *Journal of the History of Sexuality* 9, no. 1 (2000): 37–61.

Stone, Lawrence. *The Family, Sex, and Marriage in England, 1500–1800*. New York: Harper and Row, 1977.

Stout, Harry S. *The Divine Dramatist: George Whitefield and the Rise of Modern Evangelicalism*. Grand Rapids, MI: Eerdmans, 1991.

Straub, Kristina. *Sexual Suspects: Eighteenth-Century Players and Sexual Ideology*. Princeton, NJ: Princeton University Press, 1992.

Suarez, Michael F. "In Good Company: The Business of Abridgements in Eighteenth-Century England." In *Textual Transformations: Purposing and Repurposing Books from Richard Baxter to Samuel Taylor Coleridge*, edited by Tessa Whitehouse and N. H. Keeble, 153–70. New York: Oxford University Press, 2019.

Thomas, Keith. *Religion and the Decline of Magic: Studies in Popular Beliefs in Sixteenth- and Seventeenth-Century England*. New York: Scribner, 1971.

Thompson, E. P. *The Making of the English Working Class*. New York: Pantheon, 1964.

Thomson, Ann. *Bodies of Thought: Science, Religion, and the Soul in the Early Enlightenment*. New York: Oxford University Press, 2008.

Tissot, S. A. D. *Thoughts on the Sin of Onan, Chiefly Extracted from a Late Writer*. [Edited by John Wesley.] London, 1767.

Tortorici, Zeb. *Sins against Nature: Sex and Archives in Colonial New Spain*. Durham, NC: Duke University Press, 2018.

Trapp, Joseph. *The Nature, Folly, Sin, and Danger of Being Righteous Over-much*. London: S. Austen, 1739.

Trumbach, Randolph. *Sex and the Gender Revolution, Volume 1: Heterosexuality and the Third Gender in Enlightenment London*. Chicago: University of Chicago Press, 1998.

Vermeer, Leonieke. "Tiny Symbols Tell Big Stories: Naming and Concealing Masturbation in Diaries (1660–1940)." *European Journal of Life Writing* 6 (2017): 101–34.

Warner, Michael. *The Letters of the Republic: Publication and the Public Sphere in Eighteenth-Century America*. Cambridge, MA: Harvard University Press, 1990.

Warner, Michael. "The Preacher's Footing." In *This Is Enlightenment*, edited by Clifford Siskin and William Warner, 368–83. Chicago: University of Chicago Press, 2010.

Wesley, John. *An Extract of Rev. Mr. John Wesley's Journal, from Nov. 2, 1751, to Oct. 28, 1754*. London, 1788.

Wesley, John. *Thoughts on a Single Life*. London, 1765.

West, Shearer. "Wilkes's Squint: Synecdochic Physiognomy and Political Identity in Eighteenth-Century Print Culture." *Eighteenth-Century Studies* 33, no. 1 (1999): 65–84.

Wheeler, Roxann. *The Complexion of Race: Categories of Difference in Eighteenth-Century British Culture*. Philadelphia: University of Pennsylvania Press, 2000.

Whitefield, George. *The Benefits of an Early Piety: A Sermon Preach'd at Bow Church . . . Before the Religious Societies, at one of their Quarterly Meetings*. London: Rivington and Hutton, 1737.

Whitefield, George. *A Brief and General Account of the First Part of the Life of the Reverend Mr. Geo. Whitefield*. Philadelphia: B. Franklin, 1740.

Whitefield, George. "A General Account of the First Part of My Life." 1739. Pierpont Morgan Library, New York, MS MA742.

Whitefield, George. "Letter 433: To Mr. M—A—, at Morpeth, from Edinburgh, July 26, 1742." In *The Works of the Reverend George Whitefield*, 6 vols., 1:411–12. London: Edward and Charles Dilly, 1771–72.

Whitefield, George. "Sermon 14: The Lord our Righteousness." In *The Works of the Reverend George Whitefield*, 6 vols., 5:204–23. London: Edward and Charles Dilly, 1771–72.

Whitefield, George. *A Short Account of God's Dealings with the Reverend Mr. George Whitefield*. London: W. Strahan, 1740.

Whitehouse, Tessa. "Structures and Processes of English Spiritual Autobiography from Bunyan to Cowper." In *A History of English Autobiography*, edited by Adam Smyth, 103–18. New York: Cambridge University Press, 2016.

Williams, Abigail. *The Social Life of Books: Reading Together in the Eighteenth-century Home*. New Haven, CT: Yale University Press, 2017.

Winckles, Andrew O. *Eighteenth-Century Women's Writing and the Methodist Media Revolution: "Consider the Lord as Ever Present Reader."* Liverpool: Liverpool University Press, 2019.

Wood, Marcus. *Slavery, Empathy, and Pornography*. New York: Oxford University Press, 2002.

Zaret, David. *Origins of Democratic Culture: Printing, Petitions, and the Public Sphere in Early-Modern England*. Princeton, NJ: Princeton University Press, 2000.

III FANTASIES OF REALISM

SIX · *Justine S. Murison*

Secularism, Hypocrisy, and the Afterlives of Thomas Paine

Forty-five years after his death in 1809, Thomas Paine wrote a book. Titled *The Philosophy of Creation* and "transcribed" by the medium Horace G. Wood, it sought to expose the "most gross and monstrous errors" of Christian theories of creation and to provide an empirical testament of heaven from beyond the grave. The *Liberator* reprinted an excerpt of the book in the March 17, 1854, issue under the headline "Thomas Paine and His Traducers." Out of over one hundred pages of the original, the *Liberator* highlighted what might, in context, seem an ancillary point. From beyond the grave, Paine reports: "It is claimed, and believed by the religious world, that I died a most *excruciating* and *horrible* death; that my screams for mercy, and prayers of repentance, were so loud as to deafen all other sounds within a 'quarter of a mile of the "hovel" in which I died.' It is said I desired a priest to be called in, that I might be prayed for, and find favor in the sight of God; that I denounced my writings, &c., &c., to infinity."[1] Paine goes on to deny these rumors—"I died *quietly* and *calmly*, with little pain, and no terror"—but we might well ask why Paine needed to come back from the dead to set this record straight in the first place.[2] But he did. Because while Paine may have died obscurely in 1809, American Tract Society pamphlets, newspaper and magazine articles, and evangelical sermons circulating in the 1830s, 1840s, and 1850s recounted apocryphal tales of his death, claiming that he called out for both a minister and God's help—proof that "infidelity" (unbelief in God) failed even the most ardent of unbelievers at their moment of crisis.[3] These stories built up what Moncure Conway would later call the "Paine mythology," in which Paine's irreligion and immorality led to a hypocritical death.⁴ By the 1850s, Paine had come to stand for two things in the United States: On the one hand, he was the figure invoked along with Voltaire and Rousseau as the prime example of radical, openly avowed atheism, tied intimately to the French Revolution and the Terror (despite himself being thrown in prison by the French revolutionary government). On the other hand, Paine also became one of the most prominent examples of an infidel hypocrite.

Paine has always been on the margins of the panoply of "Founding Fathers." Neither a statesman nor a military leader, he was, as Edward Larkin has argued, a professional writer, and as such, he was already under a cloud of suspicion while he was still alive.⁵ If we add to this his hostile open letter to George Washington and his publication of *The Age of Reason* (1794), which this essay will consider, Paine's marginalization was solidified before the end of the 1790s. That said, Paine's antebellum identity as a hypocrite does not necessarily distinguish him from more prominent framers like Thomas Jefferson, George Washington, Alexander Hamilton, or Benjamin Franklin, all of whom have come under renewed scrutiny for their hypocrisies in both the field of early American studies and in popular US culture more broadly.

In this essay, I do not treat this heightened attention to hypocrisy as an endpoint for analysis, though; instead, hypocrisy's consistent presence in our culture as a moral judgment is an opening to see how it became salient during the early republic, the era in which the disestablishment of state churches shifted questions of religious and sexual morality to the private sphere. The wager of this essay is that Paine's cultural afterlife—as both an open atheist and, however contradictorily, a sneaking moral hypocrite—can generatively recalibrate how scholars of the early republic define "religion," and help us to explain more precisely why one's private morality came to be a public question in the United States despite the disestablishment of state churches. As I will examine it here, trying to understand the rise of hypocrisy as a moral value is not a question of the persistence of *religion* in the public sphere, but a question of how *secular society* thinks about—and disciplines—morality. In other words, I argue that pervasive accusations of hypocrisy in US culture come down ultimately to a question not of religion but of secularism.

Secularism is the ideology invested in the modern progress narrative toward rationality and away from credulity, a narrative often referred to as the "secularization thesis."⁶ One of the ideology's central myths rests on the importance of relocating to the private sphere religious beliefs and practices deemed incompatible with modernity and liberation. Through the privatization of religion, the private sphere thus became much more than a location or domicile; rather, as Saba Mahmood explains, the relocation of religion to the private sphere further entrenched state power over the "private" questions of family, sex, and sexuality.[7] As I will show, charges of hypocrisy—so rife in twenty-first-century public discourse—gained a type of public moral salience through this privatization process.

However ironically it seems, private life could no longer be truly private after the disestablishment of state churches. Instead, disestablishment—long described as the "privatization" of religion—profoundly reshaped public life around a drive for moral authenticity and a subjectivity whose "sovereignty had to be demonstrated through acts of sincerity," as Talal Asad has put it.[8] If privacy is publicly oriented, privacy's opposite is not publicity but sinful secrecy, and accusations of hypocrisy are how the US policed and continues to police this terrain. In this way, hypocrisy—which signals a disconnection between public persona and private self—has come to operate as a potent language of morality in our secular age.

This moral language is perhaps best evident not so much in tracts decrying Paine's hypocrisy—tracts with which this essay begins and ends—but with the novel at the heart of its argument, Royall Tyler's *The Algerine Captive* (1797). For it is in novels like Tyler's that eighteenth- and nineteenth-century readers learned to believe in private selves—and to desire the exposure of those selves. As the literary form most closely associated with modern subjectivity and the private lives of individuals, the novel was well attuned to emergent forms of privacy, and it was especially well attuned to the primary mechanism by which that emergent privacy would be constituted as the deepest, most authentic expression of the self: through the gesture of public revelation or exposure. Updike Underhill's fictional narrative of conversion, as I will discuss below, shows how a discourse of private conscience provided a language for acceptable forms of belief in US secularism. And his meeting with that radical deist Thomas Paine is what sets him on this trajectory toward acceptable private belief.

SECULARISM AND HYPOCRISY

The era of the early republic was an important historical pivot for the emergence of secularism in the United States. In these years, the disestablishment of state religions, fought for by an unlikely alliance of Republican deists and evangelical denominations, forged a discursive association between private religion and religious liberty. Over the course of the fifty-year process that we gather together under the single term *disestablishment*, states outlawed a variety of practices that knit a church or churches into civic life: the use of tax money to support the clergy of a favored sect or sects; religious tests for office holding; government control over theological issues and ministerial appointments; and mandatory church attendance, among other practices.[9] The movement in various states to disestablish churches (with taxation and religious tests as the most prominent targets) had, by 1790, achieved many of its goals in all but three (Connecticut, Massachusetts, New Hampshire).

It is important to state clearly what this meant: the question was not whether belief or religion should be banished from politics, but whether organized religion (i.e., a church) should be supported by and involved with the state. To the extent that this is a secularization process, we should think of it as the process by which religion was redefined as private for the nineteenth century, with both sides of the debate drawing on longer histories, theologies, and philosophies to new ends. One of those new ends can be seen as the revivals of the Second Great Awakening, which fueled both what Charles Taylor has called the "nova effect" of the secular age—the ever-increasing proliferation of beliefs and spiritualities—and the non-denominational work of such institutions as the American Tract Society and the American Bible Society all of which solidified Protestant Christianity as an "unmarked category" in American public discourse, as Tracy Fessenden has shown.[10] Above all else, the regime of "heart" religion—evangelicalism—depended on a logic of authenticity expressed in its commitment to public conversion and true, private feeling, and it was defined by its capacity to stand both for generalized "morality" *and* religious liberty.

Another effect of this process of redefining religion in the early republic was the heightened attention to moral hypocrisy. The project of what, in the eighteenth century, was often called "private conscience" was cast as freeing people from moral hypocrisy—particularly the hypocrisy of having to publicly support a religious institution while failing to truly believe in its doctrines. As Thomas Jefferson asserted in *Notes on the State of Virginia* (1785), an established church may make someone "worse by making him a hypocrite, but it will never make him a truer man."[11] This logic of authenticity was reinforced by the upswelling of Romanticism, which often stretched this Protestant framework nearly to its breaking point. "No law can be sacred to me but that of my nature," Ralph Waldo Emerson declares in "Self-Reliance" (1841), "Good and bad are but names very readily transferable to that or this; the only right is what is after my constitution, the only wrong what is against it."[12]

Hypocrisy, of course, is a moral concept with a long history. From Sophocles to Machiavelli, the uses and abuses of hypocrisy have animated theology, political intrigue, philosophical debate, and theatrical and antitheatrical theory. However, political theorists Hannah Arendt and Judith Shklar both discern a shift with regard to hypocrisy in the late eighteenth century.[13] This is the era that invested in sincerity as a political and cultural value, and it became inextricable from the rise of liberalism and the liberal nation-state. In her subtle analysis of hypocrisy, Shklar expands on sincerity as a moral code deeply embedded in liberal societies. She cites Benjamin Franklin as a prominent example of the way hypocrisy operated on the precipice of this political shift. As he recounts in *The Autobiography* (1791), Franklin obscures his deist inclinations since they upset others; he plays down his own role in starting big public projects in order to achieve consensus on them; he pays dues to all the Philadelphia churches; and he attends, above all, to the appearance of his virtue, from his early years (when he "took care not only to be in *Reality* Industrious and frugal, but to avoid all *Appearances* of the contrary") to his later accounting books for virtuous living (where, tongue in cheek, he notes that he added Humility to his list but that he could not "boast of much Success in acquiring the *Reality* of this Virtue," though he "had a good deal with regard to the *Appearance* of it").[14]

Franklin exemplifies a moral order much more oriented to a public self. Yet while his narrative shows a delight in the affordances of hypocrisy, its form—the "memoir," as the first edition explicitly named it—is exactly invested in the types of sincerity emerging in the Revolutionary era. We see the moral value accorded to sincerity when he confesses his well-meaning deceptions (and a few that were not so well meaning). When a culture values sincerity, this value is not shorn of the idea of performance. In fact, the very valuation of it depends on a public performance of one's adherence to an even more private self. Sincerity, in other words, points inward but is not a raw experience of that interiority. It is, instead, a performance of that deeper self.

With this distinction in mind, we can see how nineteenth-century American culture embraced a further investment—not just in *sincerity* but in *authenticity*. These are not opposite qualities; rather, they are degrees. A thoroughly Romantic quality still highly valued in American culture today, authenticity imagines a public self that is not performing, that is as sincere as one can be to an inner truth. Valuing authenticity means despising even the roles and poses of sincerity. Its moral value rose instead from publicly displaying a strong sense of one's authentic selfhood, which increasingly came to be synonymous with rough edges and natural emotions. Indeed, as Romantic and sentimental literature continuously show us, a culture steeped in a language of authenticity proved to be one obsessed with peeking behind the veil and rooting out the real person behind the plausible self-presentation, responses that came to seem like both a moral necessity and a sign of financial savvy. And as Shklar notes, the "uneasy fear of fraud and dissimulation" is also characteristic of democracies.[15]

RELIGIOUS PURITY AND THOMAS PAINE

The importance of hypocrisy to United States politics began with the debates over disestablishment at the end of the eighteenth century. In these years, a discursive consolidation emerged in which private religion (or, the term that was often favored in the period, *private conscience*) became the dominant way to define "religion" in general. "Private conscience" expressed the overriding emphasis (Protestant as it was) that religion began and was substantively made up of *belief*, primarily a mental consent not an embodied practice. If religion was immaterial in this way, though, it also seemed vulnerable, especially to the influence of other beliefs and more especially one's own passions; it was therefore something to be protected, nurtured, and purified.

Many of the most prominent arguments for disestablishing state churches rested on the importance of private religion to liberty. For instance, in his "Memorial and Remonstrance" to the Virginia Assembly in 1785, James Madison asserted that religious freedom was a natural right. With a hearty dose of anti-Catholicism, Madison rests this claim on a Protestant sentiment that he universalizes: that to pass church establishment laws is to deny people a fundamental right to a personal relationship with God. And he pinpoints political tyranny and its investment in church establishments for particular ire. "Rulers who wished to subvert the public liberty," Madison explains, "may have found an established Clergy convenient auxiliaries. A just Government instituted to secure & perpetuate it needs them not."[16] To Madison, corruption already riddles church establishments, even before the political tyrant comes on the scene.

Conversely, political tyranny finds in established churches a useful tool to solidify power. Relegating religion to private conscience, he implies, fights tyranny and keeps religion free.

Joining republican voices such as Madison's in the fight against established churches, denominations from Baptists to Unitarians advocated removing establishments (to which they were losing potential church revenue) based on the need to protect private conscience. As the Danbury Baptist Association wrote to Thomas Jefferson, congratulating him on his election in 1800, "Our Sentiments are uniformly on the side of Religious Liberty—That Religion is at all times and places a Matter between God and Individuals—That no man aught to suffer in Name, person or effects on account of his religious Opinions."[17] As we saw with Madison, private religion is Protestant religion in this argument, based largely on a theory that religion is a "Matter between God and Individuals" rather than church hierarchies and ritual practice.

But it is not just that private religion is free; it is also pure. In *The Age of Reason*, for example, Paine claims that the American Revolution allowed "man to return to the pure, unmixed, and unadulterated belief of one God, and no more."[18] Unlike Jefferson, Paine drew more dire conclusions about the hypocrisy lurking in societies with established churches. Not only did it encourage superstition and "priest-craft," it was the real source of infidelity. "When a man has so far corrupted and prostituted the chastity of his mind," he writes, "as to subscribe his professional belief to things he does not believe, he has prepared himself for the commission of every other crime."[19] For both Jefferson and Paine, religious freedom was constituted by a rejection of secrecy, and, in action, it stood for the opposite of hypocrisy. But we should not speed too quickly past Paine's turn of phrase for this type of hypocrisy: corrupting and prostituting the "chastity" of the "mind." When religion is imagined as consenting to a series of propositional beliefs, the wholly internal workings of this process can be threatened by passions and other unregulated ideas and urges. Paine assumes that the goal should be to purify and protect that process.

What we see in these arguments is a series of conflations: private religion is pure religion, and private, pure religion constitutes "freedom." The debate between those who favored disestablishment and their opponents often found common ground in this theory of religion. As Jefferson famously put it, "The legitimate powers of government extend to such acts only as are injurious to others. . . . But it does me no injury for my neighbour to say there are twenty gods, or no god. It neither picks my pocket nor breaks my leg."[20] Yet it is precisely this flippant attitude toward atheism—not Jefferson's mention of twenty gods but the possibility of believing in no god—that steeled their opponents, who foresaw a fearful slide from private religion into lawless, licentious chaos.

If religion were indeed to be privatized, the potential that it could also house *unbelief* needed to be significantly reined in. Consequently, the 1790s experienced rising levels of paranoia around what was often called "infidelity." As Gretchen Murphy usefully explains, in the eighteenth century "infidel" absorbed the meaning of "heretic," a term for a cultural outsider, such that "it could connote either disbelief, or unorthodox belief, or religious dissent, assigning foreign menace to them all."[21] Accusations of infidelity were on the rise in the 1790s, but this should not be confused with a groundswell of skepticism. As Christopher Grasso points out, at the end of the eighteenth century, "Christians worried about the foreign contagion of British deism and French infidel philosophy" even as the "number of Americans who had imbibed such notions was probably small."[22]

Fueling this paranoia was the French Revolution, particularly its anticlericalism and the violence of the Reign of Terror. It generated a stark partisan divide between the Federalists and Democratic-Republicans, and the specter of infidelity became a standard wedge wielded most often by Federalists for both political and religious goals. Federalists feared that, without either state churches or a belief in revealed religion and divine retribution, citizens would become vulnerable to the seductions of atheism, as they had in France. In this environment, the threat that any belief could slide into no belief became, as Eric R. Schlereth argues, "a limit to tolerable expression" and "the periphery of the acceptable," and thus infidelity "helped believers of various denominations define themselves in more general or generically 'Christian' terms."[23] As Grasso also notes, "Liberty of conscience might have to be stretched far to contain the sectarian diversity of America," but it could not go "beyond the bounds of what many considered to be common sense: morality rested in a belief in a God who would punish bad behavior even when the state could not; this belief, in turn, relied on the recognition that the Bible was God's revealed Word and that its warnings were true."[24] Or as William Linn retorted in his argument against Jefferson's election in 1800, "Let my neighbour once persuade himself that there is no God, and he will soon pick my pocket, and break not only my *leg* but my *neck*."[25]

Even more than Jefferson, Thomas Paine came to symbolize the seductive threat of infidelity for the new nation, and he continued to do so well into the nineteenth century. When he published *The Age of Reason*, Paine's stated intention was a defense of private conscience against French revolutionary attempts to dechristianize French nationalism. It was read, however, as an attack not just on organized religion but on revealed religion and therefore a grave threat to the morality of the nation. *The Age of Reason* was both popular and controversial, but not because Paine gave voice to new ideas. Indeed, Paine's argument for natural religion was not unique; Hume, Bolingbroke, and others had thoroughly canvassed these topics before him. What separated *The Age of Reason* from its cohorts was its style and wide circulation. Paine finished part 1 just as he was arrested by the French revolutionary guard, and he handed the manuscript to Joel Barlow quite literally on his way to Luxembourg Prison. Barlow managed to publish part 1 in London, where it sold for the very cheap rate of one shilling. American editions of part 1, according to Schlereth, "appeared in the shops of booksellers from Boston to Philadelphia during the summer of 1794."[26]

The second part of *The Age of Reason* had a similar trajectory, but also included Paine's self-financed shipping of 15,000 copies to the United States. Additionally, seventeen editions would be published by 1797 in the United States, and the Democratic-Republican printer and editor Benjamin Franklin Bache printed the two parts together in 1797, selling 100,000 copies in that year alone.[27] By 1800, *The Age of Reason* had gone through twenty-one American editions.[28] All that said, *The Age of Reason* proved to be most popular among college students and with urban literary circles. For instance, the Friendly Club, whose members included Charles Brockden Brown, Elihu Hubbard Smith, and William Dunlap, had "many hearty laughing-spells" while reading the second part of *The Age of Reason*, which contained the majority of Paine's barbs about revealed religion.[29]

Not quite seeing the joke that the Friendly Club did, Paine's opponents responded anxiously to what they perceived to be a print world saturated with Paine's attacks on organized religion, revealed religion, miracles, and the Bible as the Word of God, along with his defense of natural religion and deism. Thirty-five responses to *The Age of Reason* came out within a decade of the publication of part 1 in 1794, and denunciations continued strong through the first decade of the nineteenth century. The responses from ministers were often long and thorough, and they took special issue with Paine's critiques of both organized and revealed religion. Richard

Watson (Anglican bishop of Llandaff and Paine's most well circulated critic in the Atlantic world) denounced *The Age of Reason* as "the poison of infidelity" and targeted Paine's logic about the salutary benefit of following private belief over trust in organized religions and a learned ministry: "It's a maxim of every law, human and divine, that a man ought never to act in opposition to his conscience: but it will not from thence follow, that he will, in obeying the dictates of his conscience, on all occasions act right. An inquisitor, who burns jews and heretics; a Robespierre, who massacres innocent and harmless women; a robber who thinks that all things ought to be in common, and that a state of property is an unjust infringement of natural liberty:—these, and a thousand perpetrators of different crimes, may all follow the dictates of conscience."[30] Private conscience with no established church to help guide it, in Watson's account of world history, leads not to a moral society but to the Inquisition and the French Revolution. Uzal Ogden, an Episcopalian minister from New Jersey, sounded the same alarm: "When the restraints of religion are dissolved, what can be expected, but that men should *abandon* themselves to the impulse of their passions? Human laws and penalties will be *insufficient* to restrain men from licentiousness, where there is no just sense of the Deity; no regard to a future state, or to the due punishment of vice, and the rewards of virtue hereafter."[31] For both Watson and Ogden, private belief is not always reliable. Just because it is an internal voice, that does not mean it is for the good. Passions are *also* internal, and they are as likely to steer one astray as not.

Watson's argument against relying on private conscience alone was part of his larger defense of established religion (in this case, the Church of England). Paine's American detractors like Ogden, on the other hand, often voiced the fear that the unregulated passions unleashed by infidelity would subject citizens to a new tyranny. According to Ogden, Paine's treatise will "plunge us into ignorance and error; superstition and idolatry, and fix on us the fetters of slavery."[32] Slavery is the endpoint of a journey that begins with questioning revealed religion, Ogden and many others implied. The concern about tyranny often merged with a language of seduction. For example, Elias Boudinot's *Age of Revelation; or, The Age of Reason Shewn to Be an Age of Infidelity* (1801) warns the young men of the United States, "The boldness of impiety is often mistaken for knowledge, founded on an independent spirit, and thereby saps the necessary defence of simple innocence and unsuspecting modesty."[33] In a culture awash with seduction narratives, religious infidels and Jacobin radicals were easily cast as seducers and villains.[34]

In arguing in this way, Paine's critics sought to undermine his narrative of liberation. In his addresses to Yale College graduates, subsequently printed as *The Nature and Danger of Infidel Philosophy* (1798), Timothy Dwight first blasts ancient, non-Christian philosophers for drunkenness and sodomy and then excoriates modern infidels' personal, private sins. Dwight cautions his auditors that what is most seductive about deists is their confident style of writing, which is bent on convincing readers that to believe in deism is to be free: "It is boldly asserted, that the world has hitherto lain in a state of ignorance and infancy; that it has been chained by authority, and influenced by superstition, but that it has, at the present time, broken at once its bonds, roused itself into manly exertion, and seized intuitively upon the whole system of truth, moral, political, and natural."[35] Like Boudinot, Dwight insists that the problem is "boldness," that is, the clarity as well as force by which deism is pronounced. By pretending to the name of emancipators, deists like Paine confuse unwitting American undergraduates into subscribing to irreligion.

As the outcry against *The Age of Reason* makes clear, Paine's detractors attempted to counter not just his logic but his style. And they often did so through ad hominem attacks. In fact, a pattern emerges in many of the responses to *The Age of Reason*: Paine's *taste* indexes his morality. And "taste," it should be said, was quite literal. Ogden speculates that perhaps Paine turned deist because "the refulgent light of Divine Revelation, gave too much pain to his *reddened* eyes of intemperance," and adds a footnote, in case the reader was not yet clear on his meaning, that "this expression alludes to a well known fact, that, unhappily, Mr. Paine is a drunkard."[36] Or as asserted in an article in the *British Review*, which circulated in American magazines, "From the time of his imprisonment in France . . . his drunkenness, brutality, and the pestilential filth of his person, added greatly to the detestation in which he began to be held by all mankind, even by the partizans of revolution and blood."[37]

These attacks on Paine's personal vice, I want to suggest, are of a piece with the attacks on his easy and seductive style of writing, which, to quote Grasso, had the effect of "shov[ing] deism out of the gentleman's salon into the taverns frequented by artisans and laborers."[38] One article in the *American Monthly Review* bemoaned Paine's "*dashing way*"; another critic classed Paine with William Godwin as one of "those illiterate, vulgar, ignorant scribblers."[39] William Cobbett, Paine's most vociferous foe in the United States, denounced Paine's "clumsy battered pen" and declared that *The Age of Reason* "is as stupid and despicable as its author."[40] And the *British*

Review article I cited above went so far as to say that Paine had encouraged "discontent and revolutionary fanaticism" by a "broad display, in their naked and barbarous forms, of those infidel and anarchical elements, which sophistry had, till his time, refined above the perceptions of the vulgar." The reviewer continues this clothing metaphor (no doubt an allusion to Paine's first job as a stay-maker): "By stripping the mischief of the dress, though still covering it with the name and boast of philosophy, he rendered it as familiar to the capacity as it was flattering to the passions of the mob."[41] Though Paine claims to cover his crime with the name of "philosophy," what he has done is strip "fanaticism" down for all to see. In doing so, he has made his attack on, among other things, Bible truth and revealed religion too easy to follow, and thus too seductive for those artisans and other "vulgar" types who before could not follow the philosophical arguments. As this critic concludes, "The turpitude of moral as well as natural deformity should not be exhibited, without a little drapery to satisfy the demands of ordinary decorum."[42]

What Paine's critics suggest is that he has tempted the lower classes with a strumpet tricked out to look like a philosopher. But what is worse, he has done it boldly, for all to see. While hidden deists haunt the Federalist imagination, these responses to Paine are also upset by too much plainness. This might well be the crux of the problem of private religion for Federalists like Dwight and Boudinot. That religion is constituted by sincerely held belief is as old as Protestantism, but that is also why Federalist ministers were concerned about the effects of disestablishment. Without organized religion, how would individuals navigate a swirl of passions and ideas and opinions, and where would that leave the state? Passions, not just beliefs, constitute one's private self; they are powerful, if invisible, and they can absolutely lead you astray. To be sure, these are particularly Federalist criticisms, and the authors all have a political as well as religious axe to grind. Even still, what they articulate in their response to Paine is a persistent problem that would animate conversations not just about the role of privately held religion in public life but the meaning of privacy itself.

A SLAVE'S ATTIRE

The result of being seduced by Paine was to be plunged into slavery. Or so Uzal Ogden, Timothy Dwight, and Elias Boudinot all warned. Royall Tyler structured the plot of *The Algerine Captive* to represent just such a slip from infidelity to enslavement, placing Paine at the transition between the two volumes of his novel.[43] Volume 1 of the novel is a comic picaresque, but volume 2 changes tone entirely, drawing on the genres of spiritual autobiography and travel narrative and emphasizing Updike Underhill's internal conversion to Christianity and his accounts of Algeria, Islam, and enslavement (both his own and the Africans he enslaves via his duties as doctor on a slave ship). *The Algerine Captive* is but one example of the longer history of borrowing from the spiritual autobiography to construct the novel form. As Jordan Alexander Stein has argued, one of the effects of this convergence is the tendency to cast character via negative figurations (of "humility, self-effacement, and subjective vulnerability before God") that was increasingly packaged in a narrative arc.[44] Underhill's character, as expanded on in volume 2 of the novel, partakes of this tradition, and Tyler ends by affirming the importance of private Christian belief for the stability of the new nation.

Underhill meets Paine at the critical turning point of the novel, as Paine became infamous for his publication of *The Age of Reason*. Paine, in this context, is an object of fascination and denunciation, so much so that Underhill can opine, "Omitting the lions in the tower, the regalia in the jewel office, and the other insignia of British royalty, of which Englishmen are so justly proud, I shall content myself with mentioning the most singular curiosity I saw in London. It was the celebrated Thomas Paine, author of 'Common Sense,' 'The Rights of Man,' and other writings, whose tendency is to overturn ancient opinions of government and religion."[45] Meeting Paine at the house of the painter John Trumbull, Underhill calls him an English "curiosity" worthy of tourism, and thus a figure of both obsolescence and nostalgia. Underhill goes on to underscore these qualities through a description of Paine's body and clothing. Paine's "bodily presence was both mean and contemptible." Clad in the dullest and coarsest of cloth ("a snuff-coloured coat, olive velvet vest, drab breeches, coarse hose") and sporting accessories long out of style ("shoe-buckles of the size of half a dollar" and the same wig "under the shadow of whose curls he wrote, 'Common Sense' in America many years before"), Paine is behind the fashions (88). He is a memento of a time to be praised but one long passed. By adding this element of belatedness, Tyler suggests a temporal lag that reflects the diminution of Paine's own reputation and influence in these years.

When turning to the controversial publication of *The Age of Reason*, Underhill opens by noting that he never actually heard Paine rail against religion, and that he was under the impression that Paine wrote the first part as a sop to the French revolutionary government, to get him out of Luxembourg Prison. "When the reign of the terrorists ceased, an apology was expected, and, even by the pious yet catholic American, would have been received," Underhill explains, but instead "no propitiatory sacrifice was made. This missionary of vice has proceeded proselyting" (91–92). Publishing the second part of *The Age of Reason* and infamously attacking George Washington, Paine secured a new and degraded reputation. Underhill explains: "A tasteful, though irreligious scholar might tolerate a chastised scepticism, if exhibited by an acute Hume, or an eloquent Bolingbroke. But one cannot repress the irritability of the fiery Hotspur, when one beholds the pillars of morality shaken by the rude shock of this modern vandal. The reader should learn, that his paltry system is only an outrage of wine; and that it is in the ale house he most vigorously assaults the authority of the prophets, and laughs most loudly at the gospel when in his cups" (92). Paine's personal style is obsolete, and his writing and drinking are likewise anachronistic, betraying a ruder time and taste—he is a modern vandal. In fact, here again we see the two meanings of "taste" intertwine: Paine's taste for wine begets his tasteless writing. Had he been more stylistically sober, as Hume and Bolingbroke were, the crime would not have been so egregious.

After dismissing *The Age of Reason* as produced by an old, obsolescent man in his cups, Underhill embarks as doctor on a slave ship heading to West Africa, a narrative shift that will result in his own enslavement and an affirmation of his private Christianity in the face of pressure to convert to Islam. From Underhill's dialogue with a "Mollah" (mullah) to his reactions to enslavement, the novel consistently turns to the importance of privately achieved conviction. The chapter in which Underhill consults with the Mollah is written in the form of a philosophical dialogue, and, as Elizabeth Fenton observes, it continually ends in a stalemate.[46] The Mollah counters Underhill's claim to "good evidence for the truth" of the Bible, with his own claim to the same about the Koran; Underhill opines that Islam is a violent religion, but the Mollah refutes this by recounting the history of Christian violence; and, finally, echoing John Locke, the Mollah points out that theology is learned, not inherent in the soul.

Yet theology is not the issue of this dialogue at all; if Underhill converts, he can escape slavery. Thus, when the Mollah concludes his appeal to Underhill, he does so in the language of liberty: "Throw off the shackles of education from your soul, and be welcome to the joys of the true believer" (136). The Mollah suggests that Underhill might escape both a metaphoric and literal enslavement by converting to Islam—by becoming yet a different kind of "infidel" than Jefferson or Paine were accused of being. Tyler thus returns infidelity to its original meaning, and poses it as a choice that Underhill then refuses: "I have thus given a few sketches of the manner of this artful priest. After five days conversation, disgusted with his fables, abashed by his assurance, and almost confounded by his sophistry, I resumed my slave's attire, and sought safety in my former servitude" (136). In this passage, Underhill embraces the language of revealed religion, one of Paine's main targets in *The Age of Reason*. Because he has no recourse in natural religion to counter the Mollah's arguments in favor of Islam, he rewrites the Mollah's evidence and argument as "fables" and "sophistry." Underhill cannot engage in a Habermasian public debate about the comparative merits of religions, a debate that was beginning to occur with more regularity in the Anglo-American world (albeit in a way that centralized Protestant Christianity).[47] Instead, he retreats into the position of "slave," which, like the position of "woman," ideologically represented the prepolitical private, as Elizabeth Maddock Dillon has argued.[48] Choosing slavery to affirm his Christianity therefore represents the ultimate expression of private religion. The *style* by which Underhill rejects Islam and embraces Christianity is equally as important. Donning the "attire" of the slave, Underhill expresses his Christianity. On the face of it, this is a very old trope in Christian thought, in which outward poverty bespeaks inner moral riches. But this is also in keeping with the new emphasis on the purity of private religion. Underhill's simple attire reflects his refusal to hypocritically embrace Islam.[49]

As representative of private moral purity, the "slave's attire" retrospectively speaks to the reason Underhill is in Africa in the first place: the Atlantic slave trade. Tyler's representation of the slave ship ties together the moral question of slavery with the question of private morality. Underhill's job as physician is "to inspect the bodies of the slaves, to see, as the captain expressed himself, that our owners were not shammed off with unsound flesh" (96). In other words, Underhill's role is to discover the truth behind what seems an outward bearing. Thus, the foundational violation of slavery as represented by the novel (though, needless to say, not the only one) is the stark and violent public exposure of enslaved Africans' privacy. Yet he both does and does not claim responsibility for this public shaming. As he says at the end of the chapter: "I cannot reflect on this transaction yet without shuddering. I have deplored my conduct with tears of anguish; and, I pray a merciful God, the common parent of the great family of the universe, who hath made of one flesh and one blood all nations of the earth, that the miseries, the insults, and cruel woundings, I afterwards received, when a slave myself, may expiate for the inhumanity, I was necessitated to exercise, towards these MY BRETHREN OF THE HUMAN RACE" (96). This retrospective account is articulated in the negative formation of the spiritual autobiography (he "shudders" when he reflects on his transgression; he "deplores" his conduct with "tears of anguish"; and he prays to God for atonement). But, of course, here in his prayer to God, where critics have read Underhill's first articulation of antislavery sentiment, we see instead a hedge, betrayed by his use of the passive voice. He "was necessitated to exercise." Underhill deems himself both responsible and not at all responsible for the added humiliations inflicted on enslaved men, women, and children. On top of which, his prayer to God offers a type of bargain: he asks that his own enslavement expatiate for his involvement in the slave trade.

A few chapters later, when Underhill is himself enslaved within the story, he does pronounce a more ambitious, activist response. "Grant me," he cries, "once more to taste the freedom of my native country," and "I will fly to our fellow citizens in the southern states; I will, on my knees, conjure then, in the name of humanity, to abolish a traffic, which causes it to bleed in every pore." He will call out their hypocrisy and beg them to "cease to deprive their fellow creatures of freedom, which their writers, their orators, representatives, senators, and even their constitutions of government, have declared to be the unalienable birth right of man" (106). Ed White sees in this moment a "fleeting Christian antislavery sentiment," one that, in its abandonment, only affirms that the novel's overarching ameliorative approach is best produced "privately and secretly."[50] Fleeting is too true. Unlike in the earlier passage, when Underhill asks God to atone for his involvement in the slave trade by weighing it against his time as a slave, this is no retrospective voice. He is bargaining with God in the present tense of the narrative. He describes his willingness to enact his own physical abasement (that he will plead with the southern states "on his knees") and stirringly invokes revolutionary language (he will force them to adhere to the claim that liberty is an "unalienable birth right of man"). In other words, Underhill's retrospective voice, as we saw earlier, has already asked God to exonerate him, claiming "time served," so to speak; his plea here is in the present tense, a description of how he felt upon his enslavement, not how he feels as he writes the narrative later.

When we align these two pleas to God, we see Underhill (both before and after conversion) thinking of religion as one of negotiating his personal atonement with a personal God, not as a transcendent and demanding system that compels public action. Indeed, Underhill returns to the United States a moral man—and a confirmed Christian—calling for a federal unity of the nation. Abandoning calls for either sympathy with enslaved people or the rights of man, Underhill represents and reinforces the ideal effect of diffusing the threat of deism. By repositioning as antiquated those advocates for a type of religious freedom that challenges Protestant Christianity (Paine is a "great apostle" and the Mollah spins "fables"), the novel can thus champion a private Protestant morality as a type of modern freedom.

INFIDELITY'S LIFE AFTER DEATH

Writing *The Algerine Captive* in 1797 during the height of popularity of "the infidelity of the Tom Paine school," as Lyman Beecher once put it, Tyler could not fully anticipate the decline of deism's cultural purchase in the subsequent decades.[51] But even as its popularity waned, Paine continued to represent immoral infidelity in its "naked and barbarous" form, as testified by the chaos and licentiousness depicted in a George Cruikshank illustration of 1819, ten years after Paine's death (see figure 6.1). With all of the institutional trappings of religion aflame and its priests executed, phrygian caps representing the French Revolution atop the gallows and on the feet of the upside-down revelers, and Islamic and Jewish believers laughing at the spectacle, this image reflects the continued perceived threat of the French Revolution and deism in the Atlantic world, and Paine's representative role in it. In the United States, both of these threats would continue to be invoked as the dystopic ends that antebellum reformers—but most especially abolitionists—would bring about, a "topsy turvy" world in which natural and moral hierarchies had been turned upside down.

Paine as the radical deist, though, went through at least one more evolution, which is where this essay began. In the outpouring of evangelical tracts and periodicals during and after the Second Great Awakening, Paine ironically also became the hypocrite whose hidden, *real* belief in God was inadvertently revealed on his deathbed. Throughout the antebellum period, Paine made guest appearances in tracts like *Dying Testimony of Believers and Unbelievers* (1833) and *Don't Unchain the Tiger* (1833). As the former shouted from its pages, "Thomas Paine was another who, as some yet alive in the city of New-York, know, yielded up his troubled spirit in a tempest of

FIGURE 6.1 George Cruikshank, "The Age of Reason or the World Turned Topsyturvy exemplified in Tom Paine's WORKS!!," 1819. Courtesy of the American Philosophical Society, Philadelphia.

agony and despair; alternately uttering fearful execrations, and calling on the insulted of Jesus Christ!"[52]

These are the accounts that led to Paine's return from the dead. Paine culminates his report from the afterlife by saying: "I was too *independent*, too reckless of the favor of the world, to purchase it by being a hypocrite."[53] Paine, in effect, came back to dispute charges of hypocrisy—a charge much more stinging than that of infidelity, it seems. To put this more directly, his spiritualist defenders understood well what evangelicals aimed at: not infidelity so much as the *hypocrisy* of infidelity in secular society, the way, to quote the tract *The Infidel! An Authentic Narrative* (1832), someone would shed "the restraints imposed by a belief in revelation, and wholly [neglect] the institutions of Christianity" but retain, "to a considerable extent, that outward morality which forms one of the distinct folds in the accustomed drapery of the Christian religion."[54] Paine's purported antebellum hypocrisy in many ways inverts the outrage over *The Age of Reason* in the 1790s. In the antebellum period, following in the wake of the revivals, the infidel is likely to dissemble, to throw drapery over the barbarous ideas that Paine let stand naked in the public square.

Let me conclude by drawing this back out to the bigger picture about secularism. Directly after the publication of *The Age of Reason*, Paine had become an emblem of infidelity and radical revolution; after his death, he also became known as a hypocrite, especially in evangelical circles. Paine thus symbolized well a central contradiction of privacy as it would develop out of disestablishment and across the nineteenth century: privacy is afforded to those who can publicly display a properly ordered morality, and revelations of secrets—political, sexual, spiritual—increasingly became the way to enforce secular morality and a political status quo. Revelation of religious hypocrisy would be the mode by which abolitionists in the antebellum period sought to attack the South, but it was also an effective counterattack against them, as was their supposed hidden "infidelity." Abolitionists like William Lloyd Garrison, Frederick Douglass, and even Harriet Beecher Stowe were consistently accused of secret atheism. The way that religious infidelity (and Jacobinism) continued to be evoked in political debates long after disestablishment and the French Revolution points us to this moral order as a formation of the secular itself.

Turning the critical gaze on secularism, and especially the ideology's moral commitments, has the capacity to enhance early American studies beyond this particular story of Paine's life after death. Like all humanistic disciplines in the modern university, history and English—the two main fields dominating early American studies—are grounded in secular institutions and secular assumptions about the place of belief in the study of the past and its literature, and these assumptions tend to include a stable definition of both "religion" and "secular," and a stable understanding as to which of these two terms "morality" belongs. Paine's position both as deist (his own identification) or as feared infidel Jacobin is not a fact about him so much as part of the process by which certain Protestant forms of belief became valued during disestablishment and other ways of believing—or not believing—were deemed unsafe for secular institutions, including the university. To take this one step further, privacy itself is a formation of the secular; that is, it manages religious conviction, sexual morality, and the right to participate in the public sphere.

Paine's supposed hypocrisy—and the thirst to expose it—tells us a slightly different, though related, story. It would be very easy to end this essay with a punch line about how evangelical tract writers attempted to distort Paine's clearly argued deist positions to convert wayward Protestant readers back to the evangelical fold. But the story they were telling about Paine potentially had power not because it supported a theological truth but because it was an exposure of inauthenticity. Paine wasn't what he said he was. Why would that be a compelling way to combat unbelief? The answer has more to do with the moral investment in sincerity at the center of secularism, and it also reveals why a hunt for hypocrites—which Arendt and Shklar point to as concomitant with the emergence of nationalism and liberalism starting in the Revolutionary era—is a type of morality that pervades US secularism. In other words, the centrality of hypocrisy in contemporary political and cultural discourse is not a *doctrinal* or *theological* orientation but a *secular* one. It is pervasive yet invisible and is made to seem self-evident as a line of attack, but it grows out of a longer history of private conscience and the role of religion in the private sphere that followed from the disestablishment of state churches in the early republic.

NOTES

Portions of this chapter originally appeared in the introduction and chapter 1 of my book *Faith in Exposure: Privacy and Secularism in the Nineteenth-Century United States*, and they appear here with permission from the University of Pennsylvania Press.

1. "Thomas Paine and His Traducers," 45.
2. "Thomas Paine and His Traducers," 45.
3. The widespread reach of this story about Paine came about due to the role of such institutions as the American Tract Society in helping to establish the origins of "mass media" in the US. For more on evangelical print culture, see Nord, *Faith in Reading*, particularly chapters 3–5.
4. Conway, *Life of Thomas*, xv.
5. See Larkin, *Thomas Paine and the Literature of Revolution*, chapter 2.
6. Emily Ogden provides a sweeping and convincing account of credulity, which she describes as "modern enchantment." The aspiration of antebellum secularism, she argues, is to "confine, explain, and redeploy primitive religious power." Emily Ogden, *Credulity*, 9, 5, and the introduction more generally.
7. Mahmood, *Religious Difference in a Secular Age*, 21.
8. Asad, *Formations of the Secular*, 52.
9. Disestablishment varied by state and could involve some or all of the issues I list here. For a good resource on each state's particular course through disestablishment, see Esbeck and Den Hartog, "Introduction: The Task, Methodology, and Findings," in *Disestablishment and Religious Dissent*, 3–23, 6–7. See also Green, *Second Disestablishment* on how these processes played out beyond the formal disestablishment of state churches.
10. Fessenden, *Culture and Redemption*, 6.
11. Jefferson, *Notes on the State of Virginia*, 159.

12 Emerson, "Self-Reliance," 262.
13 For Arendt, the French Revolution marked a decisive shift toward a cultural preoccupation with hypocrisy and authenticity in the West. Though Arendt does exclude the American Revolution from the "never-ending" hunt for hypocrisy, Shklar more rightly includes the United States as exemplary of these political problems. See Arendt, *On Revolution*, 86–105; and Shklar, *Ordinary Vices*, chapter 2. The preoccupation with sincerity and authenticity rising in the Revolutionary era is seen, as well, in the rise of Romanticism on both sides of the Atlantic. For a study of hypocrisy and British culture in the long eighteenth century, see Davidson, *Hypocrisy and the Politics of Politeness*.
14 Franklin, *Autobiography*, 3–191, 73, 102.
15 Shklar, *Ordinary Vices*, 75.
16 Madison, "Memorial and Remonstrance."
17 Danbury Baptist Association, "To Thomas Jefferson." This association was preparing for a long fight to disestablish the Congregational Church in Connecticut, which would not happen until 1818. In response to this letter, Jefferson would assert that the First Amendment aimed to build a "wall of separation" between church and state, a phrase that would become a significant statement in religious freedom cases in the twentieth century.
18 Paine, *Age of Reason*, 665–830, 667.
19 Paine, *Age of Reason*, 667, 666.
20 Jefferson, *Notes on the State of Virginia*, 159.
21 Murphy, *New England Women Writers*, 69–70.
22 Grasso, *Skepticism and American Faith*, 14.
23 Schlereth, *Age of Infidels*, 11. See also Porterfield, *Conceived in Doubt*.
24 Grasso, *Skepticism and American Faith*, 32.
25 [Linn], *Serious Considerations on the Election of a President*, 19.
26 Schlereth, *Age of Infidels*, 49.
27 Nelson, *Thomas Paine*, 267, 269.
28 Schlereth, *Age of Infidels*, 49.
29 Smith, in *The Diary*, April 13, 1796, 156; see also Waterman, "The Bavarian Illuminati," 21.
30 Watson, *Apology*, 11, 7–8.
31 Ogden, *Antidote to Deism*, 17.
32 Ogden, *Antidote to Deism*, 13.
33 Boudinot, *Age of Revelation*, xxi.
34 Samuels, *Romances of the Republic*, 12–13.
35 Dwight, *Nature and Danger of Infidel Philosophy*, 57.
36 Ogden, *Antidote to Deism*, 15.
37 "From the British Review," 384.
38 Grasso, *Skepticism and American Faith*, 100.
39 Review of "An Answer to Mr. Paine's Age of Reason," 301; "Notice to Correspondents," 128.
40 [Cobbett], "Paine's Age of Reason," 198, 197.

41 "From the British Review," 390.

42 "From the British Review," 391.

43 Recent scholarship on *The Algerine Captive* has debated the extent to which we can see the novel in general, and its more sober second half specifically, as cosmopolitan or conservative. My argument here aligns with the readings of the novel as ultimately conservative. On the side of reading the novel as more liberal and cosmopolitan, see Holt, "'All Parts of the Union I Considered My Home'"; and Armstrong and Tennenhouse, "The Problem of Population and the Form of the American Novel." In a less overtly optimistic way, Edward Larkin argues for conceptualizing the early United States as an empire, a refocusing that allows us to see the "diversity of cultures present in the states." Larkin, "Nation and Empire in the Early US," 520. In his recent dissenting reevaluation, Ed White contends that Tyler typifies the logic of conservatism as it will emerge in the nineteenth century, in which irony allows for the appreciation and exploitation of the "constitutive gap between the conventional reality of the plebs and the cultural superiority, even transcendence of the professional class." White, "Divided We Stand," 21. Likewise, Elizabeth Fenton argues that *The Algerine Captive* turns a skeptical eye on deliberative democracy. Fenton, "Indeliberate Democracy."

44 Stein, *When Novels Were Books*, 10, and chapter 2 more extensively.

45 Tyler, *The Algerine Captive*, 87. Subsequent citations to this edition of *The Algerine Captive* will be given parenthetically in the text.

46 Fenton, "Indeliberate Democracy," 90.

47 For more on the rise of "world religions" and "comparative religions," see Masuzawa, *The Invention of World Religions*; and Jaudon, "The Compiler's Art."

48 Dillon, *The Gender of Freedom*, introduction.

49 White, "Divided We Stand," 26.

50 White, "Divided We Stand," 26.

51 Beecher, *Autobiography*, 1:43. Christopher Grasso points out that, while deism was visibly less popular in the antebellum years, there persisted widespread fears that a "vast subterranean reservoir of doubt" existed. Grasso, *Skepticism and American Faith*, 15.

52 Brownlee, *Dying Testimony of Believers and Unbelievers*, 6.

53 [Burbank and Wood], *Philosophy of Creation*, 24. The original author attribution in *The Philosophy of Creation* is to Thomas Paine. The preface, written by H. A. Burbank, explains that he and Horace G. Wood were lecturing in Vermont on "Spirit manifestations" and Paine supposedly dictated this book through Wood, but not only in his own voice but as a representative of a group of dead men that included fellow famous deist Ethan Allen.

54 [Wisner], *The Infidel!*, 1.

BIBLIOGRAPHY

Arendt, Hannah. *On Revolution*. New York: Penguin, 2006.

Armstrong, Nancy, and Leonard Tennenhouse. "The Problem of Population and the Form of the American Novel." *American Literary History* 20, no. 4 (Winter 2008): 667–85.

Asad, Talal. *Formations of the Secular: Christianity, Islam, Modernity*. Stanford, CA: Stanford University Press, 2003.

Beecher, Lyman. *Autobiography, Correspondence, Etc.* Edited by Charles Beecher. New York: Harper and Brothers, 1865.

Boudinot, Elias. *The Age of Revelation: or, The Age of Reason Shewn to Be an Age of Infidelity*. Philadelphia: Asbury Dickens, 1801.

Brownlee, W. C. *Dying Testimony of Believers and Unbelievers*. New York: American Tract Society, 1833.

[Burbank, H. A., and Horace G. Wood]. *The Philosophy of Creation*. Boston: Bela Marsh, 1854.

[Cobbett, William]. "Paine's Age of Reason." *Porcupine's Political Censor*. May 1796, 195–205.

Conway, Moncure Daniel. *The Life of Thomas Paine: With a History of His Literary, Political, and Religious Career in America, France, and England*. New York: Putnam, 1909.

Danbury Baptist Association. "To Thomas Jefferson from the Danbury Baptist Association, [after 7 October 1801]." Accessed September 19, 2023. *Founders Online*, National Archives, https://founders.archives.gov/documents/Jefferson/01-35-02-0331.

Davidson, Jenny. *Hypocrisy and the Politics of Politeness: Manners and Morals from Locke to Austen*. Cambridge: Cambridge University Press, 2004.

Dillon, Elizabeth Maddock. *The Gender of Freedom: Fictions of Liberalism and the Literary Public Sphere*. Palo Alto, CA: Stanford University Press, 2004.

Dwight, Timothy. *The Nature and Danger of Infidel Philosophy*. New Haven, CT: George Bunce, 1798.

Emerson, Ralph Waldo. "Self-Reliance." In *Emerson: Essays and Poems*, edited by Joel Porte, 259–82. New York: Library of America, 1996.

Esbeck, Carl H., and Jonathan J. Den Hartog. Introduction to *Disestablishment and Religious Dissent: Church-State Relations in the New American States, 1776–1833*. Columbia: University of Missouri Press, 2019.

Fenton, Elizabeth. "Indeliberate Democracy: The Politics of Religious Conversion in Royall Tyler's *The Algerine Captive*." *Early American Literature* 51, no. 1 (2016): 71–100.

Fessenden, Tracy. *Culture and Redemption: Religion, the Secular, and American Literature*. Princeton, NJ: Princeton University Press, 2007.

Franklin, Benjamin. *The Autobiography of Benjamin Franklin*. In *The Autobiography and Other Writings*, edited by Kenneth Silverman, 3–191. New York: Penguin, 1986.

"From the British Review." *Select Reviews of Literature and Spirit of Foreign Magazines* 6 (December 1811): 377–91.

Grasso, Christopher. *Skepticism and American Faith, from the Revolution to the Civil War*. New York: Oxford University Press, 2018.

Green, Steven K. *The Second Disestablishment: Church and State in Nineteenth-Century America*. New York: Oxford University Press, 2010.

Holt, Keri. "'All Parts of the Union I Considered My Home': The Federal Imagination of *The Algerine Captive*." *Early American Literature* 46, no. 3 (2011): 481–515.

Jaudon, Toni Wall. "The Compiler's Art: Hannah Adams, the *Dictionary of All Religions*, and the Religious World." *American Literary History* 26, no. 1 (Spring 2014), 28–41.

Jefferson, Thomas. *Notes on the State of Virginia*. Edited by William Peden. Chapel Hill: University of North Carolina Press, 1955.

Larkin, Edward. "Nation and Empire in the Early US." *American Literary History* 22, no. 3 (Fall 2010): 501–26.

Larkin, Edward. *Thomas Paine and the Literature of Revolution*. New York: Cambridge University Press, 2005.

[Linn, William]. *Serious Considerations on the Election of a President: Addressed to the Citizens of the United States*. New York: John Furman, 1800.

Madison, James. "Memorial and Remonstrance against Religious Assessments, [ca. 20 June] 1785." Accessed August 11, 2023. *Founders Online*, National Archives, https://founders.archives.gov/documents/Madison/01-08-02-0163.

Mahmood, Saba. *Religious Difference in a Secular Age: A Minority Report*. Princeton, NJ: Princeton University Press, 2016.

Masuzawa, Tomoko. *The Invention of World Religions: Or, How European Universalism Was Preserved in the Language of Pluralism*. Chicago: University of Chicago Press, 2005.

Murphy, Gretchen. *New England Women Writers, Secularity, and the Federalist Politics of Church and State*. Oxford: Oxford University Press, 2021.

Nelson, Craig. *Thomas Paine: Enlightenment, Revolution, and the Birth of Modern Nations*. New York: Viking, 2006.

Nord, David Paul. *Faith in Reading: Religious Publishing and the Birth of Mass Media in America*. New York: Oxford University Press, 2004.

"Notice to Correspondents." *Monthly Register, Magazine, and Review of the United States* 2 (January 1807): 128.

Ogden, Emily. *Credulity: A Cultural History of US Mesmerism*. Chicago: University of Chicago Press, 2018.

Ogden, Uzal. *Antidote to Deism: The Deist Unmasked; or an Ample Refutation of All the Objections of Thomas Paine, against the Christian Religion*. Newark, NJ: John Woods, 1795.

Paine, Thomas. *The Age of Reason*. In *Thomas Paine: Collected Works*, edited by Eric Foner, 665–830. New York: Library of America, 1984.

Porterfield, Amanda. *Conceived in Doubt: Religion and Politics in the New American Nation.* Chicago: University of Chicago Press, 2012.

Review of *"An Answer to Mr. Paine's Age of Reason."* American Monthly Review 3, no. 4 (December 1795): 301–4.

Samuels, Shirley. *Romances of the Republic: Women, the Family, and Violence in the Literature of the Early American Nation.* New York: Oxford University Press, 1996.

Schlereth, Eric R. *An Age of Infidels: The Politics of Religious Controversy in the Early United States.* Philadelphia: University of Pennsylvania Press, 2013.

Shklar, Judith N. *Ordinary Vices.* Cambridge, MA: Belknap Press of Harvard University Press, 1984.

Smith, Elihu Hubbard, *The Diary of Elihu Hubbard Smith (1771–1798).* Edited by James E. Cronin. Philadelphia: American Philosophical Society, 1973.

Stein, Jordan Alexander. *When Novels Were Books.* Cambridge, MA: Harvard University Press, 2020.

"Thomas Paine and His Traducers." *Liberator,* March 17, 1854, 45.

Tyler, Royall. *The Algerine Captive; or, The Life and Adventures of Doctor Updike Underhill: Six Years a Prisoner among the Algerines.* Edited by Caleb Crain. New York: Modern Library, 2002.

Waterman, Bryan. "The Bavarian Illuminati, the Early American Novel, and Histories of the Public Sphere." *William and Mary Quarterly* 62, no. 1 (January 2005): 9–30.

Watson, Richard. *An Apology for the Bible, in a Series of Letters, Addressed to Thomas Paine.* 5th ed. London: T. Evans, Cadell Davies, P. Elmsley, et al., 1796.

White, Ed. "Divided We Stand: Emergent Conservatism in Royall Tyler's *The Algerine Captive.*" *Studies in American Fiction* 37, no. 1 (2010), 5–27.

[Wisner, William]. *The Infidel! An Authentic Narrative.* New York: American Tract Society, 1832.

SEVEN · *Britt Rusert*

No Matter

Persisting Rationalisms in
Antebellum Black Thought

I say if these things do not occur in their proper time,
it is because the world in which we live does not exist,
and we are deceived with regard to its existence.

—DAVID WALKER, *APPEAL, IN FOUR ARTICLES; TOGETHER
WITH A PREAMBLE, TO THE COLOURED CITIZENS OF THE
WORLD* (1829–30)

In a few moments in his *Appeal*, black activist, intellectual, tailor, and Methodist evangelist David Walker uses the word *immaterial* in a striking way. In the sentence that follows my epigraph, Walker writes, "It is immaterial however, to me, who believe, or who refuse."[1] In another moment, he writes, "any man of colour, immaterial who he is, or where he came from, if he is not *the fourth from the negro race*!! (as we are called) the white Christians of America will serve him the same they will sink him into wretchedness and degradation for ever while he lives."[2] Read in context, Walker's *immaterial* means something like "no matter" or "it doesn't matter." Although it might sound peculiar or even idiosyncratic to twenty-first-century readers and listeners, this iteration of *immaterial* was not at all uncommon in the period. The OED defines this use of *immaterial* as "not pertinent to the case or matter in hand; that does not apply; irrelevant," and goes on to note that this use persists today in law, especially relating to evidence (as in, "The arbitrator determined that the evidence was immaterial and should be excluded"). But in the context of *Appeal*'s millenarian spiritual investments, *immaterial* also echoes with the text's occasional questioning of the existence of the earth itself; Walker's speculation that if God does not save the oppressed, it may be the case that "the world in which we live does not exist, and we are deceived with regard to its existence."[3] Such a questioning of the existence of the "world in which we live" is a powerful rejection of the status quo in a racist, slaveholding nation, but it also works to complicate the empirical investments of the text (the "read this," "listen to this," "hear this" aspects of the work that Marcy Dinius has so cogently explored), and of the purchase of empiricism more broadly for enslaved and nominally free people.[4]

Walker's musings on the unreal nature or unreal feeling of this world make complete sense in light of the surreal brutalities of enslavement as well as growing antiblack violence committed against nominally free people in the 1830s, and what Walker perceived as the unbelievable hypocrisy of white Christians who either held black people captive or supported the institution in more indirect ways. But Walker's questioning of the existence of the earth also taps into the deep nihilism of 1820s and 1830s black writing, and the forms of religious oratory from which it was derived. In this way, Walker's interest in the "immaterial" as "no matter" resonates with something like Lee Edelman's rallying cry, following the Sex Pistols, of "no future."[5] Indeed, a distinct rhetoric around the death drive is a major part of black revolutionary politics in the 1820s and 1830s, something that is on display in works like Walker's *Appeal*, but gets muted and transformed by the assimilation of early black radicalism within the mainstream movement to abolish slavery in the 1840s and 1850s. Where mainstream abolition roots itself in a redemptive futurity emblematized and enabled by the figure of the child, Walker mobilizes his rhetoric around the nonreproductivity of slavery and its abjection; the black Methodist preacher and intellectual Hosea Easton trafficked in a similar rhetoric of a damned futurity in his own manifesto published just a few years after Walker's *Appeal*. In one striking moment in his 1837 *Treatise on the Intellectual Character and Civil and Political Condition of the Colored People of the U. States*, Easton poses a question about his own existence and personhood: "I wonder that I am a man." We might read the "no future" elements of these works generically (as part of the tradition of jeremiad), or as savvy political rhetoric (the mobilization of the masses through an apocalyptic pessimism), but Walker's punk destructiveness—one that we also see in the speeches and writings of Easton, Maria Stewart, and even the Pequot intellectual William Apess in this same period—cannot be easily wished away, nor should it.

In what follows, I want to use Walker's interest in the immaterial, as well as a broader interest in "no matter" as an opportunity to revisit some of the material from my first monograph, *Fugitive Science: Empiricism and Freedom in Early African American Culture* (2017). In that project, I try to rethink the history of racial science in the nineteenth century from the perspective of black intellectuals, performers, and artists who challenged it, critiqued it, and occasionally flirted with it. Figures like Frederick Douglass and James McCune Smith penned trenchant critiques of racist science, but often from within the terms and methods of science itself. James McCune Smith's 1859 response to the fourteenth query of Thomas Jefferson's *Notes on the State of Virginia* (1785) used empirical evidence and data amassed from his own clinical practice to expose the flimsiness of Jefferson's self-admitted "speculations" about the inferiorities of the African race.[6] In the process, McCune Smith affirms that Jefferson was not only a racist, but also a shoddy scientist; in so doing, he further marks the transition to a new scientific episteme, the arrival and triumph of biology and comparative anatomy over natural history. Frederick Douglass's "Claims of the Negro, Ethnologically Considered" (1854) expresses outrage over polygenesis's heretical departure from scriptural authority on the Creation, but Douglass does not reject natural science as a whole. Citing and celebrating the Scottish phrenologist George Combe, he holds up phrenology as a model of an ethical, democratic science, in opposition to the racist despotism of craniology. Other figures, like Henry Box Brown, did not directly engage with racial science, but drew a range of popular sciences, from "electro-biology" to even mycology (the study of fungi), into his stage performances.

While I still maintain that African Americans—nominally free, fugitive, and enslaved—showed a broad interest in natural science in this period (contrary to lingering assumptions about black suspicion toward science, racial and otherwise), I've become increasingly interested in the deeply speculative purposes to which these sciences were often put. In other words, free black intellectuals, writers, and some enslaved people were interested in how the sciences of the second scientific revolution and the study of the natural world, more broadly, might be used for decidedly speculative purposes, leading them to affirm the immateriality, rather than the materiality, of the world. Here, I follow the important work that David Kazanjian has done to think about the richly speculative, lived, and often improvisatory concepts of freedom that were conveyed in the letters of African American settler-colonials in nineteenth-century Liberia.[7] A recognition of black speculative uses of empirical science might make a few different interventions: (1) it complicates liberal narratives about "African Americans in science" that are mobilized within and beyond conversations about diversity and inclusion in the STEM fields; (2) it challenges the sometimes naïve celebration of matter and a world of objects in new materialist approaches from the perspective of people who were treated, held captive, and exchanged as if they were objects; and (3) it reminds us of the long-standing importance of mysticism and theodicy in Afro-diasporic cultures, and of what Fred Moten calls the "mysticism of the flesh." I'm particularly interested in how the "no matter" strain of fugitive science might be used to rethink the centrality of empiricism within the early Americanist toolbox, especially the field's enduring "empiricist impulses."[8] In what follows, I begin with some context on the complicated status of reason amid transformations in science and religion in the early nineteenth century. I then turn to some fascinating moments in *The Confessions of Nat Turner* (1831) and Martin Delany's *Blake; or, the Huts of America* (1859), where rationalist theories of mind and intelligence come to the fore. From there, I consider how black women's antebellum manuscript cultures challenge the privileging of the individual mind's power through forms of collaboration and writing that foreground a distributed black intellect and collective genius. I end by returning to some of the metaconcerns of this volume, imagining an early American studies that is less beholden to traditional historicist approaches and more beholden to the methods of race and ethnic studies. I also humbly offer my own model of auto-critique, of revisiting and revising some of the assumptions that grounded my earlier work, as one way that scholars of early America may open themselves up to the necessary project of critique that guides this volume's concerns and priorities. The practice of critique is an ongoing, never-ending process that has the possibility to, among other things, unsettle the concealed origin narratives and ideologies that shape the field. But to truly engage in critique also means to think critically about one's own thinking, to be open to the possibility of changing one's mind, and even to the possibility of being wrong.

....

A period of scientific enthusiasm and discovery sometimes referred to as the age of the second scientific revolution, the early nineteenth century saw the strengthening of empirically rooted, data-driven science, as well as innovations in thermodynamics, electricity, biology, chemistry, and astronomy. But the second scientific revolution occurred alongside another important, paradigm-shifting transatlantic movement, another important "second": the Second Great Awakening. The confluence of the Second Great Awakening and the second scientific revolution produced a number of fascinatingly hybrid texts that traversed evangelical Protestantism and empirically rooted science. For their part, antebellum black ethnologies registered the syncretism of natural science and revealed religion in this moment and, relatedly, the ways that natural theology continued to putter along into the nineteenth century. These texts fit with Sarah Rivett's argument about the influence of the New Science on Reformed theology and practice in colonial contexts, but, in this case, the influence more often moves in the opposite direction: by mystifying empiricism itself.[9] Antebellum black ethnologies thus illuminate what Jared Hickman has identified as the use of theology among African Americans to challenge the brutal, dehumanizing heresies of polygenesis. In Hickman's reading, the American school of ethnology is understood not as a secular or secularizing science, but as a discourse embedded in a different form of religious argument. He writes, "As the largely biblicist quarrels over the justifiability of slavery became increasingly arcane and intractable, both proslavery racists like the American School [of ethnology] and radical abolitionists abandoned the conventional, biblicist ground of the argument in the hopes of changing the game and winning the day. But they abandoned biblicist arguments not for secularist, empiricist arguments, per se, but rather for broad, supraconfessional theistic arguments."[10] In other words, polygenesis cannot be simply placed within a narrative about the secularization of science, nor about the disenchantment of the world. The same can be said about African American responses to ethnology in this same period. But it's also the case that those theisms regularly exceeded Protestantism by grafting forms of conjuring and other forms of Afro-diasporic belief, practice, and mysticism onto Christianity.

In his study of early American racial theory, Bruce Dain observes that eighteenth-century theories about the environmental production of racial difference continued to be cited and circulated by black intellectuals throughout the antebellum period, even after such theories were being replaced by proto-evolutionary and proto-biological theories of race. As theories that placed pathology in shared environments, rather than in supposedly deficient bodies, climate theories of race were used to combat the increasing inflexibility and ossification of racial categories under the banner of comparative anatomy. I would like to suggest that just as climatism enjoyed a long afterlife in black intellectual cultures, rationalism also appeared with regular frequency throughout the early to mid-nineteenth century. In other words, the idea that knowledge comes from the faculty of reason, rather than from direct experience, remained an attractive idea for people who had understandable reasons for wanting to detach from the world and its oppressive wickedness, and perhaps still do. Especially in slave narratives and other narratives by formerly enslaved people, reason is often figured as divine reason. For example, Nat Turner's *Confessions* (1831), filtered through the perspective and blunt racism of the narrative's white amanuensis, presents a young Turner who has "too much sense:" restless, inquisitive, and "observant of every thing that was passing," the narrative notes that "there was nothing that I saw or heard to which my attention was not directed."[11] Turner is hyper-observant and hyper-attentive, but his knowledge comes from God, not from the false world that surrounds him. After miraculously reading without having been taught the alphabet, he notes, "When I got large enough to go to work, while employed, I was reflecting on many things that would present themselves to my imagination, and whenever an opportunity occurred of looking at a book, when the school children were getting their lessons, I would find many things that the fertility of my own imagination had depicted to me before."[12] In other words, the world does not present new information, it simply confirms what Turner has already seen in his imagination. Such miraculous occurrences establish Turner's divine inspiration and status as a prophet within his community while legitimating the 1831 Turner rebellion as authorized by divine decree. But the rationalist explanation for Turner's knowledge also establishes a form of black knowledge that does not need or care about its validation by white people. Turner's knowledge does not require the confirmation of the world, nor of his enslavers and interrogators, including his own amanuensis.[13]

Immediately following this description of Turner's divinely inspired intelligence, the text notes a youthful Turner's practice with a number of vernacular experiments, his making of materials that would presumably prove helpful for his later organization of a slave revolt: "All my time, not devoted to my master's service, was spent either in prayer, or in making experiments in casting different things in moulds made of earth, in attempting to make paper, gunpowder, and many other experiments, that although I could not perfect, yet convinced me of its practicability."[14] This form of "making" with an eye to organization and revolt is part of a genealogy of practical fugitive science that I explore in *Fugitive Science*: on-the-ground engagements with science and experimentation that were used for actual escapes and forms of revolt in the pursuit of freedom. Turner's anecdote about experimenting with molds made of earth immediately follows the text's articulation of its rationalist commitments (of knowledge that requires no worldly confirmation). This fascinating textual transition, from the realm of the sensual to the realm of the mind, points to the interanimation of the empirical and the speculative in the contexts of enslavement. It suggests, more specifically, that speculative knowledge might be useful in its capacity to foment interest in forms of experimentation that have a divine purpose. Interestingly, Thomas Gray's footnote in this section of the text further affirms Turner's knowledge and expertise with such forms of experimental manufacture, while pointing to the forms of interrogation that structure much of the slave narrative as a genre: "When questioned as to the manner of manufacturing those different articles, he was found well informed on the subject."[15] In the North, figures like Martin Delany and James McCune Smith decried the exclusion of African Americans from institutions of scientific and medical training, but still claimed the title of "Dr." and routinely pointed to their professional credentials for authorization and elevation of status both within and beyond black publics and counterpublics. When questioned about his own credentials, it's likely that Turner would have again pointed to God. Such an act of course points to the multiple uses and resources of Protestant evangelicalism for the enslaved, but also to the ways that God could be invoked as a cover for subterranean forms of knowledge production and sharing of expertise among enslaved people. We might here remember the southern laws passed in the wake of the publication of Walker's *Appeal* that sought to restrict and outlaw black movement, instruction, and literacy. Published in a post-*Appeal* moment of white panic, backlash, and surveillance, in Nat Turner's *Confessions*, God becomes a protective surrogate, or rhetorical protector, for the people who likely taught Turner to read, to organize, and to turn the materials around him into fodder for organization and revolution.

Into the 1840s and 1850s, rationalism continued to make intriguing cameos in African American texts. Most notably, Martin Delany's 1859 serial novel *Blake; or, the Huts of America* flits between scenes that emphasize the many uses of empiricism and ones that are much more interested in a kind of Kantian contemplation, or contemplating the significance of contemplation. Despite the importance of what we would today call liberation theology for many antebellum black writers, Delany is one figure that we might place within a more secular trajectory of black abolitionism in the period, one that would also include James McCune Smith and maybe even William Wells Brown. When Delany's *Blake* turns Exodus 14:13 ("Stand still and see the salvation") into a phrase meant to signal "go time" for an organized interstate and possible transnational slave revolt, he expresses a completely instrumental relationship to biblical scripture. One gets the sense that he picks this passage from the Bible quite simply because it is likely to be familiar to enslaved people across the South. More than just critiquing Christianity as an opiate for the enslaved (which he also does), Blake critiques all forms of the supernatural that, in his view, obstruct the struggle for emancipation. For example, in the heart of the Dismal Swamp, he dismisses the antiquated mysticisms of conjuring as a form of superstition unhelpful for the decidedly modern revolution he hopes to lead, though he eventually allows the group to anoint him "a priest of the order of the High Conjurors, . . . amusing enough it was to him who consented to satisfy the aged devotees of a time-honored superstition among them."[16] But beyond simply amusing him, Blake's anointment as a High Conjuror also works as a way to organize his revolutionary plot among this peculiar group in the Dismal Swamp and to give him some cachet beyond it (perhaps similar to how John Marrant's donning of Indigenous dress lends him a new status and aura of importance among family and friends once he returns to Charleston from Indian Territory). Either way, Blake ascribes no actual power to conjuring itself.

Beyond the realm of politics and religion, the almost militant materialism of *Blake* is also reflected in Delany's scientific writings. In his essays on astronomy in the *Anglo-African Magazine*, "The Attraction of Planets," the divine wonder of the galaxy is replaced by a theory that electricity is responsible for the movement of the planets. Similarly in "Comets," Delany says that comets are actually planets and that they provide an electric charge that distributes electricity throughout space. Throughout the nineteenth century, astronomers continued to nod to God as the Creator of a galaxy understood to be increasingly vast and filled with unknowns. Delany makes a similar genuflection to the "Almighty," "the Author of all Things," at the end of "Comets," though the gesture feels forced and tacked on (possibly even at the magazine editor's request, like Douglass's famous appendix to his 1845 *Narrative*).

Delany's demystified astronomy, an astronomy largely drained of divine mystery and wonder, also figures in *Blake*. I'd like to think a bit more about two scenes in the novel that have long perplexed me, two scenes in which Blake looks to the sky and reflects on what he sees there. The first appears at the beginning of chapter 22, as Blake arrives on a Mississippi steamer in New Orleans. The chapter opens: "The season is the holidays, it is evening, and the night is beautiful. The moon, which in Louisiana is always an object of impressive interest, even to the slave as well as those of enlightened and scientific intelligence, the influence of whose soft and mellow light seems ever like the enchanting effect of some invisible being, to impart inspiration—now being shed from the crescent of the first day of the last quarter, appeared more interesting and charming than ever."[17]

Displaying the moon as an object of interest to both the "slave" as "well as those of enlightened and scientific intelligence," this passage points to Delany's interest in the promotion of science among free people as well as his belief in the "enlightenment" of the enslaved masses through the efforts of the antebellum equivalent of the Talented Tenth. At first, the enchanting charm of the moon seems to offer a glimpse into a more ethereal, spiritual world, accessible through the "soft, mellow," seemingly transcendent light of the moon. But the word *seems* is important here, as Delany points to this effect as just that: an effect, a mirage, an illusion. Moreover, his use of a simile is telling: "the influence of whose soft and mellow light *seems ever like* the enchanting effect of some invisible being."[18] The moon does not offer a visible trace of God's presence; its glowing light only appears *like* "the enchanting effect of some invisible being." Delany's veiled reference to "some invisible being" is far from Nat Turner's world of fiery, divine inspiration, one in which God's plans are often made visible through signs in the natural world (on corn in the fields and leaves on the trees). Blake's look to the moon, rather, is used to impress the idea that the oppressed can only depend on themselves for their own liberation on earth.

These sentiments are reinforced in a subsequent passage at the beginning of chapter 26. Again, reflections on the deck of a steamship:

> The evening, for the season, was very fine; the sky beautiful; the stars shining unusually bright; while Henry, along on the hurricane deck of the "Queen of the West," stood in silence abaft [aloft?] the wheel-house, gazing intently at the golden orbs of Heaven. Now shoots a meteor, then seemingly shot a comet, again glistened a brilliant planet which almost startled the gazer; and while he yet stood motionless in wonder looking into the heavens, a blazing star whose scintillations dazzled the sight, and for the moment bewildered the mind, was seen apparently to vibrate in a manner never before observed by him.

> At these things Henry was filled with amazement, and disposed to attach more than ordinary importance to them, as having an especial bearing in this case; but the mystery finds interpretation in the fact that the emotions were located in his own brain, and not exhibited by the orbs of Heaven.[19]

Again, rather than looking to stellar bodies as harbingers of God's deliverance (as both Harriet Tubman and Frederick Douglass reportedly did after the famous Leonid meteor shower of 1833), Delany suppresses any possible divine explanation for the appearance of the "orbs of Heaven."[20] His temptation to attach more than "ordinary importance" to the orbs is unwarranted since the "emotions" they inspire are located "in his own brain," and not by the "orbs of Heaven," nor by heaven itself. The meteor, the comet, but especially the "blazing star" appear to point to some sign from heaven, some supernatural beyond, but in reality, they merely point back to the emotions in Delany's own head. This refusal to read "signs" in the heavens is also striking given the novel's interest in the secret signs and furtive forms of communication privileged by Masonic organizations in the antebellum period. Indeed, there is much more to be written about *Blake*'s relationship to black Freemasonry in the period.

What always strikes me about these two passages is that they do not look to the skies to *inspire* escape, resilience, or revolution among enslaved people, despite *Blake*'s focus on all three of these. In another installment, Blake instructs a group of fugitive slaves on how to use a compass and the North Star to navigate their way to freedom.[21] The narrative points to the importance of the stars for practically navigating escapes from slavery, but Delany has little use for cosmic inspiration. This might be read as a kind of pure materialism on Delany's part. Rather than putting the empirical to speculative use, he only has patience for speculative detours that might lead back to the world of action, very literally "on the ground." But each of these passages also works by shuttling between the world of the senses and the world of reason, always ending by privileging the pure powers of the mind, rather than the empirical information gleaned from acts of observation. Delany's account of astronomy is thus a rational one, one that points back to the mind itself, and its emotive and intellectual capacities. In this way, Delany's outer space is also an occasion for contemplation, and for contemplating on the nature of contemplation.

These turns to a kind of Kantian rationalism in antebellum black thought, of minds that continually refer back to faculty of reason and its own generative power, might be also understood as provocative engagements with the imperative to "prove" the equality of black intelligence. As Henry Louis Gates Jr. has long argued, early black writing in the Atlantic world largely took shape as a series of proofs of black literateness and literariness.[22] In response to arguments that people of African descent lacked the capacity for reason and imagination, and thus the capacity for self-government and freedom, black writers were beholden to an impossibly high standard: to establish the soundness and contents of their mind in every word they wrote. Texts that found black knowledge and even black genius in the mind itself, rather than in its expressions, thus do much to resist the "burden of proof" that weighted down black intellectual work throughout the period. For Turner, it is his community's belief in his "superior judgment" that matters, not displays of intelligence as proof of equality and humanity. In Franny Nudelman's terms, Nat Turner's narrative claims a "radically expanded interiority for the insurgent subject."[23] According to Nudelman, this is "first and foremost a story of Nat Turner's intellect—how his mind works and how the workings of his mind led to insurrection."[24] Across the text, Turner's mind becomes an "object of analysis," but one that remains recalcitrantly closed and inaccessible to Gray through the portrayal of Turner's "own mind as a static repository of divine knowledge."[25] By refusing the terms of will, agency, cause, and motive, Turner thus refuses the conditions of his own interrogation. He doesn't need to prove anything to anyone, and he refuses to incriminate himself or his collaborators and community. Similarly, Blake's powers of mind cannot be attributed to a benevolent white teacher, to access to education, or to some other external cause. Blake's intelligence refers back to nothing but itself.

These scenes might also be read in the spirit of Jacques Rancière's thinking on intellectual emancipation in *The Ignorant Schoolmaster*. In this text, Rancière exposes the history of liberal education as a history of intellectual stultification, rooted in beliefs about the inequality of intelligence among individuals. According to Rancière, to teach through explication is to ultimately assert the intellectual incapacities of the student: "To explain something to someone is first of all to show him he cannot understand it himself."[26] In its place, Rancière holds up the model of the nineteenth-century French schoolteacher Joseph Jacotot, the "ignorant schoolmaster," who learned that knowledge was not actually required to teach. Instead, Jacotot's success as a teacher was rooted in his philosophy that all people were equally intelligent. Jacotot understood that (equal) intelligences are served by (different) wills, wills are not served by different capacities for reason. There is no fundamental inequality of intelligence among individuals or, we might add, groups, there are only unequal wills: different types of attention, comportment, and commitments. The challenge to empiricism in antebellum thought (or the challenge to "the empiricists," who also go under the name of the "progressives," in Rancière's terms), might thus be understood as a rejection of pedagogical stultification in favor of the universal intellect. In refusing the lessons of the pedagogue, they affirm the equality of the intelligence and a model of intellectual emancipation that holds up the power of the will as the true movement of intelligence and learning. At the same time, Blake (and Delany too) is far from the model of intellectual emancipation that Rancière advocates; unlike the ignorant schoolmaster, Blake (and Delany) has clear ideas about the intellectual distinctions between enlightened free people and those held in slavery; and while he certainly believes in elevation through education, it's hard to ignore the implicit assumptions about enslaved people's inherent capacities that traverse his fiction and political essays and speeches. In this way, we might move instead to think about forms of collective study and autodidacticism in antebellum black thought, forms of study and learning in common that were not rooted in assumptions about the different capacities of reason between, for example, free people and enslaved people. Finally, we might also rethink evocations of black genius in the period through Rancière's notion of intellectual emancipation: instead of holding up the "sable genius" as an *exception* to the inferior intellect of the African people, as figures like Jefferson and others did, African Americans throughout the nineteenth century transformed figures like Phillis Wheatley and Benjamin Banneker into figures that demonstrated both the quality and equality of black intellect.[27]

....

This genealogy of rationalism in antebellum black thought becomes more complicated when we shift to consider black women's thought, writing, and engagements with science in the period. The record of black women's practice and experimentation with science is much more visible in manuscript sources, in those private and semiprivate documents that did not find their way into the public sphere through the conduit of print. For example, in the research for my book, I used the friendship albums held at the Library Company, along with the records of the Institute for Colored Youth, to trace an elusive history of black women's practice and teaching of natural history, anatomy, and physiology in antebellum Philadelphia.[28] This world of manuscripts—including scrapbooks, record books, letters, and diaries—clearly brings us back to the realm of the stubbornly material. It also raises a question about who feels privileged to reflect on the singularity and autonomy of their own intellectual prowess. This is perhaps not a particularly surprising observation, but it is worth noting that literary scenes that foreground the powers of the black mind—these scenes of autonomous, pulsating brains—appear more often in works by men rather than women. At the same time, manuscript objects like Charlotte Forten Grimké's diaries, which span much of the nineteenth century, do offer an important glimpse of a black woman as an autodidact with a largely nonutilitarian relationship to knowledge. As a sometime teacher who was often forced out of jobs due to repeated bouts of illness and convalescence, Grimké spent a significant portion of her life working, writing, and thinking on her own. She established rigorous courses of research, reading, and translation for herself, even publishing her translation of Emile Erckmann and Alexandre Chatrian's novel *Madame Therese; or, the Volunteers of '92*, with Scribner in 1869.[29]

Grimké's journals are in many ways a record of what Fred Moten and Steve Harney call the revolutionary act of black study. The prefatory entry to her first diary notes that she hoped this form of writing would "enable me to judge correctly of the growth and improvement of my mind from year to year"; but this developmentalist model of learning quickly breaks down in the journal, especially after Grimké's formal schooling ends.[30] The diaries rather track study without teleology, study without end. Relatedly, there is an important scholasticism to Grimké's interests and work, one that deserves more attention, especially as it looks forward to the scholastic, philosophical investments of someone like Anna Julia Cooper, visible in her 1892 *A Voice from the South* and other writings.

But even when black women intellectuals in the nineteenth century express an intellectualism not beholden to an instrumental—or professional—relationship to knowledge, it is rare that they present their minds as autonomous and closed to outside influence, as we saw with the narrative representation of both Nat Turner and Delany's Blake. Importantly, for example, Cooper and Grimké might also be linked through forms of intellectual kinship and connection. As Shirley Moody-Turner has discussed, Cooper worked for years studying the lives and writings of the Grimké family, including Charlotte herself. She published the *Life and Writings of the Grimké Family* in 1951.[31] Grimké's journals reflect her intense forms of personal study, both within and outside of formal schooling, but that study, as Moten and Harney also talk about it, is also undertaken in common (or in the "undercommons") through the regular exchange and borrowing of books among other black women.[32] Similarly, the friendship albums make visible networks of intellectual collaboration among black women that implicitly reject the kind of intense interiority and contemplative individualism on display earlier in this essay. Rather than pointing back to the will and agency in the individual subject and his mind, in the friendship albums, will and intellect become externalized and networked on the page.

Jasmine Nichole Cobb offers at least one way that we might begin to think about the lure of the immaterial in the Cassey and Dickerson friendship albums at the Library Company. Cobb argues that black women purposively withheld visual representations of their bodies in the pages of the friendship albums.[33] According to Cobb, the refusal to visualize and reproduce black women's bodies is particularly important given a mainstream, transatlantic visual culture that grossly caricatured Philadelphia's black community. Cobb also thinks about the refusal of visuality in the friendship albums—or for our purposes here, what we might think of as a refusal to *materialize* the black body—as a calculated strategy for dealing with the dialectics of invisibility and hypervisibility that structured, and continues to structure, black life in the United States. In her terms, invisibility is both part of the social condition of blackness in modernity as well as an important representational tactic for African Americans.[34] I would add that without the visual aid of black women's bodies, the friendship albums traffic in the forms of interiority privileged in sentimental poetics and culture. In this way, the friendship albums interestingly remove the female body from the center of sentimentality. In doing so, they redirect readers from the material and the empirical to a mind, its relationship to a broader network of black women's intellect, and to the powers of what we might theorize as a distributed intellect, a collective genius.

As this essay has traversed a number of contexts related to race, materialism, reason, religion, and the archive, I want to conclude by making a perhaps more polemical statement about the current and possible relationship between early American studies and African American studies. Although early Americanists have, of course, long studied the history of the slave trade and the role of slavery in the development of colonial regimes in North America, black studies has also, since its founding in the Black Arts/Black Power era, autonomously developed theories and methods for studying the history and cultures of enslavement. Personally, I would like to see more interanimation between black studies and early American studies, and for theoretical conversations in African American studies to be taken more seriously within early American studies.[35] I'm particularly keen to see Black studies' robust theorization of the archive brought to bear on the empiricist tendencies of early American studies. Over the past two decades, a large body of scholarship has theorized the question and problem of the archive in the contexts of enslavement and its aftermath.[36] Work largely inspired by Saidiya Hartman's influential thinking has continued to ask: Is it possible to recover the voices of the enslaved from the ship accounts, plantation ledgers, and other "master" documents that largely define this archive? What analytical tools or reading practices might be used in such endeavors? And to what end? Do we read the archive of enslavement in the name of recovery, recuperation, or reparations? Or to isolate and amplify the archive's irreparable violences, silences, and negations, insofar as they reflect or possibly symbolize the experiences of black people and the irreparable violences of slavery and colonialism in the New World? I might note here that the status of the empirical within these debates is also interesting and vexed: for example, Hartman's own deployment of "critical fabulation" as a way to glean something from the archive through speculative forms of reading possibly conflicts with her earlier arguments that knowledge of the enslaved *cannot* be gleaned from the archive.[37]

The lessons of slavery's archive might ultimately prove useful for broader conversations about and approaches to the archive in early American studies. Of course, the fragmentations, violences, and silences of slavery's archive are rooted in the historical and structural specificities of the slave trade and slavery as well as the afterlife of both in the postemancipation era. And yet, the archive of enslavement also points to the fragmentary nature of all historical knowledge, while raising crucial questions about the transparency and authority of other archives. In other words, the theorization of slavery's archive—the archive as crypt, as impossibility, as constructed by the enslaver's voice—simultaneously points to the limits of the empirical for all forms of historical and cultural inquiry.[38] Simultaneously, scholarship on colonial archives, largely inspired by Derrida and Foucault, poses a similar question: Given the archive's relationship to institutions and the power located in them, are all archives colonial archives?[39] Such questions might temper the confidence of turns to the archive for scholars working on topics outside the study of slavery, though to be honest, it's difficult to imagine any topic in this period completely untethered from slavery and the settler colonial regimes from which it was spawned. At the same time, slavery and colonialism's haunting of *all* archives might simultaneously challenge a certain utopianism that still persists around the literature and writing of nominally free people in the antebellum period, along with the "literacy as liberation" thesis that often surrounds interpretations of slave narratives.[40]

To conclude, I'd like to return to my introduction to consider how the archive might be rethought, reconceived, "critically fabulated," and, at times, perhaps even strategically discarded when it ceases to be useful. Here, I'm thinking again of the "no future" elements of David Walker, Maria Stewart, Hosea Easton, and Nat Turner, but also something much later like Ralph Ellison's burning of his manuscripts, along with the many other "shadow books" that Kevin Young discusses in *The Grey Album*, those black books that "we don't have," due to poverty, premature death, creative blocks, neglect, and censorship, and that stand spectrally behind the black books that do exist in the world.[41] Young's idea of the "shadow book"—the book that never appeared, the removed book, the lost book—might be yet another way of thinking about the limits of empirical approaches to the archive in both early African American studies and early American studies more broadly. By looking to the diversity of black engagements with empirical science and empirical methods in the early national and antebellum period, we also see that people of African descent were themselves resisting a form of empiricism that still largely shapes historical and literary approaches to the archive. In other words, these figures were themselves problematizing the transparency and authority of the archive.[42] It seems to me that scholarship that thinks about historical actors' own theorization and relationship to the archive might be a great place to continue thinking about the uses and limits to empiricism within and beyond early black archives.

NOTES

Epigraph: Quoted from David Walker, *David Walker's Appeal to the Coloured Citizens of the World*, edited and with an introduction by Peter Hinks (University Park: Pennsylvannia State University Press, 2000), 31.

1 Walker, *David Walker's Appeal*, 31.

2   Walker, *David Walker's Appeal*, 31.
3   Walker, *David Walker's Appeal*, 22.
4   Dinius, "'Look!! Look!!! At This!!!!'"
5   Edelman, *No Future*.
6   McCune Smith, "On the Fourteenth Query," 225.
7   Kazanjian, *Brink of Freedom*.
8   Max Cavitch and Brian Connelly, call-for-papers for "Situation Critical!: Critique, Theory, and Early American Studies," a conference held at the McNeil Center for Early American Studies in spring 2016, November 18, 2014, https://networks.h-net.org/node/8585/discussions/52645/cfp-situation-critical-critique-theory-early-american-studies-32016.
9   Rivett, *Science of the Soul*.
10 Hickman, "Douglass Unbound," 325.
11 Greenberg, *Confessions of Nat Turner*, 45.
12 Greenberg, *Confessions of Nat Turner*, 45.
13 The authorship of *The Confessions of Nat Turner* by Thomas R. Gray, a Southampton, Virginia, lawyer and slaveholder, of course complicates any attempt to easily retrieve Turner's voice from the narrative itself. Thus my focus is on "scenes" of rationalism, rather than Turner's own feelings and perspective on these questions. The editor's own inabilities to access Turner's thoughts and motivations for revolting might thus be also read into these sections of the narrative that meditate on the inaccessible "recesses" of Turner's mind (and brain). My reading practice here is also informed by John Sekora's foundational argument about the importance of creatively reading the silences and slippages in slave narratives; see Sekora, "Black Message, White Envelope."
14 Greenberg, *Confessions of Nat Turner*, 45.
15 Greenberg, *Confessions of Nat Turner*, 45.
16 Delany, *Blake*, 114.
17 Delany, *Blake*, 99.
18 Italics are mine.
19 Delany, *Blake*, 124.
20 See Lowry, *Harriet Tubman*, 74–75; references to Douglass and Tubman's response to the 1833 Leonid meteor shower also appear in Williams, *Prudence Crandall's Legacy*.
21 During Blake's "tour" of plantations across the US South, there is also a mention of a visit to a plantation named "Metoyers," which is presumably a reference to the Metoyers plantation in antebellum Louisiana, a slaveholding plantation owned and run by free blacks. "Metoyers," of course, also resonates with "meteors," and interestingly constellates with the other scenes in the novel attuned to astronomical phenomena.
22 See, for example, Gates, *Figures in Black*, and Gates, *Trials of Phillis Wheatley*. On black literature as a forum for "representing the race," see also Jarrett, *Representing the Race*.

23 Nudelman, *John Brown's Body*, 42.
24 Nudelman, *John Brown's Body*, 63.
25 Nudelman, *John Brown's Body*, 65, 64.
26 Rancière, *Ignorant Schoolmaster*, 6–7.
27 Accounts of collective black genius can be also found in early twentieth-century works like Benjamin Brawley, "Negro Genius," 3–9, and W. E. B. Du Bois's *Gift of Black Folk*. On evocations of Wheatley, Banneker, and other early Black Atlantic figures as geniuses in contemporary scholarship, see, for example, Vincent Carretta, *Phillis Wheatley*, and Carretta and Gould, *Genius in Bondage*.
28 See the Amy Matilda Cassey Album, Martina Dickerson Album, and Mary Anne Dickerson Album in the holdings of the Library Company of Philadelphia. See also "The Cassey and Dickerson Friendship Album Project," lcpalbumproject.org.
29 Stevenson, *Journals of Charlotte Forten Grimké*, 49. For more on nineteenth-century engagements with translation and translations among black readers and writers in the US, see Looney, *Freedom Readers*.
30 Stevenson, *Journals of Charlotte Forten Grimké*, 58.
31 Moody-Turner notes that Cooper tried to get W. E. B. Du Bois to publish a series of articles on Charlotte Grimké in the pages of the *Crisis* magazine, but Du Bois refused (54).
32 Harney and Moten, *Undercommons*.
33 Cobb, *Picture Freedom*, 91–93.
34 Cobb, *Picture Freedom*, 8–10.
35 John Sallaint's "'This Week Black Paul Preach'd'" is interested in developing a reading method that is attentive to the fragmented manuscript artifacts of early North American Black Baptists, but his hailing of an "Early African American Studies" might also be taken up in the name of producing an interface and further exchange between African American studies and early American studies.
36 The scholarship on slavery and the archive is vast. An excellent overview is offered in the editor's introduction to a special issue of *Social Text*, "The Question of Recovery: Slavery, Freedom, and the Archive." See Helton et al., "The Question of Recovery." Other meditations include Simon Gikandi's "Rethinking the Archive of Enslavement," and Lowe, *Intimacies of Four Continents*. See also Saidiya Hartman's foundational writings, including *Scenes of Subjection; Lose Your Mother*; and "Venus in Two Acts."
37 Hartman, "Venus in Two Acts," 11.
38 On the archive of the Atlantic as "crypt," see Gikandi, "Rethinking the Archive of Enslavement."
39 See, for example, Stoler, *Along the Archival Grain*; Lisa Lowe, *Intimacies of Four Continents*; Richards, *Imperial Archive*; Derrida, *Archive Fever*; Foucault, *Archaeology of Knowledge*.

40 For a less sanguine take on the ontological and political status of nominally free people in the antebellum United States, see Warren, *Ontological Terror*. Christopher Hager offers an important critique of the "literacy as liberation" thesis in his study of enslaved and recently freed manuscript writings. See Hager, *Word by Word*.

41 Young, *The Grey Album*, 11, 12–19.

42 On theorizations of the archive among the first writers to canonize and thematize African American literature, see McHenry, *To Make Negro Literature*. See Cohen and Stein, *Early African American Print Culture*, for earlier metareflections by black writers. William J. Wilson was also cannily reflexive about the fragility of African American print in the antebellum period; for his 1859 serial on African American visual arts, see Wilson, "'Afric-American Picture Gallery.'"

BIBLIOGRAPHY

Brawley, Benjamin Griffith. "The Negro Genius." In *The Negro in Literature and Art in the United States*, 3–9. New York: Duffield, 1918.

Carretta, Vincent. *Phillis Wheatley: Biography of a Genius in Bondage*. Athens: University of Georgia Press, 2012.

Carretta, Vincent, and Philip Gould, eds. *Genius in Bondage: Literature of the Early Black Atlantic*. Lexington: University Press of Kentucky, 2001.

Cobb, Jasmine Nichole. *Picture Freedom: Remaking Black Visuality in the Early Nineteenth Century*. New York: NYU Press, 2015.

Cohen, Lara Langer, and Jordan Alexander Stein, eds. *Early African American Print Culture*. Philadelphia: University of Pennsylvania Press, 2012.

Dain, Bruce. *A Hideous Monster of the Mind: American Race Theory in the Early Republic*. Cambridge, MA: Harvard University Press, 2003.

Delany, Martin R. *Blake; or, the Huts of America*. Boston: Beacon, 1970.

Derrida, Jacques. *Archive Fever: A Freudian Impression*. Chicago: University of Chicago Press, 1996.

Dinius, Marcy. "'Look!! Look!!! At This!!!!': The Radical Typography of David Walker's Appeal." PMLA 126, no. 1 (January 2011): 55–72.

Du Bois, W. E. B. *The Gift of Black Folk: The Negroes in the Making of America*. New York: Oxford University Press, 2007.

Edelman, Lee. *No Future: Queer Theory and the Death Drive*. Durham, NC: Duke University Press, 2004.

Foucault, Michel. *The Archaeology of Knowledge: And the Discourse on Language*. Translated by A. M. Sheridan Smith. 1969, 1971. New York: Pantheon, 1972.

Gates, Henry Louis, Jr. *Figures in Black: Words, Signs, and the "Racial" Self*. New York: Oxford University Press, 1987.

Gates, Henry Louis, Jr. *The Trials of Phillis Wheatley: America's First Black Poet and Her Encounters with the Founding Fathers*. New York: Basic, 2003.

Gikandi, Simon. "Rethinking the Archive of Enslavement." *Early American Literature* 50, no. 1 (2015): 81–102.

Greenberg, Kenneth S., ed. *The Confessions of Nat Turner and Related Documents*. Boston: Bedford/St. Martin's, 1996.

Hager, Christopher. *Word by Word: Emancipation and the Act of Writing*. Cambridge, MA: Harvard University Press, 2013.

Harney, Stefano, and Fred Moten. *The Undercommons: Fugitive Planning and Black Study*. Brooklyn: Minor Compositions, 2013.

Hartman, Saidiya. *Lose Your Mother: A Journey along the Atlantic Slave Route*. New York: Farrar, Straus and Giroux, 2007.

Hartman, Saidiya. *Scenes of Subjection: Terror, Slavery, and Self-Making in Nineteenth-Century America*. Durham, NC: Duke University Press, 1997.

Hartman, Saidiya. "Venus in Two Acts." *small axe* 12, no. 2 (June 2008): 1–14.

Helton, Laura, et al. "The Question of Recovery: An Introduction." *Social Text* 33, no. 4 (2015): 1–18.

Hickman, Jared. "Douglass Unbound." *Nineteenth-Century Literature* 68, no. 3 (2013): 323–62.

Jarrett, Gene Andrew. *Representing the Race: A New Political History of African American Literature*. New York: NYU Press, 2011.

Kazanjian, David. *The Brink of Freedom: Improvising Life in the Nineteenth-Century Atlantic World*. Durham, NC: Duke University Press, 2016.

Looney, Dennis. *Freedom Readers: The African American Reception of Dante Alighieri and the Divine Comedy*. Notre Dame, IN: University of Notre Dame Press, 2011.

Lowe, Lisa. *The Intimacies of Four Continents*. Durham, NC: Duke University Press, 2015.

Lowry, Beverly. *Harriet Tubman: Imagining a Life*. New York: Anchor, 2007.

McCune Smith, James. "On the Fourteenth Query of Thomas Jefferson's Notes on Virginia." *Anglo-African Magazine* 1 (1859): 225.

McHenry, Elizabeth. *To Make Negro Literature: Writing, Literary Practice, and African American Authorship*. Durham, NC: Duke University Press, 2021.

Moody-Turner, Shirley. "'Dear Doctor Du Bois': Anna Julia Cooper, W. E. B. Du Bois, and the Gender Politics of Black Publishing." *MELUS* 40, no. 3 (Fall 2015): 47–68.

Nudelman, Franny. *John Brown's Body: Slavery, Violence, and the Culture of War*. Chapel Hill: University of North Carolina Press, 2004.

Rancière, Jacques. *The Ignorant Schoolmaster: Five Lessons in Intellectual Emancipation*. Translated by Kristin Ross. Stanford, CA: Stanford University Press, 1991.

Richards, Thomas. *The Imperial Archive: Knowledge and the Fantasy of Empire*. London: Verso, 1993.

Rivett, Sarah. *The Science of the Soul in Colonial New England*. Chapel Hill: University of North Carolina Press, 2011.

Sallaint, John. "'This Week Black Paul Preach'd': Fragment and Method in Early African American Studies." *Early American Studies* 14, no. 1 (Winter 2016): 48–81.

Sekora, John. "Black Message, White Envelope: Genre, Authenticity, and Authority in the Antebellum Slave Narrative." *Callaloo* 32 (Summer 1987): 482–515.

Stevenson, Brenda, ed. *The Journals of Charlotte Forten Grimké*. New York: Oxford University Press, 1988.

Stoler, Laura Ann. *Along the Archival Grain: Epistemic Anxieties and Colonial Common Sense*. Princeton, NJ: Princeton University Press, 2009.

Walker, David. *David Walker's Appeal to the Coloured Citizens of the World*. Edited and with an introduction by Peter P. Hinks. University Park: Penn State University Press, 2000.

Warren, Calvin. *Ontological Terror: Blackness, Nihilism, and Emancipation*. Durham, NC: Duke University Press, 2018.

Williams, Donald E., Jr. *Prudence Crandall's Legacy: The Fight for Equality in the 1830s, Dred Scott, and Brown v. Board of Education*. Middletown, CT: Wesleyan University Press, 2014.

Wilson, William J. "'Afric-American Picture Gallery' (1859)." Edited and introduced by Leif Eckstrom and Britt Rusert. *Just Teach One: Early African American Print*, no. 2, Fall 2015, https://jtoaa.americanantiquarian.org/welcome-to-just-teach-one-african-american/afric-american-picture-gallery/.

Young, Kevin. *The Grey Album: On the Blackness of Blackness*. Minneapolis: Graywolf Press, 2012.

EIGHT · *Jordan Alexander Stein*

Queering Abolition

Family comes first. Such a sentiment, at least, seems to be what provoked Margaretta Mason, the wife of a Virginia senator, when Lydia Maria Child publicly offered to nurse the condemned John Brown in 1859. Calling Child's overtures of sympathy for Brown hypocritical, Mason asked rhetorically whether "*you* ever watched the last, lingering illness of a consumptive, to soothe, as far as in you lay, the inevitable fate? Do *you* soften the pangs of maternity in those around you by all the care and comfort you can give? Do *you* grieve with those *near* you, even though their sorrows resulted from their own misconduct?"[1] In response to Mason's accusations that Child and Northern women more generally did not care for the pains of those in their own communities, Child replied coolly that "I have never known an instance where the 'pangs of maternity' did not meet with requisite assistance; and here at the North, after we have helped the mothers, *we do not sell the babies*."[2]

Circulating more than 300,000 copies, this moment in the antislavery pamphlet published as *Correspondence between Lydia Maria Child, and Gov. Wise, and Mrs. Mason, of Virginia* might be considered the capstone of the inexhaustible abolitionist trope of the broken slave family.[3] With spectacular precedents, including Eliza crossing in the frozen Ohio River in Harriet Beecher Stowe's *Uncle Tom's Cabin* (1852) and the president's daughter leaping into the Potomac in William Wells Brown's *Clotel* (1852), scenes of broken slave families mobilized sentimental discourses and emphasized domestic fatality as the most consequential of slavery's many consequences. Devoting an entire chapter of *A Key to Uncle Tom's Cabin* (1853) to the "Separation of Families," Stowe propounded the view that supplies the moral force to Child's rebuff of Mason: "The worst abuse of the system of slavery is its outrage upon the family; and, as the writer views the subject, it is one which is more notorious and undeniable than any other."[4]

If indeed it is "notorious" that slavery unmade families, however, it is much less often recognized that antislavery discourse went a long way toward making them in the first place. The abundant mediascape and distribution networks of the antislavery movement committed enormous—and, more to the point, *unprecedented*—energies to edifying the agency and power of domestic life. These transformations fomented by antislavery media, and their impacts on US culture more generally, are the subject of this chapter. As we shall see, antislavery media is animated by ideological presuppositions about the inevitability of domestic familial life and the naturalness of gender roles—in short, by what the twentieth century learned to call heteronormativity.

More specifically, this chapter explores some particular examples of how antislavery media, and the later sentimental literature that takes its cues from it, tries to resolve the inhumane labor of the plantation into the sentimental scene of the home—and along the way imagines that a scheme for expropriated labor and capital accumulation (slavery) could be successfully countered by redefining the terms of social reproduction (family). The aim of this project is to elaborate how antislavery media might be understood as a historically necessary part of what Lauren Berlant and Michael Warner have called "the project of normalization that has made heterosexuality hegemonic."[5] Its argument is that antislavery media creates a version of slavery whose opposite is neither freedom nor wage labor, but heterosexuality.

....

Antislavery media refers first and foremost to the publications organized under the auspices of antislavery societies in the US, beginning about 1830.[6] As Trish Loughran argues, "Abolition unfolds itself in these years within a vast culture industry, of which it must be understood to hold itself a central share."[7] To be sure, abolitionist texts had existed in the decades prior.[8] George Bourne's *The Book and Slavery Irreconcilable*, published in Philadelphia in 1816, offers an early example of a radical abolitionist pamphlet, just as *Life of William Grimes, the Runaway Slave; Written by Himself*, published in New York in 1825, offers an early example of the narrative of a formerly enslaved person. Unconnected to organized social movements, however, these texts achieved modest circulation in single editions.[9] By contrast, publications generated under the auspices of antislavery societies after 1830 appeared on a much grander scale, often taking substantial advantage of that decade's technological developments, including the domestic manufacture of the steam press and the expansion of postal networks.[10] By 1835, the American Anti-Slavery Society's annual report announced well over a million items printed by the society that year, an output "*nine* times as great as those of last year, at about only *five* times the expense."[11] These pamphlets and tracts were disseminated via the postal system (due in part to the absence of affiliate societies in slaveholding states), and at the peak of its postal campaign in July 1835 the AASS mailed approximately 175,000 pieces to the South, "a number," according to one historian's estimate, "equal to the entire periodical output of the South for an equivalent period."[12] Though impressive by themselves, the significance of these numbers comes into relief when contrasted with earlier antislavery media. The print runs for Bourne's or Grimes's texts, for example, would have been much smaller—no more than two thousand copies—and would only have been distributed regionally, through their author's and possibly their publisher's personal networks.[13]

Because the media generated by antislavery societies took advantage of technological developments in the 1830s and after, its circulation was substantial enough to impact other abolitionist media unaffiliated with antislavery societies.[14] This is not to deny that well into the "print explosion" of the 1850s, some abolitionist media did continue to work astride the formal organization of antislavery societies—sometimes deliberately, as in the case of the *North Star* and later *Frederick Douglass' Paper*, which Douglass began to edit in Syracuse, New York, in 1847, following his break with Garrisonian abolition, and sometimes simply with a more entrepreneurial motive, as in the case of the Washington, DC–based *National Era*, owned by businessman Gamaliel Bailey, in which *Uncle Tom's Cabin* was serialized during 1851–52.[15] But even though these media outlets and the texts they produced were not beholden to any direct control by antislavery societies, they were nevertheless shaped by those societies' conventions in some important ways.[16]

Chiefly influential among those conventions was an aesthetic commitment to documentary realism. Though scholars rightly associate abolitionist media with sentimental fiction, before the Civil War sentimental fiction was widely accepted as a realist genre.[17] As Stowe wrote to Bailey in 1851, shortly after embarking on what was to become the century's most important sentimental novel, "My vocation is simply that of a painter, and my object will be to hold up in the most lifelike and graphic manner possible

Slavery, its reverses, changes, and the negro character, which I have had ample opportunities for studying. There is no arguing with *pictures*, and everybody is impressed by them, whether they mean to be or not."[18] Such an account of the aims of *Uncle Tom's Cabin* would imply that the differentiation between sentimental fiction and realism, and the former's association with popular romance and demotic genres, held little if any place in antebellum aesthetics.[19] Moreover, Stowe's claim follows on a premise well honed by antislavery media, whether fictional or nonfictional, that its most apposite aesthetic mode is that of documentation.

Beginning in the 1830s, antislavery media aspired to depict what the title of Theodore Dwight Weld and Angelina and Sarah Grimké's massive documentary compendium called *American Slavery as It Is*. Culling (especially Southern) newspapers and other publicly circulating texts, this 1839 collection collated reprehensible details about slavery by topic, including particulars of the violent punishments enslaved people received for disobedience, or the immodest garments with which enslaved mothers were supplied. The result of painstaking and highly motivated editorial work, the text was presented as a matter of "fact," on which readers were asked to deliberate in order to arrive on their own at the editors' incontrovertible conclusion.[20] The same use of documentation animates *A Key to Uncle Tom's Cabin*, and it appears in other antislavery texts all the way up to the Civil War. Lydia Maria Child's *The Patriarchal Institution, as Described by Members of Its Own Family* (1860), for instance, unflinchingly pairs excerpts from Southern antimiscegenation arguments with text from advertisements for "runaway slaves" with light hair and blue eyes.[21]

Though these texts evince a strong editorial point of view, their authors and editors emphasized the simple referentiality of their compilations and the facticity of their sources. As a consequence, in the context of antislavery media, *documentary* does not describe a merely disinterested practice of recording and reviewing official records, so much as an aesthetic or style of repurposing preprinted texts with the deliberate intention to persuade, while at the same time disavowing the significance of the context of this repurposing. By disavowing that context while privileging documentation, antislavery texts took some complex ethical leaps. Slave narratives generated under the auspices of antislavery societies required first-person testimony from formerly enslaved people but were printed with authenticating prefaces by white society members. These prefaces not only endorsed the character of the narratives' authors, but also framed their messages to suit abolitionists' assumptions, as, for example, when William

Lloyd Garrison enjoined the readers of Douglass's *Narrative* to recall that under slavery, "when the marriage institution is abolished, concubinage, adultery, and incest must necessarily abound"—points that Douglass's text itself does not much otherwise elaborate.[22] Additionally, many texts published by antebellum antislavery societies often propounded the violence of slavery against black people, and, in the name of trying ultimately to eradicate that violence, achieved what Saidiya Hartman describes as "reinforc[ing] the spectacular character of black suffering."[23] Far from merely documenting the truth "as it is," antislavery media's documentary practices generated and circulated an aesthetic that was adopted by texts produced under other auspices. Thus, a black critic of slavery like William Wells Brown, writing from London in 1852, would incorporate this aesthetic into one of the earliest of what are now called African American novels, by reprinting and repurposing his own prior writings alongside those of others.[24]

In addition to their use of a documentary aesthetic, these texts by Weld and the Grimkés, by Stowe, by Child, and by Brown, all have a further similarity. All these examples—whether produced under the immediate auspices of antislavery societies or just influenced by their conventions—share a thematic interest in domestic life. Stowe's protest against the separation of families, or Child's exposure of Southern miscegenation, or the pursuit of the heroine's legitimate paternity in Brown's *Clotel*, all evince how these authors used the documentary realist aesthetic of antislavery media to talk about familial and often highly gendered social relationships. To make this point another way, we might say that as they pursue an interest in laying bare facts about slavery, in all these texts, a further interest in domesticity consistently creeps in and often assumes central focus.[25]

....

While details about domestic and familial relationships—and other frequently catalogued details, such as those about household maintenance, dress and dishabille, and, in a more abstract sense, embodied or affective experiences among the enslaved—are, certainly, aspects of the institution of slavery, what's most striking about this emphasis on what we might summarize as "domesticity" is that, logically speaking, it is in no way what primarily justifies, rationalizes, explains, or defines the institution. Rather, slavery, by definition, is a means of (usually systematically) expropriating the labor and restricting the freedoms of another. Slavery emerges in modern political thought as an economic category, and only secondarily (and, arguably, retroactively) becomes justified as a social one. "The randomness and contingency of history nonetheless produces winners and losers," writes Hartman of the entirely casual deal struck between the Portuguese and the Akan or possibly Fante people who lived along the coast of western Africa, on what 150 years later was to become a major site of the transatlantic slave trade.[26] And with a similar sense of contingency, "It was no accident," writes Talal Asad, "that the beginnings of modern rights theories are to be found in Portugal and the Netherlands, the main centers of the slave trade at the time."[27]

Slavery is one of the very few things that perhaps can be understood primarily in economic terms, and, indeed, as a way of talking about labor, it is in many conversations primary *among* economic terms. It is due particularly to the influence of Marxism that modern Western social and economic thought regards slavery and capitalism as different things, though—as scholars including Orlando Patterson, Patricia J. Williams, Walter Johnson, and Stephanie E. Smallwood have emphasized—alienation and dehumanization are the result of making commodities of humans and human labor alike.[28] In contrast to these economic arguments, antislavery media imagines instead that slavery does damage to families, and that this damage is the fundamental problem with the institution. Antislavery media creates a version of slavery in which moral objections are more regularly trumpeted than economic alternatives.

....

Moral objections to slavery's disruption of families privilege domesticity among the problems with slavery, and they often explain this privileging with recourse to highly gendered assumptions about how families work. The above examples from Child's exchange with Mason and Stowe's *Uncle Tom's Cabin* both turn on the subtle but significant detail that the disruption of families is exemplified by the threat of separating mothers and children. Indeed, the lion's share of discourse around the disruption of slave families circles around the mother-child dyad, despite the facts that this is neither the only possible separation entailed by slavery, nor necessarily the most common, nor, in any case, the only meaningful form of kin relation.[29]

Certainly one reason for the emphasis on this particular conceit is its potential for sympathetic appeal, on the part of mothers who have lost children, for other mothers threatened with earthly separation—an identificatory relation that Karen Sánchez-Eppler has called "the exploitation inherent in [the] also empowering political alliance" between feminism and abolition.³⁰ Stowe, most famously, dramatizes this sympathetic scene in the ninth chapter of *Uncle Tom's Cabin*, wherein the death of Senator and Mrs. Bird's son motivates their abetting of Eliza's escape with her son. However, the fact that it is Senator Bird, even more than his wife, who sympathizes with a mother's plight, suggests that one does not have to be a mother to identify with a mother, any more than one has to be enslaved to identify with the enslaved. Because identification is, by definition, transitive across the bounds of identity, the emotional power of the mother-child dyad is much more easily explained than is its relatively consistent appearance in antislavery media.

Indeed, the relative ubiquity of this image seems to rely on the potential for identification to traverse the bounds of identity, as the child that is paired with the mother is more often than not a male child, and thus the incredible specificity of the image's denotative dimension is belied by the capacious generality of the image's connotative dimension. Encoded into this figure of slavery's violence, in other words, is an allegory about the welding of sexual reproduction—figured as maternal power—with social reproduction—figured as masculine youth. That is, by conjoining a mother and a male child under the sign of a threat to their bond, this image in abolitionist media figures sexual and social reproduction as dependent upon one another, such that the disruption of one entails the disruption of the other. The power that this ideological position ascribes to women is both vast and counterfactual, as anyone who has ever been a child can attest that children do not automatically reproduce their parent's conditions of living simply as a result of being born.³¹ Yet the force of this image is not that it contains a truth, so much as it offers a narrative and symbolic means for organizing and naturalizing social relationships.³²

If Stowe's scene of sympathetic identification conflates sexual and social reproduction, this conflation exists at an even more subtle level among source texts for *Uncle Tom's Cabin*.³³ Consider, for example, these lines from Grace Greenwood's 1851 poem "The Leap from the Long Bridge," which does not deploy the mother-child dyad:

She pauses, she turns, ah! will she flee back?
Like wolves her pursuers howl loud on her track;
She lifteth to Heaven one look of despair,
Her anguish breaks forth in one hurried prayer.
Hark, her jailer's yell! like a bloodhound's bay

> On the low night-wind it sweeps!
> Now death, or the chain! to the stream she turns,
> And she leaps, O God, she leaps!
>
> The dark, and the cold, yet merciful wave
> Receives to its bosom the form of the slave.
> She rises, earth's scenes on her dim vision gleam,
> But she struggleth not with the strong, rushing stream,
> And low are the death-cries her woman's heart gives
>
> As she floats adown the river;
> Faint and more faint grow her drowning voice,
> And her cries have ceased for ever!³⁴

The figuration of this enslaved person as a woman is putatively based, the poem's prologue tells us, on a true story. Furthermore, what Russ Castronovo has compellingly identified as this poem's political necrophilia—its unsentimental embrace of death as a viable alternative to slavery—leaves the impression that this enslaved woman's sex is nothing other than a fact, a historical detail preserved in redescription.³⁵ And though the poem's preface gestures to a documentary aesthetic that disclaims the distinction between a poem and a fact, the poem's deployment of the phrase a "woman's heart" mediates between the two.

A cliché during the mid-nineteenth century, "woman's heart" and related terms like "woman's feeling" show up in generically disparate locations, from here in Greenwood's abolitionist poem, to Ned Buntline's dime novels, to Rebecca Harding Davis's magazine fiction, to Maria Cummins's *The Lamplighter*. Though this phrase is the only one in the whole of Greenwood's poem that gives interpretive weight to the femaleness of this enslaved person, it does so in a way that links this figure—female but childless—with the mother-child dyads we saw above. By ascribing a "woman's heart" to this enslaved person, the poem signifies her potential for participation in a version of femininity that is both essential to women and yet worthy of comment. She matters not as a character but as a type, and yet while her circumstances are determined by the typifications of slavery, their consequences are felt according to the typifications of gender.³⁶ By figuring this enslaved person who leaps to her death as a woman, the poem makes the subtle but ineluctable suggestion that her death signifies a social, as well as a personal, fatality. Entirely in the absence of a child, "The Leap from the Long Bridge" indicates without declaring that the stakes of slavery include the disruption of families, the coextensive interruption of sexual and social reproduction.

What is sometimes considered to be the priority that women assume, as agents, in and over antislavery media turns out instead to be a mediated effect of those writings. In particular, the value that women have in the examples discussed so far is a social value. Abolitionist writings that mediate political problems by way of female figures maintain an interest in women largely insofar as these women are not individuals but types, freighted with the significant power, but also the impossible responsibility, for the reproduction of nothing less than society itself.[37]

....

This analysis of the ways that domesticity—figured as both inevitability of domestic familial life and the naturalness of gender roles—operates in antislavery media takes cues from queer critique. In an generative 1998 essay, Lauren Berlant and Michael Warner offer a succinct summary of the ways in which "queer social practices like sex and theory try to unsettle the garbled but powerful norms supporting . . . privilege—including the project of normalization that has made heterosexuality hegemonic—as well as those material practices that, though not explicitly sexual, are implicated in the hierarchies of property and propriety that we will describe as heteronormative."[38] As we have seen in the preceding section, antislavery media falls among the not explicitly sexual agents of normalization that made heterosexuality hegemonic in the imagination of many who fought for a world without slavery.

It is important to emphasize that the normativity these media conjure, enforce, and reinforce around domesticity does not reflect any kind of historical or cultural inevitability. It is simply not possible that the creators of antislavery and abolitionist media were unaware of alternatives to the domestic familial life—whether they encountered them in the urban brothel culture of cities like New York or Baltimore or New Orleans that remained little regulated and basically legal into 1840s, the free love and communal movements like Oneida or Nabosha that began in the 1820s, or, indeed, the unashamedly nonconjugal sexual arrangement of Southern slave plantations. In this respect, one way to read Garrison's hand-wringing worry about "when the marriage institution is abolished, concubinage, adultery, and incest must necessarily abound," or Senator Bird's scene of sentimental identification, or Greenwood's rhetorical figures, is, collectively, as a doubling down.[39] Abolitionists largely saw slavery as a unified object worthy of their denunciation, and not as the more complex set of various systems and practices that latter-day scholars and historians have identified. And because they were unwilling to nuance their understandings of slavery, they also failed to observe that freedom too is more than one thing.[40] These assumptions are both understandable and shortsighted.

The political difficulty with such a conclusion, however, is that one has little cause to disagree with antislavery activists that the breakup of families under slavery was morally pernicious, personally disastrous, and savagely unfeeling. Though one may well object, as this essay has, to the rhetorical sleights of hand through which nineteenth-century antislavery activists and media producers established domesticity and heterosexuality as slavery's opposite, there is little political sense in imagining that the opposite of slavery's opposite is anything good. Indeed, many scholars, including Hortense Spillers, bell hooks, and Saidiya Hartman, have identified the historical damage done to black communities in the US through what Spillers calls "an enforced state of breach," where "'kinship' loses meaning."[41] These scholars have done so, moreover, while maintaining a nuanced understanding of kinship that is in many respects compatible with a critique of heteronormativity such as Berlant and Warner articulate. To make this point absolutely clear, this essay's objection is to the particular terms in which antislavery media made its arguments, not to the political ends of antislavery itself.

While it may seem pedantic to object simply to the terms of a political argument with whose conclusions we might otherwise agree, this objection is worth making if only because it has so rarely been made. For much of the twentieth century, the historiography of antislavery viewed antebellum activists as fanatics occupying a fringe position, a view that was definitively reversed in the 1960s. Since that time, historical scholarship has elaborated the contributions that antislavery activists made to American culture as a whole, observing both points of commonality between Northern antislavery activists and Southern intellectuals, and contributions of women and formerly enslaved people to the overall shape and character that antislavery activism took.[42] Despite these significant changes in scholarship on antislavery activism, for the whole of the twentieth century, across both sides of this historiographic divide, scholars have nonetheless taken the rhetorical terms of antislavery arguments largely at face value. The fairly major rhetorical feats of championing antislavery on moral rather than economic grounds and using an embattled heterosexual domesticity as the lever for this moral position represent a powerful mythology whose existence scholars have rarely questioned.

NOTES

1. Child, *Correspondence*, 17–18.
2. Child, *Correspondence*, 26.
3. This sales figure comes from Karcher, *The First Woman in the Republic*, 423.
4. Stowe, *Key to Uncle Tom's Cabin*, 257.
5. Berlant and Warner, "Sex in Public," 548.
6. For the purposes of this essay, I will use *abolition* to refer to a broader sensibility that opposed slavery, and *abolitionist media* to refer to antislavery texts produced under auspices other than those of antislavery societies, more about which is below. On the cosmopolitan sensibility of *abolition*, see Gould, *Barbaric Traffic*, and Nwankwo, *Black Cosmopolitanism*. For a helpful overview of the term, see Fanuzzi, "Abolition." On the post-1830 periodization, see Walters, *Anti-Slavery Appeal*.
7. Loughran, *Republic in Print*, 308.
8. For a very useful overview of existing source materials, see Newman, "Bibliography."
9. On the connection between social movements and the movement of texts, see Brooks, "The Unfortunates." Grimes did reissue his narrative with some additions thirty years later in an 1855 edition, printed for the author in New Haven.
10. Tebbel, *History of Book Publishing*; Moran, *Printing Presses*, 101–9; Charvat, *Profession of Authorship in America*; John, *Spreading the News*; Henkin, *Postal Age*; Winship, "Manufacturing and Book Production," esp. 55; Pottroff, "Citizen Technologies."
11. *Third Annual Report of the American Anti-Slavery Society*, 35, emphasis in original.
12. Nord, "Benevolent Books," 243. This paragraph condenses a discussion that appears in Stein, "Whig Interpretation of Media."
13. On Grimes, see Ashton, "Slavery, Imprinted."
14. This impact was arguably most legible in the generic development of the antebellum slave narrative, as John Sekora observes: "Because they summarize what white abolitionist sponsors sought in the antislavery texts they would publish, [slave narratives after 1830] indicate the institutional conditions under which many of the narratives were composed. Despite the enormous political changes occurring in America between the time of Briton Hammon and that of Frederick Douglass, the literary continuities are arresting. While they do promote a new way of understanding slavery, the changes in vocabulary, social attitude, and philosophical presupposition follow the revised agenda of the abolitionist movement"; Sekora, "Black Message/White Envelope," 495.

15 On the antebellum print explosion, see Cohen, *Fabrication of American Literature*.
16 Roy, *Fugitive Texts*.
17 Camfield, *Sentimental Twain*.
18 Stowe, letter to Gamaliel Bailey, March 9, 1851, qtd. in Hedrick, *Harriet Beecher Stowe*, 208.
19 Dillon, "Sentimental Aesthetics."
20 Weld, *American Slavery as It Is*, 7. On the editorial process of assembling this text, see Garvey, "Nineteenth-Century Abolitionists and the Databases They Created."
21 Child, *Patriarchal Institution*.
22 Garrison, "Preface," 33.
23 Hartman, *Scenes of Subjection*, 3; see also McBride, *Impossible Witness*.
24 On Brown's "patchwork aesthetic," see Cohen, "Notes from the State of Saint Domingue," esp. 164. See also Senchyne, "Bottles of Ink and Reams of Paper"; Sanborn, "'People Will Pay to Hear the Drama'"; Greenspan, *William Wells Brown*.
25 Any attempt to explain why this happens would exceed the scope of this chapter, though Jeffrey Insko has recently made the suggestive argument that antebellum Americans tended to be more interested in a strategic presentism than in any profound commitment to history. See Insko, *History, Abolition, and the Ever-Present Now*.
26 Hartman, *Lose Your Mother*, 59.
27 Asad, *Formation of the Secular*, 131.
28 Patterson, *Slavery and Social Death*; Williams, *Alchemy of Race and Rights*; Johnson, *Soul by Soul* and "Pedestal and the Veil"; Smallwood, *Saltwater Slavery*.
29 Tera W. Hunter describes the emphasis on the part of the Freedmen's Bureau after the Civil War on reuniting husbands and wives in *Bound in Wedlock*.
30 Sánchez-Eppler, *Touching Liberty*, 10. See also Cohen's incredibly moving "Past Griefs."
31 For an excellent account of the complexity of intergenerational transmission, see Berlant, "Nearly Utopian, Nearly Normal."
32 See Warner, "Irving's Posterity": "it isn't exactly reproduction that people want from what is called reproduction; what they want is a narrative to organize a life course up to and beyond mortality" (787).
33 This story first came to public attention in a short notice by Seth M. Gates, a congressman from New York, published under the headline "Slavery in the District," on the front page of the *New York Evangelist*, on September 8, 1842. Its recirculation is tracked in the opening pages of Jackson, "Another Long Bridge."
34 Greenwood, *Poems*, 74.
35 Castronovo, "Political Necrophilia."
36 On the difference between characters and types, see Stein, *When Novels Were Books*, 21–22.

37 Edelman, *No Future*.
38 Berlant and Warner, "Sex in Public," 548.
39 Jen Manion observes that proslavery arguments frequently accused abolitions of challenging gender norms as well—a position abolitionists refused rather than embraced. See *Female Husbands*, 175.
40 Johnson, *Wicked Flesh*.
41 hooks, *Ain't I A Woman*; Spillers, "Mama's Baby, Papa's Maybe," 74; Hartman, *Lose Your Mother*.
42 The scholarship here is voluminous, but for the best recent synthesis, see Jackson, *American Radicals*. For other useful summaries from different moments in time, see Friedman, "Abolitionist Historiography, 1965–1979"; Hoganson, "Garrisonian Abolitionists and the Rhetoric of Gender, 1850–1860."

BIBLIOGRAPHY

Asad, Talal. *Formation of the Secular: Christianity, Islam, Modernity*. Stanford, CA: Stanford University Press, 2003.

Ashton, Susanna. "Slavery, Imprinted: The Life and Narrative of William Grimes." In *Early African American Print Culture*, edited by Lara Langer Cohen and Jordan Alexander Stein, 127–39. Philadelphia: University of Pennsylvania Press, 2012.

Berlant, Lauren. "Nearly Utopian, Nearly Normal: Post-Fordist Affect in *La Promesse* and *Rosetta*." *Public Culture* 19, no. 2 (2007): 273–301. doi.org/10.1215/08992363-2006-036.

Berlant, Lauren, and Michael Warner. "Sex in Public." *Critical Inquiry* 24, no. 2 (Winter 1998): 547–66.

Brooks, Joanna. "The Unfortunates: What the Life Spans of Early Black Books Tell Us about Book History." In *Early African American Print Culture*, edited by Lara Langer Cohen and Jordan Alexander Stein, 40–52. Philadelphia: University of Pennsylvania Press, 2012.

Camfield, Gregg. *Sentimental Twain: Samuel Clemens in the Maze of Moral Philosophy*. Philadelphia: University of Pennsylvania Press, 1994.

Castronovo, Russ. "Political Necrophilia." *boundary 2* 27, no. 2 (2000): 113–48.

Charvat, William. *The Profession of Authorship in America, 1800–1870: The Papers of William Charvat*. Edited by Matthew J. Bruccoli. 1968. New York: Columbia University Press, 1992.

Child, Lydia Maria. *Correspondence between Lydia Maria Child, and Gov. Wise and Mrs. Mason, of Virginia*. Boston: American Anti-Slavery Society, 1860.

Child, Lydia Maria, ed. *The Patriarchal Institution, as Described by Members of Its Own Family*. New York: American Anti-Slavery Society, 1860.

Cohen, Lara Langer. *The Fabrication of American Literature: Fraudulence and Antebellum Print Culture*. Philadelphia: University of Pennsylvania Press, 2011.

Cohen, Lara Langer. "Notes from the State of Saint Domingue: The Practice of Citation in *Clotel*." In *Early African American Print Culture*, edited by Lara Langer Cohen and Jordan Alexander Stein, 161–77. Philadelphia: University of Pennsylvania Press, 2012.

Cohen, Lara Langer. "Past Griefs." *J19: A Journal of Nineteenth-Century Americanists* 2, no. 2 (2014): 200–206. doi.org/10.1353/jnc.2014.0022.

Dillon, Elizabeth Maddock. "Sentimental Aesthetics." *American Literature* 76, no. 3 (September 2004): 495–523. doi.org/10.1215/00029831-76-3-495.

Edelman, Lee. *No Future: Queer Theory and the Death Drive*. Durham, NC: Duke University Press, 2004.

Fanuzzi, Robert. "Abolition." *Keywords for American Cultural Studies*, 3rd ed., edited by Bruce Burgett and Glenn Hendler, 1–4. New York: NYU Press, 2020.

Friedman, Lawrence J. "Abolitionist Historiography, 1965–1979: An Assessment." *Reviews in American History* 8, no. 2 (June 1980): 200–205. doi.org/10.2307/2701118.

Garrison, William Lloyd. "Preface." *Narrative of the Life of Frederic Douglass, an American Slave, Written by Himself*, by Frederick Douglass, edited by David W. Blight. 1845. Boston: Bedford/St. Martin's, 1993.

Garvey, Ellen Gruber. "Nineteenth-Century Abolitionists and the Databases They Created." *Legacy: A Journal of American Women Writers* 27, no. 2 (2010): 357–66. doi.org/10.5250/legacy.27.2.0357.

Gould, Philip. *Barbaric Traffic: Commerce and Antislavery in the Eighteenth-Century Atlantic World*. Cambridge, MA: Harvard University Press, 2003.

Greenspan, Ezra. *William Wells Brown: An African American Life*. New York: Norton, 2014.

Greenwood, Grace. *Poems*. Boston: Ticknor, Reed, and Fields, 1851.

Hartman, Saidiya. *Lose Your Mother: A Journey along the Atlantic Slave Route*. New York: Norton, 2007.

Hartman, Saidiya. *Scenes of Subjection: Terror, Slavery, and Self-Making in Nineteenth-Century America*. New York: Oxford University Press, 1997.

Hedrick, Joan D. *Harriet Beecher Stowe: A Life*. New York: Oxford University Press, 1994.

Henkin, David M. *The Postal Age: The Emergence of Modern Communications in Nineteenth-Century America*. Chicago: University of Chicago Press, 2007.

Hoganson, Kristin. "Garrisonian Abolitionists and the Rhetoric of Gender, 1850–1860." *American Quarterly* 45, no. 4 (December 1993): 558–95. doi.org/10.2307/2713309.

hooks, bell. *Ain't I a Woman: Black Women and Feminism*. Boston: South End Press, 1981.

Hunter, Tera W. *Bound in Wedlock: Slave and Free Black Marriage in the Nineteenth Century*. Cambridge, MA: Belknap Press of Harvard University Press, 2017.

Insko, Jeffrey. *History, Abolition, and the Ever-Present Now in Antebellum American Writing*. Oxford: Oxford University Press, 2018.

Jackson, Holly. *American Radicals: How Nineteenth-Century Protest Shaped the Nation*. New York: Crown, 2019.

Jackson, Holly. "Another Long Bridge: Reproduction and Reversion in Hagar's Daughter." In *Early African American Print Culture*, edited by Lara Langer Cohen and Jordan Alexander Stein, 192–202. Philadelphia: University of Pennsylvania Press, 2012.

John, Richard R. *Spreading the News: The American Postal System from Franklin to Morse*. Cambridge, MA: Harvard University Press, 1995.

Johnson, Jessica Marie. *Wicked Flesh: Black Women, Intimacy, and Freedom in the Atlantic World*. Philadelphia: University of Pennsylvania Press, 2020.

Johnson, Walter. "The Pedestal and the Veil: Rethinking the Capitalism/Slavery Question." *Journal of the Early Republic* 24, no. 2 (2004): 299–308. doi.org/10.9783/9780812207231.149.

Johnson, Walter. *Soul by Soul: Life inside the Antebellum Slave Market*. Cambridge, MA: Harvard University Press, 1999.

Karcher, Carolyn L. *The First Woman in the Republic: A Cultural Biography of Lydia Maria Child*. Durham, NC: Duke University Press, 1994.

Loughran, Trish. *The Republic in Print: Print Culture in the Age of U.S. Nation Building, 1770–1870*. New York: Columbia University Press, 2007.

Manion, Jen. *Female Husbands: A Trans History*. Cambridge: Cambridge University Press, 2020.

McBride, Dwight A. *Impossible Witness: Truth, Abolitionism, and Slave Testimony*. New York: NYU Press, 2001.

Moran, James. *Printing Presses: History and Development from the Fifteenth Century to Modern Times*. Berkeley: University of California Press, 1973.

Newman, Richard. "Bibliography." In *The Harvard Guide to African-American History*, edited by Evelyn Brooks Higginbotham et al., 3–22. Cambridge, MA: Harvard University Press, 2001.

Nord, David Paul. "Benevolent Books: Printing, Religion, and Reform." In *A History of the Book in America, Volume 2: An Extensive Republic: Print, Culture, and Society in the New Nation, 1790–1840*, edited by Robert A. Gross and Mary Kelley, 221–46. Chapel Hill: University of North Carolina Press, 2010.

Nwankwo, Ifeoma Kiddoe. *Black Cosmopolitanism: Racial Consciousness and Transnational Identity in the Nineteenth-Century Americas*. Philadelphia: University of Pennsylvania Press, 2005.

Patterson, Orlando. *Slavery and Social Death: A Comparative Study*. Cambridge, MA: Harvard University Press, 1982.

Pottroff, Christy Lee. "Citizen Technologies: The U.S. Post Office and the Transformation of Early American Literature." PhD diss., Fordham University, 2017.

Roy, Michaël. *Fugitive Texts: Slave Narratives in Antebellum Print Culture*. Translated by Susan Pickford. Madison: University of Wisconsin Press, 2022.

Sanborn, Geoffrey. "'People Will Pay to Hear the Drama': Plagiarism in *Clotel*." *African American Review* 45, nos. 1–2 (Spring/Summer 2012): 65–82. doi.org/10.1353/afa.2012.0027.

Sánchez-Eppler, Karen. *Touching Liberty: Abolition, Feminism, and the Politics of the Body*. Berkeley: University of California Press, 1993.

Sekora, John. "Black Message/White Envelope: Genre, Authenticity, and Authority in the Antebellum Slave Narrative." *Callaloo* 32 (Summer 1987): 482–515. doi.org/10.2307/2930465.

Senchyne, Jonathan. "Bottles of Ink and Reams of Paper: *Clotel*, Racialization, and the Material Culture of Print." In *Early African American Print Culture*, edited by Lara Langer Cohen and Jordan Alexander Stein, 140–58. Philadelphia: University of Pennsylvania Press, 2012.

Smallwood, Stephanie E. *Saltwater Slavery: A Middle Passage from Africa to American Diaspora*. Cambridge, MA: Harvard University Press, 2008.

Spillers, Hortense J. "Mama's Baby, Papa's Maybe: An American Grammar Book." *Diacritics* 17, no. 2 (Summer 1987): 64–81. doi.org/10.2307/464747.

Stein, Jordan Alexander. *When Novels Were Books*. Cambridge, MA: Harvard University Press, 2020.

Stein, Jordan Alexander. "The Whig Interpretation of Media: Sheppard Lee and Jacksonian Paperwork." *History of the Present* 3, no. 1 (Summer 2013): 29–56. doi.org/10.5406/historypresent.3.1.0029.

Stowe, Harriet Beecher. *A Key to Uncle Tom's Cabin*. Boston: J. P. Jewett, 1853.

Tebbel, John William. *A History of Book Publishing in the United States*. Vol. 1. New York: Bowker, 1972.

Third Annual Report of the American Anti-Slavery Society. New York: William S. Dorr, 1836.

Walters, Ronald G. *The Anti-Slavery Appeal: American Abolitionism after 1830*. Baltimore: Johns Hopkins University Press, 1976.

Warner, Michael. "Irving's Posterity." ELH 67, no. 3 (2000): 773–99. doi.org/10.1353/elh.2000.0029.

Weld, Theodore Dwight, Angelina Grimké, and Sarah Grimké. *American Slavery as It Is: Testimony of a Thousand Witnesses*. New York: American Anti-Slavery Society, 1839.

Williams, Patricia J. *The Alchemy of Race and Rights: Diary of a Law Professor*. Cambridge, MA: Harvard University Press, 1991.

Winship, Michael. "Manufacturing and Book Production." In *A History of the Book in America, volume 3: The Industrial Book, 1840–1880*, edited by Scott E. Casper, Jeffrey D. Groves, Stephen W. Nissenbaum, and Michael Winship, 40–69. Chapel Hill: University of North Carolina Press, 2007.

IV POWER, KNOWLEDGE, JUSTICE

NINE · *Matthew Crow*

Equity in the Time of *Moby-Dick*

> The more consistently the legal systems are worked out, however, the greater their incapacity to absorb what essentially defies absorption.
> —THEODOR ADORNO, *NEGATIVE DIALECTICS*

Talk of equity is just about everywhere these days, usually as an ethical indictment of unearned privilege and power. But the concept of equity, historically, is messier, and much more implicated in the problems of power and institutions than we generally appreciate. In an often-overlooked passage in his *Negative Dialectics*, the philosopher Theodor Adorno recommends Aristotle's idea of equity, "meant to be a corrective for the injustice of the law," even though the idea is often too easily dismissed as itself inequitable for introducing subjective, unaccountable discretion into an ideally rational and objective system.[1] The insight we can take from Adorno's thought here is that purported progress in the impartial administration of commercial society and its institutions will inevitably have to confront iterations of what it seeks to place safely in the past, that discretion and prerogative, the need for judgment, repressed in cold proceduralism and heated populism alike, can and will resurface with a vengeance, for good and for ill.

The intractability of discretion is a fundamental problem for modern political thought. This idea of equity as a critical, interpretive principle may well strike readers as unfamiliar, either from the normal operations of equity jurisprudence in Anglo-American legal history, from the political theology of sovereign decisionism romanticized in so much of contemporary politics, or from the progressive demands for values of diversity, equity, and inclusion in institutions today. But in each of these contexts and many others, liberal democracy confronts ancient questions of where the power to do justice sits in any institutional order, and over any case that may confront that order and comes before its constituted forms and powers of judgment. "Who's to doom," Captain Ahab asks in *Moby-Dick*, "when the judge himself is dragged to the bar?" That, too, is a meditation on equity, on the troubled legitimacy of corrective justice, and it carries with it some of the power of Adorno's insight.

Herman Melville's writing can be read as a response to these kinds of questions and problems as they arose in the wake of the age of revolutions, and in the confrontations of the normally subsuming work of imperial intellectual culture with physical, political realities that defy such absorption. Oceanic environments and overseas territories had compelled the development of discretionary powers that challenged narratives of the certainty of the rule of law replacing the arbitrary rule of men. From the powers of captains on ships to courts of chancery and admiralty, Melville was hardly alone in noticing the persistence of prerogative powers and discretionary justice up and down constitutional orders and across jurisdictional boundaries of recognized legality. He was, however, unique in his appraisal of this resurfacing of the questions of equity and discretion as questions, at bottom, of where the jurisdiction of natural justice sits, and of whether we can recognize it when it asserts itself.

Moby-Dick allegorizes the attempted absorption of equity, of natural justice and the promise of remedy and security, by the ascendancy of contract and the imperatives of a commercial legal culture. The book does so in ways that stage various episodes of the surprising institutional and wider cultural persistence of the inquisitorial and discretionary powers, and anxieties about those powers, appropriate to jurisdictional conflict and consideration of equity in early modern legal theory. Melville plays with sites of discretionary judgment, and that matters for us not because we need to endorse that power's apparent necessity or exceptionality, but because it was a critical riposte to the dominant political theory of his time, and of ours. His writing traces the relocation of the judicial responsibility to ensure justice from royal to republican institutions, or from the office of the Lord Chancellor and the power of the high courts, which drew ultimate authority from the conscience of the Crown, to the republican institutions and citizens of a postrevolutionary age telling itself stories of having left discretionary justice and arbitrary power behind.

Building on the work of Adorno and Michel Foucault, among others, the literary scholar Eric Santner has argued that modern subjectivity is a particular kind of creaturely life, an exposure to the "threshold of law and nonlaw," to the enduring, immutable historical forces that bring about law's mutability, its finitude, its ruin and decay. Modern political economy and popular sovereignty burden life with an individual responsibility for exercising judgment and maintaining the state, or at least our share of it, but that in reality makes imagining and actually constituting forms of collective judgment and action almost impossible except as intangible abstractions. "Something of the royal remains," Santner suggests, but in crumbling, increasingly anxious forms, marked by a redistribution of the medieval and early modern symbolic investiture of royal sovereignty from the body of the ruler into the citizen-subjects of liberal democracy.[2] As the powers of protective and corrective justice become questions of individual prerogative, we each feel the weight of that power but without any clear sense of what to do with it, and with that juridically charged surplus energy we become the anxious judges of ourselves and others. In response to Santner and across her own work, the political theorist Bonnie Honig has elaborated a radical-democratic political theory, describing a democratic politics of the flesh made vivid in Ishmael's experience of squeezing globs of spermaceti fluid with his fellow sailors.[3]

But for Melville, it is not sovereign decision per se but legal judgment that gets redistributed, masked, and often goes unaddressed, and Melville's work compels us to ponder the cost of banishing the early modern assumption that somewhere in the legal order there needed to be an office where the conscience of the state and the responsibility for justice could sit. Melville was obviously not naïve to the potential for abuse in this discretionary power, but he forces moderns to confront the fact that things they thought their critique of jurisdictions unchecked by republican political life had put out to sea are very much still around, especially, but not exclusively, at sea. No wonder Ahab, not unlike Jules Verne's Nemo, seems so ready to judge, and so weary of judgment! Discretion denied is discretion unleashed. Prerogative displaced is still prerogative, no less capable of cruelty and violence. Allegory and its study are some of the best resources we have to take stock of this mutual intermediation of transformation and persistence, to recognize our enmeshment in a world of powers that defy absorption in our usual understandings of law, politics, and history. We can see the fears of judgment, of being judged, of the idea of freedom as freedom from any kind of power of corrective justice so pervasive in the present as the vestiges of a settler colonial ideology whose ascendancy Melville witnessed firsthand. And we can see too the legal tools at our disposal that can acknowledge these other histories and environments as other legalities, and foster new relations with them, and among ourselves.

"I have swam through libraries," Ishmael tells us, but he yearns to "sing out for new stars."[4] This conjunction of intellectual history, of immersion in libraries, with the desire to break out into new hope and new knowledge, to have new stars with which to navigate, puts us in the realm of natural history, and allegory.[5] As Fredric Jameson hints, his late interlocutor on literary theory and history Hayden White rarely paid much attention to allegory, to that kind of narrative that surrenders claims to readily transparent meaning and identification, but the suggestion seems to be that it was lurking beneath the surface of their respectively intertwined work.[6] It is an admittedly unwieldy concept, no doubt more so in the hands of a historian. But allegory, Adorno suggests, is precisely how natural history finds its way into the humanistic corridors of intellectual history.[7] Decades after the high tide of theory in most American humanities departments, it might be time to take stock of the persistence of some of the problems critical theory posed to history about interpretative work and its possible contributions to political life. Looking for language that could capture the kinds of conjunctions of past and present Ishmael hints at above, the literary theorist Walter Benjamin turned to constellations, formulations that illuminate new possible history emerging from the ruinating forms of inherited authority. Allegory has shown up, Benjamin argues, precisely where "transitoriness and eternity confronted each other most closely," where established forms are exposed to natural history, to natural forces of ruin and decay, and birth and rebirth.[8] Slavery and empire and the oceanic environment these realities traversed exposed a kind of raw nerve in the legitimacy and durability of the new nation's laws, and Melville's writing is a response to that exposure, an exposure that reverberates in the present. The appearance of allegory is a sure sign of these reverberations from places unreconciled to written law and history. Benjamin named these oft-forgotten recesses of natural and historical reality the "allegorical depths," and those are the depths I would like to explore here.[9]

EQUITY IN TIME

As allegories of equity, Melville's writings are reflective, creatively, of history. While equitable consideration as a necessary component of legal interpretation could be traced back to Greek philosophy and Roman jurisprudence, in England the growth of the political and jurisdictional authority of the Lord Chancellor and the High Court of Chancery from the late fifteenth to the early seventeenth century created a distinctive and controversial branch of legal authority.[10] Jurisdictional conflict in seventeenth-century England was a crucial part of wider chasms in constitutional politics. Most notoriously in the Star Chamber, the equitable jurisdictions of the Lord Chancellor and other powerful judicial figures were extensions of the specifically legal power of the Crown itself: an institutional implementation of the royal prerogative and the conscience of the Crown. What it meant to incorporate conscience as a source of legal power or acknowledge it as a distinctive claim to right and authority was a tremendously important question that troubled writers and theorists in legal theory, political philosophy, and literature.

Thomas Hobbes teased out the implications of the idea of equity as a legal concept for the relationship between common law and royal prerogative, theorizing equity as the legal voice of authorized sovereign power, and therefore the guarantor of the rights of peace and security protected in the commonwealth. Custom and the artificial reason celebrated by Sir Edward Coke as the glory of the common law was in the eye of the beholder, and there were already too many beholders. Ignorant "of the causes and originall constitution of Right, Equity, Law, and Justice," people "appeale from custome to reason, and from reason to custome, as it serves their turn," Hobbes wrote in the notably titled *Leviathan* (1651), and so "the doctrine of Right and Wrong, is perpetually disputed, both by the Pen and the Sword."[11] That Hobbes and the early modern world in which he wrote shaped Melville's constructions of rule, law, and justice is beyond dispute. By the beginning of the eighteenth century, the Court of Chancery was a more regular part of the English legal system, and the use of principles of equity proved to be an important part of the development of a self-consciously modern and modernizing legal theory across Britain and the British Empire. Chancery and associated powers of discretionary judgment in higher courts also continued to be a flash point of constitutional conflict, especially in relations between British North American colonies and imperial governance.

In the antebellum period, equity remained a vehicle for working around common law constraints on property and facilitating a stable body of commercial legal precedent, but it was just as often discussed as a dangerous extension of possibly arbitrary judgment that could be as damaging as it was supportive of commercial interests and development.[12] James Kent, the Chancellor of New York from 1814 to 1823, hoped to make the Chancery Court a model for leveraging the power of the state in facilitating institutional authority, commercial development, and for expounding on the best rules within which that development could take place. Dying in 1847, he barely lived to see the end of the Chancery Court and the Masters of Chancery offices implemented by the state constitutional revision in 1846, the result of decades of ascendant populist agitation and Democratic disgust in state politics at the power Kent wielded and the ways in which he wielded it. As Amalia Kessler has argued, in case after case, most notably in *Remsen v. Remsen* (1817), Kent defended with aggressive flair the "quasi-inquisitorial," secretive, written, judge-centered methods of fact-finding and gathering testimony in chancery cases, noting their long persistence and legitimacy in English practice.[13] Concurrent with the rise of neo-Gothic architecture and High Church Anglicanism in New York City's Trinity Church on Wall Street, neighboring the offices of the Masters of Chancery in Melville's *Bartleby*, a nearly medieval legal and material culture of circulating manuscripts that was alive and well in the urban heart of modern commerce and democracy constituted a historical juxtaposition that the author could probably not help but notice.

The mature chancery jurisprudence elaborated by Joseph Story in his *Commentaries on Equity Jurisprudence* (1835), building off Kent's famous *Commentaries on American Law* (1826), communicated a relatively stable system of equitable procedure that the learned judge repeatedly and tellingly assured his readers was no more discretionary than the common law, and had little to do with what he considered the archaic notions of unchecked magisterial judgment often associated with it. Over the course of the previous two centuries, equity jurisprudence had been gradually reformulated as a predictable body of precedent for addressing disputes over wills, trusts, and contracts in a commercial age. While chancery courts were the scenes of some of the most mundane and unexceptional operations of law, in their inquisitorial case method and allowance for judicial investigative and interpretive power, those same courts were the subject of immense jurisprudential and constitutional energy and conflict, and, without far more attention to literary and intellectual history than early Americanists and legal historians have seen fit to explore, we are not in any position to understand why.

Judge Lemuel Shaw, Melville's father-in-law, crafted the authority of equity into a pragmatic interpretive tool for equitable consideration in common law cases at the Supreme Judicial Court of Massachusetts, beyond the formal limits of any chancery jurisdiction. In the 1846 case of *Atkins v. Chilson*, he presided over a dispute where the court exercised an unenumerated power to stay proceedings against a tenant for rent money, and in *Fuller v. Dame*, 1836, Shaw had voided a nominally legal contract between an attorney and the state legislature that he judged unethical, going against the general tendency of the era to enforce legal contracts whatever their unseemly origins, as Marshall had done in the US Supreme Court case of *Fletcher v. Peck* (1810).[14] In the first edition of the novel dedicated to him, Shaw would read that among the "Typee," of the island of Nuku Hiva in the Marquesas Islands of French Polynesia, "to all appearances there were no courts of law or equity," no police nor "legal provisions whatever," and yet the society worked peaceably to a degree unmatched in the Christian West.[15] In the course of Melville's novels *Typee* (1846), *Omoo* (1847), and *Mardi* (1849), however, those appearances of statelessness give way to other realities, and the novels unfold as the experience of discretionary powers of equity and protection in other people's constitutions.

Such powers fell silent in 1851, when Shaw would famously decline to protect the freedom of Thomas Sims, who escaped slavery only to be returned to Georgia under the authority of the Fugitive Slave Act of 1850. His son-in-law noticed that, too. In *Benito Cereno*, published serially in 1855, the "judicious" Captain Delano, who prides himself on his discernment of faces and the characters behind them, calmly aims to do his duty by aiding in the safe delivery of precious human commodities.[16] He reassures himself that Don Benito's unsociability was the product of an unpleasant constitution, observed in others who also "deemed it but equity" that everyone near them should share in their unkind, nervous feeling, echoing the natural jurisprudential language found in Adam Smith's dictum in *The Wealth of Nations* that it is "but equity, besides," that those who labor should have some share in the produce of their work.[17] Looking at the veneer of ordered deference and propriety that covers the threat of force and power over life and death, Delano approves of Babo: "the black here seems high in your trust," he says to Don Benito, "a sort of privy-counselor, in fact," finding the advisory role and discretionary jurisdiction exercised by the British Privy Council over legal affairs in colonial territories and imperial commerce in the personage of an apparently loyal and dependable bondsman, unbound.[18]

Enmeshment in the oceanic trafficking in human capital disturbs judgment and perception, but one thing Delano sees is right: the power to do justice to and for another has been fractured, lost or forgotten, and redistributed by the course of events, and so the facts of who has that power and what justice will be when they use it has changed incomprehensibly, even after law-preserving violence reasserts itself. "They have no memory," Don Benito says of the elements around him, "they are not human," an ascription of creatureliness that denies its own implication in a shared reality of law-made status, judgment, and reversal, a morbid response to Delano's suggestion that the trade winds on their faces should inspire them to no longer dwell or "moralize" on the past. The two free captains assure themselves, anxiously and in different ways, that they have escaped the natural judgments and actions of the enslaved. But the Spanish captain's sword, "apparent symbol of despotic command," is not really there.[19] The sword of justice familiar to royal coronation, and with it the symbolic power to wield force and even violence in the name of justice, is somewhere else. The discretionary element inherent in the very idea of natural justice has not been negated here so much as relocated and taken up by persons whom the powers that be among us had not been prepared to see wielding it.

THE WHALE

The text of *Moby-Dick* contains a playful warning not to go too far into reading the story as a "hideous and intolerable allegory."[20] And yet, it is almost a commonplace of criticism that Melville aims a critical, allegorical gaze at delusions of mastery.[21] That this sets up a substantive meditation on the related but grander myths of sovereignty and of sovereign rulers and states may well seem just as clear. After all, in his sermon Father Mapple speaks of how Jonah braves the "masterless commotion" of the sea, thinking "that a ship made by men, will carry him into countries where God does not reign, but only the Captains of this earth."[22] To obey God, which the whale does in spitting Jonah up (acknowledging the higher jurisdiction's writ of habeas corpus), is to give up control: "Woe to him who seeks to pour oil upon the waters when God has brewed them into a gale!" And delight is to him who destroys sin "though he pluck it out from under the robes of Senators and Judges."[23] As part of the contrasting contextual resonance of impotent, fractured power, of the Compromise of 1850, the role of Daniel Webster in achieving it, and Lemuel Shaw in enforcing it, Ahab is authorized by his men to redirect the ship in a ceremony of crossing rods, and in the penultimate moment, he reminds them in imagery that is strikingly reminiscent of the title page to Hobbes's *Leviathan, or, The Matter, Form, and Power of a Commonwealth*, published exactly two hundred years earlier: "Ye are not other men, but my arms and legs; and so obey me."[24]

In considering the "whiteness of the whale," the imperial whiteness of European skin and royal steeds becomes terrible in the appalling whiteness of rotting corpses, great white sharks, and Moby-Dick himself. While Ishmael delights in pointing out that royal heads are adorned by oil cut out of the heads of sperm whales by American sailors, no "whiteness" takes on as much comparative value as that which "typifies the majesty of Justice in the ermine of the Judge."[25] Melville plays on our deep ambivalence about judicial discretion, and on disturbances and remainders of our attempts to discipline conscience and judgment. Ahab rages against the implication from Starbuck's counsel that "the owners are my conscience," resisting the reformulation of the conscience of the crown as the laws of contract, and demanding that his conscience and his capacity to be judge of the situation are tied to the ship and his command of it rather than to its financiers, for "the real owner of anything is its commander."[26] If Ahab rebels against the circumscription of discretion and conscience by commerce and contract, he anchors his own conscience in the Roman maxims of absolute possession, certified by the bare fact of his command of the thing in question. But the freedom constructed from the claim of possession is as fleeting as that constructed from the claim of purchase or investment, and having purportedly freed himself from the constraints of normal circulation and exchange, Ahab finds himself a very small part of an even more daunting history, at least entertaining the idea that his attempt to possess (and even to purchase) a freedom of thought and action has only revealed a deeper reality of responsive legalities. Judgment under such conditions becomes omnipresent and impossible: "Who's to doom, when the judge himself is dragged to the bar?"[27] In the absence of the judge from their established seat, and in the imagined circumscription of discretion by the powers of contract and commerce, the responsibility for judgment is fragmented and scattered, and Ahab is as much a victim as anyone else of the epochal disjuncture of judgment from office, of decision from conscience, and of justice from law.

Melville weaves law into his narrative to the extent that its presence needs to be worked through by characters and readers alike. This is not simply a narration of law, or a drawing of law's imagined independence into the domain of literature or narrative for the sake of imaginative critique.[28] We have stories interpolated by law: law as a kind of motor of understanding and change, as a dynamic power of form and figuration rather than simply an instrument or product of political or economic power. In the extensive discussions of the legal history of whales and whaling in *Moby-Dick*, pretensions to certainty and authority are problematized, but the constructive power of law and legal thinking is taken very seriously. The whale, Ishmael cites Blackstone, is a "royal fish," not only making whaling a most respectable, even "imperial," profession, but indicating the degree to which law and legal decisions shape the conditions of possibility for thinking about what one is actually doing when whaling.[29] British whaling was an extension of the royal prerogative, and beached or found whales fell directly under royal possession.[30]

Blackstone relied on Justinian, and in matters of royal prerogative and possession Roman law played an important role in extending royal dominion and prerogative as the legal basis of overseas territories, as well as in the theory and practice of ecclesiastical, admiralty, and chancery courts in England.[31] In Scotland, civil law played an even greater role at the Court of Session, where equity and common law jurisdictions were not separated. The legal history of whaling and the powers of royal prerogative, conscience, and judicial discretion that shape that history are built with ancient, "imperial" material, and part of the implication seems to be here that even as these materials and powers are resisted or forgotten, they remain.

The reader gets to know they remain because Ishmael has studied these things, and his study illuminates a meeting between the ambitions of democratic knowledge construction and the long-accumulating histories on which those ambitions are built.[32] On account of their sexual habits and "ex lege naturae jure meritoque," Ishmael quotes Linnaeus, the whales are to be separated from fish, but Ishmael interjects that at least until 1850, the sharks and fish were to be found "dividing the possession of the same seas with the Leviathan."[33] At least two important things are going on here and in the proceeding pages on what is known of cetology, and especially where the different species of whales, dolphins, and porpoises are discussed according to size, using the standard criteria for categorizing books (the sperm whale, the largest known whale at the time, is a "folio whale"). Melville demands that readers take Ishmael's study intellectually seriously even as he makes clear the limits of scientific pretensions to certainty. Ishmael's reading of the past and present is our only guide, but more importantly, his intellectual practice illuminates an important theme throughout the book, and that is not only the constructive power and lawmaking capacity of the crew, but the allegorical nature of that constitutive activity and the necessity of it for making any legal or philosophical sense of the vast totality in which the crew sail and have their being.

Long before Ahab is humbled by the whale, Ishmael observes that even Ahab respects the customs or "sea-usages" of the whaling ship. That is to say, even if only in the prudent logic of reason of state, Ahab feels himself bound by the precedents established and built up on board his ship and thousands of others before it, and he repeatedly reinstitutes the crew's fidelity to his quest, knowing full well that they know what they are supposed to be doing instead and could easily stop him by force at any time, probably with the help of his officers. Indeed, according to Ishmael, the whalers had developed a complex framework of legal relations that had played a significant role in guidelines for dispute resolution at sea and laws and policies respecting the rightful possession of whales. The "Coke-upon-Littleton of the fist" existed side by side with a give-and-take of the distinction between fast and loose fish. The American fisherman, Ishmael reports, "have been their own lawyers and legislators in this matter," establishing a "system which for terse comprehensiveness surpasses Justinian's Pandects," making in effect a "universal, undisputed law applicable in all cases," its admirable and telling brevity necessitating "a vast volume of commentaries to expound it."[34] Again, part of what is important to note here about Melville's own vast volume is Ishmael's extensive knowledge and reflection (indeed, commentary) on the written and unwritten laws of the whale fishery, finding himself thinking and acting in a creative intellectual history of legal interpretation. In turn, it is just as important to note, the equitable procedures and principles used in deciding disputed cases are created and, ideally, mutually enforced by the whalers themselves. The men not only know and understand the rules, they participate in making and interpreting them, even universal rules that are bound by no particular code or jurisdiction.

The crew, however, are not the only ones in the story making judgments, and in turn, making law. Melville cites the 1805 case of *Gale v. Wilkinson*, decided by the Lord Chief Justice Ellenborough.[35] Reflecting the growth of the power and interpretive freedom of King's Bench in the wake of Justice Mansfield's career, and in deciding a case that originated in the North Atlantic, Ellenborough had leeway and precedent to adopt the "Loose-Fish/Fast-Fish" distinction and use it to adjudicate a case of disputed possession of a whale along with the equipment from a previously failed capture. Ellenborough disagreed with earlier decisions of the Scottish Court of Session which had relied on the principle of first taker, and found that the whale and the equipment belonged to the defendant, because when the whale took off from the first boat, as reported by Ishmael, it "acquired a property in those articles; and hence anybody who afterwards took the fish had a right to them."[36] This was a decision where equitable consideration played a significant role, and the work it does in Melville's narrative is significant, too. By Ishmael's telling, the case reveals the genius of the legal distinction of Fast- and Loose-Fish, a distinction that lay at "the fundamentals of all human jurisprudence," and revealed as no other case could so clearly that possession was the whole of the law. Even more interestingly, the story of the case includes the animal in the jurisprudential, quite literally, and like the chapter on cetology blurs the boundaries between the human and the animal to the point that both are seen as participating in a shared legal history.[37] For Ishmael, the history of empire and the history of thought alike can be seen through the prism of this distinction: What are "Republican slaves but Fast-Fish," and was not the American continent a Loose-Fish, he asks; are not "the Rights of Man and the Liberties of the World" Loose-Fish, he asks, and "what are you, reader, but a Loose-Fish and a Fast-Fish, too?"[38]

It is this perspectival expansion of who and what counts as having rights and being within the circumference of law that chiefly constitutes what can be called Melville's natural history of justice. The question of the civic identity of animals and the nonhuman more broadly recurs throughout the text, but always in a stubbornly persistent and playfully, legally humanist register. The killer whale (or orca) is described as an outlaw, "even in the lawless seas," and Ishmael goes on to reflect in chapter 65 that "no doubt the first man that ever murdered an ox was regarded as a murderer; perhaps he was hung; and if he had been put on his trial by oxen, he certainly would have been; and he certainly deserved it if any murderer does."[39] The blurriness of the boundaries between savagery and civilization, nature and society, animal and human, object and agent, and matter and man can be seen throughout the book, openly meditated upon by Ishmael and Ahab alike. In these particular cases, it is important to note, the question is not simply whether human beings choose to acknowledge animals and environments as having rights within a strictly speaking human juridical framework. The more radical and ancient question posed by Melville's narrative is whether there are nonhuman juridical frameworks that might be said to be legally binding on human beings. Nowhere are this question and its affirmative answer more explicit than in the final chapters of the book, the chase, where Moby-Dick delivers judgment on Ahab, the Pequod, and its crew. Dramatizing the seeming arbitrariness and consequentialness of such judgment, the whale repeatedly declines the opportunity to engage in destructive conflict, an instance of conflict he knows he will win. Dragging Ahab's claim of wrong and possession before the bar, Moby-Dick gives himself over to his office: as in this particular case an instrument of recalibrating, redemptive, terribly corrective justice.

Elliott Visconsi takes as title and epigraph for his excellent book words from the seventeenth-century poet Fulke Grenville, Lord Brooke: "Forming in conscience lines of equity / To temper laws, and without force infuse / A home-born practice of civility."[40] We might read the lines that tie Ahab and his doom to Moby-Dick, Ahab to Pip, and, by contrast, Ishmael to Queequeg as literalized lines of legal relationships adjudicated according to natural equity. But that equity is off balance as the madness of absolute possession, revenge, and mastery, which were all supposed to be left behind by commercial society, snap and overtake other lines of mercy, equality, justice, love, and noncoercive relation.

Holding the "monkey-rope" for Queequeg, who was dressed in "Highland costume," Ishmael sees "that for better or worse, we two, for the time, were wedded"; and should Queequeg fall off the back of the whale and drown, "both usage and honor demanded, that instead of cutting the cord, it should drag me down in his wake." Ishmael's "individuality was now merged in a joint stock company of two," and one mistake on the part of another could spell doom for him, too; "therefore," he reflects, "I saw that there was a sort of an interregnum in Providence; for its even-handed equity never could have sanctioned so gross an injustice."[41] Upon further reflection, however, by the grace of such lines go we: "If your banker breaks, you snap," and so the lines of equity that tie society together (what Scottish philosopher David Hume called "the tyes of equity") are not guarantees of security and progress, but fragile relations, laws, promises whose actual equity is situational, dependent on discretion and judgments for which we are responsible. We are tied together, and as Providence would have it, these lines of law and equity persist through the interregnum. When Queequeg goes down his coffin remains, and Ishmael is in a sense tied to it, and like Jonah, Ishmael is saved, redeemed, not from but in the judgment of Moby-Dick, who is likewise tied to other whales, gulls, fish, men, air, and the sea. This is the stuff of Melville's attempt at writing something like a natural history of justice, even, in a figure that may be too bold, a kind of negative natural jurisprudence, a jurisprudence that without conquest could be capable of relating itself to that which likes beyond its reach.

For Melville, the relational quality of law in his day was out of whack, driven by pretensions to the government of conscience and discretion and the possession of bodies, words, and things. A new kind of chasm opened up between the history of law and the history of justice. In that apparent break, equity, the principle and vehicle for law's admittance of the legitimacy and necessity of interpretive and corrective justice, became a tool with which to situate human activity in relation to the space between law and justice. In *Bartleby*, a former Master of Chancery, writing after the closure of a separate chancery jurisdiction in New York, tells the story of the slow death of his scrivener, Bartleby, who refuses to copy manuscripts of writs, reports, and testimonies in the office. The narrative proceeds as a judicial investigation not unlike the one the narrator would have presumably carried out in his regular duty of judicial fact-finding in assistance to the Court of Chancery, but in in this case the examination is oral, not written, a return to ancient, more directly inquisitorial form. He inquires after background facts, motivation, and the conscientiousness of the party before him, and makes albeit significantly uncertain and inconsistent judgments based on these findings and his own conscience, informed by a mix of sympathy and responsibility. The narrator congratulates himself more than once for his "masterly management," as it must appear to any "dispassionate thinker," for his excellent procedure in investigating, interrogating, and dealing with Bartleby, "in theory."[42] In "practice," as the Master discovers, the situation is far more complicated than simple procedure, and he seems to discover the full significance of this reality only in Bartleby's death in prison. Bartleby, he comes to understand, now rests not with angels, and not with kings alone, but with biblical "kings and counsellors," with the political officers responsible for the conscience of the crown and the polity of which the crown is the head.[43] From what little written evidence exists, the narrator learns that Bartleby had been a clerk in the Dead Letter Office in Washington, processing lost pleas for help, financial assistance, love letters, and other records of the tender mercies of private life in a commercial republic. Bartleby's passivity holds a perturbing mirror to offices and jurisdictions that are declining to use their power to protect and correct.

In seeming contrast, in *Billy Budd* Captain Vere declines to consider motive, background facts, context as it were, or the voice of his own conscience, to say nothing of the unease of his various counselors. The officers and the chaplain are troubled by the outcome of the case and the austerity of the legal procedure that led to Billy's conviction and death, but in obedience to formal duty, none publicly registers any dissent. Here, equitable consideration, or its lack, gets imported into a criminal case under martial law, at sea (Billy is only on board after being pressed into the service of the Royal Navy, impressment being maintained by the approbation of the Lord Chancellor "since Mansfield").[44] That the story stages a confrontation of nature with history is clear enough from Vere's own procedure in the trial, "scarce in equable tones,"[45] and in which he intones that in consideration of "natural justice," of course context and motive and conscience would need to be taken into consideration, but this is not, by Vere's lights, a tribunal of natural justice: "Do these buttons that we wear attest that our allegiance is to Nature? No, to the King." We are not at sea, but on a ship, Vere implies, cutting civil from natural history: "the ocean, which is Nature primeval, though this be the element where we move and have our being as sailors," yet as officers in the King's Navy, particularly in a time of war, duty lies not with what is natural, but with what is commanded, and "for that law and the rigor of it, we are not responsible."[46] Private conscience must yield to the imperial one, Vere concludes, and that is his judgment, as the events are narrated: "History, and here cited without comment."[47] That Vere acts out of felt necessity with knowing disavowal of natural justice and with at least questionable legal authority reinforces the unavoidability of discretion, that cases and events come down to judgments in specific, often individual cases, and no lines of command or commerce have alleviated the problem of responsibility, of judgment. Legal affairs and their injustices, desires and discipline, and judgments and their uncertainties are chapters in what I have called Herman Melville's natural history of justice, in which the borders between nature and history, which perhaps are only accessible or visible with the aid of art and allegory, are explored and seen, in certain cases, to transform without ever fully dissolving.

It would be easy to see in something that could be called a natural history not simply a touch of the inhuman, but a kind of fatalistic erasure of any hope for thinking and acting differently that humanistic study is, in theory, supposed to supply. Melville's study of such a history strikes off in a different direction. Afloat atop and sounding within currents of natural history, for Melville, is a history of thought, or of thinking, of the material and the activity of thinking, albeit one that is chastened by its encounter with other histories above and below.[48] The sperm whale "is both ponderous and profound," and like other great thinkers Ishmael has read, "there always goes up a certain invisible steam, while in the act of thinking deep thoughts."[49] This is an expansive history of thinking, even while it is a chastened one. Perhaps, as Melville seemed to appreciate, whales have judgments and even a jurisprudence and so a legal and intellectual history of their own. Whales and dolphins have complex cultures and histories, ancient constitutions as it were caught like ours between forces of duration and decay, and maybe Melville's intuition that the best way to think about them was, allegorically, as other legal cultures, as constitutions rather than as objects of profit or pity in our own, will prove to have had something to be said for it after all. The implications of legal and literary history's call for a radically expanded idea of what we might mean someday by international law, or the law of the sea, of jurisprudence and constitutionalism beyond the boundaries of the human, remains tantalizingly and urgently ahead for further exploration.[50] That exploration, however, if Melville has anything to contribute to it, will demand not some new ethical immediacy but something more like what Gillian Rose calls "jurisprudential wisdom," an alertness to the perduring implication of new questions and histories in ancient problems and events, in the legal history that constitutes the scene of contemporary conjecture.[51]

Oceanic environments pose real physical and theoretical challenges to our inherited categories of law, politics, and history, to the ways we humans in our humanistic endeavors have given form to the problems and potentialities of transformation and persistence that come with collective life in time. Almost in spite of itself, early American studies seems like a promising arena in which to let some of those challenges play out. David Waldstreicher has called the task of early American historiography, at its best, a jazz standard, something that requires a balance of innovation and tradition, of new and old.[52] With jazz in the air, invoking Adorno may well be the height of bad taste, but I would like to take that risk and suggest that like the world's oceans, critical theory's attention to allegory has a great deal to say to the writing of history. History and allegory are not identical, but in making any claim to narrative representation they are inextricably linked; indeed, as Adorno notes, if the allegory were merely substituted for the history, we would be degrading its capacity for "cloaking and legitimating the unreconciled world," for bringing into appearance and representation in law, politics, and history that which defies absorption in them.[53] We desperately need to imagine and explore new forms of history to care for the political conditions in which it is possible, J. G. A. Pocock writes, to write history at all, and in the coming years we may well need to reawaken missed and disregarded pieces of our traditions, of the intellectual history of law, literature, politics, and history, to innovate and think and act politically at all.[54] We will need to see our own enmeshments in histories we did not write but into which we are written all the same. We will need to just keep swimming through libraries, and we will need to *sing out for new stars*.

NOTES

Epigraph: Theodor Adorno, *Negative Dialectics*, trans. E. B. Ashton (New York: Continuum, 1973), 311.

1. Adorno, *Negative Dialectics*, 310–11.
2. Santner, *On Creaturely Life*, 15; *The Royal Remains*; and *Weight of All Flesh*.
3. Honig, "This Post-mortemizing of the Whale"; see also Casarino, *Modernity at Sea*; Fredricks, *Melville's Art of Democracy*; Milder, *Exiled Royalties*; Frank, "Pathologies of Freedom in Melville's America"; Downes, "Melville's Leviathan"; Greiman, *Melville's Democracy*.
4. Melville, *Moby-Dick*, 146, 168.
5. Benjamin, "On the Concept of History," 396–97.
6. Jameson, *Allegory and Ideology*, 355–58.
7. Adorno, *History and Freedom*, 133.
8. Benjamin, *Origins of German Tragic Drama*, 224.
9. Benjamin, *Origins of German Tragic Drama*, 166.
10. See Cromartie, *Constitutionalist Revolution*; Halliday, *Habeas Corpus*; Cormack, *A Power to Do Justice*.
11. Hobbes, *Leviathan*, 158.
12. Kessler, *Inventing American Exceptionalism*; see also Hoffer, *Law's Conscience*.
13. Kessler, *Inventing American Exceptionalism*, 55–89.
14. See Adlow, *Genius of Lemuel Shaw*, 57–63; Levy, *Law of the Commonwealth and Chief Justice Shaw*.
15. Melville, *Typee*, 200; see Rogin, *Subversive Genealogy*, 44–45.
16. See Cover, *Justice Accused*; Davis, *Problem of Slavery in the Age of Revolutions*; Nabers, *Victory of Law*; DeLombard, "Salvaging Legal Personhood"; Grandin, *Empire of Necessity*; see Forsyth, *Common Law and Natural Law in America*; Banner, *Decline of Natural Law*.
17. Melville, *Benito Cereno*, in *Billy Budd*, 62; Smith, *Wealth of Nations*, 88.
18. Melville, *Benito Cereno*, in *Billy Budd*, 79.
19. Melville, *Benito Cereno*, in *Billy Budd*, 137.
20. Melville, *Moby-Dick*, 223.
21. For a strongly dissenting perspective, see Dimock, *Empire for Liberty*; on Ahab and whiteness, see Morrison, *Playing in the Dark*; Freeburg, *Melville and the Idea of Blackness*.
22. Melville, *Moby-Dick*, 52, 53.

23 Melville, *Moby-Dick*, 54.
24 Melville, *Moby-Dick*, 618.
25 Melville, *Moby-Dick*, 205.
26 Melville, *Moby-Dick*, 517.
27 Melville, *Moby-Dick*, 592.
28 On narrative form in law, legal argument, and literature about law and legal processes, see Cover, "Nomos and Narrative"; Thomas, *Cross-Examinations of Law and Literature*.
29 Melville, *Moby-Dick*, 121; Deal, "Fast-Fish, Loose-Fish."
30 Blackstone, *Commentaries on the Laws of England*, 410–12.
31 See MacMillan, *Sovereignty and Possession in the English New World*.
32 Indeed, early knowledge of whales was dependent on the archive of logbooks and journals collected in whaling ports and, today, whaling museums; see Dyer, *O'er the Wide and Tractless Sea*.
33 Melville, *Moby-Dick*, 147; see Burnett, *Trying Leviathan*.
34 Melville, *Moby-Dick*, 432–33.
35 Deal, *Law of the Whale Hunt*; Tomlins, "Animals Accurs'd"; Fernandez, *Pierson v. Post*, 310–18.
36 Melville, *Moby-Dick*, 434.
37 The place of the animal in natural law and the application of natural law in the commonwealth was something at least contemplated by Hobbes in early work; see Hobbes, *Hobbes: On the Citizen*, 105–7; Brett, *Change of State*.
38 Melville, *Moby-Dick*, 434–53.
39 Melville, *Moby-Dick*, 327.
40 Visconsi, *Lines of Equity*.
41 Melville, *Moby-Dick*, 349.
42 Melville, *Bartleby*, in *Billy Budd*, 41.
43 Melville, *Bartleby*, in *Billy Budd*, 53; Arsić, *Passive Constitutions*; Vismann, *Files: Law and Media Technology*; Whyte, "I Would Prefer Not To"; Dayan, "Bartleby's Screen"; Sbriglia, "From Sublimity to Sublimation."
44 Melville, *Billy Budd*, 261; Mansfield was never the Lord Chancellor, but he was instrumental in implementing the growth and legitimation of equity and increased jurisdictional authority of King's Bench, particularly in marine and merchant law. Thus, Melville toys with the very real problem of jurisdictional confusion at sea as a problem on land as much as on the ocean; indeed, a removed line from the manuscript elaborates the problem of the decision Vere has to make and the uncertainty of the criteria on which he has to make it: "not seldom an impracticable abstraction even in civil life and under the most liberal form of it"; on Melville's purposeful problematizing of reports of fact, see Samson, *White Lies*.
45 Melville, *Billy Budd*, 306.
46 Melville, *Billy Budd*, 308.
47 Melville, *Billy Budd*, 311.

48 See Hurh, *American Terror*.
49 Melville, *Moby-Dick*, 409.
50 For a start, see Mawani, *Across Oceans of Law*; see also Gilroy, "Never Again."
51 Rose, *Dialectic of Nihilism*, 212. This at once dialectical and allegorical approach contrasts with actor-network and posthumanist theories, especially with how law gets discussed in and around the work of Bruno Latour, for whom, in an approved description, "the content of law is not only irredeemably bound up with its conditions of enunciation, but is *fully identical with those conditions.*" See McGee, "On Devices and Logics of Legal Sense," 64; see Barter, "Bartleby, Barbarians, and the Legality of Literature," 304–30; Latour, "Strange Entanglement of Jurimorphs," in McGee, *Latour and the Passage of Law*, 335.
52 Waldstreicher, "Revolutions of Revolution Historiography."
53 Adorno, *Aesthetic Theory*, 69.
54 Pocock, *Discovery of Islands*, 310.

BIBLIOGRAPHY

Adlow, Elijah. *The Genius of Lemuel Shaw*. Boston: Court Square Press and the Massachusetts Bar Association, 1962.

Adorno, Theodor. *Aesthetic Theory*. Edited by Gretel Adorno, Rolf Tiedemann, and Robert Hullot-Kentor. Translated by Robert Hullot-Kentor. Minneapolis: University of Minnesota Press, 1998.

Adorno, Theodor. *History and Freedom: Lectures, 1964–1965*. Edited by Rolf Tiedemann. Translated by Rodney Livingstone. Cambridge: Polity, 2006.

Adorno, Theodor. *Negative Dialectics*. Translated by E. B. Ashton. New York: Continuum, 1973.

Arsić, Branka. *Passive Constitutions or 7 1/2 Times Bartleby*. Stanford, CA: Stanford University Press, 2007.

Banner, Stuart. *The Decline of Natural Law: How American Lawyers Once Used Natural Law and Why They Stopped*. Oxford: Oxford University Press, 2021.

Barter, Faith. "Bartleby, Barbarians, and the Legality of Literature." In *Latour and the Passage of Law*, edited by Kyle McGee, 304–30. Edinburgh: University of Edinburgh Press, 2015.

Benjamin, Walter. "On The Concept of History." In *Selected Writings, Volume 4, 1938–1940*, edited by Howard Eiland and Michael W. Jennings, translated by Edmund Jephcott, 389–400. Cambridge, MA: Harvard University Press, 2003.

Benjamin, Walter. *The Origin of German Tragic Drama*. Translated by John Osborne. London: Verso, 1998.

Blackstone, William. *Commentaries on the Laws of England, Volume 1*. Chicago: University of Chicago Press, 1979.

Brett, Annabel S. *Change of State: Nature and the Limits of the City in Early Modern Natural Law*. Princeton, NJ: Princeton University Press, 2011.

Burnett, D. Graham. *Trying Leviathan: The Nineteenth Century New York Court Case That Put the Whale on Trial and Challenged the Order of Nature*. Princeton, NJ: Princeton University Press, 2007.

Casarino, Cesare. *Modernity at Sea: Melville, Marx, Conrad in Crisis*. Minneapolis: University of Minnesota Press, 2002.

Cormack, Bradin. *A Power to Do Justice: Jurisdiction, English Literature, and the Rise of the Common Law*. Chicago: University of Chicago Press, 2007.

Cover, Robert M. *Justice Accused: Antislavery and the Judicial Process*. New Haven, CT: Yale University Press, 1975.

Cover, Robert M. "Nomos and Narrative." *Harvard Law Review* 97, no. 4 (1983): 4–68.

Cromartie, Alan. *The Constitutionalist Revolution: An Essay on the History of England, 1450–1642*. Cambridge: Cambridge University Press, 2006.

Davis, David Brion. *The Problem of Slavery in the Age of Revolutions, 1770–1823*. Ithaca, NY: Cornell University Press, 1975.

Dayan, Colin. "Bartleby's Screen." *Leviathan* 17, no. 2 (June 2015): 1–17.

Deal, Robert. "Fast-Fish, Loose-Fish: How Whalemen, Lawyers, and Judges Created the British Property Law of Whaling." *Ecology Law Quarterly* 37, no. 1 (2010): 199–236.

Deal, Robert. *The Law of the Whale Hunt: Dispute Resolution, Property Law, and American Whalers, 1780–1880*. Cambridge: Cambridge University Press, 2016.

DeLombard, Jeannine Marie. "Salvaging Legal Personhood: Melville's *Benito Cereno*." *American Literature* 81, no. 1 (March 2009): 35–64.

Dimock, Wai Chee. *Empire for Liberty: Melville and the Poetics of Individualism*. Princeton, NJ: Princeton University Press, 1990.

Downes, Paul. "Melville's Leviathan." In *Melville's Philosophies*, edited by Branka Arsić and K. L. Evans, 315–36. London: Bloomsbury, 2017.

Dyer, Michael D. *"O'er the Wide and Tractless Sea": Original Art of the Yankee Whale Hunt*. New Bedford, MA: New Bedford Whaling Museum, 2017.

Fernandez, Angela. *Pierson v. Post, the Hunt for the Fox: Law and Professionalization in American Legal Culture*. Cambridge: Cambridge University Press, 2018.

Forsyth, Andrew. *Common Law and Natural Law in America: From the Puritans to the Legal Realists*. Cambridge: Cambridge University Press, 2019.

Frank, Jason A. "Pathologies of Freedom in Melville's America." In *Radical Future Pasts: Untimely Political Theory*, edited by Romand Coles, Mark Reinhardt, and George Shulman, 435–58. Lexington: University of Kentucky Press, 2014.

Fredricks, Nancy. *Melville's Art of Democracy*. Athens: University of Georgia Press, 1995.

Freeburg, Christopher. *Melville and the Idea of Blackness: Race and Imperialism in Nineteenth-Century America*. Cambridge: Cambridge University Press, 2012.

Gilroy, Paul. "Never Again: Refusing Race and Salvaging the Human." 2019 Holberg Prize Lecture, https://holbergprisen.no/en/news/holberg-prize/2019-holberg-lecture-laureate-paul-gilroy.

Grandin, Greg. *The Empire of Necessity: Slavery, Freedom, and Deception in the New World*. New York: Picador, 2014.

Greiman, Jennifer. *Melville's Democracy: Radical Figuration and Political Form*. Stanford, CA: Stanford University Press, 2023.

Halliday, Paul D. *Habeas Corpus: From England to Empire*. Cambridge, MA: Belknap Press of Harvard University Press, 2010.

Hobbes, Thomas. *Hobbes: On the Citizen*. Edited and translated by Richard Tuck and Michael Siverthorne. Cambridge: Cambridge University Press, 1998.

Hobbes, Thomas. *Leviathan*. Edited by Noel Malcolm. Oxford: Oxford University Press, 2012.

Hoffer, Peter Charles. *The Law's Conscience: Equitable Constitutionalism in America*. Chapel Hill: University of North Carolina Press, 1990.

Honig, Bonnie. "'This Post-mortemizing of the Whale': The Vapors of Materialism, New and Old." In *Ahab Unbound: Melville and the Materialist Turn*, edited by Meredith Farmer and Jonathan D. S. Schroeder, 197–226. Minneapolis: University of Minnesota Press, 2022.

Hurh, Paul. *American Terror: The Feeling of Thinking in Edwards, Poe, and Melville*. Stanford, CA: Stanford University Press, 2015.

Jameson, Fredric. *Allegory and Ideology*. London: Verso, 2019.

Kessler, Amalia D. *Inventing American Exceptionalism: The Origins of American Adversarial Legal Culture, 1800–1877*. New Haven, CT: Yale University Press, 2017.

Latour, Bruno. "The Strange Entanglement of Jurimorphs." In *Latour and the Passage of Law*, edited by Kyle McGee, 331–53. Edinburgh: University of Edinburgh Press, 2015.

Levy, Leonard W. *The Law of the Commonwealth and Chief Justice Shaw*. Oxford: Oxford University Press, 1957.

MacMillan, Ken. *Sovereignty and Possession in the English New World: The Legal Foundations of Empire, 1576–1670*. New York: Cambridge University Press, 2006.

Mawani, Renisa. *Across Oceans of Law: The* Komagata Maru *and Jurisdiction in the Time of Empire*. Durham, NC: Duke University Press, 2018.

McGee, Kyle. "On Devices and Logics of Legal Sense." In *Latour and the Passage of Law*, edited by Kyle McGee, 61–92. Edinburgh: University of Edinburgh Press, 2015.

Melville, Herman. *Billy Budd, Bartleby, and Other Stories*. Edited by Peter M. Coviello. New York: Penguin, 2016.

Melville, Herman. *Moby-Dick or, The Whale*. Edited by Andrew Delbanco. New York: Penguin, 2003.

Melville, Herman. *Typee: A Peep at Polynesian Life*. Edited by Mary Bercaw Edwards. New York: Penguin, 1996.

Milder, Robert. *Exiled Royalties: Melville and the Life We Imagine*. Oxford: Oxford University Press, 2006.

Morrison, Toni. *Playing in the Dark: Whiteness and the Literary Imagination*. Cambridge, MA: Harvard University Press, 1992.

Nabers, Deak. *Victory of Law: The Fourteenth Amendment, the Civil War, and American Literature, 1852–1867*. Baltimore: Johns Hopkins University Press, 2006.

Pocock, J. G. A. *The Discovery of Islands: Essays in British History*. Cambridge: Cambridge University Press, 2005.

Rogin, Michael Paul. *Subversive Genealogy: The Politics and Art of Herman Melville*. New York: Knopf, 1983.

Rose, Gillian. *Dialectic of Nihilism: Post-Structuralism and Law*. Oxford: Blackwell, 1984.

Samson, John. *White Lies: Melville's Narratives of Facts*. Ithaca, NY: Cornell University Press, 1989.

Santner, Eric L. *On Creaturely Life: Rilke, Benjamin, Sebald*. Chicago: University of Chicago Press, 2006.

Santner, Eric L. *The Royal Remains: The People's Two Bodies and the Endgames of Sovereignty*. Chicago: University of Chicago Press, 2011.

Santner, Eric L. *The Weight of All Flesh: On the Subject-Matter of Political Economy*. Edited by Kevis Goodman. Oxford: Oxford University Press, 2015.

Sbriglia, Russell. "From Sublimity to Sublimation: Hegel, Lacan, Melville." In *Subject Lessons: Hegel, Lacan, and the Future of Materialism*, edited by Russell Sbriglia and Slavoj Žižek, 227–48. Evanston, IL: Northwestern University Press, 2020.

Smith, Adam. *The Wealth of Nations*. Edited by Edwin Canaan. Chicago: University of Chicago Press, 1976.

Thomas, Brook. *Cross-Examinations of Law and Literature: Cooper, Hawthorne, Stowe, and Melville*. Cambridge: Cambridge University Press, 1987.

Tomlins, Christopher. "Animals Accurs'd: *Ferae Naturae* and the Law of Property in Nineteenth-Century North America." *University of Toronto Law Journal* 63, no. 1 (2013): 35–52.

Visconsi, Elliott. *Lines of Equity: Literature and the Origins of Law in Later Stuart England*. Ithaca, NY: Cornell University Press, 2008.

Vismann, Cornelia. *Files: Law and Media Technology*. Translated by Geoffrey Winthrop-Young. Stanford, CA: Stanford University Press, 2008.

Waldstreicher, David. "The Revolutions of Revolution Historiography: Cold War Contradance, Neo-Imperial Waltz, or Jazz Standard?" *Reviews in American History* 42, no. 1 (March 2014): 23–35.

Whyte, Jessica. "'I Would Prefer Not To': Giorgio Agamben, Bartleby, and the Potentiality of the Law." *Law and Critique* 20 (2009): 309–24.

TEN · *John J. Garcia*

Antebellum or Interbellum?

Franklin Pierce confided in his diary on July 25, 1847. Most scholars would fit this day and year into the antebellum era of American history, but Pierce was writing in the midst of another war. The man who later became the fourteenth president of the United States at that time was a brigadier general in Winfield Scott's army, which was participating in the US armed invasion of Mexico (1846–48). Writing from Xalapa, Pierce was struck by the openness with which rural landowners, who were nominally his enemies, traded with Pierce's troops to provide supplies. Such kindnesses perplexed and confused his sense of how war was to be waged.

In the 1847 diary entry, Pierce argued that the war with Mexico must include violent actions deliberately left out of the written record.

> Has this the appearance of war? *Our* Gov't does not comprehend *this* Gov't. I say Gov't, because a *people*, in our acceptation of the term there is none. Most evidently nothing like an intelligent people framing their own laws & controlling their own Government. *War* has been *declared*, but with all our battles, all our brilliant victories, and the loss of all the valuable lives *war* has not yet been *prosecuted*. I could desire that it may not be, but from the little I have observed I believe, that it *must* be before a peace can be "*conquered*." I mean war as it has been recognized for 200 years in the most civilized nations. No not as it has been recognized, but *war* as it has actually been carried. War, with its fruits & its results. *War*, that actually carries, widespread woe & despoliation to the *conquered* and tacitly at least, allows pillage & plunder with accompaniments not even to be named during a campaign like this even in a private journal.[1]

For Pierce, as for other commentators, Mexico was not considered a sovereign republic for reasons that included religious prejudice, racism, and ignorance of the political history of this foreign country. The fighting Pierce saw firsthand didn't conform to his expectation, steeped in the ideology of the nation-state, that governments ruled by a sovereign people confront each other directly. Because he couldn't see a "people" represented by enemy forces, Pierce's ideals of legitimate warfare failed him. The proximity throughout the campaign of Pierce's men to civilians and guerrilla insurgents prompted his regiment to commit atrocities ("widespread woe & despoliation," unnamed "accompaniments"). Referencing centuries of military precedent, the future president argued that his men obeyed the rules of early modern warfare, wherein victorious armies were expected to murder, rape, and plunder. The US-Mexico War was no exception to this violent tradition.[2] "Tacitly at least," a good leader was to look the other way when violence took place. Looking the other way also meant not documenting violence, "even in a private journal."

Pierce theorizes the Mexican War as a vanishing public event. Keenly aware of the press's role in popularizing "brilliant victories," he purposely restricts what his diary will record because he knew it could enter the public domain. Five years later, in 1852, Nathaniel Hawthorne published a widely read campaign biography of Pierce that helped his friend secure the presidency. The novelist strained to reframe Pierce's undistinguished military career as proof of his leadership capabilities. To accomplish the goal Hawthorne reproduced Pierce's Mexican diary, but the omissions are telling. The passage quoted above was deliberately left out. Hawthorne characterized the Mexican diary as "mere hasty jottings-down" and claimed the freedom of a professional editor to select the best parts. Editing the diary raised a contradiction. Should it be reproduced verbatim, as an example of the whole man, or redacted to trim away Pierce's bad qualities? Hawthorne wished to bring the voting public close, but not too close, to Pierce in Mexico. Omitting the confusing "has this the appearance of war" paragraph that I cited simplified Pierce and the war itself, adding a secondary censorship from Hawthorne on top of the silences Pierce adopted to conceal military violence. Hawthorne therefore followed Pierce's tortured logic. Both agreed that the unglamourous parts of war should be allowed to vanish.

Franklin Pierce's elusive moment of overlooking Mexican War violence exemplifies a disappearance of atrocity from historical memory. Although recovering Pierce's "accompaniments not even to be named" is impossible, careful analysis of the archive allows us to make meaning out of the erasure. Centering omission transforms the Mexican War into a vanishing public event: a series of military actions that cannot go public and a public discourse on war structured by these erasures. This essay pursues that dynamic. Examining manuscripts, pictures, and contemporary histories that document the invasion as it transpired, I merge bibliography with critique to unsettle the Mexican War's periodization. Centering the patterns of effacement deployed by Pierce and his contemporaries, I argue, upends traditional understandings of this military conflict. The Mexican War archive offers glimpses into the US soldier's experience of time and social fragmentation. Careful bibliographical parsing of textual transmission—the translation of manuscript into print and the spatial distribution of published wartime experiences—delineates the mechanisms by which the war in Mexico exposed officers, soldiers, and citizens to a temporality that differed from the ordering paradigms of the nation-state.

AN UNTIMELY MEXICAN WAR

The Mexican War demands a more ambitious critical intervention than historians have yet attempted. Recent developments in material culture studies, history of science, and philosophy have prompted greater reflection on how objects knit together "pleats" of time, in the words of Michel Serres.[3] Serres identifies two aspects of temporality. On the one hand, his understanding of "polychronic" time denotes the yoking together of materials or techniques from different points in history as constitutive elements of a single artifact. On the other hand, the "multitemporal," in a subtle yet consequential difference, involves the apprehension of different temporal orders prompted by the polychronicity of the object. Such temporalities dovetail, in terms of historicist method, with the assemblages of persons and things associated with the work of Bruno Latour. Serres and Latour together highlight how artifacts and events can be elaborated in terms of their polychronic and multitemporal meanings for historical actors.[4] Hawthorne's *Life of Pierce*, for example, is somewhat polychronic by weaving together a wartime diary from 1847 into an 1852 presidential campaign biography, but that text also draws attention to multitemporal interpretations of the Mexican invasion that held real purchase on the US military. Mexico's archaeological remnants of ancient civilization, combined with popular interest in the Black Legend, prompted the army to imagine itself as living a "Second Conquest."⁵ Too easily subsumed under the heading of romanticism, the conceit of a second conquest that repeated world-historical events captivated soldiers, some of whom believed they stepped backward into history as they marched forward from Veracruz to Mexico City.

This war, more than other US imperial events, significantly reconfigured the scale of time. Military experiences blurred epistemology and ontology for the participants, not with philosophical precision, but out of the sheer messiness of social interactions. Much of Zachary Taylor's and Winfield Scott's respective armies experienced war as boredom, since weeks could pass without any fighting. Consequently, many soldiers sought entertainment through activities that resembled tourism. John Wolcott Phelps felt he was transported into a different time when he pondered human sacrifice atop a pyramid in Cholula: "The dark drop curtain of 500 by-gone years seemed suddenly lifted, and the priests were seen again around the sacrificial stone, their chiefs lifting the still palpitating heart of the victim towards heaven." Phelps made imaginative leaps in response to the historicity of stone. His sense of being lost in an imagined prehistory was prompted by artifacts gathered by children whom he paid to collect bones, pottery fragments, and obsidian weapons. "The latter," Phelps writes, "leave no doubt but that they are the broken and worn out knives which were used in the sacrifices."⁶ These found objects were indexical markers of premodernity. Across Mexico, officers, volunteer soldiers, and enlisted regulars shared this sense of stepping outside the bounded time-space of the US nation, in the process experiencing what Siegfried Kracauer called chronological extraterritoriality.⁷ Popular history disseminated by US publishers commodified the step backward into time by cloaking war in the language of heroism and romantic adventure, resulting in archaic narratives punctuated by sensational violence and martial manhood, as I discuss below.

The erasure and untimeliness discussed in this essay differ from a number of reigning scholarly paradigms. Describing the war with Mexico as a forgotten conflict is a well-worn trope of the historiography, but this is not a surrogate for studying the forgetting internal to the war's prosecution. Most of all, the Mexican War isn't an antebellum phenomenon, and that latter assumption must be critiqued. The routine invocation of the antebellum as a periodization for the decades preceding the Civil War is a historiographic prejudice. There can only be an antebellum history if we subordinate the Mexican War within a broader container. Scholars such as Jesse Alemán and Shelley Streeby have already challenged these assumptions.⁸ However, cultural studies of this phase of US imperialism rely too heavily on fiction. Novels by George Lippard and Ned Buntline, though widely read, fail to exhaust the war's cultural meanings. Furthermore, critical theory has not directly engaged with the war's vast archive, despite the fact that the conflict coincided with the early stirrings of a mass culture that resonates with aesthetic and political theories proposed by the Frankfurt School and Jacques Rancière.

Historiography, cultural studies, and critique come together in my focus on amateur writings by US soldiers (including the Pierce diary), on the war's memorialization and forgetting, and on its visual representations. As agents of cultural production, soldiers wrote letters and diaries that were published in newspapers and popular histories. At the same time, artists and engravers rushed to issue prints for US audiences. Well before the 1848 Treaty of Guadalupe Hidalgo ended the conflict, lithographed prints entered the marketplace. Audiences curious about the war relied on visual representations along with the printed word; many of these books were profusely illustrated with wood engravings, and some of the pictures were designed by soldiers-turned-artists. All of these representations (manuscript, print, image) linked sites of warfare to the mass public of the United States. Here the "history of the book," particularly that scholarly field's attention to the distribution of texts through the book trade, opens avenues to retrace the mechanisms that shaped the Mexican War's reception. Within the book trade, middlemen such as peddlers and pushcart salesmen disseminated war to audiences. Illustrations, popular histories, and soldier writings traveled through subscription publishing networks that disseminated print in cities and rural areas.⁹ The book trade mediated soldiering into a mass culture of national proportions.

This essay's foray into critique blends concepts from W. W. Greg, Siegfried Kracauer, and Georges Bataille. While the trio may seem incommensurable, putting them in dialogue with the Mexican War demonstrates what critical theory can do with the resources of bibliography. Siegfried Kracauer's relevance stems from his posthumous treatise *History: The Last Things before the Last* (1969). There the Frankfurt School–aligned writer offers insights into fallacies of historical periodization: "The typical period is not so much a unified entity with a spirit of its own as a precarious conglomerate of tendencies, aspirations, and activities which more often than not manifest themselves independently of one another."¹⁰ Kracauer proposes a more capacious investigation of temporality, but with the consequence that the historian's period, as such, loses solidity. Given that "antebellum America" is featured so conspicuously in countless monographs, articles, dissertations, and syllabi, it may be time to consider whether the phrase is being used in the uncritical fashion critiqued by Kracauer.[11]

The polychronic and multitemporal experiences of US soldiers disfigure antebellum history precisely because their present wavered between imagined pasts and futures. Inspired by the literary scholar Jesse Alemán, I propose adopting the term *interbellum* to reimagine one war in particular. The prefix *inter* evokes death, burial, and disinterment. With these figurations the Mexican War takes the form of a hemispheric unheimlich that unsettles familiar interpretations.[12] What would the interbellum look like? Such an emergent concept would emphasize the Mexican War as a dynamic interval whose position in-between entails from structuring erasures, overlapping times, and widespread mobilization. Soldier experiences are the glue holding together this conceptualization. Here, Bataille's writings on war, waste, and sacrifice resonate with Pierce's thought of a secret military conflict. Pierce recognized with some discomfort that the US invasion paved the way for what Bataille called wasteful expenditure. Indeed, one of Bataille's maxims, "Man is the most suited of all living beings to consume intensely," paraphrases what the war means for reckless soldiers such as Samuel Chamberlain, whose memoirs celebrate behaviors Pierce thought best left unrecorded.[13]

Recuperating vanishing wartime events requires thinking through patterns that don't necessarily refer to identifiable actions. I wager this is a mode of critique that speculates on (and in) historical flash points that resist transparent meaning. Indeed, the difficulty of ethically reporting any war for the sake of public discussion is one of contemporary theory's most pressing interventions.[14] Counterintuitively, not assuming to know, and holding on to ambiguity, can be theoretically productive. It's almost too easy to imagine Pierce's "accompaniments" as evidence of murder, theft, and so on. But leaving hints of a fleeting past untheorized forecloses other interpretive findings. My position is that the antebellum periodization has calcified our vision in ways that inhibit critique. Antebellum racism and period labels such as Manifest Destiny wouldn't add anything substantially new if we just confirmed our suspicions of what Pierce alludes to. Following the through line of Pierce's thinking requires holding on to circumlocution and self-censorship as a target of analysis. The diary shifts between the actual and the virtual without siding with either, and Pierce subjects his thoughts to muddy qualifications ("No not," "tacitly at least," "not even to be"). One thing is clear. Pierce didn't want the diary to go public. He scribbled "*on no account to be published*" elsewhere in his diary. And Pierce was not alone to withhold detail. On the ground, eyewitnesses struggled to articulate egregious activity. Afterward, the war's historians redacted narratives to make them palatable for the booksellers' market.

Critique's restless negativity could move beyond familiar explanations of race, martial manhood, and empire by asking how and why the Mexican War's legitimizing constructs held themselves together. The political justifications of securing new territory for slavery or free white labor do not necessarily explain the mechanisms of the war's reception. Why not also inquire into what was gathered, secreted, kept intact in a soldier's murky reporting? What linked a wartime diary to the mass public? When did pictures share the circumlocutions that inflected soldier writing? Such questions depart from the antebellum historian's Mexican War. Given that the volunteer members of the American army tended to act with relatively few restraints, their radical freedom bracketed the conflict, at least temporarily, from the national politics of slavery and expansion that shaped the war in the US and in the succeeding decades. With Kracauer, one way forward is to decipher the movements and trajectories of ephemera produced by the military. Diaries, sketchbooks, and correspondence reveal themselves, to borrow from Lisa Gitelman, at the nexus of "authority and amnesia."[15] Like Pierce's diary, the texts discussed below don't hide meaning so much as accumulate it when circumlocution becomes constitutive of history.

CRITICAL BIBLIOGRAPHY

W. W. Greg defined critical bibliography as "the science of the material transmission of literary texts."[16] As a textual scholar, Greg thought of the life cycle of writing in terms of descent and contingency, both in the work of copying manuscripts and the multiplication of copies through print editions. Transmission denotes "the whole history of the chances that have befallen [a text] in the course of its precarious survival."[17] Careful reading of Greg proves that the time of the text is not chronologically linear. This means that bibliography is a way into the polychronic and multitemporal:

> A text is not a fixed and formal thing, that needs only to be purged of the imperfections of transmission and restored once and for all to its pristine purity, but a living organism which in its descent through the ages, while it departs more and more from the form impressed upon it by its original author,

exerts, through its imperfections, as much as through its perfections, its own influence upon its surroundings. At each stage of its descent a literary work is in some sense a new creation, something different from what it was to an earlier generation, something still more different from what it was when it came from the author's hand. Moreover, it will differ likewise from place to place. . . . And this is just what bibliography, with its impartial outlook, recognizes, when it treats each step in the history of the text as potentially of equal significance.[18]

Greg never states that each textual iteration severs previous ties; rather, we cannot assume those prior marks are wholly determinative of a text's future. Bibliography's "impartial outlook" communicates its findings by understanding texts as assemblages with complex timings. Greg anticipated the whole range of the history of the book with this statement on critical bibliography. Robert Darnton's well-known "communications circuit," as well as revisionary models indebted to that formulation, already find expression in descent and transmission.[19] Greg's version of bibliography is more ambitious (i.e., critical) because of his willingness to keep texts agentive. Here Greg is somewhat in disagreement with himself. As a bibliographer, he naggingly insists the contents of a book are irrelevant for understanding the material artifact. Examination proceeds by setting aside meaning or subject matter. Instead, a bibliographer studies "arbitrary marks."[20] But the mark still exerts pressure on society; otherwise, bibliography couldn't have the broad applicability to which Greg aspires. There is therefore a labor of the mark upon the world (and vice versa), an "exertion" that will vary according to context.

Transmission is also a question of conveyance, not just a matter of copying. The labor of distribution is one way texts differ "from place to place." However, some of book history's most influential models do not easily comprehend distribution. The communication circuit problematically separates "shippers" from "booksellers" even though both are concerned with conveyance. Thomas Adams and Nicolas Barker argue that distribution is the "dynamic phase" of a book's life, but without demonstrating how that dynamism approximates Greg's ideas of textual variation.[21] Extending critical bibliography in ways responsive to early American contexts, broadly conceived, provides two insights. First, bibliographical critique can read processes and moments embedded in an artifact's materiality to show how texts are never fixed in meaning or location. Second, the microscopic scrutiny of manuscript and print can connect documents to the larger field of cultural production, ideological belief systems, or social and economic formations. Critical bibliography stitches the detail with larger frameworks in ways that unsettle interpretive models that favor linguistic meaning over materiality. If materiality is that which exceeds the linguistic, as social anthropology has proposed, then bibliography is a tool to reconsider writing as if we don't know in advance what writing is, does, or can be.[22]

SOLDIERING AS MASS CULTURE

The invasion inspired soldiers to record their experiences. One New York periodical satirized the voluminous written output (see figure 10.1). In a wood engraving titled "Latest from The Army," more attention is paid to writing than to combat, and one soldier composes a letter with no regard for a corpse at his feet. For *Yankee Doodle*'s urban audience, this "triumphant and scribbling soldiery" marked the difference from earlier wars and provided fodder for satire.[23] Contemporary memoirs from soldiers mention frequent letter writing. One author noted that the US subsidized correspondence. Volunteers and regulars received "sheets of paper from the officers, (to whom, every quarter, a quantity is allowed by the government)."[24]

"Latest from The Army" visualizes the performative power of writing the history of a war still in progress. The soldier at left absentmindedly scribbling above the dead body replicates, on the visual level, the disavowals shared by Pierce. This detail visualizes a fracture in verifiable reporting elsewhere unconsidered in Richard Caton Woodville's celebrated *War News from Mexico* (1848), the well-known painting depicting an array of citizens crowded around a newspaper. Woodville's picture of public space posits the newspaper as arena of public opinion, but it doesn't meditate on the fact that war reporting from Mexico could be censored and self-censoring. And *War News* wasn't the most popular image from the conflict. Other mediums—engraving and lithography—took precedence, and they sometimes foregrounded the work of distributing agents. An engraving entitled "The Mexican Express" connects news and its emotional effects to acts of transmission. A central scene of mother and child weeping for a dead soldier, the effect of news, is traceable to its proximate cause, a newsboy fading out of sight (pictured in the window at left) (see figure 10.2).[25] More emphatically than Woodward, "The Mexican Express" dramatizes how a

FIGURE 10.1 Soldiers in the US Army writing home from Mexico in the middle of combat. "Latest from The Army," *Yankee Doodle*, December 12, 1846.

communications network could collapse the distance between remote Mexico and bourgeois homes, making the foreign war startlingly domestic. The plate thematizes the agency of peddlers who distributed texts that originated from the soldiering depicted in "Latest from The Army." The two images complement one another, revealing two sides of war (fighting men and despondent families) shaped by the movements of paper documents.

Many soldiers stationed in Mexico participated in the publishers' networks. The mails had become more accessible than ever due to the 1845 expansion of postal services. This infrastructural development explains why so much correspondence transpired between soldiers and families.[26] Transmitted back to the US through the mails, the soldier's voice fueled a print marketplace perfectly timed for widespread distribution. Men like William McKittrick noticed when their letters appeared in American newspapers.[27] Occasionally the amateur authors reflect on the relation between large-scale events and their own experiences. "I shall not describe the movements of the army or give a History of the War only so far as they are intimately connected with myself," wrote Benjamin Scribner, "nor do I promise to keep a regular diary."[28] Similar to Franklin Pierce, this volunteer recorded what he saw while being careful not to incriminate himself. And compared to the original manuscript, the published edition of Scribner's narrative sidesteps unsavory moments, just like Hawthorne did with Pierce.

FIGURE 10.2 A family receives news of a soldier killed in the Mexican War. "The Mexican Express," *The Odd-Fellow's Offering, for 1852*, (New York: Edward Walker, 1852), 256–57. Courtesy American Antiquarian Society, Worcester, Massachusetts.

Scribner's wartime diaries were published in a widely read book, *Camp Life of a Volunteer* (1847), that popularized the genre of the camp narrative. Stories from the camps packaged the Mexican War as tourism, with officers and volunteers finding time to sample cuisines, drink, carouse, and gather mementos. Line by line examination of Scribner's manuscript reveals divergences that occurred when the diaries were forwarded to a Philadelphia publisher. Every divergence shows how the war's memorialization could be regulated down to the smallest details. In one incident from *Camp Life*, volunteers set out at night to a village looking for a fandango. Stumbling upon one such party, the visitors were "received with great trembling by the women." Our narrator, if he can be believed, portrays the soldiers as well behaved, but the subtext is untethered masculine aggression.[29] As with Pierce's unnamable accompaniments, it's tempting to imagine the party erupting into violence. And yet Scribner ends up repeating Pierce's hesitations in recounting tense interactions. "The more I see of vice and dissipation," states the published version, "the firmer I believe a moral and virtuous life constitutes the only sure guarantee of happiness."[30] We don't know what those vices were, when they occurred, or to what degree Scribner was culpable. He claims to be "acting a part in which my own character is not represented. I have dipped into all the temptations that have come in my way, but I do not think that the effect will be demoralizing or its impressions lasting."³¹ He later concludes that "the future has nothing in store for me." However, readers never got to read these passages, because they were redacted.³²

Not all soldiers were equal on the battlefield or in the written record. Historians point out that the US military was internally divided between regulars and volunteers. The volunteers, who dominate the written record, were literate men who had families to write home to.³³ Volunteers were more likely to exercise gratuitous violence against the enemy and occasionally each other. "Service in a volunteer regiment," Peter Guardino writes, "was in a sense like being in a saloon or election-day crowd, except that it lasted for months rather than a few hours."³⁴ Volunteers had time to write, drink, fight, and kill. Two complementary points regarding the structure of military life pertain to this discussion moving forward. On the one hand, the volunteer's identity depended upon freedom from rigid discipline and corporal punishment that kept the regular soldiers in check. On the other hand, the volunteer's rampant individualism lent itself to chronological extraterritoriality, the fantasy of reliving the days of Cortés, and engaging in sprees not tolerated at home. Volunteers described living intensely in the moment, looking ahead to uncertain futures, and encountering unfamiliar surroundings that partook of premodernity. Some committed suicide; others turned violent against friends and family.³⁵ It cannot be accidental that such experiences took root in a foreign conflict. "The march of our armies into Mexico, was an emigration as well as an invasion," muses the narrator of the novel *Talbot and Vernon*, whose protagonist is a young artist recruited to paint Mexican "sieges, marches, bivouacs, camps, etc. etc."³⁶

THE SUBSCRIPTION PUBLISHING NETWORK

Publishers stoked interest in the war by selling military histories peddled by traveling agents. As late as 1857, a humorous war history could be sold exclusively by subscription and reach a wide readership. In books like *Chile con Carne*, readers looked upon the Mexican War as a heterotopia, an alternative nonnational space of martial valor. No evidence in any copy of *Chile con Carne* indicates that subscription agents sold the book; a lone salesman's prospectus is the only evidence of its transmission.³⁷ Book trade archives and ephemera are therefore necessary to recover unnoticed pathways of the war's print dissemination.

Subscription bookselling emerged in the second quarter of the nineteenth century as an offshoot of an industrializing book trade. Publishers established a far-flung network beyond the urban centers of New York, Boston, and Philadelphia. Mexican War histories were subscription bestsellers in the decade before the Civil War.[38] The evidence survives only in fragments, since most sample volumes have not been preserved. Each surviving copy of a canvassing book is unique, since it made the rounds of particular communities while being carried by a specific agent. A list of names carried by the agent could be persuasive. Each new customer would see the growing list of signatures as the manifestation of a reading community they too could join. Instructional manuals emphasized this moment of presentation: "the unfolding of the subscription list, when the *array of signatures* strikes the person with a sort of mesmeric influence."[39] Canvassers understood that they gathered readers into aggregates visible only in these lists.

In the essay "The Mass Ornament," Kracauer discusses cultural ephemera in ways that recall the agentive force of the subscription list. For Kracauer, the spontaneous formations of popular culture articulate unspoken patterns of community belief. A mass ornament "does not emerge out of the interior of the conditions, but rather appears above them."[40] The lists of names recorded in canvassing books could be a nineteenth-century version of Kracauer's abstracted social body, since they gather together (in Latour's sense) thousands of participants in artifacts that acquire value out of the cascading lists of names. For instance, W. H. Brown peddled John Frost's *Pictorial History of Mexico and the Mexican War* (1849) across North Carolina. Brown secured ninety-three orders for six different book titles, but well over half opted for Frost's war history. The sample book was the apparatus that knit together these scattered readers, offering a snapshot of a reading public—or, more accurately, a virtual public manifested on paper.[41] While Brown's numbers might seem small, he was but one man among thousands of agents doing this work across the US.

Agents and their canvassing techniques forged direct links between rural people, urban publishers, and authors and illustrators of Mexican scenes. By definition, subscription had its own temporal cycles of anticipation and delivery, since this kind of distribution required reiterative contact between peddlers and readers. Lewis D. Clawson of Florida mounted a certificate to his order book that specified the amount of time it would take to get the books into the hands of subscribers. Orders taken in November would be expected to arrive in February or March. Of seventy-six Floridians who ordered from Clawson, twenty-nine chose Frost's *Pictorial History of Mexico and the Mexican War*.[42] Clawson and W. H. Brown worked on commission for Philadelphia's Thomas, Cowperthwait & Co., a company employing hundreds of agents to disseminate histories and maps related to Mexico. Between 1848 and 1852, the firm sold over twenty-thousand subscriptions to Frost's book. Mexican War histories were sold by agents in Massachusetts, New York, Pennsylvania, Ohio, Illinois, and all of the major southern states.[43] The Philadelphia firm distributed other Mexican War titles.[44] Other publishers used this model as well. An earlier title by Frost, *The Mexican War and Its Warriors* (1848), was published in Hartford, Connecticut, a center of the subscription trade.[45] Another Hartford firm, A. C. Goodman & Co., issued *History of the American Wars*, giving prominent attention to Mexican battles.[46] Publishers in other cities, such as Cincinnati's J. A. & U. P. James and W. H. Moore & Co., employed traveling agents.[47] Philadelphia's Grigg and Elliot, publisher of Scribner's *Camp Life of a Volunteer*, also sold military histories by subscription.[48]

Luxury books about the war were also sold by subscription. The most expensive history on the market, George Kendall's *The War between the United States and Mexico Illustrated* (1851), was a folio collection of battle narratives accompanied by hand-colored lithographs made by the Parisian firm Lemercier. Production details of the expensive publication show the subscription network extending across countries and continents. Lemercier's twelve lithographs were copied from portraits made by Carl Nebel in Mexico. Workers in London, Berlin, and Brussels did the hand coloring.[49] A New York bindery turned the engravings into books.[50] Kendall, who had connections with the New Orleans *Picayune*, called upon newspaper editors in many US cities and towns to sell the expensive work.[51]

Reviews of *War between the United States and Mexico Illustrated* acknowledged the role of images for the war's memorialization. "With admirable judgment," one newspaper reported, Kendall's artists "limn, from life, the bloody front of war." "Thus accoutered, he is an active participant in nearly every battle that distinguished the war with Mexico . . . and now, before the immense territory won in that brilliant war is placed, and its metes and bounds appointed, the country is presented at a munificent expense of labor and money unprecedented, with this noble book."[52]

Kendall's book was a "participant" in the war; the same could be said of Scribner's *Camp Life* or Frost's *Pictorial History*. Subscription, in this regard, made the war participatory beyond the battlefields. When American subscribers registered their names, they ratified and validated the invasion. Perhaps difficult to perceive from our own hypermediated situation, my claim here is that public representations intersected with a mode of distribution that inflected the Mexican War with a peculiar ontology and an epistemology. More precisely, the army's aspiration and its actuality could be confused in pictures. The war "happened" in fictive images, a procedure bound to perpetuate inaccuracies. Winfield Scott's famous assault on Veracruz, published in Frost's *Pictorial History* as a foldout lithograph facing the text's title page, erroneously shows the port city engulfed in flames.[53] Here is a nineteenth-century version of Jacques Rancière's distribution of the sensible: a substitution of violence that didn't happen for the violence that did occur in the real invasion. This substitution was accomplished through lithography's allure as the most "democratic" of the popular arts.[54]

CHRONOLOGICAL EXTRATERRITORIALITY
AND THE SACRIFICIAL VICTIM

Kracauer's *History* contests the assumption that people "belong" to empty, homogenous time. The film theorist challenges a venerable tradition in the philosophy of history which understands time as unidirectional. For Kracauer, the idea of disparate peoples belonging to their times is dependent on the simultaneity elaborated in Walter Benjamin's famous essay on the concept of history. Kracauer argues further that historical periods are the back formations of homogenous time: "The period seems so indispensable a unit that it is invented after the fact if it cannot be discovered in the material."[55] But this is not simply a rejection of traditional history. Kracauer sees a fundamental antinomy between time's unidirectional passing and the alternatives of recurrence, anachrony, or nonprogression. For present purposes the twin concepts of polychronicity and multitemporality offer an analytical opportunity to unhinge time from its vulgar conception. I've recounted above how the Mexican War lured the US Army to experience the commingling of different scales of time. As such, the archive offers the chance to redeploy Kracauer's idea of chronological extraterritoriality.

But what is chronological extraterritoriality? It is not equivalent to the transcendental homelessness of György Lukács (whom Kracauer admired), but is instead an "unsettled settlement" captured in images and texts. Gerhard Richter has offered the most penetrating analysis of this idea. Extraterritoriality is the "experience that allows for the articulation and mobilization of the ways in which territoriality is at odds with itself, a liberation of the terror that always already was hauntingly at work in territoriality, if only as a form of dissimulation."[56] Richter's explanation locates an uncanny within extraterritoriality, where territory generates a terror of exile and the fear interior to settlement. While helpful, that reading doesn't yet unpack *chronological* extraterritoriality, but we can extend Richter's insight to questions of temporality. Following Richter, we can conclude that *History: The Last Things before the Last* expands the unheimlichkeit of extraterritoriality to time, to actors within history, and to the historian. Space does not permit a thorough discussion of Kracauer's writings. I will instead examine a document that instantiates how invasion and unsettlement confounded the soldier's sense of time.

Kracauer's interest in ephemera and cultural detritus would favor figure 10.3, an untitled watercolor by John Darragh Wilkins, an officer who had fought in the Battles of Contreras and Churubusco. The enigmatic image channels the war into a theologically inflected scene of punishment and abjection. Two demons flagellate a man who lies prostrate, blindfolded, and chained. An angelic figure on the right shields its face. A bolt of lightning descending from above reiterates the angel's theological judgment. Unquestionably, this sketch translates the war's violence into a different order of time. Other illustrations by Wilkins confirm his preoccupation with the multitemporal. The same sketchbook includes a pencil illustration of knights on horseback, as if on a kind of medieval crusade. Another drawing depicts "Catholic Irish" men taking communion in a church at Coyoacán. The book therefore replays the time-bending war adventures we have seen in writings from Scribner and other soldiers and officers, but in this instance manifested in a horrific image. The scene in figure 10.3 represents the war as delirium and lived mythology. Here violence is experienced as "expelled and expelling, as the cutoff and the cutting off," to cite Rodolphe Gasché's paraphrase of Georges Bataille.[57]

A theoretical critique of the Mexican War requires that the analysis of bibliographic documents (per Greg) and their temporality (per Kracauer) moves in the direction of the soldier's immersion in myth, or, to be precise, Batailleanan sacrifice. French theory's oracle of the dépense would be the best resource for theorizing the war's archive of killing and hedonism. Lest readers object, recall that Bataille was bibliographically minded from his career at the Bibliothèque Nationale, where he worked in numismatics

FIGURE 10.3 An angel shields its face as demons flagellate a blindfolded man. Watercolor by John Darragh Wilkins, Memorandum and Letters, 1846–1848. Beinecke Rare Book and Manuscript Library, Yale University.

and printed books for nearly twenty years. His professional life provided access to manuscripts that inspired some of his most probing essays on religion, aesthetics, and material culture, including several pieces where he was drawn to philosophize on Aztec society.

Bataille took interest in early Mexico's "bloody eccentricity." Like William Prescott before him, Bataille was fascinated by the Aztecs' sheer alterity to European ordering paradigms. In the 1928 essay "Extinct America," Bataille admired the "amazingly joyous character" of Aztec sacrifice for its alternative to an early American history tied to the US nation. "Nothing in bygone America can equal Mexico."[58] Pre-Conquest Mexico epitomized the concept of expenditure he elsewhere treasured in the Lascaux cave paintings, as if Mexican representations of bloody ecstasy rivaled the anthropological significance of Lascaux. We'll briefly turn to the Lascaux essays, but "Extinct America" is noteworthy for temporal workings that mirror the imaginative investments of the Mexican War diarists. In "Extinct America," Bataille consults William Prescott's *History of the Conquest of Mexico* (1843) but finds the latter's descriptions inadequate. Bataille moves backward by consulting Juan de Torquemada and Bernardino de Sahagún, supplemented by visual evidence from the Codex Telleriano-Remensis. The latter manuscript, held by the Bibliothèque Nationale, was probably consulted in person. As Robert Johannsen noted in the classic cultural history of the war, many soldiers and officers knew Prescott's history, some even carried copies with them.[59] Going backward from Prescott to Mesoamerican history was a thought experiment shared between Bataille and literate members of the US military.

Though teasingly brief, "Extinct America" demonstrates Bataille's interest in a subversive anthropological reading of early Mexico. He clearly sees Aztec culture as epitomizing a lived ontology defined by sacrifice and myth that fit his transgressive philosophy of history. This essay echoed philosophical themes explored in Bataille's other writings on prehistoric art. In several art historical essays, Bataille positions the paintings at Lascaux as an allegory of executioner turned sacrificial victim: "He who gives death enters into death."[60] But Lascaux, for Bataille, precedes the practice of warfare, which only arrives with the abundant resources produced by agricultural societies. Ancient Mexico, with its administrative state, belongs to a later stage whose economic surplus required the periodic expenditure of excess resources. He believed this relief from surplus was accomplished through war or ritual sacrifice.

Cues in the watercolor reproduced in figure 10.3 necessitate a Bataillean perspective. I will therefore conclude this essay with a closer reading. The prone figure, like the devils torturing him, has an undeniably ecstatic and erotic quality that exemplifies Bataille's preoccupation with war and sacrifice (which is also war as sacrifice). The victim is *charged* by the encounter to such an obvious degree that he risks making the lightning bolt redundant. That ecstasy in giving and receiving punishment, dimly seen in the victim's face, who could be a displaced representation of Wilkins or someone he knew, can plausibly be read as reflecting the American military's untethered masculinity I earlier examined. The angel also partakes of chronological extraterritoriality. Rather than simply rejecting the violence at the picture's center, the angel's *angle* betrays a sliding movement toward the middle in a way that makes attraction to violence a constitutive element of its moralizing repulsion. In turning away, the angel, as well as the artist, falls into the terrifying maelstrom.

The Mexican War watercolor should therefore be understood as a Bataillean movement of expenditure, where the wasting away of the body and exhaustion of the ego are distributed across the various figures. It's as if our artist produced the watercolor to say, "I made this in Mexico out of the pain I have witnessed (or inflicted), but I've lost track of which figure best represents me, because I've forgotten who I am." This visual expression of chronological extraterritoriality leads to multiple identifications: victim, demon, and angel.

CONCLUSION: THE INTERBELLUM

Bataille leaves us with a loosely defined idea of an early Mexico that potentially defamiliarizes our notions of early and antebellum America. However, despite this chapter's best efforts, the term *antebellum* will surely continue to be used in articles, monographs, and dissertations. But theorizing the US-Mexico War upsets neat demarcations of American history. Lasting just two years, the invasion took place amid the early stages of industrial publishing that foretold the rise of war reporting in mass culture. This cultural and technological convergence altered the possibilities of public culture by making visible a mass spectacle of war. The term *interbellum* makes conceptual this widespread imaginary of an event that took place elsewhere. It doesn't simply deny the antebellum, since the *betweenness* preserves, even as it disfigures, the paradigm indexed when we invoke the antebellum unreflectively. The concept of an interbellum seeks to foreground the Mexican War as a vanishing public event, where what appears is already disappeared. Images and texts accomplished this work of forgetful recollection, in differing ways, sometimes in the same published books and elsewhere in letters, diaries, and notebooks.

As we have seen, the US invasion of Mexico included moments when the extraterritorial work of invasion prompted some military personnel to lose hold of their times. And the magnitude of violence perpetuated by the United States prompted others to struggle over how it should be represented. Hence Pierce wrote: "I hope I have an incorrect view of things when I am so foolish as to think that in this 19th Century *war* to be effectual must be *war* not a mission of civilization and humanity." The mask of restrained leadership almost fell off here, but the cruel sentiment was quickly retracted: "I hate war in all its aspects, I deem it unworthy of the age in which I live & of the Gov't in which I have borne some part."[61] The diary articulated the difference between an illusion of a restrained conflict and the realities of violence that Pierce and his contemporaries sought to keep out of the historical record.

NOTES

1. Franklin Pierce, Mexican War Diary, HM 61, The Huntington Library, San Marino, California.
2. Guardino, *Dead March*; Foos, *Short, Offhand, Killing Affair*.
3. Serres and Latour, *Conversations*, 60.
4. Harris, *Untimely Matter*, 3–4.
5. John Darragh Wilkins Memorandum and Letters, Western Americana Collection, Beinecke Rare Book and Manuscript Library, Yale University.
6. John Wolcott Phelps, July 17, 1847, Diary S.4, Manuscripts and Archives Division, New York Public Library.
7. Kracauer, *History*.
8. Streeby, *American Sensations*.
9. Hackenberg, "Subscription Publishing."
10. Kracauer, *History*, 66.
11. Hager and Marrs, "Against 1865."
12. Alemán, "Other Country."
13. Bataille, *Accursed Share*, 37; Chamberlain, *My Confession*.
14. Butler, *Frames of War*.
15. Gitelman, *Always Already New*, 6.
16. Greg, "What Is Bibliography?"
17. Greg, "Bibliography—an Apologia," 116.
18. Greg, "Bibliography—an Apologia," 135.
19. Darnton, "What Is the History of Books?"
20. Greg, "Bibliography—An Apologia," 122.
21. Adams and Barker, "New Model," 22.
22. Fleming, *Cultural Graphology*; Pinney, "Things Happen."
23. *Yankee Doodle*, December 12, 1846.
24. Furber, *Twelve Months Volunteer*, 418.
25. The engraving illustrates a poem by E. Anna Lewis titled "The Mexican Express," in *The Odd-Fellows' Offering, for 1852* (New York, 1851), 256–57. The image appears on unnumbered pages between the first and second pages of the poem.
26. Henkin, *Postal Age*.
27. William H. McKittrick Letters, Beinecke Rare Book and Manuscript Library, Yale University.
28. Benjamin Franklin Scribner's Private Journal, University of Texas at Arlington Library Special Collections.

29 Scribner, *Camp Life*, 44–45.
30 Scribner, *Camp Life*, 28.
31 Scribner, Private Journal, September 7, 1846.
32 Scribner, Private Journal, September 20, 1846.
33 Winders, "Composed of a Different Material."
34 Guardino, "Gender, Soldiering, and Citizenship."
35 D. Williamson McNulty to Thomas Jefferson McKean, October 4, 1850; Richard Coulter Journal, April 9, 1848, William L. Clements Library, University of Michigan.
36 McConnel, *Talbot and Vernon*, 108, 54–55.
37 *Chile con Carne*, salesman's sample copy, American Antiquarian Society.
38 Hackenberg, "Subscription Publishing."
39 *Agent's Companion. A Manual of Confidential Instructions* (Philadelphia, 1866).
40 Kracauer, *Mass Ornament*, 77.
41 *A General View of the World*, salesman's sample copy, Beinecke Rare Book and Manuscript Library, Yale University.
42 *Pictorial Life of George Washington*, salesman's sample copy, American Antiquarian Society.
43 Thomas, Cowperthwait and Co., Account Book, 1846–1852, American Antiquarian Society.
44 Edward D. Mansfield, *Life of Winfield Scott* (New York, 1846); *Taylor and His Generals* (Philadelphia, 1847); Henry Montgomery, *Life of Major General Zachary Taylor* (Auburn, NY, 1847).
45 John Frost, *Mexican War and Its Warriors*, salesman's sample copy, American Antiquarian Society.
46 R. Thomas, *History of the American Wars* (Hartford, CT: A. C. Goodman, 1847).
47 J. A. and U. P. James published Philip Young, *History of Mexico* (Cincinnati, 1848), and Furber, *Twelve Months Volunteer*. W. H. Moore published Raphael Semmes, *Service Afloat and Ashore During the Mexican War* (Cincinnati, 1851).
48 Nathan Covington Brooks, *Complete History of the Mexican War* (Philadelphia: Grigg and Elliot, 1849).
49 "Scrapbook of Clippings," Kendall Family Papers, University of Texas at Arlington Special Collections.
50 Kendall to Mathews and Rider, May 1851 to November 1852, Kendall Family Papers, University of Texas at Arlington Special Collections.
51 *Prospectus*, Kendall Family Papers, University of Texas at Arlington Special Collections.
52 "Scrapbook of Clippings," Kendall Family Papers, University of Texas at Arlington Special Collections.
53 Wagner and M'Guigan, lithographers, "Landing of the troops at Vera Cruz."
54 Marzio, *Democratic Art*.
55 Kracauer, *History*, 147.

56 Richter, *Thought-Images*, 114.
57 Gasché, *Georges Bataille*, 104.
58 Bataille and Michelson, "Extinct America."
59 Johannsen, *To the Halls of the Montezumas*.
60 Bataille, *Cradle of Humanity*, 172.
61 Pierce, Mexican War Diary.

BIBLIOGRAPHY

Adams, Thomas R., and Nicolas Barker. "A New Model for the Study of the Book." In *A Potencie of Life: Books in Society*, edited by Nicolas Barker, 5–43. London: British Library, 1993.

Alemán, Jesse. "The Other Country: Mexico, the United States, and the Gothic History of Conquest." *American Literary History* 18, no. 3 (2006): 406–26.

Bataille, Georges. *The Accursed Share: An Essay on General Economy, Vol. 1: Consumption*. New York: Zone, 1991.

Bataille, Georges. *The Cradle of Humanity: Prehistoric Art and Culture*. Edited by Stuart Kendall. Translated by Michelle Kendall and Stuart Kendall. New York: Zone, 2005.

Bataille, Georges, and Annette Michelson. "Extinct America." *October* 36 (1986): 3–9.

Butler, Judith. *Frames of War: When Is Life Grievable?* New York: Verso, 2010.

Chamberlain, Samuel. *My Confession: Recollections of a Rogue*. Austin: Texas State Historical Association, 1996.

Darnton, Robert. "What Is the History of Books?" *Daedalus* 111, no. 3 (1982): 65–83.

Fleming, Juliet. *Cultural Graphology: Writing after Derrida*. Chicago: University of Chicago Press, 2016.

Foos, Paul. *A Short, Offhand, Killing Affair: Soldiers and Social Conflict during the Mexican-American War*. Chapel Hill: University of North Carolina Press, 2002.

Frost, John. *Pictorial History of Mexico and the Mexican American War: Comprising an Account of the Ancient Aztec Empire, the Conquest by Cortex, Mexico under the Spaniards, the Mexican Revolution, the Republic, the Texan War, and the Recent War with the United States*. Philadelphia: Thomas, Cowperthwait & Co., 1849.

Furber, George C. *The Twelve Months Volunteer*. Cincinnati: J. A. and U. P. James, 1849.

Gasché, Rodolphe. *Georges Bataille: Phenomenology and Phantasmatology*. Translated by Roland Végsö. Palo Alto, CA: Stanford University Press, 2012.

Gitelman, Lisa. *Always Already New: Media, History, and the Data of Culture*. Cambridge, MA: MIT Press, 2006.

Greg, W. W. "Bibliography—an Apologia." *Library*, 4th ser. 13 (1932): 113–43.

Greg, W. W. "What Is Bibliography?" *Transactions of the Bibliographical Society* 12, no. 1 (1913): 39–54.

Guardino, Peter. *The Dead March: A History of the Mexican-American War*. Cambridge, MA: Harvard University Press, 2017.

Guardino, Peter. "Gender, Soldiering, and Citizenship in the Mexican-American War of 1846–1848." *American Historical Review* 119, no. 1 (2014): 23–46.

Hackenberg, Michael. "The Subscription Publishing Network in Nineteenth-Century America." In *Getting the Books Out: Papers of the Chicago Conference on the Book in 19th-Century America*, edited by Michael Hackenberg, 45–75. Washington, DC: Center for the Book, Library of Congress, 1987.

Hager, Christopher, and Cody Marrs. "Against 1865: Reperiodizing the Nineteenth Century." *J19: The Journal of Nineteenth-Century Americanists* 1, no. 2 (2013): 259–84.

Harris, Jonathan Gil. *Untimely Matter in the Time of Shakespeare*. Philadelphia: University of Pennsylvania Press, 2009.

Hawthorne, Nathaniel. *Life of Franklin Pierce*. Boston: Ticknor, Reed, and Fields, 1852.

Henkin, David M. *The Postal Age: The Emergence of Modern Communications in Nineteenth-Century America*. Chicago: University of Chicago Press, 2006.

Johannsen, Robert W. *To the Halls of the Montezumas: The Mexican War in the American Imagination*. New York: Oxford University Press, 1985.

Kendall, George Wilkins. *The War between the United States and Mexico Illustrated*. New York: D. Appleton, 1851.

Kracauer, Siegfried. *History: The Last Things before the Last*. New York: Oxford University Press, 1969.

Kracauer, Siegfried. *The Mass Ornament: Weimar Essays*. Translated, edited, and with an introduction by Thomas Y. Levin. Cambridge, MA: Harvard University Press, 1995.

"Latest from The Army." *Yankee Doodle*, December 12, 1846.

Lewis, E. Anna. "The Mexican Express." In *The Odd-Fellows' Offering, for 1852*, 256–57. New York: Edward Walker, 1852.

Marzio, Peter C. *The Democratic Art: Pictures for a 19th-Century America: Chromolithography, 1840–1900*. Boston: David R. Godine, 1979.

McConnel, John Ludlum. *Talbot and Vernon: A Novel*. New York: Baker and Scribner, 1850.

Pierce, Franklin. Mexican War Diary, HM 61, The Huntington Library, San Marino, CA.

Pinney, Christopher. "Things Happen: Or, from Which Moment Does That Object Come?" In *Materiality*, edited by Daniel Miller, 256–72. Durham, NC: Duke University Press, 2005.

Richter, Gerhard. *Thought-Images: Frankfurt School Writers' Reflections from Damaged Life*. Palo Alto, CA: Stanford University Press, 2007.

Scribner, Benjamin Franklin. *Camp Life of a Volunteer: A Campaign in Mexico, or a Glimpse at Life in Camp*. Philadelphia: Grigg and Elliott, 1847.

Serres, Michel, and Bruno Latour. *Conversations on Science, Culture, and Time*. Translated by Roxanne Lapidus. Ann Arbor: University of Michigan Press, 1995.

Streeby, Shelley. *American Sensations: Class, Empire, and the Production of Popular Culture.* Berkeley: University of California Press, 2002.

Winders, Robert. "Composed of a Different Material: Democracy, Discipline, and the Mexican War Volunteer." In *Papers of the Bi-National Conference on the War between Mexico and the United States,* edited by Douglas A. Murphy, 117–23. Brownsville, TX: National Park Service, 1997.

LIST OF CONTRIBUTORS

MAX CAVITCH is associate professor of English at the University of Pennsylvania, where he also codirects the program in psychoanalytic studies. He is the author of *American Elegy: The Poetry of Mourning from the Puritans to Whitman* (2007) and dozens of articles on American and African American literature, cinema studies, poetry and poetics, and psychoanalytic studies. His new edition of Walt Whitman's *Specimen Days* is forthcoming in 2023, and he is completing two new books: *Ashes: A History of Thought and Substance* and *Passing Resemblances: World Autobiography from Enheduanna to Knausgård*.

BRIAN CONNOLLY is associate professor and chair of the Department of History at the University of South Florida. He is the author of *Domestic Intimacies: Incest and the Liberal Subject in Nineteenth-Century America* and editor of *History of the Present: A Journal of Critical History*. He is completing a book on family, psychoanalysis, and history, *The Family and the Phallus*.

MATTHEW CROW is associate professor of history at Hobart and William Smith Colleges in Geneva, NY. He is the author of *Thomas Jefferson, Legal History, and the Art of Recollection* (2017), currently completing a second book project about Herman Melville, oceans, and early modern law and empire, and beginning future work on the intellectual histories of legal, ecclesiastical, and oceanic history.

JOHN J. GARCIA is director of scholarly programs and partnerships at the American Antiquarian Society. He is completing a critical edition of an illustrated diary from a nineteenth-century children's author who was institutionalized in European and American insane asylums.

CHRISTOPHER LOOBY is professor of English at the University of California, Los Angeles. He edits a series entitled *Q19: The Queer American Nineteenth Century*, the most recent volumes of which have been Margaret J. M. Sweat's 1859 novel *Ethel's Love-Life* and Charles Warren Stoddard's 1903 novel *For the Pleasure of His Company: An Affair of the Misty City, Thrice Told*.

MICHAEL MERANZE is professor of history at the University of California, Los Angeles. He is the author of *Laboratories of Virtue: Punishment, Revolution and Authority in Philadelphia, 1760–1835*, and numerous articles on the intellectual and legal history of early America and the history of punishment.

MARK J. MILLER is associate professor of English at Hunter College, CUNY, where he teaches early American literature, early Native American literature, and literary theory. His work considers public-sphere religious organizing, race, and sexuality in the eighteenth and nineteenth centuries. He is the author of *Cast Down: Abjection in America, 1700–1850*.

JUSTINE S. MURISON is professor of English at the University of Illinois, Urbana-Champaign. Her research and teaching examine nineteenth-century American literature with special attention to its relation to the intertwined histories of health and religion. She is the author of *The Politics of Anxiety in Nineteenth-Century American Literature* and *Faith in Exposure: Privacy and Secularism in the Nineteenth-Century United States*.

BRITT RUSERT is professor of Afro-American Studies at the University of Massachusetts Amherst. She is the author of *Fugitive Science: Empiricism and Freedom in Early African American Culture* (2017) and coeditor of *W. E. B. Du Bois's Data Portraits: Visualizing Black America* (2018). She is finishing a book manuscript about William J. Wilson's "Afric-American Picture Gallery" (1859) and is also writing a history of mutual aid organizing in the long nineteenth century.

ANA SCHWARTZ is assistant professor of English at the University of Texas at Austin. She is the author of *Unmoored: The Search for Sincerity in Colonial America* and is researching her second book, a social history of the soul.

JOAN W. SCOTT is professor emerita in the School of Social Science at the Institute for Advanced Study in Princeton, New Jersey. Her most recent books are *On the Judgment of History* and *Knowledge, Power, and Academic Freedom*.

JORDAN ALEXANDER STEIN teaches in the English department and the Comparative Literature Program at Fordham University, where he is also affiliated faculty in African and African American studies. He is the author most recently of *When Novels Were Books*.

INDEX

abolition, 203, 224–25, 229, 233n6
abolitionism, 9, 22, 192, 208, 223–25, 229–31, 233n14; historiography of, 232; and media, 223–29, 231–32, 233n6, 233n14
Adams, Thomas, 270
Adorno, Theodor, 6, 23, 241, 242, 244, 256; on allegory, 23, 244, 256; *Negative Dialectics*, 241
affect, 5, 7, 38, 145, 150, 163, 227. *See also* annoyance
Alcock, John, 118–23, 127
Alemán, Jesse, 266, 268
allegory, 23, 229, 243–44, 248, 255–56, 280
American Revolution, the, 3, 8, 66–67, 183
American studies. *See* early American studies
American Tract Society, 22, 177, 180, 196n3
Anderson, Misty, 150
annoyance, 75–77, 81–93
Apess, William, 203
archives, 2, 5, 8, 9, 24, 39, 41–42, 216–17; digitization of, 41; Mexican War, 275; problem of, 216–17; and slavery, 216–17, 221n36
Arendt, Hannah, 181, 196, 197n13
Aristotle, 69n22, 241
Asad, Talal, 179, 228
astronomy, 206, 209, 211
atheism, 18, 178, 184, 195
Atkins v. Chilson (1846), 247
Augustine, 124–25, 131, 135n42; *City of God*, 135n42; *Confessions*, 124–25
authenticity, 22, 179–82, 196, 197n13. *See also* sincerity

Banneker, Benjamin, 213, 219n27
Barker, Nicolas, 270
Barrough, Philip: *The Method of Physick*, 120

Bataille, Georges, 23, 267–68, 278–82; "Extinct America," 279–80
Beecher, Lyman, 193
belief, 2, 22, 34, 37, 122, 193–96, 206, 212, 271; Foucault on 4; Kracauer on, 275; private, 186, 188; vs. secularism, 45, 179–80, 182–89, 195; and sexual character, 144, 148; Weber and, 45. *See also* Christianity; fantasy; ideology; Protestantism; Puritanism; religion
Benjamin, Walter, 7–8, 15, 23, 244, 277
Bentley, Nancy, 18
Berlant, Lauren, 231–32
Bersani, Leo, 17
Best, Stephen, 10
Black studies, 215–16
Blackstone, William, 250
Blake, William, 164
Bolingbroke, Henry St. John (viscount), 185, 190
Boudinot, Elias, 186–88
Bourne, George: *The Book and Slavery Irreconcilable*, 224–25
Bray, Alan, 103–4, 111, 113, 114, 133n23, 133–34n26
Brower, Brady, 40
Brown, Charles Brockden, 185
Brown, Henry Box, 204
Brown, John, 223
Brown, Kathleen, 15
Brown, William Wells, 209, 223, 227; *Clotel*, 223, 227
Buck-Morss, Susan, 9
Buntline, Ned, 230, 267
Butler, Sara, 146

Castronovo, Russ, 230
Certeau, Michel de, 36, 38, 40, 42–43

character, 144–47, 149, 151–60, 162–63, 165
Cherniavsky, Eva, 111, 113, 115, 123, 129
Child, Lydia Maria: *The Patriarchal Institution, as Described by Members of Its Own Family*, 223
Chow, Rey, 13
Christianity, 58, 84, 88, 90–91, 99, 117–18, 141–42, 145–49, 157, 177, 180, 184–94, 206, 209. *See also* belief; conversion: narratives of; morality; Protestantism; sin
citizenship, 46, 65
Cobb, Jasmine Nichole, 215
Cobbett, William, 187
Coke, Sir Edward, 245, 251
collectivity, 205, 215
colonialism, 1, 2, 9, 18–19, 21, 37, 74–75, 93, 100n4, 216–17, 267
Combe, George, 204
confession, 105–6, 117, 124, 139, 143–44, 146–49, 157, 159, 161–63, 206–8; and print culture, 148–49. *See also* diary; privacy
conversion: narratives of, 139, 141–42, 149–51, 155, 161, 163–64, 179
Conway, Moncure, 177
Cooper, Anna Julia, 214, 219n31
Copjec, Joan, 37–38
Cornell, Saul, 15
Coviello, Peter, 38, 146
crisis, 1, 6–7, 8, 20, 127, 132–33n15
critical race theory, 9
critique, 2–20, 22, 24n9, 33, 159, 205, 231, 267–70, 278; and auto-critique, 205; bibliographical, 270, 278; histories of, 159; ideology, 10; immanent, 6, 8–9; and indeterminacy, 33; limits of, 9; and negativity, 269; queer, 231
Crowder, Richard, 104, 111, 113–14, 120, 125, 133n21
Cummins, Maria: *The Lamplighter*, 230

Dain, Bruce, 206
Darnton, Robert, 270
Davis, Kathleen, 16
Davis, Rebecca Harding, 230

death drive, the, 9, 22, 45, 203
Delany, Martin, 22, 205, 208–14: "The Attraction of Planets," 209; *Blake; or the Huts of America*, 205, 208–14, 218n21; "Comets," 209
democracy; indeterminacy of, 46, 47
Derrida, Jacques, 6, 24, 41, 116, 216; *Archive Fever*, 41; on hospitality, 6
desire, 6, 18, 20, 35–37, 55, 57–58, 87–88, 92–93, 111–12, 116, 121, 124, 131, 145–47, 150, 156, 164, 253, 255, 263; and *Ion*, 63, 67; and *Oedipus Rex*, 55, 57–58, 67; sexual, 111–12, 116, 121, 124, 131. *See also* Euripides: *Ion*; fantasy; Foucault, Michel; Freud, Sigmund; psychoanalysis; Sophocles: *Oedipus Rex*; sex; sin
Detienne, Marcel, 59
diary: of Grimké, Charlotte Forten, 214; of Pierce, Franklin, 263–65, 267–69, 272, 282; of soldiers, 273, 281; of Whitefield, George, 153–54, 156; of Wigglesworth, Michael, 17, 21, 103–6, 110–21, 123–25, 128–30, 131n2, 132n11, 133–34n26, 135n42
Dickinson, Emily, 1, 7, 8
Dillon, Elizabeth Maddock, 12, 191
Dinius, Marcy, 203
discipline, 57, 73–74, 76, 86–87, 91, 150, 161. *See also* Foucault, Michel; repression
disestablishment, 1, 22, 178–80, 182–83, 188, 195, 196, 196n9
domesticity, 22, 73, 224–25, 227–28, 231–32. *See also* family, the
Donzelot, Jacques, 46
Douglass, Frederick, 195, 204, 209, 211, 225, 227, 233n14; "Claims of the Negro, Ethnologically Considered," 204; *Narrative of the Life of Frederick Douglass, an American Slave*, 209
Downes, Paul, 9
dreams, 21, 33, 35, 37, 39–41, 55, 103–5, 110, 112–16, 123–25, 127–30, 133–34n26, 135n42. *See also* Freud, Sigmund; psychoanalysis
Drexler, Michael, 13
Du Bois, W. E. B., 38, 219n31

Dunlap, William, 185
Duparc, François, 35
Dwight, Timothy, 187–88

early American studies, 5, 10, 13–17, 19, 29n13, 178, 195, 205, 215–17, 256
Easton, Hosea, 203, 217
Edelman, Lee, 45–46, 112, 203
Edwards, Jonathan, 116
Ellison, Ralph, 217
emancipation, 209, 212–13, 216; intellectual, 212–13
embodiment, 104, 105, 117. *See also* sex
Emerson, Ralph Waldo, 94, 180–81; "Self-Reliance," 180–81
empiricism, 17–19, 21–22, 34, 203–6, 208, 213, 217; Black speculative use of, 9, 22, 204–5, 208, 211, 216; challenges to, 213, naïve, 2, 5. *See also* fact; neoempiricism
Engen, Abram van, 92
equity, 22–23, 44, 241–50, 253–54, 258n44
ethnology, 34, 206
Euripides: *Ion*, 62–65, 67
evangelism, 143–46, 148–51, 155–56, 161–64, 177, 193–95, 202. *See also* print culture; writing: evangelical

fact, 12, 17–19, 21–22, 39, 58, 75, 84, 226, 230, 258n44; -finding, 246, 254. *See also* empiricism; truth
family, the, 18, 21–22, 45, 73, 147, 179, 191, 223–25, 226. *See also* domesticity; heteronormativity
Fanon, Frantz, 37
fantasy, 1, 33, 35, 43, 46, 73, 111, 274 *See also* desire; ideology
Fassin, Didier, 11
Fassin, Eric, 24n9
Felski, Rita, 10
feminist theory, 15, 44–45
Fenton, Elizabeth, 190, 201
Fessenden, Tracy, 180
Fletcher v. Peck (1810), 247
Foote, Samuel, 164

Foucault, Michel, 4, 5, 15, 20, 34, 37–38, 46, 52, 53–67, 68n22, 117, 131n2, 146–48, 157, 216, 242; *Care of the Self*, 58; *Confessions of the Flesh*, 135n42; *Discipline and Punish*, 58; *The Government of Self and Others*, 62; *The History of Sexuality: Vol. 1*, 58, 60–61, 73, 117, 146–47; *Lectures on the Will to Know*, 52–58; and *Oedipus Rex*, 52–67; *On the Government of the Living*, 59; *Use of Pleasure*, 58; *Wrong-Doing, Truth-Telling*, 59, 61
Franklin, Benjamin, 152, 158, 163, 178, 181, 185, 197; *The Autobiography of Benjamin Franklin*, 181
freedom: academic, 66; Black conceptions of, 204, 212; emotional, 93; from judgment, 243; interpretive, 251; limits of, 18; in *Oedipus Rex*, 62; religious, 1, 21, 139, 182–83, 192–93, 197n17; and slavery, 3, 9, 22, 204, 208, 211, 232; of speech, 64; of volunteer soldiers, 269, 274. *See also* abolition; abolitionism; sovereignty
Freeman, Lisa, 143
French Revolution, the, 178, 184–85, 190, 193, 195
Freud, Sigmund, 20, 33–41, 43, 45, 47, 48n4, 48n17, 48n29, 52, 54–55, 58, 73, 75, 79, 85, 86, 87; "Analysis Terminable and Interminable," 87; and gender, 43–47; *Moses and Monotheism*, 34, 35, 39, 48n12; post-Freudian, the, 37–39; "Psychopathology of Everyday Life," 48n4; "Repression," 73–75; *Totem and Taboo*, 34, 35, 47
Frost, John: *Pictorial History of Mexico and the Mexican-American War*, 275–77
Fugitive Slave Act (1850), 247
Fuller v. Dame (1836), 247
futurity, 6, 8–9, 11, 14, 34, 39, 48n29, 203, 217, 268, 270, 274; rejection of, 203, 217

Gale v. Wilkinson (1805), 251
Garrison, William Lloyd, 195, 225, 227, 231
Gates, Henry Louis, Jr., 210

gender, 18, 22, 43–47, 131, 144–46, 155–63, 224 230, 231, 235n39; history, 15; norms, 144, 162–63, 235n39
Gitelman, Lisa, 269
Godbeer, Richard, 92, 111, 113
Godwin, William, 187
Goffman, Irving, 143
Grasso, Christopher, 184, 187, 198n51
Gray, Thomas, 208, 218n13
Greenblatt, Stephen, 85, 86, 90
Greenwood, Grace: "The Leap from the Long Bridge," 229–31
Greg, W. W., 267, 269–70, 278
Grimes, William: *Life of William Grimes, the Runaway Slave; Written by Himself*, 224–25
Grimké, Angelina: *American Slavery as It Is*, 226–27
Grimké, Charlotte Forten, 214
Grimké, Sarah: *American Slavery as It Is*, 226–27
Guardino, Peter, 274
Guelzo, Allen, 9

Hager, Christopher, 220n40
Hannah-Jones, Nikole: *The 1619 Project*, 3–4, 9, 66, 67
Harney, Stefano, 214–15
Hartman, Saidiya, 216, 227–28, 232
Hawthorne, Nathaniel, 73, 264–65, 272; *Life of Pierce*, 264–65, 272
Hegel, Georg Wilhelm Friedrich, 6, 9
heteronormativity, 9, 22, 224, 232
Hickman, Jared, 206
historiography, 42, 89, 232, 256, 266–67
history: and empiricism, 33–35; indeterminacy of, 20, 33–47; and knowledge, 33–35; and the nation, 39; and psychoanalysis, 39–43
Hobbes, Thomas, 9, 245, 249
Hogarth, William, 162
Honig, Bonnie, 243
Hooke, Robert, 140
hospitality, 6
Hughes, Walter, 111, 113, 115, 133n22

Hume, David, 185, 190, 253
Hunter, Tera W., 234n29
hypocrisy, 12, 18, 22, 65, 151, 163, 177–83, 192, 194–96, 197n13, 203

ideology, 15, 57, 116, 122, 178, 243, 264
immateriality, 22, 182, 202–204, 215
imperialism. *See* colonialism
Insko, Jeffrey, 234n25
intellect: distributed, 205, 215
interiority, 2, 5, 12, 17, 85, 90, 93, 181, 212, 215
Islam, 189–91, 193
interpretation: and character, 144; and Freud, Sigmund, 34–35, 39; indeterminacy of, 47; legal, 244–45, 251. *See also* critique

Jameson, Fredric, 6, 14, 24n34, 244; on allegory, 244; and historicization, 6; *The Political Unconscious*, 6
Jefferson, Thomas, 110, 180, 183–85, 191, 197n17, 204, 213; *Notes on the State of Virginia*, 180, 204
Jephson, Ralph, 142, 162–63
Johannsen, Robert, 280
Johnson, Edward, 17, 21, 74–88, 90–94: "New England's Annoyances," 74–81, 83–85, 88–89
Johnson, Walter, 228
Jones, Anne, 78
Jong, Mayke de, 146
Jordan, Mark, 157
justice, 12, 19, 22–23, 55, 112, 242–49, 252–55; natural history of, 23, 252–55. *See also* equity

Kant, Immanuel, 6, 8–10, 208, 211
Katz, Jonathan, 111, 113
Kazanjian, David, 9, 85, 204
Kendall, George: *The War between the United States and Mexico Illustrated*, 276–77
Kent, James, 245–46
Kessler, Amalia, 246
Klosowska, Anna, 155

knowledge, 4, 5, 11, 20, 33–34, 37–39, 41, 42, 46, 53, 55–62, 207–8, 212, 214, 216, 244, 250–51; black, 207–8, 212, 214, 216; medical, 155; self-, 93–94; sexual, 142. *See also* empiricism; intellect
Kompridis, Nikolas, 6
Kordela, A. K., 45
Kraayenbrink, Taylor, 111, 113
Kracauer, Siegfried, 266–69, 275, 277–78: *History: The Last Things before the Last*, 267–68, 278; "The Mass Ornament," 275
Kupperman, Karen, 90–91

Lacan, Jacques, 37, 43, 45, 57, 85
LaFleur, Greta, 145, 155
Laplanche, Jean, 37, 43
Laqueur, Thomas, 145–46, 155
Larkin, Edward, 178, 198n43
Latour, Bruno, 5, 259n51, 265, 275
law, 2, 19, 23, 39, 44, 46, 47, 202, 241–57; constitutional, 3; divine, 147; and equity, 241–57; natural, 180, 258n37; and *Oedipus Rex*, 52–53, 55–58, 61, 63, 65; state, 24n12. *See also* justice
Law, Edward (Ellenborough), 250–51
Lefort, Claude, 46–47
Lemay, Leo, 76–77, 85
Lévi-Strauss, Claude, 52, 54, 55
liberalism, 1, 181, 196,
Linn, William, 184
Linnaeus, Carl, 250
Lippard, George, 267
Locke, John, 1, 153, 190
Looby, Christopher, 145
Loughran, Trish, 224
Lúkacs, György, 277

Machiavelli, Niccolo, 181
Madison, James, 182–83; "Memorial and Remonstrance," 182
Mahmood, Saba, 179
Manning, Susan, 144
Marcus, Sharon, 10
Marx, Karl, 6, 48n29, 85

Mason, Margaretta, 223, 228
materialism, 211. *See also* immateriality; new materialism
material textual studies, 21, 104
Mather, Cotton, 122, 130, 133n21, 161
McCune Smith, James, 204, 209
McDowell, Paula, 156
McLeod, Allegra, 11
medical humanities, 104, 130
Melville, Herman, 23, 242–57, 258n44; *Bartleby, the Scrivener*, 246, 254; *Benito Cereno*, 247–48; *Billy Budd*, 254–55, 258n44; *Mardi*, 247; *Moby-Dick*, 23, 242, 248–53; *Omoo*, 247; *Typee*, 247
memory, 33, 35, 41, 74, 75, 91, 94, 125, 135n45, 156, 248; historical, 23, 264
Meranze, Michael, 166n40
Mexican War, the, 23, 264–69, 271–82
Michelet, Jules, 42
Miller, Perry, 20, 80
Moody-Turner, Shirley, 214
morality, 161, 178–80, 184–87, 190–91, 193–195
Morgan, Edmund S., 97n68, 105–106, 110–14, 117, 120, 125, 132–33n15
Morgan, Jennifer, 18
Moten, Fred, 205, 214–15
Murphy, Gretchen, 184
Myles, Anne, 153
mysticism, 205–206, 209

nation-state, 2, 3, 5, 19, 23, 24n12, 34, 39, 45, 47, 89, 181, 185, 189, 264, 265
neoempiricism, 5, 10
Nietzsche, Friedrich, 6, 57
Nudelman, Franny, 212

Ogden, Emily, 196n6
Ogden, Uzal, 186–87, 188
origin stories, 1–2, 4, 19–20, 35, 39, 67
Orlemanski, Julie, 10
orthography, 103–31; and queerness, 103–31
Ostler, Jeffrey, 90

Paine, Thomas, 8, 18, 22, 177–91, 193–96, 196n3, 198n53; *The Age of Reason*, 178, 183–87, 189–91, 195; *The Philosophy of Creation*, 177, 198n53
parrhesia, 4, 12, 20, 52, 63–67, 69
Patterson, Orlando, 228
Pepys, Samuel, 110, 140
performance, 86, 140, 143–46, 150, 152–58, 163–64, 181. *See also* theatricality
periodization, 5, 15, 16, 22–23, 41, 263–82
phallus, the, 46–47, 51n44, 125, 128–29, 141
Phelps, John Wolcott, 266
Phillips, Adam, 37
Pierce, Franklin, 23, 263–65, 267–69, 271–73, 281–82
pleasure, 42, 104, 113, 120, 123, 125, 133–34n26, 135n45, 140, 150, 152. *See also* sex
Pocock, J.G.A., 256–57
Poovey, Mary, 18
postcolonial theory, 37, 45
postcritique, 2, 5, 10–11
Prescott, William, 279–80
print culture, 139, 159, 164, 205, 267, 274, 281. *See also* public sphere
privacy, 18, 21–22, 178–79, 188, 191, 195–96, 199, 213
Protestantism, 18, 73, 81–84, 87, 93, 140, 143, 146–48, 180, 182–83, 188, 191, 193, 195, 206, 208. *See also* morality
public sphere, 4 11, 21, 143, 145–49, 154–55, 159, 161, 164, 178, 195, 213; and print, 21, 143 *See also* evangelism
psychoanalysis, 17, 20, 33–47, 85, 86, 87, 147; and history, 20, 39–43
Puritanism, 1, 9, 18, 20–21, 105, 113, 131n2, 142, 149, 161

queerness, 5, 17, 18, 21, 110–15, 130, 131n2, 133n21, 150, 231
queer theory, 44, 45, 104, 231
Quijano, Anibal, 1

race, 9, 19, 20, 37–38, 44–45, 202–17, 269; and racialization, 2; and racial science, 204, 206. *See also* critical race theory

racism, 1, 3, 9, 37, 45, 207, 264, 268
Radel, Nicholas F., 111–12, 113, 133n22
Rancière, Jacques, 212–13, 267, 277: *The Ignorant Schoolmaster*, 212–13
Raskolnikov, Masha, 155
rationalism; 207, 208, 211, 213, 216n13; and antebellum black thought, 213
realism, 14, 22, 225–27
Reign of Terror, 184, 190. *See also* French Revolution, the
religion, 18, 88, 144, 146–47, 164, 178–88, 189, 190–96, 205, 206, 209, 215; privatization of, 179; and purity, 182–88. *See also* belief; Christianity; disestablishment; Islam; Protestantism; sin
Remsen v. Remsen (1817), 246
repression, 5, 17, 21, 35, 37, 41–42, 73–75, 85–91,
revisionism, 36
revolution, 2, 3, 66, 67, 178, 181, 183–85, 187–88, 193, 195–96, 203, 208, 209, 211, 214, 242; and black revolutionary politics, 203, 208, 209, 211, 214; scientific, 204–206. *See also* American Revolution, the; French Revolution, the
Richter, Daniel, 15
Richter, Gerhard, 278
Rieff, Philip, 48n29
Rivett, Sarah, 206
Roitman, Janet, 20
Rolnik, Eran, 33, 38
Romney, Susana Shaw, 93
Rose, Gillian, 256

sacrifice, 23, 127, 190, 266, 268, 278, 280
Salecl, Renata, 37
Sallaint, John, 219n35
Sánchez-Eppler, Karen, 228
Santner, Eric, 242–43
satire, 140, 142, 157–58, 162–64, 271; erotic, 142, 158, 162–64
Schlereth, Eric R., 184–85
Schor, Naomi, 37
science, 146, 204–8, 210, 213, 217. *See also* astronomy; empiricism

Scott, Joan Wallach, 1
Scott, Winfield, 263, 266, 277
Scribner, Benjamin: *Camp Life of a Volunteer*, 272–73, 276, 278
Second Great Awakening, 180, 206
secularism, 1, 18, 21, 45, 178–79, 195–96, 196n6
Sedgwick, Eve Kosofsky, 11, 12, 145
Sekora, John, 218n13, 233n14
sentimental fiction, 182, 215, 223–26, 230
Serres, Michel, 265
sex, 21, 43–44, 47, 111–14, 117–22, 133–34n26, 139, 141, 145–50, 157–58, 161–63, 179, 231; masturbation (Onanism), 18, 21, 105, 124, 140–65
Sex Pistols, 203
sexuality, 2, 5, 17–18, 19, 20–21, 37, 43, 57, 85, 111–12, 148, 153, 157, 179; history of, 58, 61, 103–5, 145–48, 163; queer, 103. *See also* queerness; sex
Shaw, Lemuel, 246–48
Shelton, Thomas, 103, 106–10, 115–17, 129, 132n11
Shklar, Judith, 181–82, 196, 197n13
Shuger, Debora, 135n42
Sims, Thomas, 247
sin, 115–118, 122, 124, 129, 140–143, 145, 146, 148–154, 156–163
sincerity, 179, 181–82, 196, 197n13. *See also* authenticity
Slauter, Eric, 12, 13
slave narratives, 208, 233n14
slavery, 1, 3, 19, 22, 66, 186, 188–93, 203, 206, 211, 215–17, 219n36, 223–32, 233n14, 244, 247, 269; and archives, 216–17, 219n36. *See also* abolition; abolitionism
Smallwood, Stephanie E., 228
Smith, Adam: *The Wealth of Nations*, 247
Smith, Elihu Hubbard, 185
Sophocles: *Oedipus Rex*, 52–63, 65–67, 181
Souza, Igor de, 157
sovereignty 1, 5, 9, 12, 19–20, 22, 46, 52, 54, 59, 62, 63, 179, 243, 248. *See also* freedom; law; subjectivity
spectacle, 23, 74, 94n6, 193, 281
Spiegel, Gabrielle, 10

Spillers, Hortense, 37–38, 232
Spivak, Gayatri, 97n68
Stahuljak, Zrinka, 157, 158
Stallybrass, Peter, 78
Steedman, Carolyn, 41
Stein, Jordan Alexander, 86, 131n2, 189
Stewart, Maria, 203, 217
Stowe, Harriet Beecher, 195, 223, 225–29; *A Key to Uncle Tom's Cabin*, 223, 226; *Uncle Tom's Cabin*, 223, 225–29
Story, Joseph, 246
Streeby, Sheeley, 266
Stuelke, Patricia, 11
subjectivity, 2, 4, 5, 17, 19, 38, 41, 60, 117, 153, 179

tachygraphy, 21, 103, 106–10, 115
Taylor, Charles, 180
Taylor, Zachary, 266
theatricality, 143–44, 146, 151, 161, 163–65. *See also* performance
Thiessen, Marc, 9
Thompson, E. P., 150
Tissot, Samuel-Auguste: *L'Onanisme*, 145, 155
Tortorici, Zeb, 148
truth, 4, 5, 10, 18, 19, 20, 35, 37, 39, 52–53, 55–66, 117, 182, 187–88, 190–91, 196, 227, 229; and power, 56–66; and sovereignty, 52; truth-value, 2
Tubman, Harriet, 211
Turner, Nat: *The Confessions of Nat Turner*, 205, 207–8, 210, 212, 214, 217, 218n13
Tyler, Royall: *The Algerine Captive*, 22, 188–89, 191, 193, 198n43

Underhill, John, 92
Underhill, Updike, 189–90
Upham, William P., 106, 129–30

violence, 2, 5, 11–12, 19, 21, 22, 23, 64, 65, 75, 89–90, 92–94, 184, 190, 203, 227, 229, 243, 248, 264, 274, 277–78, 280–82; antiblack, 203; Christian, 190; sexual, 64; and slavery, 227, 264. *See also* slavery; war
Visconsi, Elliott, 253

Waldstreicher, David, 258
Walker, David, 22, 203–4, 208, 217
Wallerstein, Immanuel, 1
war, 5, 22, 23, 80, 92, 255, 263–82; temporality of, 263–82. *See also* American Revolution, the; French Revolution, the; Mexican War, the
Warner, Michael, 143, 224, 231, 232, 234n32
Washington, George, 178, 190
Watson, Patricia A., 122
Watson, Richard, 186
Weber, Max, 1, 45
Weber, Samuel, 48n44
Webster, Daniel, 248
Weld, Theodore Dwight, 22, 226–27
Wesley, John, 141, 149, 155, 156
Wheatley, Phillis, 213
White, Ed, 13, 192, 198n43
White, Hayden, 244
Whitefield, George, 21, 139–65; diary of, 153–54, 156; *A General Account of the First Part of My Life*, 139–65; *Journals*, 139, 160; *Sermons*, 139
Whitehead, A. N. 8, 9
whiteness, 249

Wigglesworth, Michael, 17, 21, 87–88, 91, 94, 103–31. *See also* diary
Wild On Collective, 14
Wilkins, John Darragh, 278–80
will, the, 123–29, 213, 215
Williams, Patricia J., 228
Williams, Raymond, 117
Wilson, Elizabeth, 38
Wilson, William J., 220n42
Winslow, Edward, 76, 77, 91
Winthrop, John, Jr., 80–82, 84, 89, 118, 122, 134n29
Wolfe, Patrick, 93
Wood, Horace G., 177
Woodville, Richard Caton, 271
Woodward, Walter W., 122
writing: evangelical, 20–21, 73–94, 103–31, 139–65; scientific, 209; secret, 112; seductive style of, 187–88. *See also* diary; orthography; tachygraphy
Wynter, Sylvia, 37, 85

Young, Kevin, 217

Zupančič, Alenka, 43

www.ingramcontent.com/pod-product-compliance
Lightning Source LLC
Chambersburg PA
CBHW051049230426

43666CB00012B/2624